3 1994 01269 4656

2/07
02/07 (10/07)

A SON OF THUNDER

HENRY MAYER

A Son of Thunder

PATRICK HENRY
AND THE
AMERICAN REPUBLIC

GROVE PRESS
New York

B HENRY, P. MAY
Mayer, Henry
A son of thunder

$17.00
CENTRAL   31994012694656

Copyright © 1991 by Henry Mayer

All rights reserved. No part of this book may be reproduced in any form or by
any electronic or mechanical means, or the facilitation thereof, including
information storage and retrieval systems, without permission in writing from
the publisher, except by a reviewer, who may quote brief passages in a review.
Any members of educational institutions wishing to photocopy part or all of
the work for classroom use, or publishers who would like to obtain permission
to include the work in an anthology, should send their inquiries to
Grove/Atlantic, Inc., 841 Broadway, New York, NY 10003.

First published in 1986 by Franklin Watts, New York and Toronto

This Grove Press edition is published by special arrangement with the
University Press of Virginia from their 1991 edition.

Printed in the United States of America

Library of Congress Cataloging-in-Publication Data

Mayer, Henry, 1941–
    A son of thunder : Patrick Henry and the American Republic / Henry
Mayer.
        p. cm.
    Originally published : New York : Franklin Watts, 1986.
    ISBN-10: 0-8021-3815-2
    ISBN-13: 978-0-8021-3815-6
    1. Henry, Patrick, 1736–1799. 2. Virginia—Politics and government—
1775–1783. 3. United States—Politics and government—1775–1783. 4.
United States—Politics and government—1783–1789. 5. Legislators—
United States—Biography. 6. United States. Continental Congress—
Biography. I. Title.

E302.6.H5 M35 2001
973.3'092—dc21
[B]   00-066344

Grove Press
an imprint of Grove/Atlantic, Inc.
841 Broadway
New York, NY 10003

Distributed by Publishers Group West

www.groveatlantic.com

06 07 08 09 10   10 9 8 7 6 5 4 3 2

For Betsy
and
For Eleanor and Tommy

CONTENTS

A SON OF THUNDER

PREFACE

We don't really know much about him. Patrick Henry's fame rests upon a single resounding sentence that rattles somewhat emptily in our heads, devoid of context and separated from the man. We know, vaguely, that his oratory helped propel the colonies toward independence, but we have forgotten that a dozen years later his dissenting voice, directed against the proposed Constitution of 1787, nearly defeated the measure and forced its proponents to adopt the conciliatory amendments known as the Bill of Rights.

Patrick Henry survives in memory as an agitator, not as a statesman, even though he served three busy terms as Virginia's first governor and dominated the state assembly for a decade longer. In an age of reason he was emotional; in an era of aristocratic stewardship he voiced the demands of the inarticulate. In a time when men regarded statecraft as a science he remained indifferent to theory and impulsively reached for whatever argument best suited his immediate need.

Henry combined an actor's flair with a preacher's fervor, and he evoked a rapport with ordinary folk that changed the face of Virginia's—and later, America's—politics. An ambitious, self-made man who aspired to gentry status while challenging the style of gentry politics, Henry seemed to thrive upon controversy, and his career moved explosively from one confrontation to another. His rivals, who included Thomas Jefferson and James Madison, considered him a schemer and a demagogue. They deprecated his narrow education and his country manners; they disparaged his character as too grasping, too eager for fame and money, and they found something shameful in the way Henry could mobilize popular passion toward political ends. Their antagonism has become history's vantage point, although it more properly forms a subject for analysis.

Understanding a man as unusual as Patrick Henry is made more difficult by the failure to recognize the high degree of partisan and philosophic controversy within the American Revolution, the struggle wisely described many years ago as a question both of home rule and of who should rule at home. The Revolution had a dimension of violent confrontation and internal quarreling that two centuries of mythmaking have done much to obscure. Like the other great engineer of the Revolution, Samuel Adams of Boston, Henry was a new man in politics, the son of an undistinguished family who rose to power in the imperial crisis and brought a newer, more plebeian element into the political coalition required to oppose the British ministry. Adams's constituents were Boston craftsmen and mechanics; Henry's were Virginia's poor white farmers and religious dissenters. Within the old aristocratic forms of colonial politics, then, Henry's success heralded the changes that would shape the more democratic politics of the half century that followed independence.

Tension, however, existed from the beginning. A volatile alliance of aristocrats and commoners made the Revolution together, but this uneasy combination of elite and democratic tendencies had to strike some new balance of power. Good revolutionaries found themselves at odds with one another in the effort to determine the extent of democratic participation in government, to define the pace and direction of economic growth, and to sift the conflicting claims of personal liberty and energetic government. Each party claimed "liberty" as its polestar and presented itself as the faithful guardian of revolutionary values.

The struggle over the Constitution and the Bill of Rights caught up all these issues and became in truth the last battle of the American Revolution. Two hundred years later, however, the constitutional convention is draped in legend and its proposal venerated as the miracle of Philadelphia. The violent, bitter contest over ratification has shrunk into a peevish minor quarrel mounted by "men of little faith." But Patrick Henry did not think himself sacrilegious in opposing what issued from Philadelphia. The delegates had violated their instructions and instead of amending the existing form of government had proposed a more ambitious, more aristocratic plan that sacrificed "the rights of man for the dignity of government." In Henry's view the convention delegates were the men with insufficient faith in self-government and the state governments a revolutionary people had created for themselves.

Losers get little credit from history, for in retrospect a lasting victory will always seem inevitable. The Framers can be made out to be our contemporaries while their adversaries seem only curious antiques. Yet to understand the Revolution fully we need to know why its Patrick Henry—like its Sam Adams—saw the Constitution as betrayal, not fulfillment, and why he risked his reputation one more time in liberty's name.

This book will be a political biography, for Henry was a political man, working out the consequences of a profound revolution, and it is his public life that claims our attention. I hope to dramatize the political conflict that was his life's blood and to recreate the political culture in which his career took shape and found its justification.

A brief word about sources. Biographers, said Catherine Drinker Bowen, should aim "not to startle with new material but to persuade with old." I think that this is a reasonable dictum, especially since I can lay no claim to a cache of hitherto unexplored evidence: no secret diary, no dusky mistress, not even a rough draft of the "liberty or death" speech. I have worked principally from the available primary sources in order to evoke both man and era with as much immediacy as possible. Most of the documents dealing with Virginia in the revolutionary era can be found in published collections; Henry's papers (such as they are) are also available in print. He did not always commit his thoughts or intentions to paper, however, and made no systematic effort to save or organize the documents he had. So there are great gaps in our knowledge of Henry's activities and only very scanty material on his domestic life. I have examined the material that exists with a fresh eye and tried to fashion from it a lively and persuasive portrait of the man.

The impulse to tell this story comes from several sources. As an eighth-grader, having just moved to North Carolina, I felt an odd kind of pride at learning that my adopted state had refused to ratify the Constitution until it had been amended with a bill of rights. That struck me as an act of great integrity, and I wondered why it had come about. Some years later, as a secondary-school teacher, I found myself uncomfortable with the usual formula that "Some people were unhappy because the Constitution lacked a bill of rights, so they added one." Who added it?, I wanted to know, and who made the promise necessary? Was a bargain actually made at some meeting, or was this statement one of those generalizations that texts and teachers use for getting past a complicated topic and on to the War of 1812?

My questions took on more urgency when I taught back-to-back courses on the American Revolution and contemporary civil liberties. I wanted something that would bridge the gap of centuries and encourage students to think about the relationship between ideas of the Revolution and twentieth-century values. Using my own collection of documentary material, I found students greatly excited when they realized how much the Framers had to struggle with conflict, uncertainty, and ambivalence about the relationship between individual liberty and the authority of the state. I also found both students and their parents surprised that this should have been so; for them the dead hand of the past was inert indeed and "the intent of the Framers" a sacrosanct and weighty concept that impeded their own ability to think.

It became clear that the Bill of Rights had an uncertain standing as the Revolution's stepchild, for it had emanated not from the Framers but from the pressure of now-forgotten adversaries like Patrick Henry. This circumstance is, in itself, a profound lesson in the history of dissent. That patriots could be so at odds comes as something of a surprise and, I think, serves as an encouragement to independent thought.

No greater tribute could be paid to Patrick Henry on the 250th anniversary of his birth than to realize anew how his forceful dissent helped to secure protection for civil liberty in the U.S. Constitution. In celebrating, moreover, the bicentennial of that document, we need to remember that it emerged from conflict and that the constitutional system has defined itself through debate, through highly partisan conflict, and through the tragedy of civil war. To exalt the Framers by denying their partisanship and forgetting their opponents both distorts the past and diminishes our ability to understand the present.

This book, I hope, will invite us to consider the claims of patriotism in its broadest sense and give us a new appreciation of the legitimacy, indeed the necessity, of political conflict in a free society.

Berkeley
January 1986

PROLOGUE

"The Great Adversary"

People set out early, harnessing steaming horses in the post-dawn chill or walking across stubbled fields still drifted in mist. The veins of frost in the rutted trails Virginians called their "High Waies" returned to mud under the pale wintry sun, and farm wagons and the gentry's coaches alike struggled across the hilly, broken ground of Prince Edward County, through the long stretches of pine forests separating the tobacco and wheat fields and the peach, pear, and apple orchards not yet in bud. They came from thirty miles around, fording creeks or the meandering Appomattox, then climbing one more ridge to the crossroads hamlet that was Prince Edward Court House.

It was the third Monday in March 1788, and the third Monday was "court day" for Prince Edward, a traditional holiday in the isolated region. There were no towns or newspapers in the county, and court day provided the only opportunity for a general gathering of the populace. The county court handled all the local public affairs—road repair, bridge building, regulation of mills and taverns, militia organization—as well as legal matters, such as probating wills, recording deeds, and hearing civil suits and minor criminal cases. People came in on court day to do business, to complain to the magistrates, to shop and trade, to enjoy the theatrical flourishes the lawyers would be sure to provide, to swap news and gossip at the tavern, to see the blooded horses someone would likely have brought to show, and to watch the races and the wrestling matches that could be counted on to spring up as the day wore on and spirits rose. On this morning, too, word had gone round that there was to be a special election, and that meant there would be "treats" for the voters—barrels of rum and ginger cakes supplied by friends of the candidates—and the likelihood of some fine speaking and excitement.

Prince Edward Court House hardly counted as a village; it was no more than a wide spot where the clay roads parted around the public square. An acre of ground held a motley group of buildings: the frame courthouse, with two brick chimneys and a clapboard facade badly in need of fresh paint; the cabin of rough-hewn logs that served as the debtors' prison; the county clerk's cottage; and the stocks, pillory, and whipping post. Across the road stood Smith's Tavern, with its spacious porch, agreeable taproom, stables, and outbuildings. Thirty years before, when Prince Edward was a fledgling county on the frontier of settlement, the first county courts had met in the tavern itself, and it remained an arena for much unofficial business.

By midmorning Prince Edward's monthly hubbub was well underway. The creak of carriage wheels and the cries of the hostlers filled the air near the stables, along with shouts from the spectators at the cockfight in the hayloft. Several young boys yelled and shrieked at their droves of hogs, trying to keep the animals together while their fathers arranged a sale. The courthouse yard was awash in conversation, a current of murmurs and laughter rippling from one knot of men to the next. Itinerant peddlers hawked their tin and pewter along the roadside, and under a grove of locust trees an auctioneer hollered up his crowd for bidding on several batches of black slaves, all "Virginia-born and in the best of health." The tavern porch rumbled under the stomping of muddy boots, and inside, the fiddler's tunes flowed merrily along with the rum punch and good Virginia brandy and cider.

The talk rambled over the usual run of country matters: the weather, the crops, the horses, the land that might be up for sale, the bridge that might still be out. And it ranged over the local political and economic news: more delays in the scheme to clear the Appomattox down to Petersburg so that flatboats might carry tobacco directly to the warehouses there; the scarcity of hard money in the county and the hopes that tax payments could be deferred again this year, or paid in warehouse notes or even in paper money; and the expectation, given all these tax troubles, that the court would appoint deputies to reassess property more equitably.

Prince Edward was not a wealthy county: like the rest of "Southside," the region below the James River, it had thin-looking, fragile soil. George Washington, who had an eye for such matters, pronounced it "indifferent . . . of an inferior quality . . . a good deal mixed with pine," a sure sign for him of sandy, acidic tilth lacking in nutrients. Although more than half the white farmers worked their lands with slave labor, the county had few great planters and only a dozen or more who owned as many as twenty slaves. The middling planters found themselves constantly in debt. They had no elegant mansions, just decently weatherboarded houses, often in need of repair, whose brick chimneys were their chief claim to grandeur. The county lay too far from markets to be a growing commercial area, and its people hoped more for self-sufficiency than for profits.

Eventually talk came around to the pending election, more a ceremony, really, than a contest. The county was to send two delegates to a special state ratifying convention, called for Richmond in June, to consider a new Constitution drawn up at Philadelphia for the American states, and everyone expected that Prince Edward's representatives in the state assembly would stand unopposed for this extra duty. The county was fortunate, people said, in having experienced men for the job. General Robert Lawson had served seven terms in the assembly since the first revolutionary convention in 1774, and he had compiled a worthy record as commander of Virginia's battalion in the war against the British. He was a solid, eminent character and a firm patriot, who could be relied upon to give the county respectability in Richmond and to remember his friends at home. The county's second representative was a newcomer to their midst but an old favorite in their hearts, the intrepid and eloquent Patrick Henry. He had retired to Prince Edward a little more than a year before, after his fifth term as Virginia's governor; he had bought some land along the Appomattox up near Venable's and Woodson's where he hoped to recover some money from farming and intended, after a time, to resume his once-lucrative law practice.

Henry had served in nearly every Virginia assembly since 1765, except for his five years in the governor's chair, and he had represented Virginia at two Continental Congresses. He had a brilliant reputation as an advocate and a talent for political maneuvering that had made him as many enemies as friends. An amiable man, seemingly indifferent to fashion yet mercurial and ambitious, he came from an undistinguished family and had worked his way into prominence, his own cause advancing along with the independence movement he helped engineer.

Next to General Washington he was the leading man in Virginia, and among ordinary farmers Henry held an even higher place in their hearts. Everyone believed that he understood the common people, and "he was naturally hailed as the democratic chief," Governor Edmund Randolph wrote. "Identified with the people, they clothed him with the confidence of a favorite son." As an advocate of debtor relief measures, Southside had considered him its champion for years. Henry loved the woods and hills of the Piedmont, and he had lived for some time at an even more remote plantation, eighty miles west of Prince Edward, on the headwaters of the Dan River. His career oscillated between intense engagement in public affairs and complete withdrawal into modestly prosperous farming. His Prince Edward venture was his latest effort to cultivate his private interests, but his political drive remained strong, and he had barely settled on his new land before he allowed the Prince Edward electorate to send him back to Richmond as a delegate in the most recent assembly.

People were saying that Mr. Henry opposed the scheme for a new constitution, that indeed he had parted company with General Washington on the issue. The news was confused, of course, and only fragments of the story could be fitted together from the tattered, much-handled, and somewhat out-of-date newspapers being passed around. It seemed, however, that the prominent men of Virginia were sharply divided. George Mason and Governor Randolph had left the convention without signing the document, and it was said that the powerful Richard Henry Lee had joined them in opposition. General Washington favored the plan, as did the eminent jurist Edmund Pendleton and many of the wealthy planters of the northerly Tidewater counties. On Southside, however, men generally seemed to be against the plan. It sounded complicated, expensive, unwarranted, and very much a threat to liberty. It gave too much power to a distant government, threatened a host of new taxes, and, some said, was truly a plot to throw the country back into the hands of the monarchists.

Expectations ran high in the courthouse yard that Mr. Henry would go beyond the customary brief word of greeting usually expressed by candidates and favor the people with a public address on the question. A speech from Patrick Henry would be an even greater treat than the ample drafts of punch and plates of barbecue being served up on the lawn by friends of the candidates. Indeed, by voting time a great crowd had gathered in front of the building, perhaps as many as five hundred people, about three hundred of whom were property owners eligible to vote, and the rest overseers, managers, tenant farmers, and the adult sons of prominent landowners who had not yet come into their legacies. The crowd was overwhelmingly male—the racy, sweaty, drunken atmosphere of court days and politics excluded women—and predominantly white, although a smattering of black slaves who had driven their well-to-do masters to court stood off to the side, turning bland impassive faces away from the crowd and pretending not to listen to the speeches.

Patrick Henry had mingled pleasantly in the crowd during the morning, chatting with the others about hunting and horseflesh or stepping to one side to confer earnestly with someone who had heard that the governor was taking legal cases again. Henry did not stand out from the crowd; indeed, he looked undistinguished, "like a common planter who cared very little for his personal appearance," one observer wrote. He was dressed in a worn and rumpled suit of black homespun with a brown camlet cloak draped over his shoulders. His brown wig, as usual, "exhibited no great care in the dressing," and the youngsters in the crowd hoped that they would get to see Henry take off his wig and twirl it during his speech, as he was said to do when making a point before juries.

There were huzzahs and applause when Henry, accompanied by his son-in-law and several of the magistrates, made his way through the "immense concourse" and mounted the brick steps of the courthouse to make his address. Henry stepped forward, stoop-shouldered and strikingly wrinkled for a man of fifty-two, looking as gloomy as a preacher. His sallow cheeks enhanced the deep, dark impression of his eyes, half hidden beneath bushy brows, and his long face seemed tensed on the verge of a scowl, a look of such severity, habitual with him when assuming the rostrum, as to imply a sense of anger and contempt suppressed only by rigid control. He wore spectacles though he carried no notes, and his manner was so grave and penetrating that, someone said, "you would swear that he had never laughed at a joke."

His "solemn and impressive" manner hushed the crowd, and he began to speak, casually at first, almost indolently, drawing his listeners in, forcing them to press forward and concentrate hard to catch his words. Henry had an actor's mastery of timing, and he used the theatrical trick of suddenly straightening his slouched body to his full height, just over six feet, to emphasize a point, his body rising with his voice, his argument gaining force as his stature increased. He also knew when to pause, and he punctuated his outbursts with long rests, "riveting the attention more by raising the expectation of renewed brilliancy," one listener wrote. "His lightning consisted in quick successive flashes, which rested only to alarm the more."

Henry presented himself as a sentinel over the people's rights. He wished for an appointment to the ratifying convention because he conceived the republic to be in "extreme danger." The proposed change of government threatened the people's liberties. The convention that put it forward had been convened only to amend the Articles of Confederation, but it had violated its instructions and concocted an entirely new government—a consolidated affair of vast and threatening new powers. Even worse, the convention had so arranged the scheme that it would go into effect whenever any nine states agreed to it, thus driving a wedge into the Union and breaking the solemn promises the thirteen states had given each other when they had agreed to confederate: changes in their system would be made with the consent of all.

Henry did not join in the abuse some had heaped upon the Confederation. It had safely concluded a long and dangerous war and secured a western territory "greater than any European monarch possesses." The people lived in peace and security, enjoying the fruits of their labors, but the partisans of the new plan, Henry charged, were trying to "terrify us into an adoption" by spreading reports of tumults and disorders elsewhere. Such exaggerated tales, he thought, had no bearing upon the tranquil atmosphere of Virginia, where, as he saw it, the chief danger came from the proposed new Constitution itself.

Henry did not want the sovereign independent states—the soul of the Confederation—to be taken over by one general government whose extensive powers—the purse in one hand and the sword in the other—would be used to oppress and ruin the people. He painted a gloomy and frightening portrait of "energetic government," with two sets of tax gatherers, state and federal sheriffs, distant and oppressive courts, and excise men armed with powers of search and seizure. His characterization vividly recalled the colonists' case against heavy-handed royal government fifteen years before, and Henry emphasized that the proposed Constitution envisioned a revolution as radical as that which had separated the colonies from Great Britain.

Virginia's independent constitution began with a Declaration of Rights to protect the people against the possibility of an oppressive state government. The new national Constitution offered no such protection. The rights of conscience, of trial by jury, of liberty of the press, all the privileges and immunities of the citizen would be in jeopardy, if not lost entirely, in the "alarming transition." In all his speeches Henry had special words of warning for his Baptist and Methodist friends, for the proposal remained silent—darkly silent—about the hard-fought, newly acquired rights of religious dissenters.

Virginia's voice would be decisive, Henry said. The commonwealth should take time to consider, to offer amendments, or even to stand by for a while and see the effect of adoption by the other states. Virginia had a rich staple crop and friends in other nations; it could do very well on its own, perhaps even better than at present if, as feared, the new Congress handed control of the Mississippi River back to Spain in order to win trade concessions for the northern states.

The zealous proponents of the Constitution insisted that it was to be "this, or nothing," that there could be no amendments until the plan was passed. The science of government ought to be simple and plain, Henry thought, and a constitution should, like Caesar's wife, be not only good but unsuspected. No one but a lunatic would accept a constitution that was avowedly defective in the hope of having it amended afterward.

Henry looked upon "that paper" as "the most fatal plan that could possibly be conceived to enslave a free people." He would never consent to it without amendments first, not even if all but one-half of one state favored it. As a guardian of the Revolution he felt obliged to oppose this threat to liberty, and oppose it he would, no matter how harshly he were criticized for it.

Partisans of the Constitution had already castigated Henry for "blowing the trumpet of discord." He was an "implacable" opponent, a man of "very bold language," they said, who "diffused his poison" through "industriously propagated" speeches that made "the people much disposed to be his blind followers." He had the Baptists in an uproar and the Kentuckians in a sweat, and his demagoguery so roused passion in each neighborhood that the Constitution's friends claimed they had to adopt a prudent silence. George Washington believed that Henry had "no great objection to the introduction of anarchy and confusion," and James Madison, principal architect of the new plan, thought that "desperate measures will be [Henry's] game."

Henry "artfully prejudiced" people's minds with low "artifice" and "scandalous misrepresentations," his critics charged, and even as he spoke to the crowd, a college student unobtrusively took down his speech in shorthand so that his cunning design might later be exposed. "I can not find that he has ever once specified the amendments he would have in the project," one of Madison's lieutenants reported after canvassing Southside, and "it is therefore fairly to be concluded that his views are a dismemberment of the Union." "Disunionist" became the epithet whispered against Henry all across Virginia, along with the gossipy accusation that Henry intended to throw the Southwest into a confederacy with the Spaniards. The talk of amendments deliberately "concealed" his real design, they said, but those who had specific objections to the Constitution were easily recruited into opposition by Henry's maneuvers. The old governor's influence had deeply penetrated even Madison's home county, and, under great pressure from family and friends, Madison reluctantly agreed to return from New York to run for a seat in the ratifying convention himself. Henry, he knew, "would strike at the essence of the System," and he would have to be stopped. Madison had come into politics as Henry's admirer, but they had battled for years in Virginia's legislature. As the old governor spoke in Prince Edward, Madison prepared to leave New York to work for ratification in Virginia against Henry, the suspected disunionist whom he unflinchingly recognized as "the great adversary who will render the event precarious."

The cheers rang out for many minutes after Henry had finished speaking, and many punch cups were raised in toasts to the old governor, to liberty, and to Virginia. Finally, the sheriff, William Bibb, appeared on the steps to call for order and conduct the election. After reading the legal papers calling for the election, Bibb simply looked out across the crowd and declared, in the customary phrase, that "upon the view" of the freeholders it was plain that Governor Henry and General Lawson had their approbation, and he would so certify their election. Cheers broke out anew, and then the crowd began to dissipate. As Patrick Henry made his way out of the courthouse yard, an old squirrel hunter, dressed in buckskin, came up to give him a sharp tap on the shoulder. "Old fellow, stick to the people," the hunter said; "if you take the back track, we are gone."

Part One

1736–1766

CHAPTER 1

Backcountry Gentry

In the second quarter of the eighteenth century eminent
Virginians conceived a passion for mansions of brick. They
wanted baronial manor houses that would rival the country
seats of their distant English cousins, and by poring over
published books of English designs and construction draw-
ings, by importing master workmen, by setting gangs of
slaves to quarry clay and fire bricks, and by sparing no
expense in furnishings, the planters got what they desired.
"You perceive a great air of opulence amongst the inhabitants,
who have sometimes built themselves houses, equal in magnificence to many of our superb ones at St. James," an English
visitor wrote admiringly in 1746. "The planters live in a
manner equal to men of the best fortune" at home.

Governor Alexander Spotswood had set the pace in 1710
with his handsome new mansion at Williamsburg, three stories
high and gracefully proportioned, with four central chimneys
and a charming two-tiered cupola in the center of the roof.
Spotswood had cunningly grouped the kitchens, artisans'
shops, stables, and other outbuildings behind a symmetrical
forecourt, following the best Italianate villa style, as adapted
for England by Inigo Jones and Christopher Wren. Acres of
shrubbery and gardens, wonderfully arranged, further enhanced the magnificence of the edifice. Detractors thought
that Spotswood had "lavished away" too much public money
on the building and derisively called it the governor's "palace,"
but the opulent residence captivated the leading planters.

The Carters and the Randolphs, the Harrisons, Beverleys, and Lees soon undertook their own mansions along the broad reaches of the James, the Rappahannock, and the Potomac, seating the new dwellings upon knolls and terraces with commanding views of the river and their wharves. They sought the most advanced English styles, reworked them to their own advantage, and added something unique to set their estates apart from others.

If Spotswood had a cupola, then at Turkey Island the Randolph mansion would be surmounted by a dome visible for a great way downriver and topped by an aerial structure "called the bird cage, because many birds do hover and sing about it." If the governor's "palace" had four chimneys, then at Stratford the Lees would have two central chimneys with four stacks apiece, joined by archways to form pavilionlike bell towers. If others had remained with the steep hipped roofs of the old Virginia cabin, then the Harrisons would build Berkeley with a pedimented gable, a more heroic-looking affair that expressed the first turn of fashion toward the classic revival. If Landon Carter built his Sabine Hall of variously shaded red brick with a mile-long view down to the river, then his brother Robert would situate Nomini Hall on a piece of high ground above the Potomac so that the mansion, its brick stuccoed white, could be seen from six miles off. At Westover, William Byrd II, perhaps the most erudite man in Virginia, fused the elements admired by the planters into the most accomplished and stylish of the new mansions. Built of soft red brick along lines of the utmost purity and restraint, Westover stood three stories high and had four massive chimneys, marble pedimented doorways, and two flanking wings, one of which housed Byrd's four-thousand-volume library, the largest in America. Gracious brick walls enclosed the garden and screened the outbuildings at a convenient distance. From the James River visitors approached Westover through an ellipse of tulip poplars, and Byrd balanced this elegant avenue with an equally imposing land entry through wrought-iron gates, imported from London and unrivaled in craftsmanship. With his initials worked into the design and suspended from ten-foot brick piers capped with falcons perched on gilded globes, the gates could be read as a rebus for the master's name and power.

Westover and its contemporary expressions of order and repose seemed to consolidate generations of headlong development. They supplanted older, more ramshackle dwellings, built for the moment and carelessly, artlessly expanded to meet pressing needs. The stately new halls crowned the achievements of Virginia's first century. The colony had grown up along its rivers, long fingers of tidal water extending one hundred miles or more into the sandy forests of the coastal plain, a region lying so low and flat and so divided by waterways that to the European eye it appeared only recently reclaimed from the sea. The Virginia barons, too, bore the marks of fresh minting, their fortunes only three or four generations old, their progenitors drawn from the middling ranks of English merchants and craftsmen. They had engrossed enormous tracts of land and, especially since 1700, imported cargoes of enslaved Africans to clear the forests and produce tobacco for the European markets. They had braided family connections into a tight knot of social and political control. Half of the consequential men in the assembly belonged to fewer than a dozen families, and their political and matrimonial alliances worked together to extend their hold upon the land. The new county boundaries the assembly drew upon Virginia's map followed and extended the progress of their family lines, as sons established new branches upriver and slipped easily into the new political offices opened up through extension and subdivision of the counties.

The great rivers gave Virginia its highways and its history and tied the flourishing colonists to the British Isles they still called home. The grandees of Virginia faced their new mansions toward the water, but their thoughts increasingly turned west, toward a second Virginia, the beckoning region of rising ground between the tidewater falls and the mountains. Indeed, Governor Spotswood had no sooner finished his palace than he led a great party of gentlemen on the first expedition over the mountains in 1716. Upon their return he presented each of his companions with a golden horseshoe studded with valuable stones and symbolizing membership in what Spotswood called "the tramontane order."

Within a few years the select Knights of the Golden Horseshoe had laid claim to huge tracts of land on both slopes, and the entire region had been organized into Spotsylvania County, its western boundary dreamily reaching over the crest of the Blue Ridge toward the misty regions of the Mississippi and Ohio. When the Spotswood party toasted King George I atop the Blue Ridge in 1716 only 80,000 souls inhabited the colony, all of them dwelling east of the line of rocky rapids and falls that marked the limit of oceangoing navigation. Twenty years later, in the year of Patrick Henry's birth, the population had doubled, and it had increased by half again to 230,000 by the time of his marriage in 1755. The number of counties had doubled, too, and the tide of settlement had pushed over the mountains into the great valley of the Shenandoah and pressed southwest toward the rich bottomlands of Kentucky. Virginians could dream of a continental empire vested, as an enthusiastic mapmaker put it, "with all the Wealth and Power that will naturally arise from the Culture of so great an Extent of good Land, in a happy Climate." Henry was a son of this second Virginia. His family looked west for an increase in fortune, having occupied for generations a respectable but far from opulent position on the margins of Tidewater. Yet Patrick Henry never owned a mansion of brick and came to challenge the political power of those who did.

"Pamunkey" meant "sweat house" to the native people who first inhabited its banks, and the Bristolmen who were Patrick Henry's forebears could understand why. The steamy expanse of lowland that forced the York River to divide forty miles upstream from the bay was a place of agues and fevers, but once seasoned to the land's vapors a man could make his fortune on it. Still, the Winstons (Henry's mother's folk) preferred to push on upstream another thirty miles or so to plant themselves on healthier ground. There the land began a gentle rise; from the slight upswells in the clearings one could see the ridges separating one creek's path from the next, and the trees no longer seemed to grow directly out of the river itself. Indeed, so far inland, the Pamunkey narrowed into a meandering, sluggish stream, its uncertain channels no longer hospitable to the large oceangoing vessels. It took great faith and a mighty hunger to believe that one could become rich by setting a few barrels of tobacco on a shallow-draft sloop and expecting it to coast forty miles on the ebbing tide out to the broad channel of the York, where the *Lark*, the *Lively*, or the *John and Mary* rode at anchor, taking on the cargoes of tobacco, staves, and deer and beaver skins with which backcountry men hoped to turn their forest land to coin.

Hopeful Virginians in the late seventeenth century acquired land under a system of "headrights." In order to populate the colony, the assembly offered fifty acres for every person one transported into Virginia. Poor people gained their passage by signing indentures obliging them to repay the cost of transportation with labor, so that the importer gained hands to work his land or realized some cash by selling the indentures to someone else. The first Winston in Virginia may well have come over from Bristol as an indentured servant, but eventually he accumulated enough land to give his sons an independent start. The second generation of Winston brothers—William, Anthony, and Edmund—used the headright system to patent more than five thousand acres of New Kent County, on the upper stretch of the Pamunkey where Totopotomoy's Creek met the river. At first indentured servants cleared and drained the marshy creek bottoms, but then the Winstons bought a few slaves to make the tobacco crops that brought the family into prosperity.

The Winstons lifted themselves from subsistence to respectability, although their situation never became favorable enough for them to match the operations of Tidewater magnates like the Carters or Byrds. In 1720, however, when their section grew thickly enough settled by Virginia standards to become the separate county of Hanover, the next generation of Winstons moved smoothly into seats on the new county court and the parish vestry. Just emerging from the frontier stage of settlement, Hanover (named to honor the new royal house of Britain) had only about two thousand "tithables"— the white men and the Negroes of both sexes over sixteen counted in the levying of taxes. Only a few families possessed holdings on a grander scale than the Winstons, while the great majority had simply cleared a few tobacco patches on their hundred-acre tracts and begun to do largely subsistence farming with the aid of one or two servants or slaves.

Anthony Winston's son, Isaac, distinguished in a thin-haired family by an exceedingly bald head, had worked up a stake in the export business and made a good marriage early in the new century with Mary Dabney, the daughter of an equally enterprising English family that tried to gloss its humble origins by claiming a French connection—*d'Aubignes, s'il vous plaît*. Isaac and Mary had six children, and while young William (known as "Langloo") displayed an untoward wild streak, running off to the West to hunt and trap among the Indians half the year, the daughters had made good marriages right in the county.

Sarah, born in 1710 as their fifth child, made an especially advantageous match. Colonel John Syme was a gentleman, born in Scotland, who had made his fortune in Virginia. An older man and a widower who had inherited a great deal of Tidewater property from his first wife, Syme held extensive land patents in the hilly, western portion of Hanover reaching across to the upper James River. Moreover, he had some skill as a surveyor, which allowed him to keep a close eye on land developments throughout the region. He had assumed a seat on the parish vestry and the county bench, and he had served one term in the House of Burgesses. Sarah gave birth to their first child, John, Jr., in 1729, and the new family had every prospect of success on the Syme home plantation, "Studley," a choice expanse of higher ground not far from Sarah's parents, a mile or so back from the Pamunkey River and ribboned with fertile meadows in the creek bottoms.

Syme's quarrelsome style had got him in political trouble, however, and in 1731 he tried to augment his waning power by organizing a major surveying party to establish the boundary between Hanover and the newly organized county of Goochland lying southwest along the James. He stood to gain a great many more patents himself and the favor of planters whose tracts would be confirmed by the line. Unfortunately, Syme dropped dead in the forest before the job was done. Sarah had to sue the county to recover some of the expedition's expenses, and the promise of land and patronage passed to other entrepreneurs.

The Widow Syme apparently bore up well, for when the great William Byrd II called at Studley some months later she impressed him as an exceedingly cheerful woman who "seemed not to pine too much for the death of her husband." Her lack of reserve captivated the flirtatious grandee, who was wearily nearing the end of a three-week "progress" across "the more retired part of the country" lying north of Westover. Only a few families could match Byrd in rank. He passed a few rainy days with the Randolphs at Tuckahoe, where the company "killed the time and triumphed over the bad weather" by reading aloud *The Beggar's Opera*. He had a pleasant and informative time with the Chiswells at "Scotch-town" in upper Hanover, and at Germanna he toured former Governor Spotswood's mines and forges. For the remainder of the trip, however, he took lodgings with a succession of local colonels and justices, drank much cider and wine, and engaged in dull conversation until he "gaped wide as a signal for retiring."

Then he met the Widow Syme. He had spent the day along the Pamunkey inspecting some of his "quarters," outlying plantations run by overseers with groups of twenty or so slaves, and although he had found everything in good order and his "people" well, Byrd felt tired and out of sorts by the time his overseer conducted him to Studley, where he could expect decent quarters for the night. The place seemed well kept, the outbuildings in good trim; and while the long, low one-story house did not look as large as the library wing at Westover, it had solid brick foundations and stood at the end of a charming lane of locust trees.

The widow struck Byrd as grave at first ("suspecting I was some lover," Byrd surmised), and the traveler must have feared another dreary rustic evening of forced conversation and feigned sleepiness. Mrs. Syme, however, "brightened up" as soon as she learned her visitor's distinguished identity, and before long they had "tossed off a bottle of honest port" and "relished it with a broiled chicken."

Byrd looked at his hostess closely and was thoroughly charmed. He saw a "portly, handsome dame . . . with much less reserve than most of her countrywomen." Her heartiness was very becoming, he thought; it set off her other agreeable qualities to advantage. Byrd had heard some malicious talk in the neighborhood, but to his eye her child certainly bore the "strong" (that is to say, ugly) features of the late Colonel Syme. The man was rather a "saracen," Byrd knew, coarse and uncouth, not at all like his cheerful, practical widow. If the philandering Byrd sensed an amorous opportunity, the moment passed unseized, for his account of the evening concludes demurely: "At nine I retired to my devotions and then slept so sound that fancy itself was stupefied, else I should have dreamt of my most obliging landlady."

The morning brought another amiable meeting over milk and tea. The "courteous widow" invited Colonel Byrd to rest a day from his travels and accompany her to church, "but I excused myself," Byrd says, "by telling her that she would certainly spoil my devotion." The widow reminded the colonel that her house would always be his home when he visited his plantations in the neighborhood. Byrd bowed low and thanked her very kindly.

The hospitable widow had another admirer for whom Studley had already become home. He was John Henry, a Scotsman from Aberdeenshire like her late husband, and he had made his way to the Syme plantation shortly after his arrival in Virginia in 1727. Colonel Syme had taken his countryman into the household; the young man had some skills in mathematics, and he joined Syme in his surveying projects. When his host died, John Henry stayed on at Studley, undoubtedly making himself useful in managing the plantation affairs. Within a year or so of Colonel Byrd's visit, the Scotsman married the Widow Syme. In another year their first son was born and named William for his mother's frontiersman brother, and on May 29, 1736, their second son arrived. They named him Patrick for his father's older brother, an Anglican minister who had just come from Scotland to take up the vacant pastorate at St. Paul's, Hanover.

The match was a lopsided one. By marrying the Widow Syme, née Sarah Winston, John Henry acquired an interest in a promising plantation, a fistful of up-country land patents, and a connection with one of the county's better families. In marrying John Henry, Sarah Winston Syme acquired a husband more educated than most local men, including her father and brothers, but a man without much pedigree or, as it turned out, business sense.

The Henrys (or Hendries) had eked out a living as farmers and herdsmen in a quiet parish outside Aberdeen on Scotland's rugged northeastern coast. The family had a reputation for probity but not much else beyond its good name. John's older brother, Patrick, had won a scholarship to Kings College, Aberdeen, and had taken his degree there in 1718. John, too, showed enough promise to be given some early training in a parish school, after which he passed the stiff competitive examination and enrolled at Kings in 1720. If tradition held, he would have brought with him the sack of oatmeal upon which scholarship boys were expected to sustain themselves all term.

John Henry's name appears on the college rolls for four years, but he left abruptly for America when either academic failure or some infraction of the cloister's rules denied him a degree. Some combination of desperation and hope led him to endure nine weeks aboard a crowded vessel where "betwixt decks," a countryman wrote, "ther was some sleeping, some spewing, some pishing, some shiting, some farting, some flyting, some damning, some Blasting their leggs and thighs, some their Liver, lungs, lights and eyes, And for to make the scene the odder, some curs'd Father, Mother, Sister, and Brother."

The grueling voyage over, John Henry gratefully inhaled the sweet and prosperous air of Virginia. Everyone ate wheat bread there, immigrants soon learned, and they had their work done by servants, in one Scotsman's terse description, "as Black as the D——s A——se." John Henry settled in his brother's parish and sought out his fellow Scots for assistance in making a fresh start. With Syme's help he patented some land in western Hanover in 1727, but made no move to open it to cultivation. On January 28, 1733, a few months after Byrd's visit to Studley, John Henry (now writing "Gent." after his name) received a grant for twelve hundred acres between Fork and Roundabout creeks in upper Hanover. The property adjoined land patented by Sarah Winston Syme.

John Henry had taken a traditional shortcut on the road to wealth and power. He had married up, stepping into the shoes and bed of a spirited entrepreneur and expecting to carry forward the late colonel's affairs in a rewarding manner. Sarah Winston had displayed her family's penchant for taking the handiest solution. Young widows seldom remained by themselves for long; she might have returned to her father's house at Laurel Grove or operated Studley independently with some assistance from her brothers. Yet Providence had set in her path a civilized successor to her brutish late husband, and Sarah, with her sharp intelligence but rudimentary schooling, also seized an opportunity to marry up.

At first things went swimmingly. As a literate, college-trained man, well spoken if somewhat pedantic and tedious, John Henry had obvious qualifications for leadership. With the strength of Winston connections he had no trouble securing entry into the county's governing circle, becoming an acting justice of the peace in 1737, a year after Patrick's birth, and an officer in the county militia. He had enough standing, moreover, to enjoy political favors from the Governor's Council in the form of readily granted patents for extensive tracts of land on the upper stretches of the James River; some he held in his own name, others in partnership with his father-in-law Isaac Winston or his brother the parson. He sold the parish some land for its glebe and minister's house, took his place on the vestry, and served his turn as church warden. The distinguished Colonel William Byrd called occasionally at Studley, taking eight hours to drive the forty miles from Westover in his coach and then enjoying fowl and bacon at "Major Henry's" table, along with a friendly game of cards and some talk about Hanover land the grandee had decided to sell.

The mood of the county matched the major's optimism. In 1736 and again in 1737, the leading gentlemen organized a St. Andrew's Day Fete that proclaimed their exuberant satisfaction amid banners and toasts, the beating of drums, and the sounding of trumpets. Rough Virginia planters from the poor fringes of Scotland and the West Country strolled with their ladies about "the Old Field" (with permission kindly granted by its proprietor, the Honorable William Byrd) like country squires back home. They avidly bet on the horse races and lustily cheered the cudgeling bouts, the foot races, and the fiddling contests. After a goodly feast the entire company listened to "a number of Songsters" with "Liquor sufficient to clear their windpipes" perform "a Quire of Ballads."

Hanover gentlemen had large hopes for the county's economic growth. John Henry helped to underwrite the building of a wooden bridge across the Pamunkey near a tobacco warehouse, and as the local surveyor he drew up an ambitious plan for a town at the site. It would be called Newcastle, after the flourishing port in England, and Henry envisioned a grand main street sixty feet wide running parallel to the river with a major cross street leading to the bridge. He laid out fifty lots above the riverbank. Colonel Meriwether, who owned the warehouse, bought six, and Major Henry spoke for one himself, intending to build a town house there someday when Newcastle outstripped Williamsburg and had perhaps become the capital of the province.

Unfortunately John Henry's ambitions far outran his talents. Hanover remained a backwater, and Henry's fortunes sank into the morass of failed dreams. Within a few years the Pamunkey bridge fell into disrepair and opinion divided about the wisdom of bothering to repair it. The river silted up frequently and made navigation hazardous. Newcastle remained no more than a crossroads, although when the Capitol at Williamsburg burned to the ground in 1747, Hanover interests unsuccessfully tried to persuade the assembly to rebuild on the Pamunkey. The bulk of the interior tobacco trade shifted twenty miles south where Colonel William Byrd's scheme for laying out a town called Richmond on the hills above the James had caught on. Byrd's father had long maintained a profitable trading post at this strategic spot, and the son had added mills and warehouses to the enterprise.

John Henry found it difficult to make Studley a commercially successful operation. He lacked farming skill and the patient attention to earthy detail it required, and he made unfortunate choices in overseers. While the plantation generated enough to keep his growing family fed and clothed, Henry accumulated little capital. He lacked the acumen required for far-flung operations. He found it hard to do anything with his western holdings and did not capitalize on his skill as a surveyor to get in on more profitable ventures. He did maintain his social position for some time, however. When his fellow justices chose him as sheriff in 1744, he took the post for more than reasons of prestige; he needed the income provided by the fees.

By 1749, however, John Henry realized that the family would have to move. His stepson, John Syme, Jr., would soon reach his majority and assert his rightful claim to Studley and much of his mother's property. (Long and complex litigation by the heir of Colonel Syme's first wife had whittled away a fair portion of the estate.) The Henry boys, William and Patrick, approached adolescence and their futures had to be decided, and there were a half a dozen younger daughters with pressing needs as well. By selling off his shares in some of the more grandiose western speculations, John Henry raised enough money to finance a move to the western edge of Hanover, twenty miles beyond Studley and a full day's ride through heavily wooded country from slumbering Newcastle. On the crest of a hill above the creek-sized South Anna River Henry built a small frame house and took heart in the Virginian's traditional remedy of plowing up fresh land. Henry optimistically called his new estate "Mount Brilliant," but for many years the family called it, more accurately, "The Retreat."

CHAPTER 2

The Dilapidated Colonel's Son

Patrick Henry grew up knowing that although he came from a good family, nothing much could be done for him. His father, riding to Hanover Court House on a fine horse, dressed in silks and wearing the gentleman's periwig, received the homage of his humbler farming neighbors, but the people who counted knew that Studley was not the best managed of estates, and young Patrick knew more keenly than most that its extensive lands, stocks, and slaves would pass in a few years to his older half brother, John Syme, Jr. The Henry boys could watch their father strut at the head of the county's militia company on muster days, listen to him toast the king in grandiloquent language, and jump excitedly as the company fired off volley after volley in salute to their father's generosity in providing the punch that always concluded the day's business. Yet Patrick knew, too, that Major Henry did not confine his drinking to muster days, that large tracts of the fabled western lands that were to be their salvation could easily change hands at the card table, and that behind the appearance of grandeur lay only insubstantial hopes.

He could hardly remember a time without trouble in the family: not only the nag of money matters and the unease of precarious station, but the heat and fury of religious dispute. The "red hot Comet" of the evangelical revival had raced through Hanover in the 1740s, as indeed it had throughout the colonies, kindling what its partisans praised as "a great and general Awakening" of the spirit and what its critics termed "a rueful Conflagration" that "would soon set the World on Fire in good earnest." The Henry family smoldered for years in its embers.

Patrick's mother, perhaps sensing hollowness at the core of her family's life or seeking a remedy for a "kind of lethregie" plantation women sometimes felt, had accepted the warm embrace of the Presbyterian revival, her soul newly awakened to the beauty of Christ's grace. Patrick's grandfather, Isaac Winston, also experienced what the evangelists called "the new birth" and went with the dissenters; indeed his own conversion helped ignite the Hanover revival. He had stopped attending services at the established (Anglican) church, having grown dissatisfied with the "general strain of preaching." His unease could not be put into so many words, but people like him tended to say that they wanted more "savour" in preaching, more piety and less discourse. He had grown less interested in worldly things and more concerned about the state of his soul. Without ever having heard of the New England evangelist Jonathan Edwards, Old Isaac had come to embody that preacher's observation in defense of the emotional revivals sweeping his church: "Our people do not so much need to have their heads stored as to have their hearts touched."

Instead of Anglican services, Isaac Winston participated in a reading group of like-minded souls gathered in their own homes. They studied a much-worn pamphlet of printed sermons by the celebrated revivalist George Whitefield, "the greatest orator since the Apostles," people said, whose tour of the colonies in 1739–40 had set the churches ablaze. Grandfather Winston had allowed itinerant preachers—full of the new gospel and ready to touch the emotions of their listeners— to speak in his home at Laurel Grove, and he had contributed to the building of "reading houses" when the eager crowds grew too large for front parlors. For all these affronts to the laws regulating religious worship, Isaac Winston had stood several times before the Hanover magistrates, including his son-in-law John Henry, to pay fines for "willfully" absenting himself from church services and to stare grimly at his benighted accusers.

Major Henry remained a vestryman, however, a pillar of the church and a staunch defender of every aspect of the church establishment, including the character of the parish rector, his brother Patrick. The dissenters called Parson Henry "a stranger to true religion," and one, Roger Shackleford, went so far as to say publicly that the minister had "preached damnable Doctrine" and ought to be pitied as an "unconverted graceless man." The "new light" enthusiasts held that true Christians could tell whether a minister had experienced his own new birth by the manner of his preaching, and by the revivalist standard the entire Anglican clergy seemed cold-blooded and lacking in conviction. They read dull homilies, sanctimonious lectures on virtue, in velvet tones perfectly tuned to the gentry's own complacency. Indeed, clergymen gained praise for taking on the traits of the gentlemen in their parish: they were good-humored, conversant about business as well as books, "good Christians without appearing stoicks," as one approving minister put it, and above all, willing "to give up a small matter rather than create disturbance and mischief."

Parson Henry would not suffer the mischief-makers in silence. Young Patrick, the cleric's namesake, heard his uncle fulminate against the "new preachers that have lately seduced some unwary people in this parish," and he would watch wide-eyed as his uncle related with horror how the revivalists stamped and beat their pulpits, raised their voices, made spectacles of themselves, and frightened their listeners into convulsions. Patrick listened to his uncle and his father fashion an introduction to a pamphlet from New England entitled *An Impartial Trial of the Spirit*, which attacked itinerant preachers so soundly that the Henry brothers sought to reprint it for circulation in Virginia. Their preface branded itinerants as "a set of incendiaries, Enemies not only to the Established Church, but also common Disturbers of the Peace." If factious and restless people could be led to put up meetinghouses as they pleased without leave or license, the brothers reasoned, the security of both religion and society would become very precarious. They ridiculed the revivalists, moreover, as mountebanks who had stepped into the pulpit directly from "the Plough," "their pretended conversion supplying the place of learning."

At nine years old, Patrick was old enough to remember the commotion surrounding George Whitefield's visit to Hanover in October 1745. Major Henry and his brother consulted for many anxious hours after word arrived that the great evangelist would pass through the county, and the parson ultimately decided to allow Whitefield, an ordained Anglican minister now in the fold of the Methodist revival, to speak from his own pulpit. "If I had refused him access to the Church, he would have preached in the Church yard, or very near it," Henry told his superiors, "and then the whole congregation would have gone over to him."

Parson Henry extracted a concession or two from the revivalist, who agreed not to baptize any children in the parish and to preface his sermon with the customary litany from the Book of Common Prayer. Thus assured that his authority as parish minister would not be undermined, Henry stepped aside, "for all the people to a man had a great desire to hear the famous Whitefield." Young Patrick pressed into the church along with everyone else, making "the church itself hot with their breath," as Whitefield once wrote in his diary about the crowds at his appearances, "that the steam would fall from the pillars like drops of rain."

More itinerants followed Whitefield, and Parson Henry came frequently to Studley to consult with Major Henry on how best to stop them. Over and over again the boy heard of the distracted condition of the parish and future disturbances his elders feared. The revivalists "screw up the People to the greatest heights of religious Phrenzy," his uncle said, "and then leave them in that wild state, for perhaps ten or twelve months, till another Enthusiast comes among them, to repeat the same thing over again." Yet when the Presbyterians tried to get their ministers licensed, the Henry brothers worked hard (used their "Interest with our Court," as they put it) to block such action, trying to avoid all encouragement that could be legally denied.

In 1747 the Reverend Samuel Davies came to Hanover from Pennsylvania, assigned by the Presbyterian Synod to take up a regular mission in Virginia. A young widower, educated at one of the new academies the dissenters had established in the middle colonies to train clergymen, Davies entered a room "like the ambassador of some mighty King." He proved a stunning diplomat. Slender and solemn, with winning manners and unshakable integrity, he minced no words about the "swarms of prayerless families" in Virginia, the people who ate no "spiritual food" or—far worse—grew "nauseated" on the thin gruel served up to them, and the deferential clergy who manifested the "cringing compliance of worms to worms, of clay to clay, of guilt to guilt." Yet instead of denouncing the government's intransigence, as had some of his itinerant predecessors, he sweetly complied with all the tedious requirements for a license, signed the necessary declarations without a murmur, and blithely agreed to whatever the governor, William Gooch, asked of him. At the same time he wittily countered the Henry brothers' reprinted pamphlet with one of his own, entitled *The Impartial Trial, impartially tried, and convicted of Partiality*. Licensed at last, Davies took up a pastorate in Hanover that included about 150 families in two meetinghouses. Before long he had married a local woman, started a family of his own, and undertaken circuit-riding assignments in the adjoining western counties. He attracted hundreds of listeners and established three more meetinghouses, all of which he managed to get duly licensed after the fact. "Where I go amongst Mr. Davies people," a visiting Presbyterian exclaimed, "religion seems to flourish; it is like the suburbs of Heaven."

Sarah Henry, like everyone else, found Davies's preaching close to sublime. She took her little girls with her to the services and had their older brother Patrick, now entering his teens, drive the carriage. On the way home she would make Patrick repeat aloud the substance of the sermon.

Davies spoke with uncommon artistry, and Patrick sat in church transfixed. The sermons had a seamless unity, with emotion and reason flowing simultaneously to a series of excited climaxes. The man could modulate his voice into a great variety of tones, booming and hushed, lyrical, penitent, frightened. He could enact, right before the congregation's eyes, the majestic scenes of resurrection and judgment so that his listeners could see and feel the cosmic drama unfold. He would put them in the immense crowd gathered at the Judgment Seat, warn them that the Judge's eye "will be as particularly fixed on every one of us as though there were but one before him," and portray the piteous scene as the Judge divided the multitude upon his right and left hands.

"But O! when I think what unexpected separations will then be made, I tremble lest I should miss some of you there," Davies would moan, then stare down from the pulpit for a long, silent moment. "Are you not afraid lest you should miss some of your friends, or some of your families there?" Davies spoke from notes alone, keying his examples and varying his tempo with the response of his listeners. His sentences stood plain and unadorned. No elaborate constructions concealed their meaning, and no textual or logical proofs crippled their pace. He addressed the congregation directly, and he could arrest attention with a single word.

"Awake."

"Arise."

"Exert yourselves."

"I would you were cold or hot," Davies would cry, and the one word would shiver and the other glow. "Either make thorough work of religion, or do not pretend to it."

No wonder that on the long drives home Patrick would find himself half standing as he retold the sermon, find himself shaping words and phrases in echoes of Davies's style. No wonder, too, that observers likened Davies to "a skillful pleader before a jury," mingling principles, facts, and feelings with "resistless effect," or that in later years Patrick Henry would claim Davies as the greatest speaker he had ever heard and the most profound influence upon him.

Yet Patrick, for all the power of Davies's sermons and his mother's earnest solicitation, never experienced "the new birth." He watched and he listened, but he held himself aloof. He enjoyed the spectacle, the mingling, and he sensed the power of the voice to unite a multitude, but Davies never swayed him from his father's church. Perhaps Patrick had already spent too much time in the world of men to be entirely comfortable in the "beloved community" his mothers and sisters had formed among themselves. Moreover, Patrick could plainly see that with the exception of his Winston kin and a handful of other gentlefolk, the evangelical dissenters came primarily from the lower ranks of ordinary farmers and tenants. The better sort of people had remained firmly within the Anglican parish, and, as an ambitious youth who would have to make his own way, Patrick did not want to turn his back upon the sociability of a Virginia Sunday.

The crowd of gentlemen would gather early in the churchyard to hear the news, swap business letters and advertisements, consult about the current prices of tobacco and grain, and set up horse races and cock matches. Patrick could stand with his father in this elite circle and enter church with them in a body, just as the sexton made ready to close the doors. St. Paul's had built a gallery in 1745, "appropriated to the use of the Gentlemen Justices, vestry men, and their Families," and Major Henry would take his place above the main floor with a pride made fierce by the felt absence of his wife. Services would be brief, the prayers read hastily and casually, and from his balcony perch Patrick could survey the community below, seated in ranks as the church wardens thought fit. Patrick, too, could see the top of his uncle's head, barely visible to the rest of the congregation above the deep sides of the lectern, as Parson Henry read his short lecture on some point of sound morality. After church, the "polite assembly" would stroll about the yard, exchanging pleasantries and invitations to dinner, while young beaux took opportunities to display their gallantry with the ladies and perhaps arrange for an afternoon of racing or the barbecue of some lambs or hogs.

Patrick thus had a dual upbringing. From the evangelical world of his mother he gained a sense of ardent fellowship, an appreciation of the power of "enthusiastick" emotion and zeal, and a striking sense of theater. Whitefield's "enchanting Sound," it was said, "would equally have produced the same Effects whether he had acted his Part in the Pulpit or on the Stage." For Patrick the many days in the clapboard Presbyterian meetinghouse proved the equivalent of long evenings at Garrick's in London, and in time he would become a superb political actor. From his father's genteel Anglicanism Patrick retained some commitment to form and propriety. He never left the Episcopal church, and he mastered the affability of gentry style, even when he came to challenge gentry power.

There were immediate domestic consequences. Sarah Henry withdrew much of her participation in genteel social life. She set herself against the drinking, gambling, and dancing that comprised her husband's chief diversions and the stuff of gentry political life. For his part, John Henry stood alienated from his well-connected father-in-law. When the Trans-Allegheny West was opened to patent in 1749, the Winstons got in on a major grant of fifty thousand acres, but John Henry was excluded from the deal. The move from Studley to the new farm at Mount Brilliant soon followed. John Henry ceased to be a vestryman in his brother's parish, and no one invited him to take on the duties of church government in his new neighborhood.

Influenced by his mother's standing rebuke to his father, Patrick acquired an unusual degree of personal abstemiousness —an indifference to fashionable dress, fine furnishings, and good liquor—but he remained ambitious, eager for success, and comfortable with tavern and courthouse politics. Ultimately Patrick Henry would amalgamate the evangelical and gentry styles into a powerful political identity. He would mingle with the gentry and understand its quiet paths to power. Yet he would always be an outsider, a man who could reach out to ordinary people, speak to them with fire and conviction, meld them into one community of belief, and turn that massed opinion into a new tool of political control.

It would take time to perfect and fuse the roles. Young Patrick, not surprisingly, proved to be a shrewd observer, alert yet noncommittal. He developed what contemporaries termed "a remarkable facility of adapting himself to his company" and a "most extraordinary talent" for finding out others' views without disclosing his own. He watched closely, listened carefully, and asked seemingly irrelevant questions, yet "nothing escaped his attention."

A moody boy, inclined to keep to himself, he took off alone on long hunting and fishing expeditions. He was the most patient fisherman imaginable, his friends all said, a fellow who could sit for hours angling at the same spot if he sensed that something might eventually bite. When Patrick hunted with companions he still jockeyed for the solitary stand or hung back to study birdcalls or lose himself in the immense silence of the wood. The forests teemed with squirrels, hares, partridges, wild turkeys, and an occasional red deer. Wild swans and geese clustered on the marshes, and great flocks of ducks coasted easily on the river. Patrick proved "remarkably fond of his gun" and would have learned much from his uncle "Langloo" Winston, who lived at least half the year in remote mountain cabins, hunting deer and trading with the distant Indians. Langloo preferred buckskin to broadcloth, was whispered to have had Indian wives, and kept his distance from the polite society of Tidewater. Throughout his life Patrick maintained a fondness for the solitude of the back-country; he frequently picked out-of-the-way corners for his periods of retirement, and hunting remained a favorite diversion. Even as a circuit-riding lawyer, he would pause along the trail to stalk game and arrive at the courthouse, people said, with a brace of ducks across his saddle and his blood-stained leather hunting jacket still upon his back.

Patrick had a fun-loving, even mischievous streak, however. Fishing from a dugout canoe, he could suddenly propose a swim, shuck off his clothes, and dive from the canoe in a way that would capsize the craft and drench his still-clothed, slower companions. He could be a daredevil at treeclimbing and would swing across the creeks from the branches of ancient overhanging beeches. He coaxed the little servant boys into feats even more outlandish than his own, paying out his pennies to see the blackamoors climb tall pines feet first.

Although he preferred the isolation of the countryside, Patrick did not come across in company as bashful. He dressed presentably, had the knack of pleasant conversation, and enjoyed the display of country dancing. He had a good ear for music, and he could entertain passably upon the violin, his repertoire composed of familiar airs and rustic fiddler's tunes rather than the polite trio sonatas favored in the drawing rooms of Williamsburg and the Tidewater mansions. He also learned to play the flute, puzzling out the instrument for himself and not relying upon the books of tunes published for gentlemen musicians.

His method of learning always led him to intuitive and practical paths rather than to formal or bookish approaches. In this he proved like other Virginians who, one visitor said, "are more inclinable to read men by business and conversation, than to dive into books, and are for the most part only desirous of learning what is absolutely necessary, in the shortest and best method." Henry "was not a man of regularity or system," his son-in-law Spencer Roane recalled, and the youthful Patrick seemed to learn more by osmosis than by reading. Neither the boy nor the man he became ever had a reputation as a bookworm or scholar. He once told Roane that he considered Montesquieu's *Spirit of the Laws* to be a perfect companion for a journey by stagecoach, for a half hour's reading would provide ample material for a day's reflection. "Such was somewhat the proportion," said the son-in-law, "between Mr. Henry's education as drawn from reading and from observation and reflection."

Patrick had only the scantiest of elementary schooling. His father had given both boys some fundamental instruction in reading and arithmetic, and Parson Henry added some work in the catechism. The boys may have spent a few months at a neighborhood "English" school studying grammar and spelling from the traditional hornbooks, but their lessons generally took place at home, at odd intervals depending upon the plantation routine and their teacher's persistence. Patrick did learn to write and spell respectably and to keep careful accounts. As the boys approached their teens, their father, proud of his new rank of colonel, set them to a course in Latin and then added a smattering of Greek and ancient history. Samuel Davis had once described Colonel Henry as a man "who knew his Horace better than his Bible," but despite this faint praise John Henry was not especially noted for the vigor of his intellect. His curriculum consisted of oddments remembered from his own years in Aberdeen and the exhortations by which mediocrity justifies routine. None of this did much harm, but it hardly kindled sparks of lasting intellectual excitement. Patrick's father's teaching undoubtedly leaned toward the pedantic elements of grammar rather than the poetry or drama of the texts and could not have been as soulful or as sweeping as the sermons of the Reverend Davies in opening vistas for the young man's contemplation.

Formal education, such as it was, ended when Patrick reached fifteen, only a few years after the family's move up-country to Mount Brilliant. His hard-pressed father could not afford to send the boy "back home" to study in England or at his alma mater, Kings, in Scotland. Nor could money be spared to establish young Patrick in Williamsburg for a term or two at the struggling College of William and Mary, the colony's only formal institution of higher learning. The failure to provide his sons with an education comparable to his own grieved John Henry. He was a university man, his patina of erudition his only strong suit; in a few years his literacy would become his livelihood when money problems reduced him to operating a plantation school for the children of his well-to-do neighbors.

Instead of being sent off to Williamsburg, London, or Aberdeen, Patrick found himself back on the banks of the Pamunkey. His father arranged a position for him as an apprentice clerk with one of the Scotch merchants in Newcastle. Patrick would return to his half brother's house at Studley to live while he learned the mercantile business. The position, humble as it sounded, was something of a plum, however. The Glasgow owners of the upriver concerns did not like to take on local youth, believing that in the wilds of America young men acquired "a reluctance to confinement and drudgery" with "too many passions to serve before they can be serviceable to any man." But someone did John Henry a favor by giving his son a few months of training, after which the colonel purchased a small stock of goods on credit and established Patrick, along with brother William, in a small store of their own.

Dr. Johnson's dictionary defined a merchant as "one who trafficks to remote countries" in contrast to the shopkeeper, "a trader who sells in a shop; not a merchant who deals only by wholesale." By these usages John Henry was setting his sons up as shopkeepers, or what Virginians styled "traders," in a small-scale enterprise with almost no potential for growth. In Virginia the great Tidewater planters also acted as merchants by importing goods directly to their own wharves and reselling some of their "stores" to neighboring people. As settlement spread beyond Tidewater, a number of Scotch mercantile houses, especially in Glasgow, bypassed the planters and their London connections to establish networks of stores at strategic inland points. From crude beginnings as utilitarian cabins at the end of a river landing these storehouses grew into elaborate concerns with brick residences for the resident agent, large warehouses, barns, craft shops, and inventories running to thousands of pounds. At Newcastle and Hanover Town Scotsmen such as Francis Jerdone and A. Gordon worked as import merchants for overseas firms and local retailers. They handled the planters' tobacco, wrote the all-important bills of exchange that kept men afloat with credit, and took orders for European goods. A small crossroads store, such as John Henry proposed for his sons, could not compete with the larger outfits and merely existed on their fringes. Country traders generally farmed as well as tended store, or sold goods to the neighborhood as an adjunct to a milling or smithy operation.

Yet Patrick and William Henry had to make their whole living from the sale of hairpins and padlocks, snuff and shoes, pocket knives, candle molds, and piece goods. By living at Studley, where John Syme, Jr., had taken some bold steps to increase the income from the plantation, they could meet their basic needs for food and shelter at little or no expense. All the more reason to expect two high-spirited adolescents to be indifferent, careless shopkeepers, impatient with detail and far too casual about credit. In the way of balky children, too, Patrick suddenly developed a profound interest in reading and could scarcely be persuaded to look up from his newspaper or his worn editions of "Don Quick Zotte" or "Robertson Crueso" when the infrequent customer ventured into the cabin with its haphazardly stocked shelves.

The store sank into its inevitable bankruptcy within a year. Colonel Henry was not pleased. He exiled the rowdy and profligate William to a patch of unoccupied land fifty miles west on Fluvanna Creek, where the young man took hold as a farmer, married, and ultimately turned into a prosperous, solid citizen. Patrick escaped whatever plan his father had formulated for him by seizing the hour of insolvency to get married.

Her name was Sarah Shelton; the family called her Sallie. She had a pretty, round face, dark brown hair, and deep brown eyes. Her family lived at Rural Plains, only a few miles from Studley, and Patrick had known her all his life. He would have paid his "addresses" in the whirl of barbecues and dances that county society enjoyed, strolling under the ample shade trees, breaking away from the drunken capers, the loud young men singing the same bawdy songs over and over again, the pulling and hauling of the fancy reels and jigs in which partners outdid each other in solo display. The parties often lasted all night; "every gentleman here has ten or fifteen beds which is aplenty for the ladies," a Virginia buck explained to a friend in England, "and the Men Ruffs it."

The Sheltons were good people, surely respectable if not

quite in the upper echelon. John Shelton farmed extensively and owned the profitable tavern across the road from Hanover Court House. His wife, Eleanor, had recently inherited a considerable sum from her father, William Parks, a printer and bookseller in Williamsburg, who had established the colony's first and only newspaper, the *Virginia Gazette*, in 1736, the year of Patrick's birth.

At eighteen Patrick was marrying four or five years earlier than most Virginia males of his station, and Sallie, too, at sixteen, was bowing out of the giddy courting society somewhat abruptly. Minors in Virginia needed their parents' consent to wed, and the two families reluctantly agreed to let the marriage proceed. The Sheltons had misgivings about the impecunious young man and the deteriorating reputation of his family, while John Henry no doubt hoped that Patrick would someday make a more prosperous and elevating match, as he had himself attempted. The families, however, had little choice. The ardent couple pressed their claims in overpowering fashion and, conceivably, told their families with some embarrassment that passion had raced ahead of the parson, making an early wedding suddenly necessary.

In October 1754 the two families and their assorted kinfolk crowded into the small front parlor of the Sheltons' modest house to hear the Reverend Patrick Henry read the ceremony by which his impulsive nephew married his sixteen-year-old sweetheart. John Shelton gave three hundred acres of land and six black slaves as his daughter's dowry. The farm, inauspiciously known as Pine Slash, lay half a mile down a winding road from Sallie's parents' house, and on it Patrick would have to make a living from tobacco planting. The land was sandy, partially cleared and somewhat worn from prior crops, with a second growth of scrub pine, some serviceable farm buildings, and a modest frame house. (Patrick's father had taken him aside to promise some fresh land farther west in Louisa County but had explained that it would be some time before he could actually convey it.)

Patrick had to clear some new fields on the piney land if he expected much return beyond subsistence, and like the other struggling farmers of the neighborhood he would have to work in the fields himself. He had never farmed before, nor had he much experience at directing the labor of slaves. With the exception of an older woman to help Sallie manage the kitchen and household (and cope with baby Martha, nicknamed Patsy, who arrived early in the summer of 1755), the dowry slaves proved to be youngsters—an investment in the future, to be sure, but more helpful with the cooking, washing, and farmyard chores than with the staple crop.

With one or two black youths a few years younger than himself, Patrick labored through the long months of a tobacco season. They cleared planting beds in March, burning off the grass, then plowing the ground and breaking it up with hoes and rakes. They mixed their seed with ashes and pressed it into the soil, covering the patch with brush to protect against late frost. While the seedlings grew, they prepared the fields, plowing, manuring, and shaping mounds three feet apart and the height of a man's knee. Then came the transplanting, after a rain shower so that the little plants could be moved easily, one to each mound. There followed long weeks of weeding, removing leaves growing too low to the ground, nipping off the flowering tops and keeping the plant trimmed to the nine leaves everyone allowed was the best size. Then the awful midsummer task of "worming"—endless marches up and down the rows to pick off the hawkmoth in its larval stage and crush the fat lumps underfoot. Finally, Patrick and his help would harvest the leaves, hang them to dry on rows of sticks in a dark shanty, sort the results, and—at last—"prize" the crinkly wafers into great barrels for shipment, as the geese flew south overhead and the morning mists broadcast the sweet scent of the finished crop.

A rough and sweaty existence, it dispelled Patrick's reputation for indolence, but it must have wracked his heart to realize that he had sunk to the level of a rude husbandman. How long would the homes of gentlefolk be open to him if he had to work all day right alongside the darkies, with only a few hogsheads of mediocre weed the result? At Studley, John Syme, Jr., only six years older, had enough people to grow a large crop, and, what was more, with the profits he was buying more slaves to work his western lands. Syme had already become a county justice and had stood for a seat in the House of Burgesses, and here Patrick stood up to his ears in tobacco worms. In six years Pine Slash would still be no more than a dirt farm, and Patrick could see himself as defeated as the sorry land itself.

Patrick Henry had the misfortune to take up farming in a year plagued first with summer drought and then with early frost. Hanover produced only 1,550 hogsheads of tobacco, instead of the previous year's 4,000. "The poor people are now very much pinched," the merchant Francis Jerdone advised his associates early in 1756. Although the short crop had driven up prices, Jerdone explained that trade had nearly stopped owing to the alarm spreading from the frontier, where "French Indians" were "laying waste the back country by fire and flood."

Virginia had begun to feel the consequences of Britain's worldwide war with France for colonial empire. In July 1755 word had reached Hanover that General Braddock had died in an unsuccessful attack on Fort Duquesne and that a young Virginia colonel, George Washington of Potomac River, had bravely regrouped the tattered regiment and conducted it to safety. The House of Burgesses resolved to place Washington at the head of a new Virginia regiment that would resist French encroachments, and in Hanover John Syme, Jr., and other gentlemen, including Patrick's intrepid uncle, Langloo Winston, sprang to form their own cavalry troop. Samuel Davies preached a thrilling sermon at the courthouse intended to recruit men for Colonel Washington.

"Shall Virginia incur the guilt, and the everlasting shame, of tamely exchanging her liberty, British liberty, her religion, and her all, for arbitrary Gallic power, and for Popish slavery, tyranny, and massacre?" Davies asked the crowd.

"Virginians! Britons! Christians! Protestants! if these names have any import or energy, will you not strike home in such a cause?

"We fight," he said, "for the cities of our God."

The prospect of military glory must have tempted Patrick as an escape from his domestic and economic trap, but he resisted Davies's call to arms and remained in stubborn battle with the soil. In the spring of 1757, however, with an infant son, John, added to the family, his circumstances worsened. Fire destroyed the young family's house and most of their possessions, and they had to set up temporarily in a dilapidated overseer's cabin one hundred yards away from the charred ruins. The place had only three rooms, connected to each other in a straight line, with some "jump" rooms under the roof for sleeping. A six-foot-wide chimney afforded fireplaces in two rooms downstairs, but it was by far the rudest dwelling in which Patrick or Sallie had ever lived. They struggled through the summer and another poor harvest, but by fall it became clear that they could not go on. John Shelton offered his daughter and her growing family a place in the tavern he owned at Hanover Court House.

Hanover Tavern consisted of a long rectangular structure with a broad porch running the length of one side, butt end to the road. An ordinary Virginia cabin stood attached at the rear of the opposite wall, with the ground-floor basements of both buildings joined into an L-shaped taproom and eatery. Patrick tended bar across from the large fireplace and looked after the lodgers upstairs, while Sallie set up family housekeeping in the cabin. The tavern, situated on the main road to Williamsburg and Richmond, did a lively business, and Patrick proved a genial host. "Generally clad in an Oznaburg Shirt Jump, Jacket and Trowsers of Ozna or checks, and very often barefooted," a Winston cousin recalled, "he was very active and attentive to his guests and very frequently amused them with his violin."

Patrick also decided to make another try at storekeeping. He sold off a few of his Negroes and bought a small stock of goods. This time he hired a clerk, while he divided his time among tavern, store, and farm. The new store fared better than the earlier one, at least at first. Patrick's relatives made small but frequent purchases, although his father evidently arranged for Patrick to pay off some of the colonel's small personal debts out of the store's accounts. Some of the court-house trade filtered past the store, located on the main road about a mile south of the little center. Mr. Pollard, the court clerk, bought a few notebooks and expressed his regards. As with any store, people would stop by to chat for hours and then perhaps, like Pleasant and John Stanley on September 6, purchase a button for one shilling threepence. Patrick opened for business in the summer of 1758 and only took in about £10 during the hot months preceding the harvest.

Weeks went by without rain, the weather stayed "mighty hot and very dry," flies and worms ate their fill, and people started saying it would be the worst crop in many years. Good customers like the Widow Barnett came into the store to buy large supplies of "Brown Holland," "Linnen," and "Ozna-brug" cloth and a sufficient quantity of thread, pins, and buttons for the winter's sewing, but most of the trade went on the book as credit advanced by the storekeeper. At the year's end, Patrick could look at paper profits of about £100, but he was still obliged to feed his family out of the tavern's kitchen garden and tend bar to keep the roof over their heads. The next year saw another damaged harvest, and the debt columns in the large account book grew longer and darker. Patrick lost his capital and owed money, but everyone was in the same fix, and he remained unperturbed. The combination of pursuits had given him the sense of being a man of affairs; he had recovered his self-esteem.

When Patrick took his family to his parents' house at Mount Brilliant for Christmas 1759, he spent much time socializing at the nearby home of Colonel Nathaniel West Dandridge, a man of large means and good connections through his marriage to Dorothea Spotswood, the late governor's daughter. The parties were lively and gay, with wine, toddy, cider, and lemon punch flowing merrily, card games aplenty in every room, and minuets, reels, jigs, and marches performed in the ballroom to the accompaniment of violins and horns. At an interval in the dance, the ladies dined first and then the gents nimbly jockeyed for position at the tables filled with hams, fowls, hot breads, and an assortment of sweetmeats and syllabub.

Dandridge's house guests included the seventeen-year-old Tom Jefferson, on his way from his father's Albemarle County plantation to the college at Williamsburg. Jefferson recalled many years later that Patrick Henry's misfortunes could not be "traced, either in his countenance or conduct." He displayed, Jefferson recalled, only "a passion for music, dancing, and pleasantry," and although "his manners had something of coarseness in them," he so "excelled" at sociability that "it attached everyone to him." At least one of the guests was "a man of science," Jefferson remembered, but Henry could not be drawn into any serious talk. Absorbed in "the usual revelries of the season," however, the two became "well acquainted," Jefferson said, "although I was much his junior, being in my seventeenth year and he a married man."

Only six years older than Jefferson, Patrick Henry could see in the tall, sandy-haired youth from the flourishing Piedmont the path he had not been able to follow. Jefferson's father came from a poor family and had made his way as a surveyor and land speculator while marrying into one of the most reputable families in the colony, the vast Randolph clan. Unlike John Henry, however, Peter Jefferson had continued to prosper, had developed a sizable estate in the upper James River Valley, and could now send his eldest son off to Williamsburg, where Tom would spend the next five years in serious reading and contemplation. In the equivalent five years of his life Patrick Henry had failed in one business venture, married, fathered three children, brought a languishing farm into some modest renewal of productivity, started a second business, and kept himself afloat by mixed work as a bartender, innkeeper, farmer, and proprietor of a country store. Yet here he was, frolicking at the esteemed Colonel Dandridge's with the best people of the region, cutting a fine figure on the dance floor, carrying on with all the respectability and grace the gentry expected of its own. Behind so confident a performance Henry secretly harbored a plan that he hoped would give him the place and income he thought he deserved.

CHAPTER 3

"Bold License"

Henry had decided to become a lawyer. From his vantage point at Shelton's Tavern he had had ample opportunity to observe the members of the bar of justice in their informal moments. He listened carefully to the swirl of talk about covenants, declarations, and pleadings, and he grew intrigued with the discussions of stratagems and the boasting about how one had outfoxed another on some obscure point or technicality. On court days he joined the crowds gathered on the wooden benches of the courtroom across the road to follow the spectacle of the monthly sessions. He became fascinated with the stylish ways of the attorneys and the tangled web of emotions revealed in every case as members of a passionately acquisitive community went about the business of getting everything they could. Henry knew, too, that lawyers prospered from their fees and that increasingly the law provided a successful entry into political preferment and public office.

Not many routes to legal training existed. Henry could not even dream about a sojourn in one of the Inns of Court, although at least forty Virginians of his generation—the scions of the great planters—would study in London at an annual cost to their families of £250–300. English training carried weight, but many questioned its utility, since Virginia conditions were so different, its judges often laymen, and most case decisions unreported. But the few colonial colleges offered no specific courses in the law, although many provincial lawyers had at least studied philosophy, logic, and languages in them as useful intellectual foundation. Henry could not afford formal study of any sort, and he was too desperate and impatient to apprentice for several years as a law clerk with some older practitioner. To become a lawyer Henry would have to learn enough on his own to pass the entrance examination devised by the assembly in 1745 to keep the unscrupulous and unskilled from stirring up contention in order to enrich themselves. Under the new professional system, the Governor and his Privy Council would appoint a panel of distinguished attorneys to examine candidates for the bar upon their "capacity, ability and fitness." The exam would be conducted orally, examiners would question the candidate individually, and the signature of two examiners would be required for a license. Henry persuaded himself that he could meet the test.

He began to listen more closely to the lawyers' conversation in the taproom. He started to ask more questions about the cases he had heard argued in court, he asked to look at some of the legal papers the lawyers had crammed in their pockets, and he inquired after the odd terms—*ejectment, abatement, assumpsit, replevin, trover, tender,* and *demurrer*—he had heard the gentlemen employ. Attorneys traveled with their few law books in their saddlebags, and a law dictionary would be brought forth to confirm a definition or settle an argument provoked by differing answers to Henry's questions.

If Henry had pressed the friendly disputants to suggest a book for him to read, he would have heard only one name.

"Cook."

"Cook 'pon Littleton."

"Cook's Institutes."

They would all be talking about Sir Edward Coke's great treatise on the laws of England, first published in 1623, the fountainhead of learning upon the common law and the starting point for every fledgling lawyer in King George's great domain. Every novitiate read it, hated it, and solemnly recommended it evermore. "I do wish the Devil had old Cooke," Jefferson would complain a year or two later, "for I am sure I never was so tired of an old dull scoundrel in my life."

If one of the lawyers, John Lewis of Hanover most likely, had loaned Henry a copy of what Coke himself described as "a painful and large volume," he would have discovered that Coke upon Littleton consisted of one great jurist's comments upon another's work. Littleton had written a monumental fifteenth-century treatise on feudal tenures that Coke had annotated copiously with what amounted to a history and distillation of centuries of the common law on landholding. As Coke carefully put it in his subtitle, the work was "a commentary upon Littleton, not the name of the author, but of the law itself."

Henry supposed he knew enough Latin to understand the technical phrases of the law, but Coke's crabbed English would have given him pause. Hunched over the huge folio volume, Henry would have confronted ribbons of closely printed columns, one for Littleton's original text in a mixture of legal French and Latin, a second for Coke's translation into English, and a third for the comments, which sometimes ran far longer than the texts, covering all three columns and going on for pages about philosophy, philology, and precedent. Before starting the first chapter on fee simple, Henry might have found comfort in Coke's prefatory advice that one should read "no more at any one time than he is able with a Delight to bear away, and after to meditate thereon, which is the Life of Reading."

Henry had no time for meditation. Tradition holds that he set off for his bar examination having read only Coke upon Littleton and a digest of the laws of Virginia. He is supposed to have accomplished this study in six weeks, although some say the time was closer to six months. Even allowing the whole winter or extending the time to a year or more of long hours by candlelight and many days of courtroom observation and earnest discussion at the tavern, there is no question that Henry had only haphazard and skimpy preparation when he took advantage of a break in the stormy spring weather to ride to Williamsburg about the first of April 1760.

"A lawyer must have an iron head, a brazen face, and a leaden breech," ran an old saying at the Inns of Court. But for a twenty-four-year-old innkeeper to confront the luminaries of his intended profession on the strength of a winter's reading suggests a degree of presumption that might make even a barrister blush. Ambition, self-confidence, and desperation drove Henry to the little capital. His first cousin Edmund Winston regarded him now as "a virtuous young man, unconscious of the Power of his own Mind, in very narrow circumstance, making a last effort to supply the wants of his Family."

Henry spent two days traveling the fifty miles between Hanover Court House and Williamsburg. He had to detour many miles to negotiate crossings of the overflowing creeks, and his horse found the muddy, rutted road slow going. Approaching the town, he saw first the grounds of the College of William and Mary on the western edge of town, then the spacious three-story college building, first "modeled" from a design by Sir Christopher Wren. From the cupola, which offered a superb view of the James and York rivers, each about three or four miles away, visitors could look out across the town, a neatly ordered cluster of two hundred houses, uniformly set back from the streets, on half-acre lots, with gardens and orchards separating the wooden dwellings and inhibiting the congestion which might lead to fire. The spacious main street, nearly as broad as the college grounds, ran almost a mile straight across to the handsome brick Capitol at its opposite end. Midway along, the line broke for the market square, with its cluster of taverns and shops, the public armory, and a greensward running north toward the stately Governor's Palace. At "Publick Times," such as the assembly session just concluded, the town filled with visitors, there were splendid entertainments, and at night the public buildings glowed with lanterns placed at every window. But with the legislature in recess and the courts adjourned, Henry made his way about a sleepy village, no more than a thousand souls, white and black. To a young man just in from a backwater hamlet, however, the streets seemed as thronged as if it were court day back home.

At least four of the gentlemen deemed enough "learned in

the law" to examine candidates for attorneys' licenses had homes in Williamsburg. They were George Wythe, who shortly became Jefferson's tutor and later held the first law professorship in America; John and Peyton Randolph, sons of the late and distinguished attorney general, themselves both trained at the Inns of Court, and each at times the colony's attorney general; and Robert Carter Nicholas, educated at William and Mary and soon to be the colony's treasurer and later its chief judge of chancery. All four sat in the House of Burgesses, the Randolphs and Nicholas came from families of vast wealth, and Wythe had a Tidewater gentleman's plantation income in addition to his sizable legal fees.

In the morning Henry walked across the Palace Green to George Wythe's square brick town house standing high along the drive just north of the churchyard. He had good reasons for going there first. Wythe had begun his legal practice under the auspices of Zachary Lewis, father of Henry's lawyer friend John Lewis, and had married John's sister Anne. Although the young woman had died in childbirth and Wythe had remarried after moving to Williamsburg, the family and social connection would give a starting point to Henry's meeting. Then, too, of the four potential examiners, only Wythe had not had formal training himself, having apprenticed in his uncle's office and then gained practical experience in courts of Spotsylvania and the other Rappahannock peninsula counties. Henry might thus have expected a sympathetic hearing from Wythe, who, moreover, had a reputation for such mildness that in his presence "even a surly dog would unbend and wag his tail."

Henry waited in the first-floor study, a smallish room with a fireplace faced with marble and cupboards filled with law books and scientific apparatus. Wythe turned out to be a stocky man, shorter than Henry, kindly-looking, with a very round head, the first traces of a double chin, and striking blue eyes, inquiring yet soft and cheerful. Henry presented his compliments from John Lewis and produced his certificate signed by the Hanover justices, who numbered among them his father, his half brother, and three cousins, thus assuring

Wythe that the awkward young man standing in front of him was no quack or charlatan, that he had a good name and connections who would answer for him.

Nothing is known of the examination but its outcome. Wythe signed the license. Perhaps he saw something of his own first groping study in the young man's practical absorption and with a teacher's instinct had no desire to pinch a budding curiosity. Possibly he was impressed by Henry's determination and the force with which he could speak about the limited knowledge he had already acquired. The examination requirement was primarily intended to keep out the ignorant and the irresponsible, after all, and Henry did not appear to be either. Wythe brought forth a parchment on which he wrote down the formal phrases of the license, which declared that he had found Patrick Henry "duly qualified" to practice law in the county courts of the colony. In the lower right-hand corner he signed his name in a clear, round hand and affixed his seal.

At John Randolph's spacious estate on the south edge of town Henry underwent an examination of several hours' length. Tradition holds that Randolph was put off by the applicant's rustic appearance and at first had not wanted to examine him at all. Learning, however, that Wythe had already signed the young man's license, Randolph consented to pose some questions and proceeded to lead Henry on a hopeless chase through thickets of philosophy, the law of nations, feudal systems, and other abstruse topics before coming to the ground of ancient history, in which Henry could speak with at least a measure of force and confidence. Then Randolph moved into an examination on the common law and pretended to disagree with one of Henry's answers. Randolph used all his courtroom subtleties to shake the applicant's position but at last gave up and congratulated the young man upon the natural force of his reason, saying that if his industry were only half equal to his genius Patrick Henry would become an ornament to the profession. Randolph affixed his signature and seal to the parchment, laughingly vowing that he would never trust to appearances again.

The very next week Henry rode thirty miles west from Hanover to Goochland Court House on the upper James, where on Tuesday, April 15, 1760, he stood impatiently in the courtroom as the gentlemen justices set the new rates for the county's taverns, reviewed the state of the roads, and heard the case of a man charged with failing to educate an orphan boy bound into his care. Finally, it was Henry's turn to step forward. He produced his license, placed his hand upon the Bible, and took a series of oaths to the Crown and the court. He then had the unalloyed pleasure of watching the clerk write in the long narrow columns of his record book, "Patrick Henry Gent. [being now sworn] is entitled to practice at this barr." Later in the court session the new lawyer filed his first papers, a petition on behalf of William Harding, who was trying to recover £30 owed him by a man named Webber, whom the sheriff reported could not be found "within my Bailiwic." The court received the petition favorably and ordered Webber's goods and chattels attached for the requisite amount. Henry charged Harding the prescribed fifteen-shilling fee and went home. Pleas at the bar obviously accumulated shillings faster than selling buttons did.

Over the next few months lawyer Henry presented his license at Hanover Court House and in the other counties of the region. He filed numerous small actions for the recovery of debts, and his family connections brought minor work his way. He drew some papers for John Shelton, and his cousin John Winston hired him to press a damage suit against a man who had called him a "hog stealer." When his grandfather Isaac Winston died midway through the year, Henry did "sundry writing" for the executors of the estate. (Old Ike left his grandsons nothing; among the Henrys only Sarah and her Presbyterian daughters received small bequests.) Henry found his way through much of this early work by relying upon a volume setting forth the forms of various pleas and declarations given to him by his cousin Peter Fontaine upon his return from Goochland. On the flyleaf he exuberantly signed his name in French: "Patrice Henry le Jeune, son livre. Avrille 18, 1760. Le don de Pierre de la Fontaine."

Early in September the busy lawyer closed his store. He sold several hundred yards of Brown Holland, Black Shaloon, and India Dimity to his Richmond suppliers for £25, turned a page in his account book, and started to record his legal fees. By the end of the year he reckoned that he had handled 176 cases for 75 clients, two-thirds in Hanover and Goochland, and that he had collected about half the £123 in fees owed him.

Over the next three years he spent many weeks riding the circuit of courthouses in the hundred-mile swath of developing country west of Hanover. A number of Scotch merchants, especially in the vicinity of Richmond, became his clients, and he began to serve as a broker in some of their complicated credit transactions. He also performed the wide range of services required of country lawyers. He wrote conveyances for springs and drew up arbitration bonds; he looked over estate accounts, wrote written instructions respecting property transfers, drafted wills, and rode boundary lines; he filed actions against men who felled trees in their neighbors' swamps or sold someone else's Negroes on commission and then pocketed all the money. By the end of 1763 his practice had more than doubled, and he had collected £200 in fees. This was only a third of what he was owed, but it was more money than he had ever made in his life, and he could at last begin to think about moving his family from the tavern. He had learned a great deal about legal practice in a short time and had earned favorable notice from his colleagues. Peter Lyons, the King's Attorney for Hanover, said that he could prepare his legal papers while sitting in the courtroom no matter what else was going on, "except when Patrick rose to speak." Even on "so trifling a subject as a summons and petition for twenty shillings," Lyons said, he "could not write another word" until Henry had finished his presentation.

In December 1763, Lyons felt the brunt of Henry's developing power when the two faced each other in a case that turned the obscure young lawyer into a political celebrity. Nominally an action for the recovery of a debt—a minister suing the parish tax collector for an unpaid portion of his salary—the case formed one strand in the tangled affair known as "the Parsons' Cause" and placed Patrick Henry squarely in opposition to his father and his uncle.

The problem originated with the terrible harvest of 1758. Since tobacco—or, more accurately, warehouse notes for tobacco inspected, weighed, and ready for shipment overseas—circulated as a means of exchange in Virginia, the scarce crop meant that people found it hard to accumulate enough notes to meet their obligations. In response to much public clamor for relief, in September 1758 the assembly passed legislation granting debtors the option of paying their bills—both private and public—either in tobacco notes or in money at the rate of twopence per pound of tobacco. By fixing the cash value of tobacco at an artificially low rate the assembly eased the pressure on taxpayers and denied creditors a windfall profit, the price of tobacco having soared to sixpence per pound. The "Two-Penny Act" would be in effect for one year only, and in all respects it repeated the provisions of a similar law enacted as a temporary relief measure in the drought year of 1755.

Only one group of creditors, the Anglican clergy, reacted with outrage to the Two-Penny Act. Their salaries, fixed by law since 1696 at sixteen thousand pounds of tobacco annually, would be 300 percent lower if paid in money than in kind, and they believed the "option" law put a disproportionate burden of the colony's economic woes upon their black-robed shoulders. The ministers did more than mutter about breach of contract, however. They called a convention. Worried as they were about the steady rise of dissenting congregations and already embroiled in a long dispute with the assembly over control of the College of William and Mary, the churchmen felt certain that the Two-Penny Act had the hidden motive of further undermining their position in the colony. The convention thus resolved to appeal the validity of the act to the Board of Trade in London. They argued the high ground that the law was unjust and the technical ground that it was invalid because the measure did not contain a routine clause, required for several classes of legislation, suspending its operation until the Crown had granted approval. The ministers urged that the Two-Penny Act be declared null and void *ab initio*, "from its inception."

The clergy's appeal stirred up a vituperative debate and pamphlet warfare and raised the murky sort of constitutional issues that officials on both sides of the ocean always sought to avoid. A pamphleteering cleric charged that the assembly had treasonably tried to usurp the Crown's supremacy over the clergy and bind the king's hands on legislation. Outraged burgesses retorted, amid loud professions of loyalty to church and king, that the assembly had a right to pass emergency legislation for the relief of the people when the Crown could not extend "its beneficient Hand . . . in Time." The most fundamental rule in the English constitution, they argued, was *salus populi est suprema lex*, "let the welfare of the people be the supreme law," and no minor technical violation could invalidate an act "intended to produce the most salutary End, the Preservation of the People."

Disputes over the extent of a colonial assembly's power went on throughout the eighteenth century, but they generally pitted the legislature against the royal governor. In this case, however, Governor Fauquier had sided with the assembly, and the clergy had blundered quite severely in antagonizing him. New to Virginia, but an experienced diplomat—elegant, learned, fond of gambling, and a devotee of the violin—Fauquier had found easy acceptance among genteel Virginians, and he did not want to antagonize the local powers during his very first legislative session. He calmly told the Board of Trade in London that he had assented to the Two-Penny Act without the regular suspending clause because he thought one unnecessary in a temporary measure due to expire long before approval could be communicated from England; because his predecessor had—without censure—approved a very similar law, also lacking the suspending clause, three years earlier; and because public opinion and the assembly so strongly favored the act that to veto it, "as an entire stranger to the distress of the country," would severely jeopardize his position and make it difficult to finance and prosecute the war against the French and their Indian allies.

London officials hated such disputes. They could find no precedent for declaring laws void *ab initio*, as the clergy wanted, and to establish one would invite a howl of protest up and down the coast of North America, hardly desirable in the midst of a long war fought in large measure by colonial troops. To uphold the validity of the act, however, would condone the absence of the suspending clause and might imply acceptance of the Virginia assembly's claim to emergency powers. No prudent administrator would grant such an inch to politicians so many miles away. In the end the Privy Council put the burden back on its man in Virginia, Governor Fauquier. The Council declared the Two-Penny Act "disallowed, void, and of none effect," which sounded severe but left the pivotal question unresolved. When would this disallowance take effect? Was it an annulment from its inception or was it a repeal henceforth? When the official news of the Council's action arrived in Virginia, months after the 1758 act had expired, Governor Fauquier proclaimed it now "repealed," which left the clergy with no grounds for claiming back pay. The governor confidently said that the disappointed ministers could challenge his interpretation in the county courts, and the assembly, with equal assurance, said it would bear the expenses of any local officials sued.

Several ministers immediately filed lawsuits against their parish vestrymen and tax collectors for back pay and damages, but in the first two cases the courts of King William and York counties upheld the validity of the law; repeals, they ruled, always took effect when the word arrived in Virginia and was duly proclaimed by the governor. The third case, brought by the Reverend James Maury of Louisa County, took a different and, ultimately, spectacular turn.

Maury was a reserved and thoughtful man, very much interested in education, who had at first counseled against his brethren's protests, believing that "each individual must expect to share in the misfortunes of the community to which he belongs." The ensuing years of bitter quarrel and the rising tide of animosity toward the clergy had persuaded him to take a stand, however, and in 1762 he decided to sue Thomas

Johnson, collector of the parish levies, to recover the balance of his 1759 salary. Maury's attorney, the distinguished Peter Lyons, prudently filed the suit in neighboring Hanover County for two reasons. The defendant Johnson wielded immense political influence in Louisa, where he sat on the county court and regularly won elections to the assembly. A change of venue would help Maury in any case, but Hanover looked especially attractive because the presiding judge there, Colonel John Henry, had learned most of what he knew about the case from his brother, the Reverend Patrick Henry. If the parson had the justice's ear as fully as many supposed, Maury could expect success.

Lyons had his best hopes realized. When the case finally came to trial in November 1763, the issue presented itself with the utmost clarity. Johnson's attorney raised the Two-Penny Act in his defense, and Lyons demurred, insisting that the law had never been binding. Colonel Henry, firmly under his brother's thumb, led the court in sustaining Lyon's point; the law—for the first and only time in a Virginia court—was declared invalid *ab initio*, as the clergy had contended all along. Maury had won his legal case, and the court directed that a select jury be called at the next court day to fix the amount of damages. At this point, Johnson's attorney, John Lewis, withdrew, for he had essentially lost, and turned the matter over to his young friend, Patrick Henry, Jr. In the face of his father's ruling, the young lawyer's only task could be to try to minimize the damages to be awarded by the jury.

The Hanover verdict in the Parsons' Cause had shocked public opinion, and a very large crowd—farmers, gentlemen, and a delegation of ministers—pressed into the tidy brick courthouse on December 1, 1763, expecting a showdown. When Parson Maury saw the perfunctory manner in which the jury was chosen, he sensed trouble. The sheriff, Maury said later, merely passed through a room of gentlemen, "told his errand," and "immediately left the room, without summoning any one person there." Next, he went out on the green, excused a gentleman he met there on the grounds that he was a church warden and hence too interested a party, and proceeded "among the vulgar herd." After he had made up a list of names Maury accosted him and objected, stating that the panel was not as "select" as the court had ordered, the summoned jurors "being people, of whom I had never heard before."

Lawyer Henry, meanwhile, came up and insisted that the proposed jurors were "unexceptionable," since they were all "honest men." But at least three or four of them were "New Lights," Maury groused, dissenters who did not look kindly upon the Anglican clergy, "which the Sheriff, as they were all his acquaintance, must have known." The jury was immediately called and sworn, however, and Patrick Henry was surely pleased to see among the panel Samuel Morris, the bricklayer who had started the first dissenting "reading house" in the county, and Roger Shackleford, the outraged parishioner who had once publicly damned Parson Henry as an unconverted wretch. Maury sat quietly in his place at the bar, now more than ever convinced that Johnson had deliberately brought Patrick Henry into the case for some dark political purpose.

The trial proceeded very quickly. Lyons called two witnesses, the leading tobacco dealers in Hanover, who testified that in May and June 1759 tobacco had generally sold for fifty shillings a hundredweight. That was all the jury needed to hear, Lyons said, and he rested his case. In response Henry introduced as evidence a receipt signed by Maury indicating that he had received from Thomas Johnson £144, the value of the tobacco due him as provided by the Two-Penny Act. Claiming this was the full amount allowed to Maury by law, the defense rested.

Lyons, ponderous and corpulent, stood up and began his argument to the jury. The defendant had no business reopening the question of the law, he said, for the court had already ruled it invalid. The jury was sworn to try a single point—the amount of salary due Maury—and it could discharge its obligation by making one simple calculation, figuring the difference between the £144 already paid and the value of sixteen thousand pounds of tobacco at fifty shillings per hundredweight or sixpence the pound. Lyons should have stopped right there, but sensing the undercurrent of feeling against the clergy, he tried to disarm it by launching into more than a few well-chosen words about their benevolence and the respect owed them by the community. When he sensed the risible effect of these platitudes among the jurors, however, he concluded his remark and confidently seated himself.

Henry rose to speak. He started slowly and quietly, but as he warmed to his theme, his body seemed to grow more lofty, his voice more mellifluent, and his language so stirring and passionate that people started to rock and nod as if they were at Mr. Davies's church. No one seemed unmoved, and afterward some claimed that they had even seen tears running down Colonel John Henry's cheeks as he sat hunched forward in the center of the judges' bench.

The lawyer's talk lasted nearly an hour. He insisted upon the assembly's power to make laws for the good of the people, defended its use of emergency powers, and maintained that free-born Virginians had never before heard that the British constitution gave the Crown the right to declare laws void from their inception. Henry knew better than to press these points of law in a hearing for damages, but the court made no move to stop him. In soaring language he insisted, as had defenders of English legislative supremacy for nearly a century, that king and people were bound by solemn compact, that the king secured protection for the people by assenting to the just laws of Parliament, and that in exchange the people gave obedience to the Crown. The Two-Penny Act of 1758, he urged, had every characteristic of a good law and could not, consistent with the original compact, be annulled from its inception. To disallow a salutary law in such a fashion would be "an instance of misrule" or even tyranny, would violate the compact, and would cause the people to "consult their own safety" by continuing to adhere to the act of their assembly.

Some of the jurors nodded their heads in enthusiasm, but murmurs of "treason" buzzed through the crowd, and Peter Lyons, red-faced and furious, pulled himself to his feet to express astonishment that the worshipful bench could listen to such treasonable talk. It was a predictable charge, always raised when partisans of legislative power stated their case too boldly, and hurled back and forth for years in the Parsons' Cause. But Henry backed off. He had said enough to probe his jurors' feelings, and, liking what he saw, he passed on to a discussion of the relationship between the clergy and the people.

An established clergy, Henry contended, should be expected to enforce obedience to law. Since the Virginia clergy had so notoriously counteracted and defied the purposes of the colony's own legislature, the ministers had forfeited their useful position as members of the community and had become its enemies. Instead of receiving damages, they ought to be punished with severity. He launched into a tirade against the clergy, calling them "rapacious harpies" who would "snatch from the hearth of their honest parishioner his last hoe-cake." Yes, Henry conceded, by the ruling of the court the jury must find for the plaintiff, but they need not give him more than a farthing's worth of damages. That would teach the clergy not to have the temerity to dispute the validity of laws made in accordance with the hallowed constitution. If the jury let this opportunity slip away, he warned, they would be riveting the chains of bondage about their own necks.

The torrent of words ceased abruptly. Henry turned from the jury box, his body taut and his head reeling with the power suddenly unleashed. The spectators erupted into wild commotion, admirers pressed forward to slap the shoulders of the unsuspected orator, and before the bailiff could restore order, the jury had filed out, then right back in again to announce its verdict. The plaintiff Mr. Maury, they decided, should receive damages in the amount of one penny.

Amid the clamor of the audience at this sensational outcome, Peter Lyons sputtered a series of rapid-fire motions attempting to set aside the decision. Colonel Henry had lost control of his court, however, and in the pandemonium Lyons's requests were denied. He vowed to carry the case on appeal to the General Court, which the justices agreed was his right. By this time zealous farmers had hoisted Patrick Henry to their shoulders and paraded him across the courtyard to Shelton's Tavern, where they celebrated his triumph long into the afternoon. The talk went round and round that the people needed men like Henry in the assembly, and his client, Thomas Johnson, vowed that he could get him elected from Louisa as quick as lightning.

The Reverend Maury went home convinced that Henry had staged the whole business just to make himself popular and claimed that the lawyer had admitted as much to him in a brief, apologetic exchange outside the courtroom. Virginia's presiding minister professed shock at the upstart young lawyer's attack upon both mitre and sceptre and complained to London that Henry "received no Check from the Court, nor has hitherto been taken notice of by any other power . . . ." Colonel John Henry shook his head in bewilderment at the day's events. "Patrick spoke," he said, "in a manner that surprised me, and showed himself well informed on a subject of which I did not know he had any knowledge."

It was a stupendous performance, a bold strategy brilliantly managed with superb oratory and shrewd politics. In one inspired stroke Patrick Henry, age twenty-seven, made himself a force in Virginia politics. He defended the prerogatives of the local elite by the unorthodox means of mobilizing the emotions of the lower ranks of religious and political outsiders. A contemporary said later that he had distilled the sympathies of the dissenters, "unlocked the human heart and transferred into civil discussions many of the bold licenses which prevailed in the religions." There was no telling where such potent daring might lead.

CHAPTER 4

"Ancient Rights and Privileges"

In 1763, the year of Patrick Henry's triumph in the Parsons' Cause, Great Britain and France signed the treaty ending their bitter Seven Years' War for empire. The vanquished French handed over their North American possessions to King George III and quit the continent. "We in America have abundant reason to rejoice," declared a Boston lawyer named James Otis. "The heathen are driven out and the Canadians conquered. British dominion now extends from sea to sea and from the great rivers to the ends of the earth; liberty and knowledge, civil and religious, will coexist, improve and preserve, to the latest posterity. What God in his Providence has united let no man dare to put asunder."

A generation earlier Virginia's Governor Spotswood had portrayed the connection between colony and metropolis with a similarly connubial figure. "I look upon Virginia as a rib taken from Britain's side," he said, "and believe that while they both flourish as living under the marriage compact, this Eve must thrive so long as her Adam flourishes, and I'm persuaded that whatever serpent shall tempt her to go astray and meddle with forbidden matters will but multiply her sorrow and quicken her husband to rule more strictly over her."

Spotswood pointed his warning at the Virginia assembly, which had successfully blocked some of the governor's more ambitious proposals in the name of its own prerogatives. Over the next forty years his successors also had to contend with a legislature ready and eager to assert itself, but they managed to reach an accommodation that, in the colonists' view, paralleled the relationship between Crown and Parliament at "home."

Georgian Virginia felt British liberty embodied most fully in its own House of Burgesses. The representatives met in a chamber modeled after St. Stephen's Chapel at Westminster, where the House of Commons sat on ranks of benches running the length of the temple parallel to the walls, then curving in to meet the Speaker's great carved chair where the altar once had stood. Virginia's Speaker sat bewigged and gowned, as did his counterpart in England; he guided the House with the aid of well-perused copies of the precedents of Parliament lying upon the clerk's table along with the silver mace that, in Williamsburg or London, symbolized the power of the House. At the opening of each session the House chose its Speaker by sober procedures chiseled into ceremony by centuries of English use; the Speaker would then go before the governor—the Crown's representative in this pageant—to "beg protection" that the House "might enjoy their Ancient Rights and Privileges, such as Freedom of Speech and Debate, Exemptions from Arrests, and Protection for their Estates." The same petition long intoned at Westminster, it would receive the carefully gracious, time-honored answer that the governor "should take Care to defend them in all their just rights and Privileges."

So did Britons in Virginia enact the simple rites of self-government and bring into their House of Burgesses the solemn presence of English liberty. Significantly, they had retained the ancient name. "Burgess" had come to mean representative, as of a borough, but its roots reached deep into the rich medieval mold of the language to draw strength from the municipal rights of the burgher, the protection of the burrow and the castle, the independence of the bourgeoisie. Virginia's great families indeed found their political home within the House of Burgesses. By the 1730s and 1740s the Governor's Council—the goal of the wealthiest settlers for much of the colony's first century—no longer had enough places to accommodate the political ambitions of all the Virginia grandees and their numerous sons. From their handsome new mansions along the rivers and the new outposts up-country the Virginia gentry rode to Williamsburg to take their places in the expanding House of Burgesses, where they aggressively sought political influence to match their economic and social power. By mid-century, under a series of able Speakers, the House had come to dominate Virginia politics, and the gentry dominated the House. In its eminence and influence the House of Burgesses had assumed the mingled legacy of liberty and property for which Parliament had come to stand. The burgesses gloried simultaneously in their independence and their British pedigree.

Patrick Henry first presented himself for admission to the august House of Burgesses in the middle of May 1765, less than two weeks before his twenty-ninth birthday. Younger than most of the members and decidedly lacking their common prior experience of public service as vestrymen and county magistrates, Henry owed his unusual and rapid political elevation to the notoriety he had gained in the Parsons' Cause and the continued patronage of his client in that case, the influential Louisa County magnate Thomas Johnson.

In an important sense, Henry had become Johnson's steward. He took on a number of civil cases for him, wrote bonds, attested to surveys, and otherwise looked after Johnson's interest. Henry even made plans to move into Johnson's bailiwick, the heavily wooded foothills of Louisa County twenty miles west of Colonel Henry's place at Mount Brilliant and a long two-day ride from his father-in-law's tavern at Hanover Court House. Colonel Henry had finally deeded over some acreage on Roundabout Creek he had promised his son as a wedding present, and in the summer of 1764, with the increased prosperity of a growing caseload, Henry hired a mulatto farm hand to cut boards for what would be a modest four-room dwelling on a hillside overlooking a quiet valley. The fresh land offered the promise of a better tobacco crop, and the homestead lay less than a mile from Johnson's manor house, a two-story gabled affair locally known as Roundabout

Castle. While Henry devoted more and more weeks to riding the courthouse circuit and launching operations in Louisa, Sallie and the children (now three) remained at the Hanover Tavern.

Despite Henry's burst of popularity in Hanover, political circumstances there did not favor his immediate election to the House. His half brother John Syme held one of the county's seats; his old friend Colonel West Dandridge became embroiled in a bitter contest to retain the other and had asked for Henry's legal assistance in that fight. With prospects blocked in Hanover, Johnson and Henry came up with another stratagem that would allow the intrepid young advocate to capitalize on his fame before it wore off: they would take advantage of the election law which allowed freeholders to vote and hold office in every county in which they owned property. Henry could easily win election in Louisa, a less populous, simpler constituency that had been represented for more than a decade by Thomas Johnson and his brother William. What could be easier than to appoint William county coroner and have Henry "stand the poll" in his place? A goodly crowd, including at least forty of Henry's Hanover friends who owned property in Louisa, turned up at court day to drink the candidate's rum and sugarloaf and vote in the special election that placed Henry, unopposed, in the vacant seat.

Henry set right off for Williamsburg, a good four-day ride away, for the House session had already begun. On Monday, May 20, 1765, he worked his way through the crowd of planters, merchants, and ship captains gathered to swap news and settle accounts on the grassy field outside the Capitol known as "the exchange" and walked into the trim red-brick building. The burgesses met in the east wing of the H-shaped structure, and after depositing his bundle of election papers in the clerk's office at the end of the connecting arcade, Patrick Henry entered the House itself.

The chamber looked plain and somewhat small. Not a great deal larger than the backcountry courtrooms he was used to, the room measured only ten paces across and perhaps fifteen paces in length from the polished entry rail to the great oaken Speaker's chair, with a carved pediment and elegantly tapered legs, that dominated the far wall. About 60 burgesses—slightly more than half the total membership of 116—listened from the benches running lengthwise on each side of the room as Henry took the prescribed oaths and was duly "admitted to his place in the House."

The Speaker ordered that Mr. Henry be added to the committee on courts and justice and amid handshakes and smiles the new member from Louisa took a seat and turned his attention to the day's business.

First, Henry heard the final reading of a bill intended "to prevent the raising of Hogs, and suffering them to run at large in the Town of Richmond." Next came several messages from the Governor's Council. Then followed bills treating the sale of useless military stores in the magazine at Williamsburg, an alteration of the jurisdiction of the courts in Norfolk, and amendments to the various acts requiring owners of mills, hedges, and other barriers along the rivers to provide openings for the free passage of fish. This measure was referred to committee, after which Henry's first day as a legislator ended with an adjournment until the next morning at ten o'clock.

Henry had entered a tobacco planter's club. The wealthiest members—the great Tidewater magnates and their sons—wore elegant silks and satins and gloried in the whirling mix of politics, commerce, and merriment that at "Publick Times" turned the sleepy village into what Virginians fancied the sprightliest of capitals. Although members from the upland districts tended to dress more plainly, some even attending the sessions in buckskins and riding boots, by and large they tended to be the men of substantial property in their neighborhoods, well favored with gentry connections and extensive tracts of fresh land.

Although the formal rules of the House made every member equal in the privileges of debate, a handful of truly aristocratic gentlemen held most of the power. The committee chairmen all came from safe Tidewater constituencies, and they invariably numbered one or more chieftains from the Randolph, Carter, or Beverley clans, with major lieutenants drawn from the headmen among the Lees, Harrisons, Burwells, and Blairs. For the past forty years at least half the men of political consequence in the House had come from fewer than a dozen families, themselves intertwined beyond measure, so that claims of blood and public interest could scarcely be disentangled. For thirty years now John Robinson —a Beverley on his father's side, a Randolph on his mother's, and kin to nearly everybody else through his three advantageous marriages—had occupied the Speaker's chair and held unchallenged sway over the House.

Robinson did not look particularly impressive, even in the Speaker's dark gown and rolled wig; he was short and fleshy, with a roundish face, rather full lips, and heavy-lidded eyes. But this bland man, with a reputation for being "liberal, friendly, and rich," proved a "perfect master" of legislative detail and worked the rules of procedure like a magician. "Whatever he agreed to was carried and whatever he opposed dropt," one member complained privately, "for there he sits and what he can't do himself he prompts others to do by his nods." When Robinson indicated his displeasure with pained looks or veiled remarks, "no stone was unturned to please the worthy gentleman." He knew how to "convince the reluctant" with the "delicious incense" of "the thousand little flattering attentions which can be scattered from the chair," one politician recalled, and he further augmented both his power and his income with a second office, treasurer of the colony.

Although some muttered under their breaths about Robinson's vast power, referring to him as "the bashaw" or "the big man," and a few cynics had begun to entertain the idea that the Speaker's much-lauded generosity might be more with public funds than his own, only one man in recent memory had challenged Robinson directly. That was Patrick Henry's mentor, Thomas Johnson. During the session of 1759 the House, at Robinson's bidding, had ordered Johnson censured for having told a group of his constituents that the

House leadership squandered the public money on schemes to enrich themselves. "One holds the lamb while another skins," he was reported to have said. Johnson stood silently while Robinson intoned a reprimand for this malicious remark, but as the Speaker finished, Johnson pursed his lips and "set up a loud whistle, which brought down the House in a roar of laughter, and converted the whole affair into a farce."

Robinson had a long memory. While Henry's oratory in the Parsons' Cause had defended the power of the legislature and should have found favor with the Speaker, the young lawyer's rise was too abrupt, his origins too cloudy, his connection with Johnson too suspect, for the leadership to court the new member from Louisa.

Henry quickly confirmed that he would be as refractory as Robinson suspected. On Henry's third day in the House he loudly opposed a proposal for a public loan office advocated with some urgency by Robinson and his protégé, a Caroline County attorney named Edmund Pendleton. The complicated plan envisioned that Virginia would borrow nearly a quarter million pounds from merchants in England, to be repaid over fourteen years by means of a new schedule of taxes on tobacco. The colony would use nearly half the loan to buy up the steadily depreciating paper money it had been forced to issue to meet wartime expenses; the rest of the borrowed sum would be used to secure a public loan office, which would issue bank notes at 5 percent interest to those with "permanent security" and thus rescue a number of seemingly wealthy planters from the terrible web strung by low prices, scarce credit, devalued currency, and their own undiminished extravagance.

The plan rested upon the dubious proposition that British merchants, deeply embittered at the Virginians' failure to pay their bills, would lend the colony money to refinance the debt. Henry did not attack the plan's logic; he concentrated instead upon its inequities. Everyone would be taxed to underwrite the new scheme, but only the most aristocratic gentlemen would reap the advantage of new mortgages that supplanted their British creditors with the presumably more understanding treasurer of Virginia, John Robinson.

Henry stunned the House with a condemnation of favoritism and an attack upon the idea that the day of reckoning should be postponed. The fierce energy of Henry's attack "electrified" his audience, including the young law student Thomas Jefferson, listening intently at the doorway. Jefferson never forgot Henry's "remarkable exhibition," especially the ardent exclamation that disdainfully punctured the idea: "What Sir, is it proposed to reclaim the Spendthrift from his dissipation and extravagance by filling his pockets with money?"

Henry had a hungry man's talent for sensing resentment and capitalizing upon it. By casting a grim eye upon the gentry's prodigal ways, Henry evoked not only the spirit of his mentor, Thomas Johnson, but the abstemious principles of the ever-growing number of dissenters in the western counties. In his first formal speech to the House he skillfully rode the undertow of animosity the western members felt toward both Robinson and the heady casualness of Tidewater finance. "While the men of rank, fortune, and fashion from the lower counties would typically augment a public servant's stipend for the sake of dignity," one contemporary recalled, "the men from the interior would insist upon a strict calculation of the labor to be performed." The attitudes had not collided earlier because the western men lacked the coherence a leader provides; suddenly, right before their eyes, the newcomer spoke their feelings with an almost reckless candor. All the western burgesses joined Henry in opposing the bill.

Henry also sparked Pendleton's enmity. Tall, handsome, and smooth-spoken, Pendleton had come into the ruling circle from humble circumstances—worse than nobody's son, someone said, he was the son of a nobody. His charm, his undoubted abilities, and his obliging services for Robinson had propelled him upward. In the new man Pendleton could sense an ambition to rival his own and a crude energy that in his acquired hauteur Pendleton had come to detest.

Although Pendleton and Robinson saved face by mastering sufficient strength to win passage, the loan office scheme became sidetracked in the Council, apparently with their tacit consent, in order to appease the sudden outburst of criticism. It was not a project that could stand close scrutiny and, alarmed by Henry's attack, the leadership prudently abandoned it.

Henry's eloquence, however, crystallized a spirit of confidence in the western delegates that encouraged them to seize initiative from the leadership on an even more provocative issue. The capital hummed with the distressing but unofficial news that Parliament had finally passed the fateful Stamp Act, and a good many of the western delegates wanted the House to enact some strong resolutions of protest. The "men of weight," however, advised caution until more official news arrived from England and the political situation there could be accurately assessed. They believed the House would demonstrate sufficient principle by standing with decent firmness upon the petitions against the act it had sent to king, lords, and commons six months earlier.

Henry recognized the political challenge at once. Virtually every man of affairs in Virginia regarded the proposed Stamp Act as unconstitutional and subversive of the rights of Englishmen, and everyone had been saying as much—officially and privately—in the fourteen months since the ministry in London had first put forward the scheme of taxing the colonists by requiring that revenue stamps be purchased for almost every act of official business. If the act had indeed now passed, despite all the maneuvering and quiet protest against it by the colonies, they could hardly accept it uncomplainingly without seeming like blustering fools. Some way must be found to keep the argument alive, and if the westerners in the House could successfully flex their muscles on this issue against the counsel of the established leadership, there would be other dividends as well.

Before his first week as a burgess ended, Henry found himself "in conclave" at Lewis's Tavern, caucusing with a trio of backcountry men to plot a legislative course. Henry already knew the senior member of the group, John Fleming, a strong-minded lawyer from "Maiden's Adventure" in Cumberland, just across the James River from Goochland Court House, where both men frequently appeared. After ten years in the House, Fleming had moved away from an earlier attachment to Robinson and Randolph and seemed ready for a strong statement. George Johnston of Alexandria had a large law practice in the Northern Neck and a good-sized Potomac River plantation; he had a well-supplied library, more cultivated tastes than Henry and Fleming, and a precise, logical manner that helped anchor their flamboyance. The fourth man, Colonel Robert Munford of Mecklenburg, also had literary aspirations, which he had trouble nourishing in the isolation of his Staunton River plantation in the hinterland near the Carolina border. All four undoubtedly brought to the task of formulating strategy a sense that popular feeling on the long-simmering issue ran more deeply than the leadership realized.

George Grenville, the British exchequer, had first served notice in March 1764 that he would ask Parliament to approve a schedule of revenue stamps for the colonies as part of a comprehensive fiscal program. The ministry intended to raise from the colonies funds adequate to meet the staggering financial burdens of the lately concluded war as well as the cost of defending and administering the much-expanded North American domain. In effect, Grenville proposed a tax on all administrative transactions within the colonies, but since the ministry did not understand local procedures well enough to formulate specific legislation, the matter could not come before Parliament until royal officials could collect technical information from the colonies and draft an appropriate bill. This interval gave the colonies time to maneuver against the proposal as an infringement of the Englishman's right to be taxed only by his representatives. In Virginia, the House registered its displeasure in a series of intricately contrived statements filled with humility. "Nothing is further from our Thoughts than to shew the least Disposition to any

Sort of rudeness," one passage cooed, "but we hope it cannot be taken amiss that we, apprehending ourselves so nearly concern'd, should, at least while the Matter is in Suspence, humbly represent against it, and take every Measure which the Principles and Laws of our Constitution appear clearly to justify, to avert a Storm so very replete with the most dangerous Consequences."

Even as the collaborators at Lewis's reviewed copies of such serpentine petitions, they received proof positive of their failure from the latest newspapers. On May 2 the clever and outspoken editor of the *Maryland Gazette* had printed the unofficial text of the new Stamp Act across the entire front page of his newspaper, which Virginians read avidly since their local printer, a tool of the governor, had kept his pages free of controversy. The Marylander had both the text and news of its passage from a ship's captain freshly arrived in Annapolis, and this latest intelligence transformed rumor into incontrovertible fact. The legislation ran to sixty-three sections and contained a great number of repetitive, formulaic clauses that the printer ingeniously abbreviated with asterisks, curlicues, and other typographical devices, which both conserved space and gave the act an irreverent, pockmarked, and stuttering appearance.

A printer's subtle ridicule, however, diminished no one's fury at the act's provisions. The lawyers anxiously reading the newspaper by lantern light at the tavern found themselves the first group affected. "For every skin or piece of vellum or parchment, or sheet or piece of paper," the schedule began, "on which shall be ingrossed, written, or printed any declaration, plea, replication, rejoinder, demurrer, or other pleading . . . a stamp duty of three pence." Two shillings for bail papers, one and six for chancery pleadings, ten shillings for writs of appeal, five shillings for probating a will or obtaining writs of entry and recovery, four shillings for any judgments or decrees, and on and on through every category of document the lawyers used in their daily work. Hardly mastering their anger, Henry and his friends could discern from the monotonous regularity of the articles the thoroughness with which Grenville's agents had studied colonial activity. Every license and bill of lading would be taxed, and every letter of appointment, every promissory note or bond, every land survey and deed, every indenture, every warrant, every diploma, every bill of sale, every sheet of every newspaper, every copy of small pamphlets, every almanac and advertisement, and every pack of cards and pair of dice—all would require stamps, which would have to be purchased in cash.

Heretofore the Virginians, and colonists elsewhere, had protested the idea, the phantasm even, of unconstitutional oppression; reading the legislation directly gave them a staggering view of actual and burdensome expense to be imposed on virtually every facet of public life beginning November 1. The riled-up burgesses at Lewis's redoubled their conviction that the House must declare its opposition in far stronger terms than before. But the tavern draftsmen wanted the House to take a firm stand, not only to impress Parliament but to rally popular opinion in Virginia. Consequently they sought a text that would be plainspoken and terse, devoid of ambiguity and capable of being read aloud in every tavern and courthouse in the colony. They began with the premise, stated in a brief preamble, that since the House of Commons had lately "drawn into question" the extent of the Virginia assembly's power to levy taxes, the burgesses must enact resolutions "for settling and ascertaining" the issue for "all future Times." Next, they condensed the thick choral passages of the previous year's petitions into four single sentences conveying the essential constitutional argument with drum-roll clarity.

- The first settlers of Virginia did not forfeit their British privileges and immunities by emigrating to America.
- Royal charters from the time of King James I confirm that the colonists have the same liberties as those subjects born in England.
- Taxation only by representatives chosen by the people themselves is "the distinguishing characteristic of British freedom" and the basis of the ancient constitution.

Virginians have "uninterruptedly" enjoyed the right of being taxed only by their assembly, a practice "constantly recognized" by the kings and people of Great Britain.

From these premises, finally, the indignant draftsmen drew three, related conclusions.

"Resolved therefore, That the General Assembly of this Colony" has "the only and sole exclusive Right and Power" to levy taxes upon the inhabitants of the colony;
"That his Majesty's Liege People, Inhabitants of this Colony, are not bound to yield Obedience" to any tax laws—such as the Stamp Act—not passed by their own assembly;
"That any Person who shall, by Speaking, or Writing, assert or maintain" that some public body other than the assembly has the right or power to tax "the people here" should be "deemed an Enemy" to the colony.

Even after being worked up by the several hands of Henry, Fleming, Johnston, and Munford, the resolutions proved only one-fifth as long as the 1764 petitions, but they were incalculably more audacious. The tavern conclave had formulated an aggressive program not only of opposition but of resistance. Like the evangelical preachers who had taken firm hold in their constituencies, these politicians sensed the power of a crowd and the persuasiveness of a great outpouring of spirit. They shrewdly realized that any campaign for repeal of the Stamp Act would require more pressure than high-minded resolves alone could bring, and so they sought a statement that, with evangelical directness, would convey the imperative of choice and prepare the ground for acts of defiance. They would have the House not only declare its power, but extend the populace a license to protest.

Despite the excitement the caucus did not exaggerate its strength. The draftsmen prudently decided to wait until the end of the session to undercut the governor's implicit threat to dissolve the House if it approved such forthright propositions. They would, however, mobilize what power they had. The earnest Johnston, a diminutive figure of strong intellect but only modest speaking ability, thought that their dauntless new colleague, so impressive in the loan office debate, ought to make the leading speech in support of the resolutions. Much flattered and eager to consolidate his reputation, Henry accepted the invitation.

CHAPTER 5

"Young, Hot, and Giddy"

Only thirty-nine members sat on the green serge benches of the chamber on the morning of Wednesday, May 29, when George Johnston broke into a droning hour of bill reading to move that the House "immediately" resolve itself into a committee of the whole "to consider the Steps necessary to be taken in consequence" of the impending stamp duties. The caucus had waited as long as it dared. The burgesses were packing up. Pendleton had left at the weekend; Landon Carter had gone home earlier; and the silent Colonel George Washington and a number of other planters, bent on minding the season's advancing business, had left the day before. Attendance always dwindled toward the end of a session, especially in a warm, dry spring like this one, although the westerners could not but wonder whether rumors of their impending assault on the stamps had sent some members scurrying for cover.

Henry seconded Johnston's motion, which passed at once, and the burgesses fell silent as the Speaker stepped down from the great chair, removed his wig and robe, and assumed an ordinary member's place on a front bench. Peyton Randolph, corpulent and keen-witted, would preside over the Committee of the Whole from the clerk's desk; his brother John, the clerk, removed the mace, placing it under the table to signify the less formal parliamentary situation.

Randolph directed Johnston to proceed, but Johnston startled the House by deferring to his colleague, the member from Louisa. Henry rose slowly, almost languidly. His long face looked solemn; the earnestness in his features riveted the attention of every member. Fixing his eye directly upon Randolph in the chair, Henry put forward the resolutions his group had drafted at Lewis's Tavern. The accustomed leaders of the House sat stern-faced as Henry in effect defied them to endorse arguments they had previously made themselves, but which he now expressed in sharpened words and with far riskier consequences.

The weighty gentlemen—George Wythe, Robinson, Randolph, the scholarly Richard Bland—one by one rose to dispute the premise behind Mr. Henry's resolutions. No further statements were necessary, their argument ran, until the House received answers to its earlier petitions. If indeed the rumors creeping into the House that the act had passed eventually were confirmed, appropriate rebuttal could be made when all the facts were known. Further protest now would be imprudent and might do more mischief than good; softer language would be advisable if it were later judged necessary to warn the citizens against admission of the stamps. The motion at hand would only inflame and aggravate a most delicate situation.

Henry responded with a "manly eloquence" that left another young western newcomer, Paul Carrington, speechless with admiration. Johnston and Fleming backed him with "solid reasoning," arguing in sum that the passage of the act was certain knowledge, that most gentlemen had known of it for several weeks, and that a letter from Virginia's agent in London containing the terms of the measure was even now privately circulating among the members. Parliament had not deigned to answer the previous petitions, except with the asperity of the tax itself, and the House could not silently acquiesce in this infringement of its rights.

The long day in committee showed the old leaders that they could not quash the protest. Caught in the difficult position of opposing both the Stamp Act and the statements proposed to attack it, the leaders finally agreed that the resolutions might be reported to the House. They began the onerous task of modifying them into acceptability. They first excised the preamble, probably on the technical grounds that the House could not respond to resolutions from the Commons it had not officially received. Then they started in on the resolutions themselves, but how far they went before reporting the text to the House cannot be ascertained.

With John Robinson once more occupying the Speaker's chair, and barely enough members to maintain the quorum, the House convened at ten o'clock on Thursday, May 30. The leadership promptly struck back at Henry. Peyton Randolph reported that the Committee on Privileges and Elections had reviewed the writs returned by the newly elected members. Only one return, Mr. Carrington's from Charlotte County, was in completely proper order, the committee found, but the errors in four others could be repaired in the customary way by the clerk at the table. The returns from Louisa, however—all heads turned toward Henry—so deviated from the form prescribed by law that the county sheriff should "be sent for in Custody to amend his said return." This indirect insult hinted at the leadership's power to harass its opponents, although the influential gentlemen had apparently—and wisely—decided not to press the point so far as to deny Henry the floor until his papers proved more satisfactory.

While the House murmured at this unexpected turn, several routine bills received their final reading and the clerk of the council delivered a few messages. Finally, Peyton Randolph stood once more to report that the Committee of the Whole had come to several resolutions "concerning the charging of Stamp Duties in the Colonies" which they desired to place before the House. Stoutly concealing his repugnance, this generally good-natured gentleman performed the disagreeable duty of reading the resolutions aloud to the tense but silent House. Knots of eager listeners at the windows and the doorway pressed forward, straining to hear the argument.

The first three resolutions—nothing more than historical truisms—won quiet acceptance by narrow majorities, a solid bloc of western votes providing the backbone of support and the Tidewater leaders uniformly opposed. The debate grew warmer when the fourth resolution came up for approval. In Henry's draft it held, "his Majestie's liege People of this most ancient Colony have uninterruptedly enjoyed the Right of being thus governed by their own assembly in the Article of their Taxes and internal Police and . . . the same hath never been forfeited or any other way given up but hath been constantly recognized by the Kings and People of Great Britain." Virginia should be described as "this most ancient and loyal Colony," someone insisted, and amid vehement cries of "Hear! Hear!" such an amendment easily carried. Then the established leaders, who prided themselves upon their knowledge of charters and precedents, attacked the resolution on more legalistic ground. The motion erred, they argued, in implying that Virginia was governed by the assembly alone. The colony would win no friends with so careless a statement. Virginians enjoyed the inestimable right of being governed by laws derived "from their own consent" on the one hand, "with the approbation of their Sovereign, or his substitute," on the other. If the motion were so rephrased, the scholars insisted, the true genius of the constitution would be more aptly expressed, and less offense could be taken at the principle maintained.

The amendment won acceptance. The leading gentlemen's concern for erudite precision revealed that beneath the tactical differences over the wisdom of renewed protest lay a more subtle contest over the nature of discourse and its intended audience. The elder statesmen spoke the private language of parliamentary diplomacy, filled with elaborate qualifications and designed to persuade the necessary few with subtlety and finesse. They believed in "cool and deliberate proceedings" and felt they deserved honor and respect for their "firm but decent representations" of the session before. Their challengers, however, instinctively employed a simpler style, less mindful of niceties and aimed not so much at courtiers as at the crowd on the courthouse green. The much-mentioned petitions had sailed unnoticed through the usual channels of the colonial office. Henry's new resolves aimed to create a fresh wave of popular opinion. But to the old leaders it seemed that the westerners sought to bully Parliament by whipping up the people. They would risk the dignity of the House for "paper'd resolutions," mere rhetoric, impetuous and meaningless, except to vault certain designing men into a mischievous popularity.

This subterranean current of resentment burst out into flowing rage when the debate turned to Henry's final resolution. As conceived by the tavern draftsmen, it asserted the assembly's "only and sole exclusive Right and Power to lay taxes" and then went on to absolve Virginians of obedience to the Stamp Act and cast obloquy upon those who publicly defended it. This was too much for Tidewater aristocrats to bear. An assertion of right was one thing, an exhortation to defy the law another; perhaps the House could divide the motion and consider its clauses separately.

Tempers flared, and language grew stronger. The "most bloody" mood shocked Jefferson, standing at the doorway again, unwilling to miss a word. The cautious leaders found themselves arguing for quiet submission in the most angry terms. This was no time for hot-headed, ill-considered, and possibly treasonous assertion, they insisted. If Parliament had indeed passed a law subversive of their civil rights, they reasoned, their only recourse was to suffer patiently without breaking the public peace, to lay their complaints humbly and dutifully once again before the Crown in a quiet effort to have the unjust law repealed, and to rest content in the assumption that if the colonies conducted themselves decently, it would be base indeed of Parliament to disdain such moderation.

Henry countered these arguments with "torrents of sublime eloquence" that "plucked the veil from the shrine of parliamentary omnipotence," holding forth with a dramatic, even epic grandeur that prompted young Jefferson to think that his friend "spoke as Homer wrote." None of the established leaders, except the absent Pendleton, could speak with even a fraction of Henry's power, and indeed, they had always influenced the House more by their social standing than by their oratory. The newcomer seemed to be changing the unwritten rules. "His style of oratory was vehement, without transporting him beyond the power of self-command," Peyton Randolph's nephew wrote later; "not always grammatical, and sometimes coarse in his language, he taught his hearers how to forget his inaccuracies by his action, his varying countenance, and voice."

That voice! It was monotonous and insistent, like a Baptist preacher's whine, yet somehow melodious as well. Henry now employed his splendid voice in a harangue unlike any heard before in the royal Capitol. He cited no charters, quoted no precedents, but instead seized the imagination of his listeners by enlisting them in a vivid personal drama. Just as he had made the Hanover jury feel the selfishness of the established clergy, so now he evoked before the burgesses the brutal face of tyranny. Like the Reverend Samuel Davies enacting the solemn division of Judgment Day before his enthralled congregation, so did Henry create the spectacle of virtuous liberty triumphant over oppression. This was no complex and invisible operation of diplomacy and the mechanics of repeal; this was a matter of manhood and self-assertion. Boldly and dexterously he took his listeners' minds from the intricacies of parliamentary negotiation to the emotional heart of the matter, their dependence upon the distant power of the Crown. He shockingly raised the specter of regicide.

"He had read," a French traveler standing in the doorway heard Henry say, "that in former times Tarquin and Julius had their Brutus, Charles had his Cromwell, and he Did not Doubt but some good american would stand up, in favour of his Country."

Henry paused for breath. Then, as he was adding a qualifier—"but in a more moderate manner"—Speaker Robinson rose from his chair shouting, "Treason! Treason!" In cold fury Robinson rebuked the House, declaring his shame that not one member was loyal enough to stop the man before he had gone so far.

The Speaker glared into the chamber. Then Henry launched into a silky apology. "If he had affronted the speaker, or the house, he was ready to ask pardon," the Frenchman understood Henry to say. "He would shew his loyalty to his majesty King George the third, at the Expence of the last Drop of his blood, but what he had said must be attributed to the Interest of his Country's Dying liberty which he had at heart, and the heat of passion might have led him to have said something more than he intended, but again, if he said anything wrong, he begged the speaker and the houses pardon."

It was a gracious retreat. Just as in the Parsons' Cause, he had probed the effect of an idea and drawn back tactfully as soon as he overstepped the boundary of what his audience was prepared to accept. Nevertheless, he had badly miscalculated in provoking the Speaker so grievously, and Henry's elaborate apology indicated that he realized the error. His friends rallied to his defense, and the affair was dropped. When the vote came soon thereafter, a division was called, and amid much hullabaloo the Speaker declared that with twenty ayes and nineteen nays, the resolution had carried.

Peyton Randolph lumbered into the entryway, red-faced and angry. "By God, I would have given 500 guineas for a single vote," he stormed, and his young cousin Jefferson, standing in earshot, knew exactly what he meant. "As this would have divided the house, the vote of Robinson the speaker would have rejected the resolution."

In the wild uproar, and the welter of cross-motions and attempted amendments, men claimed different results. The protesters believed the resolution had passed intact and dispatched the text to the newspaper. The Speaker's cousin thought the dreadful last clause—styling those who defended the Stamp Act as Virginia's enemies—had been cut; the Frenchman thought a majority had favored it. Jefferson believed the clause inviting Virginians to disregard the act had carried and that it had occasioned his cousin Peyton's wrath.

To a man like Peyton Randolph—privileged, polished,

and proud—the crude, emotional tactics of a Patrick Henry were simply too galling. Randolph had first covered himself with glory ten years earlier by personally negotiating in England the successful resolution of a similar dispute involving the governor's imposition of a licensing fee without the assembly's consent. Experience had buttressed his belief in diplomacy and decorum and led him to resist the injection of religious enthusiasm into politics. Randolph's furious oath bespoke the frustration of a gentleman politician who felt himself bested by a rabble-rouser, the outrage of a tribune who felt his state, in an hour of crisis, falling into the hands of untested and untrustworthy men.

Henry unaccountably left Williamsburg that evening, whether savoring his victory or worried that although members' remarks were privileged some highly placed official might harass him with a warrant, the record does not show. In his absence, however, his opponents launched a stunning counterattack.

Jefferson realized that unusual business was afoot when, arriving early at the Capitol the following morning, May 31, to claim his doorway listening post, he encountered one of the Randolphs (his mother's cousin Peter, who had served as his father's executor and Tom's guardian) at the clerk's table "thumbing over the volumes of Journals to find a precedent of expunging a vote of the house, which he said had taken place while he was a member, or clerk of the house." The curious student peered over Randolph's shoulder as the old gentleman turned the leaves until the house bell rang.

The Speaker called the House to order with unusual dispatch. Despite the extremely thin attendance, he entertained no calls for a quorum and made no count of the members. Robinson quickly recognized Peyton Randolph, who moved that the House strike from its journals the text of the resolutions passed the previous afternoon. With the House awash in bitterness, Fleming and Johnston moved that the vote be taken serially, and the motions to strike the first four resolutions were all defeated. On the momentous fifth resolution, however, the House proved evenly divided (Henry's absence alone would have made it so, but there may have been others missing, too), and the Speaker cast the decisive vote that ordered the resolution erased. When the neophyte Paul Carrington went later to find the manuscript page from the journal containing the erasure, it was missing. In its place rested a freshly copied sheet that recorded only four resolutions and made no mention of the motion to expunge.

The bashaw and his friends had done their work efficiently and thoroughly. Now they could all go home. Governor Fauquier obliged by dissolving the assembly the next morning, June 1. He coldly omitted the customary civility of a parting speech and, more ominously, set no date for convening a new session.

Williamsburg remained in a grim mood. A crowd threatened to burn an effigy of George Grenville in the market square, but the authorities prevented the affair without causing an even greater tumult. Even this hint of defiance made the governor edgy, for he sensed the populace to be "uneasy, peevish, and ready to murmur at every occurrence." Public sulkiness made the King's Birthnight festivities at the Governor's Palace a few days later on June 4 a rather lame show. The French traveler attended eagerly, expecting a glittering company, but "was Disappointed" to find "not above a Dozen of people," and he left before the governor led the handful of celebrants in to supper.

Fauquier made no mention of the tepid party the next morning when he drafted a careful account of the political insurgency for his superiors in London. "Young hot and giddy members," carried along by the "very indecent language used by a Mr. Henry," a young lawyer new to the House, had "overpowered" the accustomed leaders, who had "strenuously opposed" such "rash heat." The resolutions would never have passed, Fauquier said, if more burgesses had "done their duty by attending to the end of the session," but he also recognized that the uprising hinted at a major realignment. The governor doubted that "cool reasonable men" would be chosen for the next assembly, and consequently John Robinson ("a gentleman who has always assisted me in carrying on the King's service") might not be re-elected Speaker. Perhaps, Fauquier added, he might be permitted to show some special favors to Robinson in order to shore up his position.

Other writers endeavored immediately to have Henry's audacity condemned in London. One dispatch, printed anonymously in the London newspapers by midsummer, regretted that instead of being "sent to the Tower" for "blazing out" against the king, Henry "rode off in triumph" after getting "some ridiculous violent resolves" passed. Another report, directed to the Bishop of London by his deputy in Virginia, the Reverend William Robinson (the Speaker's cousin and neighbor), emphasized how the upstart lawyer had gratified his desire for popularity by striking out first against the clergy and now against the authority of Parliament and the king. In the assembly just concluded Henry had violently compared His Majesty to Caesar and Charles I, "not sparing insinuations that he wished another Cromwell would arise," Robinson said. "He made a motion for some outrageous resolves, some of which passed and were again erased as soon as his back was turned." The clergyman regarded Henry's conduct as one more sign of the gathering power of religious dissenters. "Too many of his party . . . have wrong notions respecting both property and legal authority," Robinson fumed, and they are using the new Stamp Act as "an opportunity of breaking out." The minister thought such political unruliness should have received an "early and spirited check." Instead of being punished, Mr. Henry has become a popular hero and has now "gone quietly into the upper parts of the country to recommend himself to his constituents by spreading treason and enforcing firm resolutions against the authority of the British parliament," Robinson said. "This is at least the Common report," he added.

Henry's action had indeed made him a local champion. When the French traveler who had listened to the debates in Williamsburg passed through Hanover County a week later, everyone talked excitedly of "the Noble Patriot Mr. henery."

To a man the inhabitants defended his action, the Frenchman found, and they said "publicly that if the least injury was offered to him they'd stand by him to the last drop of their blood."

Detained by a heavy rainstorm for twenty-four hours in Newcastle, the hamlet first surveyed into lots by Henry's father, the Frenchman found his innkeeper interested in no other subject than resistance to the stamps. One patron, a militia officer named Boswell, swore that he would "sooner die than pay a farthing and was sure that all his countrymen will do the same." Other denizens grumbled, much to the Gallic visitor's amusement, that if the French were still in Canada the British Parliament "would as soon be damned as to offer what they do now." "Let the worst come to the worst," someone muttered, "we'll call the French" back to our aid.

As he moved north into Maryland, the Frenchman found convivial crowds at every tavern, eager to denounce the stamps and ready to hear the traveler's account of how bravely the patriotic "Henery" had spoken in the Virginia assembly. Enjoying Annapolis in the midst of the June court session, none of the Frenchman's esteemed company went to bed sober, what with "feasting and drinking, after the King's health, the Virginia assembly, and then damnation to the stamp act and a great deal to that purpose."

At Marlboro, Tulip Hill, and Baltimore, the Frenchman heard more rousing talk, with his own account prompting rowdy huzzahs for Henry and the Virginia assembly. But then a curious thing happened: the traveler began to meet his story coming the other way. At a banquet in Annapolis in early July, before the Frenchman could launch into his by now much polished account, a lawyer visiting from Philadelphia proved full of praise for the Virginians and told of opinion inflamed as far away as Boston, where, he solemnly reported, "their first toast after dinner is the Virginia Assembly."

The rash Virginians, it seems, had craftily let their words get loose. An anonymous hand, undoubtedly one of the draftsmen, mailed a copy of the rough version of the resolutions drafted at the Lewis's Tavern conclave to an interested correspondent in Philadelphia, who passed them in privacy to some gentlemen in New York, who entrusted them to a northbound traveler, and as was hoped from the start, they eventually got into the newspapers. The *Newport Mercury* published them on June 24, with the clear implication that the Virginia House had heroically endorsed the lot, and two Boston papers reprinted them a week later. Simultaneously, the *Maryland Gazette*, whose printer claimed he had received several manuscript copies from gentlemen in Virginia, published the propositions, again with the impression that all had won approval. (Only the *Virginia Gazette*, firmly under Robinson's control, kept silent and failed to print any of the resolves.) As the summer wore on, reports kept echoing like gunshot in virtually every colonial newspaper that the Virginia House had acquitted itself nobly with its firm resolves. Everywhere men stirred to action on their own, and the royal governor of Massachusetts wrote that the publication of the Virginia resolves had sounded "an alarm-bell to the disaffected." A Connecticut minister used a more incandescent figure; the resolves "came abroad," Ezra Stiles wrote, "and gave fire to the Continent."

An unprecedented continental mobilization over the next few months nullified the Stamp Act before it could take effect. In July the Frenchman heard that the legislature of Massachusetts was urging all the colonial assemblies to send delegates to New York in October to consult upon united measures of opposition, and he discerned at once what the colonial office would spend months denying: the Americans were sophisticated enough to overcome their diversity and mutual animosities when confronted by a common threat. By the time the traveler himself reached New York in August, conversation there centered on the "spirited" action of the Bostonians who had recently forced the appointed stamp distributor to resign his commission; a crowd had surrounded the wealthy gentleman's house and threatened to level it to the ground if he did not meet their demand to renounce all connection with the stamp business. Mobs later attacked the homes of well-placed officials in Boston, Newport, and other towns, partly to protest their complicity with the Stamp Act and also to settle grudges against their monopoly of local power. Everywhere, the Frenchman heard, men spoke of manufacturing necessary goods at home and buying "not a farthing's worth of anything from England."

In September the colonial assemblies of Rhode Island, Pennsylvania, and Maryland all passed resolutions—some virtually copied from Virginia's—denouncing the act, urging repeal, and in some cases indemnifying local officials who refused to comply with its provisions. Other legislatures chimed in as the autumn advanced.

Editors and pamphleteers rehearsed the case against the tax. To the familiar constitutional arguments, they added new charges that the British ministry plotted against liberty, since violators of the Stamp Act would be tried, without benefit of juries, in the admiralty court at distant Halifax, Nova Scotia. Moreover, they began to link the Stamp Act with the other elements in the ministry's colonial program, now regarding the tightening up of the customs service, the stationing of new regiments, and the new restrictions on western land grants in a far more ominous light as part of a concerted effort to stifle colonial entrepreneurship and maintain dependence upon Britain.

Merchants in the port cities vowed to discontinue trade until the tax was lifted. The boycott idea spread among lawyers and judges, too, who pledged to close their courts rather than operate with the hated stamps. Every town, moreover, had its noisy parades, its hanging of effigies, and other menacing rituals, while groups styling themselves "Sons of Liberty" turned out crowds to intimidate the recalcitrant.

Mob action and high-minded resolve worked in tandem to defeat the Stamp Act. By the end of October, the British military commander in New York was ready to call the tumultuous outpouring of opinion an "insurrection." "From the highest to the lowest," people refuse "to take the stamps," General Thomas Gage reported, and they threaten "to plunder and murder" those who will comply with the law.

"The Spirit of Democracy is strong amongst them," Gage warned; the lawyers started the clamors, and the merchants have hired mobs of sailors to continue them. Only a "very considerable military force," Gage thought, could enforce the act.

Virginia had experienced its share of argument, pageantry, and rough stuff. Peyton Randolph and George Wythe endeavored to "prevent any ill Impress from the Spurious" resolves circulating in Virginia's name by sending the colony's London agent "a true Copy . . . properly authenticated" of the four resolutions on the assembly's journal. While they looked backward to protect their flanks, public opinion, as Patrick Henry had sensed, eagerly moved forward into resistance. The countryside witnessed numerous exhibitions in which the Stamp Act was pilloried or stabbed to death by "the genius of liberty" and then burned "to prevent infection from the stench." At Dumfries, in the upper Potomac River country, a late summer crowd paraded an effigy of a stamp distributor through the streets of the little tobacco town. "Hundreds of all ranks" followed the figure seated "on Horseback, with its Face toward the Horse's Tail," and a copy of the hated law "tied round its neck, with a Halter." The effigy received "the Insults of the Congregation," which included caning, cropping, and undoubtedly the enthusiastic slinging of manure.

Richard Henry Lee, an influential burgess somewhat hostile to Robinson but absent from the galvanic May session, made amends by staging an equally lurid funeral procession at Westmoreland's court day in September. The stately Lee, dressed as the hangman, dispatched effigies of Grenville and George Mercer, the Virginia stamp distributor, and then reported to the crowd that the condemned officials had acknowledged the justness of their punishment.

The Westmoreland justices of the peace made their own demonstration the next day, publicly signing a notice to the governor that they would decline to act as magistrates after November 1, when thenceforward tax stamps would be required. Several other county courts followed Westmoreland's lead, and many others crowded their October calendars, sitting in extra sessions to prepare for a longer-than-customary recess. More cautious magistrates, like Henry's rival Edmund Pendleton, grew alarmed at the rowdy, potentially riotous parades and the shocking impropriety of gentlemen haranguing crowds. They endeavored to keep their benches in session and transact as much local administrative business as could be accomplished without the use of stamps. "The appearance of courts may convince the people that there is not a total end of laws tho' they are disabled to act in some instances," Pendleton advised his friend, Squire James Madison of Orange County. But Madison apparently took a harder view, for his court did not sit during the next few months.

Planters wrote anguished letters to their correspondents in Britain, complaining of the insuperable burden imposed by the tax and the threat to prosperity on both sides of the ocean. The colony was in "a ferment," one gentleman wrote to his broker in Bristol. "Our affections are alienated through oppression," he warned, "and we are full of discontent . . . and resentment."

Virginia's embodiment of royal authority—the sixty-one-year-old governor, Francis Fauquier—regarded the burgeoning resistance to the Stamp Act as the most vexing problem he had ever faced. The son of an exiled Huguenot physician who had become a director of the Bank of England, Fauquier knew how to cut his way through political thickets, and he had earned a good deal of respect in his decade-long administration. But now Fauquier felt that he wandered in a wilderness, off balance and uncertain of his judgment. He would call the assembly into session if he were only sure that the reliable veterans would retain control and repudiate Henry's resolves and the outbursts they had encouraged. Such a happy outcome seemed only wishful. The veterans, he realized, would have to step lively lest they be tossed out altogether for inadequately appreciating the popular mood and a dozen Patrick Henrys put in their places. He also feared that the colony would slide into "general outlawry" if the courts shut down. (Fauquier was mindful that in Boston, the lieutenant governor had fled his elegant home just ahead of a mob, which spent a riotous hour sacking and destroying it.) But if he tried to shore up the courts by finding new justices, he might provoke the meaner sort either to take the places the first gentlemen had resigned or to boycott them altogether.

Fauquier temporized. He took no official notice of the judicial resignations, if such they were, and he postponed from month to month the anticipated call for new elections. By this stratagem he kept the assembly adjourned and thus unable to send delegates to the intercolonial protest meeting in New York, but his laggardness further convinced public opinion that the authorities were embarked on a campaign to suppress all liberty.

At the end of October Fauquier protected the newly arrived stamp distributor, George Mercer, from an angry Williamsburg crowd bent on securing his resignation. Mercer capitulated anyway, promising not to distribute stamps until he had received further orders from England, "and not then without the assent of the General Assembly of this Colony."

On November 1 Governor Fauquier rode his coach through strangely quiet streets to the Capitol for the opening of the scheduled quarterly court session. When he entered the paneled courtroom, his councilors were seated on the bench as usual, but the area within the bar was empty, save for Peyton Randolph, the attorney general, sitting glumly at his accustomed table. Fauquier ordered the crier to proclaim the opening of court, but not one lawyer and not one litigant appeared in response to the ancient call of "oyez, oyez . . ." No Wythe, no Pendleton, no Henry. Fauquier had averted violence in his capital, but the Stamp Act had met a bloodless end.

The stamps passed the entire winter quietly gathering mildew on His Majesty's Ship *Rainbow*, anchored in the middle of the York River, and Virginians remained stubbornly close-minded toward their use. Patrick Henry's sense that popular opinion, rallied by legislative resolve, could defeat the tax proved triumphantly correct, not only in

Virginia but all along the seaboard. Henry's name cannot now be linked with any of the demonstrations, not even the closing of the courts in Louisa and Hanover, but the actions grew directly from his rousing talk in May.

His outspokenness had received quick vindication. Other writers took up his themes. Newspaper polemics rang changes on the theme of treason, turning Speaker Robinson's insult into a compliment. It is "not Treason in Englishmen to be sensible when they are oppressed . . . and not Treason in any Legislature to Pronounce, Declare, and Resolve" upon the grave subject of liberty, one writer declared. The real treason, he went on, was "to attempt the Subversion of the Most happy Constitution upon Earth." Another Virginia pamphleteer took up Henry's reference to Charles I and reminded his audience that it was Parliament that not only remonstrated against taxes imposed without its consent but voted "the voluntary payers, as well as the Ministers who levied it, betrayers of the Liberties of England." Most deliciously, however, the man who had first felt the power of Henry's oratory against him, the Reverend James Maury, now made common cause. Maury insisted that although some brand us "with the odious name of rebels," others will "applaud us for that generous love of liberty which we inherit from our glorious forefathers."

Spirits stayed firm all winter, buoyed by fresh pamphlets and occasional marches by the Sons of Liberty to intimidate the few merchants who refused to honor the nonimportation agreements. Meanwhile the Grenville ministry had fallen and merchants in England were lobbying the new Rockingham government for repeal.

On May 1, 1766, a passenger fresh off a ship in the York River tied his lathered horse to the post in front of the printing office in Williamsburg and burst in with the news that Parliament had repealed the Stamp Act two months earlier. Next day, the newspaper heralded the "Great and Glorious News to America" and bubbled, "Let the cheerful song go round, for Britons, Britons never will be slaves."

Norfolk, Virginia's largest port, held a day-long celebration. On the front of the courthouse the citizens hailed "a well executed piece of painting" that depicted a grateful America prostrate before the king, who was attended by Virtue and Mercy, with a sun rising behind the throne in "full meridian splendour." Manufactures, Agriculture, and Commerce were seen "raising their drooping heads" while Tyranny, Slavery, and Oppression looked morosely toward the deep pit waiting to receive them.

In June, when the General Court convened in Williamsburg for the first time in nearly a year, the town put on a general illumination, with candles in every window and a grand ball at the Capitol, where Governor Fauquier amiably joined in drinking "all the loyal and patriotick toasts." The celebration in Williamsburg had a mournful and uncertain tinge, however, for along with triumph coursed the unsettling news that John Robinson had died several weeks earlier. The next session of the House, now the palladium of American liberty and opened to more vocal politics, would choose a new Speaker for the first time in thirty years.

Part
Two

1766-
1773

CHAPTER 6

"We Are All in Parties"

Patrick Henry hired a mason in the spring of 1766 to white-wash the walls of his new farmhouse on Roundabout Creek. While the agitation over the Stamp Act made the name of the "noble patriot" known up and down the continent, Henry worked hardest at putting his own household in order. He brought Sallie and the children up from Shelton's Tavern. The Roundabout house wasn't much to brag on—just three rooms downstairs and the usual Virginia jump half story above—yet, as the first place Henry had ever owned out-right, it suited.

Good fresh land, plenty of water and timber, and a comforting view across the snug creek valley made Round-about attractive, and the homestead—with its slave cabins, promising new orchard, smokehouse, and stables—quickly took on a prosperous air. Henry had an overseer to look after crops and hands and several tenant families on nearby acre-ages to increase the farm's production. Louisa was still a thinly settled county, with fewer than a thousand white men, but Henry's place lay advantageously between two paths to market. He could ship tobacco out along the "mountain" road that wound down from Albemarle and Orange along the South Anna River, past his father's place at Mount Brilliant and across Hanover to the familiar warehouses at Newcastle. Or he could choose the more southerly "Three-Chopt Road," named for its guideposts of triple axe marks, that meandered along the border with Goochland and led to "Shaccoes," the flourishing trading post and warehouse that was growing into the town of Richmond.

To the courthouse six miles north, however, Henry generally walked, "carrying his gun and hunting by the way." He would appear at the bar in his short hunting jacket and greasy leather breeches and between cases make plans for longer expeditions in which he would go off "with overseers, and people of that description," Jefferson recalled, in search of deer, "of which he was passionately fond." For a fortnight he would sleep under a tent, before a fire, "wearing the same shirt the whole time and covering all the dirt of his dress with a hunting shirt." Unlike the gentry, for whom fox hunting offered a daylong occasion for displaying prowess with horses, dogs, and drink, Henry took a more plebeian pleasure in his hunting trips, leaving care behind and returning, refreshed, with a full larder of meat.

Louisa County retained a backwoods flavor that appealed to Henry's simple tastes. His account books are filled with barter transactions: bonds and writs swapped for sheep or cider, cases tried in exchange for elk skins and venison or a few days' hire of a slave with special skills. There were still a few Indian traders based in Louisa. Most of the people were self-sufficient farmers, and even the few families of wealth, like Henry's mentors, the Johnsons, lacked the cultivated manners of Tidewater aristocrats. Louisa's people twanged their words, danced to their black folks' banjoes, and admired the simple gifts of their famous young neighbor, whom they all called "Pahtrick." Henry deliberately clung to his country ways. "Naiteral parts is better than all the larnin' upon yearth," he once declared to a well-bred gentleman in Williamsburg. When sophisticates talked of fine wines, Henry would extol the delights of drinking water from a gourd dipped into a wooden cask beside the cabin door.

When the courts reopened in the summer of 1766, following repeal of the Stamp Act, the pace of Henry's law practice quickened substantially. He had taken what cases he could manage without actually filing papers or making appearances, but his fees had dropped by nearly 80 percent in the year of protest and agitation. In 1767, however, he earned about as much as he had in 1764 and 1765; fees charged in about 550 cases amounted to approximately £425, of which he actually collected about £300.

As before, his legal work varied. Merchants brought him a great deal of business. The Scotsmen working their stores in Hanover and Richmond wanted him to sue their laggard customers (thirty or forty cases a year from each of half a dozen merchants meant considerable fees), and as word of his deftness got around the merchants from Norfolk and other Tidewater ports asked him to file actions for them, too. Land speculators wanted his advice on claims and titles and surveys, and his practice soon spanned the Piedmont and began to reach over the mountains as well. Almost immediately upon resuming the legal circuit in August 1766, Henry rode the seventy-five miles up to Staunton to qualify for practice in Augusta County, then Virginia's most westerly, embracing most of the Blue Ridge and the Shenandoah Valley.

The county courts tried to organize their sessions so that the members of the bar would not be pulled in too many directions at once, but a busy attorney might be continually making the courthouse rounds. Henry typically would appear on the first Monday of the month in Henrico or Charlotte, and on the first Thursday in Hanover. He could then ride home to Roundabout and Louisa's court on the second Monday. Then he would be off to Albemarle or Caroline on the second Thursday, Prince Edward on the third Monday, Goochland on Tuesday or perhaps a long trip over to Augusta, with a return via Cumberland on the fourth Monday. Quarterly trips down to Williamsburg for the General Court in April and October and the Court of Oyer and Terminer, which heard criminal cases (a lucrative part of Henry's practice, given his talent before a jury) in June and December.

Making the courthouse rounds had its evident hardships: long absences from home, long days in the saddle, and long nights in the "ordinaries," which, one English visitor sniffed, "have not their name for nothing, for they are ordinary enough." If he continued to be served nothing but bacon and chicken in these indifferent establishments, the visitor lamented, he would surely "be grown over with Bristles or Feathers."

Patrick Henry, however, left no complaints about life as a country lawyer; it gave him a very good living and kept him in the midst of public affairs. The courthouse crowd, moreover, afforded him a political platform and source of power that, in ever greater measure, compensated for his lack of family connections and ample wealth.

Court days in the summer of 1766 proved thick with startling political gossip. Speaker John Robinson had gone to his grave in May with the tributes of a grateful colony, but before the *Gazette* could finish printing all the memorial verse people began to murmur that Robinson, long presumed to be one of Virginia's wealthiest gentlemen, had run up a secret and staggering debt.

In early June a public notice in the *Gazette* asked that persons indebted to John Robinson's estate "make immediate payment" since the affairs of the estate were "so circumstanced as not to admit of delay or indulgence." The deceased gentleman had—from "the goodness of his heart"—advanced "large sums of money to assist and relieve his friends," Edmund Pendleton explained for the executors. Respect for "the memory of so kind a friend and benefactor" now requires that those so favored "pay immediately what they owe, without further trouble or application."

This notice set off new waves of rumors. The estate's largest creditor, the story ran, was the colony itself. Had Robinson's munificence not all come from his own pocket? Could it be that the most powerful politician in Virginia "had no great command of his fingers"? As Henry traveled from one county to the next he heard these sly words give way to uglier ones. "Misappropriation," "defalcation," and "embezzlement" began to be whispered, then charged openly, and by midsummer a cascade of newspaper articles confirmed that Virginia faced a scandal of considerable dimension.

Robinson, as his few critics had suspected for years, had made private loans from the colonial treasury to his friends, using the paper money he was supposed to have destroyed when the sheriffs returned such temporary tender as collected taxes. Robinson's estate owed the treasury about fifty thousand pounds, the gossip ran, and the executors' urgent plea sought to recoup that vast sum before its extent became public knowledge.

Courthouse politicians and lawyers speculated about the choices facing Edmund Pendleton, Robinson's grateful protégé and now his principal executor. Pendleton's fiduciary duty, as every man of the bar understood, required him to proceed unswervingly against the debtors, but such action would disgrace an untold number of very prominent gentlemen and possibly drive them into bankruptcy. If he proceeded leniently, collecting the debts slowly and repaying the treasury on some orderly and reasonable basis, he might not act in the most responsible manner that the court and his client, the Speaker's widow, had every right to expect, but he would prevent the financial wreck of a fair portion of the aristocracy and presumably, with the assistance of the grateful debtors, preserve the Robinson group's political power.

While the talk raged around him, Pendleton maintained a public silence. Only he knew the secrets contained in the crumpled notes and cryptic columns of Robinson's account books. As Pendleton worked his way through the disorderly papers, he kept finding new names. Two of the executors owed money to the estate, as did two of the estate's sureties, five of the six gentlemen justices on the probate court, twenty Tidewater burgesses, and half the Governor's Council. In the aggregate these gentlemen owed more than sixty thousand pounds to the estate, and hence to Virginia.

Faced with this distressing private information Pendleton made what he ever after regarded as the most public-spirited decision. He would protect his friends. While he would do what he could for Mrs. Robinson, surely she would have to understand the need for discretion and patience. Once the late Speaker's friends, under Pendleton's careful leadership, had elected Robinson's most intimate political collaborator, Peyton Randolph, as Speaker—and treasurer—in his place, matters could be quietly arranged to everyone's satisfaction.

Patrick Henry may not have divined Pendleton's plan at

once, but he knew from his own correspondence that the succession would not be so simple. The esteemed Robert Carter Nicholas, whose piety lent rectitude to his ambition, wrote to every burgess to hint discreetly at a different plan. Nicholas had volunteered himself as interim treasurer and had publicly pledged to investigate the rumors and to render equal justice to the Speaker's memory and the colony's assets. If he gave the public satisfaction, Nicholas said, "I shall think myself extremely happy, and own that I then shall not be without some hopes of being continued in that office."

In the oblique fashion of Virginia politics Nicholas was suggesting that the offices of Speaker and treasurer be separated. For years the Board of Trade had urged from London that the posts be severed, but Governor Fauquier had risked his superiors' displeasure because he had not wanted to disrupt his good relationship with Robinson. The safest course after Robinson's death, Fauquier thought, would be to continue the old arrangement with Peyton Randolph in both posts. If, however, the lately "virulent" House were to choose as Speaker some less reliable gentleman "remarkable for opposing all measures of government," Fauquier would happily veto any act appointing him treasurer. The governor realized that the Speakership was more important to the Crown's welfare than the plum of plural office holding. To protect Randolph's chances for the chair, he declined to place him in the treasury immediately and accepted Nicholas's offer instead.

Randolph was not pleased. He had ostentatiously declined service as a Robinson executor because he expected to take over the treasury at once. By letting Nicholas in the door, Randolph knew, the governor was giving the young hotheads led by Patrick Henry a respectable shield for their mischief. With the treasury even temporarily separated from the Speakership, the disruptive members would be free to rally opposition directly against Randolph.

Henry quickly sensed the opportunity, but he also realized that he need hardly say a word himself. Enough division existed among the senior members to mount an effective challenge to Randolph using the separation of offices as a wedge. The saddlebags were stuffed with letters from the burgesses all summer. Richard Bland declared his willingness to become Speaker and publicly stated that he believed "the Treasury ought to be put upon a new establishment, and not united to the chair, as it has been heretofore." Richard Henry Lee had also revealed "his views of the Chair," various correspondents reported, and had endorsed Nicholas as treasurer. Lee's animosity toward Robinson was well known, however, and his ambitions now were blocked by the sudden public charge that, in 1764, he had sought the office of stamp distributor before realizing the depth of colonial opposition to the scheme. Lee had rebuffed the most scurrilous attacks, but, tagged as "Bob Booty," he had little chance of succeeding a scandal-tinged leader.

The Randolph-Pendleton group vehemently maintained that the old arrangement should be continued under the eminently trustworthy Randolph, but the more they insisted, the louder the insurgents declared that no man—or group of men—could be trusted with unrestricted power. The public had to guard itself against the "confederacy of the great in place, family connections, and that more-to-be-dreaded foe to public virtue, warm and private friendship."

Henry need only say amen. The new popular spirit of the Stamp Act agitation would ventilate the previously closed byways of local politics. The warm agitation, one Virginian boasted in a New York newspaper, already had "the salutary Effect of correcting the haughty Spirits of some of our great Men, who from their Fortunes, Connections, and Stations, had conceived very high ideas of Self-Importance,—but are now convinced that, 'A Bashaw opposed against a Man, is but a Man.' "

Aristocratic connection, long unchallenged as the sinew of Virginia politics, suddenly faced public censure in the Robinson affair, and the opprobrium intensified that summer when a Piedmont tavern brawl left the Robinson-Randolph party discreditably involved in a murder case. When word first went around that the eminent Colonel John Chiswell had killed someone at Cumberland Court House, across the James River about thirty miles south of Louisa, no one expressed much surprise. "Chizzel" (as the name was pronounced) had a choleric nature and a large enough reputation for quarrelsome behavior to have made bloodshed seem inevitable. It was a pity, of course, that Chiswell, a magistrate and former burgess who owned vast tracts in Hanover and Goochland, would have to be imprisoned and stand trial, but surely there would be a compelling show of self-defense and the matter would be disposed of quietly.

But Chiswell did not go to prison, even though the examining court in Cumberland so ordered. When the county's under sheriff reached Williamsburg with the colonel in custody, intending to turn him over to the keeper of the public jail behind the Capitol, the somber party was met by a clerk of the General Court. Three judges "out of session" had authorized the worthy colonel's release on bail, and he went off, a free man, to his nearby town house.

The judges had called no witnesses and examined no record before taking this unprecedented action, an anonymous critic charged in the *Gazette*. "Is it not in fact a rescue, under pretence of law, of a person charged with an atrocious crime?"

This accusation—that the judges had behaved like highwaymen forcibly removing one of their number from the hands of the law—stunned Virginia. No one had ever put favoritism in such an ugly light before. Once implied, however, the charge soon became explicit. Chiswell, after all, was exceedingly well connected. His wife was a Randolph, the formidable Peyton's first cousin no less; the eldest Chiswell daughter Susannah had become Speaker John Robinson's third wife (now his widow), their match sealed by the gift of the lordly Chiswell plantation at Scotchtown. Two of the three judges who had freed Chiswell, moreover, were his friends and business partners.

The finger of favoritism and collusion pointed beyond the judges, too. Peyton Randolph, the King's Attorney, had not appeared at the Cumberland hearing, nor had he dispatched a deputy, which, the critics said, "must, in the eyes of all men who are not blind, look extremely dark." The judges, it turned out, had taken advice on the legality of the bailment from three of Randolph's intimates: his brother John, George Wythe, and Edmund Pendleton. Wythe, in line to become King's Attorney if Peyton Randolph became Speaker, later scurried to disassociate himself from the action while the others kept their silence.

Chiswell's case became a zesty public scandal. Assisted by a conveniently supplied newspaper diagram, every tavern crowd could divert itself by retelling the story of the "most unhappy drunken affair" that had left the popular merchant Robert Routledge dead at the point of Chiswell's sword. The men had hurled cups of punch and candlesticks at each other along with insulting words. Evidently the men were standing on opposite sides of a table in the taproom when Chiswell called Routledge a "rebel Presbyterian fellow," and the merchant retorted that he thought himself "as good a fellow as John Chiswell." Most of the witnesses said that the colonel lunged forward and stabbed Routledge while the merchant's friends tried to take him from the room; one Thomson Swan became well known for his account of standing so close to Routledge that Chiswell's sword passed first through Swan's coat, three buttonholes up from the bottom. But nasty rumors held that certain friends of Chiswell's would swear that they had been restraining the colonel's extended arm when the unfortunately inebriated Routledge hurled himself at his antagonist and landed upon the unsheathed sword.

Popular opinion approved the Cumberland magistrates' decision to hold Chiswell on charges of murder, and wherever Henry went in the Piedmont he heard people grousing about the "act of wonderful partiality" that had countermanded a local court. An "atrocious murderer" had gone free "by means of great friends," the country people were saying, and if some scrupulous soul endeavored to point out that Chiswell had only been admitted to bail until a trial could be held, a dozen cynics would respond that the colonel would doubtless object to the Cumberland venire and his protectors would "take care to have a menial or pliable tribe of bystanders ready to supply their place." There was ugly talk, too, that Routledge's friends would "take proper revenge" for his murder if the law could no longer be counted upon to render justice. "The middle and lower ranks of men" are "extremely alarmed," one correspondent informed the *Gazette*, and they will "never permit the assassin, and his abettors, to pass with impunity."

The heated debate matched the sweltering summer. Three Negroes dropped dead in Tidewater cornfields during one week in July, as did a white workman repairing the roof of a house. A gardener in Williamsburg mocked the excessive heat by baking an egg on his master's flagstone terrace, but most just complained and fumed. In so sultry a climate it did not take long before the Robinson and Chiswell affairs became intertwined as a double warning against trusting even the most eminent men with too much power. If the union of Speaker and treasurer had concentrated power unduly, perhaps the same might be said for allowing members of the Council to be judges.

With mob action threatened and constitutional arrangements questioned, Virginia's aristocracy deplored the spirit of "licentiousness" unleashed by the Stamp Act and now turned distrustfully upon the colony's distinguished men. But "distrust," one polemicist retorted, "is a political virtue of unspeakable utility." Had this virtue been properly exercised in some recent assemblies, he went on, some prominent gentlemen would not now be taxing the public's credulity by endeavoring "to metamorphose a notorious breach of the publick confidence into charity and munificence."

"We are all in parties," Chiswell's attorney complained, and it was true that the attacks upon the bailment had originated with men hostile to Peyton Randolph's efforts to occupy Robinson's dual offices. Robert Bolling, the most persistent of the critics, had supported Henry's resolves against the Stamp Act; Bolling's first cousin, John Fleming, not only had collaborated with Henry on the resolves but had also presided over the Cumberland court that had ordered

Chiswell jailed. Bolling's stepfather, moreover, was Richard Bland, whose readiness to become Speaker was well known.

One of the judges Bolling had criticized so harshly, William Byrd III, tried to end the public clamor by suing Bolling and the newspaper editors for libel, but the grand jury in Williamsburg would not return an indictment. Meanwhile, Chiswell silenced his critics with even more finality. Two weeks before his case was to be tried the colonel was found dead in his home. His physicians swore under oath that the colonel had perished from "nervous fits, owing to a constant uneasiness of mind," but the public took this to mean suicide. The most bitter, and perhaps the most knowing since their number included Peyton Randolph's acerbic wife, said that Chiswell felt abandoned by his friends and expected to be thrown to the vultures of public opinion. Yet so great had mistrust grown that some in the general populace suspected the death notice to be a ruse for spiriting Chiswell out of the country. A huge crowd stormed Chiswell's funeral in Hanover and halted the proceedings until a trustworthy person had the coffin opened and satisfactorily identified the remains.

Such suspicious tempers could not be ignored. As the assembly session neared, the wind blew toward accommodation. The assembly convened on November 6, 1766, for the first time since its dramatic session of May 1765. Patrick Henry had entered that house a neophyte and left it notorious. Now he returned, his reputation consolidated more by events than by his own efforts. The successful repeal of the Stamp Act had vindicated his boldness, while the upsurge in anti-aristocratic feeling and the odium which news of Robinson's embezzlement cast upon the established leaders only enhanced the fresh voice he had introduced into Virginia politics. Others would follow where Henry seemed ready to lead.

Everyone anticipated a "very warm" session. Since "the blood of the people is soured," Governor Fauquier reported to London, "party feuds will run high." The governor might have added that a certain instability might be expected also, owing to the largest turnover of membership in memory. One-third of the new House would be newcomers, some succeeding retired or deceased burgesses, but others replacing gentlemen who had opposed Henry and the Stamp Act resolves and thus incurred the displeasure of the electorate. Most of the western phalanx that had stood with Henry won reelection, however, and among the new members there were some who considered themselves, first and foremost, Mr. Henry's friends.

As always, much of the business would be concluded beyond the meeting chamber ("out of doors," as the politicians phrased it) amid the roistering entertainment and avid commercial conversations of the capital in "publick times." Ships' captains sought fresh cargoes, and land speculators searched out fresh capital. Patrick Henry's half brother, John Syme, a burgess from Hanover, was looking out for two plow horses, supposedly stolen "by a tall black fellow with remarkable white teeth," and he went into the complexities of the case with anyone who would listen. No one could stop talking about the tumultuous hailstorm that had struck a few weeks earlier. The noise of the storm was dreadful, everyone agreed, and they all laughed at how "the people" (meaning the Negroes) had thought "the last day was at hand."

When the House formally convened, 101 members (double the number present at the opening of the previous session) "took their places" on the long green benches and proceeded to the election of their Speaker. Despite the agitation and the turnover, the dissident burgesses could not prevent Randolph's elevation. He gracefully assumed John Robinson's imposing carved oak chair, knowing, however, that he could not rule with the bashaw's monumental power.

Randolph acknowledged the new order of things the very next morning. In appointing the first of the session's innumerable ceremonial committees, this one to count the votes for doorkeeper, Randolph identified the spectrum of influence in the House by naming Richard Bland, Richard Henry Lee, Edmund Pendleton, George Wythe, and Patrick Henry. When the House, as its next order of business, voted to establish a special committee to investigate the state of the treasury, Randolph appointed virtually the entire leadership of the House. Bland would be chairman; Lee, Wythe, and Henry would join him along with seven additional members including Archibald Cary, John Blair, and Landon Carter for the Tidewater conservatives partial to Robinson and John Fleming and Paul Carrington for the restive Piedmonters. Only the influential Pendleton was missing, barred by the blatant conflict of his position as Robinson's executor. Finally, the new Speaker completed the morning's business by naming the standing committees of the House, and Patrick Henry heard Peyton Randolph flatter him for the third time in as many hours with appointments to the two most influential bodies: Propositions and Grievances, and Privileges and Elections.

These conciliatory gestures may have soothed the dissidents but did not entirely win them over. Randolph watched helplessly as the House awarded the largesse of printing all public documents to William Rind, the bold printer whom the Stamp Act radicals had brought in the year before and whose newspaper had aggressively attacked the leadership on both the Robinson and Chiswell scandals. This vote signaled that an even more stinging defeat lay ahead.

On November 11 Richard Henry Lee moved, and Patrick Henry seconded, that the offices of Speaker and treasurer "shall not be united in the same person" and that "the Speaker shall not be concerned as an Officer of the Treasury in any manner whatsoever." Lee argued that the House should follow the maxim that liberty could best be protected by "dividing places of power and profit." He warned of the corruption that had undermined Rome and urged that Virginia should not "seal her own ruin" by uniting in one person "the only two great places in the power of her assembly to bestow." Henry lent his own determined eloquence to the proposition, and eventually the House adopted the measure by a decisive vote of sixty-eight to twenty-nine. Peyton Randolph, who would have paid five hundred guineas for the single vote needed to defeat Henry's resolution the year before, did not have the resources to stem rebellion this time. His chagrin was scarcely modified by the House's subsequent decision to compensate the Speaker for the loss of treasury fees with an annual salary of five hundred pounds; the money was the least of it. After all, he was willingly giving up the lucrative sums earned by the attorney general in order to become Speaker. The loss of authority rankled more. Being an astute politician, however, he bravely accommodated himself to the fresh political forces seeking recognition and built a new coalition on the ruins of his predecessor's reputation.

While the House anxiously awaited the results of the treasury investigation, it occupied itself with the session's routine business. Much concerned land: titles needed to be cleared, swamps drained, entails docked, disputed surveys disentangled, and growing counties subdivided. The rest concerned money: ferry operators needed to increase their fees; frontiersmen wanted compensation for wounds incurred from Indians; farmers sought recompense for tobacco stolen from a public warehouse or a horse that had died while on loan to a sheriff's deputy for public business.

Colonel John Henry was among the supplicants in Williamsburg that season. He wanted the burgesses to subsidize his latest scheme for recouping his fortune: mapmaking. He would measure the roads and prepare accurate maps of the entire colony as well as each county, to be printed in London and sold by subscription. "The advantages arising from such an undertaking are obvious to any who will duly attend to the Nature of such a work," he asserted in his petition, which was referred to committee. Patrick Henry, who had heard his father run on tediously about the project for months, did nothing to advance it, and the House declined to support it.

Henry wearied of the routine business and took ten days' leave in midsession to pursue his own private affairs. (George Washington, too, had taken advantage of the lull to inspect the progress of a land drainage scheme near the Great Dismal Swamp.) Finally, in early December, the House heard the staggering news that Robinson's estate owed the colony more than one hundred thousand pounds. Edmund Pendleton presented a petition with figures showing that Robinson's personal assets in land and slaves, if liquidated, could make up about one-third of the deficiency and that the late Speaker had posted performance bonds that would more than cover the remainder if the persons in debt to the estate failed of repayment. Pendleton asked the House to grant the estate three years' time in which to settle the affair.

The House did not yet know just how many of its own members owed money to the Robinson estate, but the sorry business produced much dissension. Robinson's friends, led by Randolph and Pendleton, forestalled any attempt to have the late Speaker's actions condemned. Officially, no violations of law had occurred, only a breach of trust; the Speaker had not intended to enrich himself but had acted solely to prevent financial calamity for his friends.

But the angry mood could not entirely be denied. Henry and the other dissidents would not grant Pendleton the indulgent hand he desired. They wanted to put some public and legal pressure upon the executors; the governor should order lawsuits against the estate, they insisted, to add interest penalties to what the colony was owed. The governor should also press for judgments against those who had pledged security for Robinson's performance and his estate. Those gentlemen ought to make good the difference between what Robinson owed and what his property would yield.

The House, not without debate, approved these measures, along with Pendleton's three-year repayment scheme, and the Speaker appointed Henry head of the committee to acquaint the governor with the resolutions. On the closing day of the session, Patrick Henry had the exquisite pleasure of standing in front of the House to report that the governor had heard their address and "that he was pleased to say that he would give Directions that the said suits should be commenced immediately." The theatrical Henry knew how to make an impression even in a minor role; while serving as ceremonial messenger he managed to communicate the upstart's ascendant power.

CHAPTER 7

"Hunting Out Good Land"

Patrick Henry invariably retreated deeply into private affairs after a session of public business. He seemed depleted and worn out, sometimes even feverish, and wanted nothing more than the solace of woods and fields and the comforts of family life. His circle was growing larger, too. In the summer of 1767, Sallie gave birth to another daughter, Anne; Henry's elder daughter Patsy had passed her twelfth birthday, and the boys, Johnny and Billy, delighted their father by running "as wild as young colts." They ran barefoot most of the time and, with their father's blessing, spent hardly any time at book learning. Several law clerks also boarded with the family, and they paid their addresses to their employer's younger sisters, who frequently called at Roundabout from Mount Brilliant.

Plantation life alternated between long stretches of tedium and frolicsome interludes of sociability. There would be evenings of dancing, with Henry taking his turn at the fiddle. The young clerks and the sisters and cousins danced the energetic jigs country people favored, an uninhibited, even competitive style that struck English visitors as more Bacchanalian than polite and tested the endurance of fiddler as well as dancers. There would be high-spirited singing, too, with the hundred or more verses of "Old Chevy Chase" lasting far into the night. Then the visitors would leave and the days subside into a routine so familiar that people would say that one "never saw two peas more alike than our yesterday and today."

Although Henry now earned a very good living, his tastes remained simple. He did not import many of the luxury goods favored by the Tidewater gentry; no "Turkey carpet" for the cabin floor and no elaborate silver service for the table. But the women in the family did consume yards of Irish linen and crimson shalloon and wore shoes made of rich callimanco fabric checked with satin; they rode upon fashionable saddles and talked of getting a two-wheeled coach or "chariot."

Henry had cash enough to help take care of his father's numerous small debts. John Henry tried to make ends meet by conducting a boarding school at Mount Brilliant, but he endlessly diverted himself with talk of his mapmaking project and a possible trip abroad in pursuit of subscriptions and subsidies. When William Christian, one of the Henry law clerks, asked for permission to marry Patrick's sister Annie, the elder Henry said he had nothing for a dowry. Writing to the young man's father, the prominent Staunton merchant Isaac Christian, Colonel Henry said, that while "the match is as good as concluded . . . it seems to depend chiefly on you—for as I can at present do nothing worth mentioning . . . I should be pleased to know what you can do" for your son. As always with the colonel, there were future possibilities. "At my wife's death, and mine, there will be some considerable estate to be divided among my daughters," Henry told the elder Christian, "but it is of such a nature that it must be kept together for our support."

Sallie Henry's father, John Shelton, also experienced financial reverses, and Patrick drove a hard bargain in coming to his father-in-law's relief. When Shelton was "greatly distressed for money" and his estate "like to be seized for a trifle," Henry wrote, "I resolved to advance some money for him." In exchange Henry wanted to step into Shelton's place as a land speculator. Shelton had to mortgage six tracts of highly touted western land to Henry, who even charged his father-in-law for the minor fees owed to another attorney, Thomas Jefferson, for witnessing the papers. When Henry subsequently learned that the land was liable to be forfeited for nonpayment of quitrents, he made sure that Shelton signed over an "equity of redemption," so that as mortgagor Henry would be able to redeem the property from default. Henry paid out the delinquent fees, but charged the money to his account with Shelton.

Henry also raised money for Shelton by selling the Pine Slash tract that had been Sallie's marriage portion. The two men had a falling out about repayment, and Henry groused for quite some time that he had never received all that Shelton had promised to settle as dowry, a deficiency that greatly "overbalanced" whatever claims Shelton was making against Henry to mitigate the mortgage debt.

Like many ambitious Virginians, Patrick Henry saw western land as a way to wealth. Tidewater gentlemen holding patents for vast stretches of what were now the settled Piedmont counties had prospered as this second Virginia grew. Now the Piedmonters themselves looked west toward a boundless third Virginia beyond the Blue Ridge. The colony's charter described Virginia as extending two hundred miles northward and southward from the entrance to Chesapeake Bay and within those bounds westward "from sea to sea," as far as the king's domain did run. On the flimsiest of patents—and only the sketchiest notion of American geography—Virginia gentlemen airily built their castles.

But land speculation had become a tricky business in the aftermath of the French and Indian War. In 1763 the Crown had temporarily ordered royal governors to allow no more land grants or surveys "beyond the Heads or Sources of any of the Rivers which fall into the Atlantick Ocean from the West and North-West." The "proclamation line" seemingly did not invalidate the vast grants made earlier to shareholders in Virginia's large land companies, but the uncertainty necessitated much diplomatic and political maneuvering in order to protect the potentially privileged status of these older ventures. His father-in-law's holdings, which stemmed from surveys of a 120,000-acre grant made in 1749, admirably suited Henry's purpose. Shelton's six tracts were only the surveyed part of his share in a land company headed by James Patton and Dr. Thomas Walker, two of Virginia's most intrepid land brokers, and Henry assumed his father-in-law's standing in this venture in land "lying on the waters of the Mississippi."

Buying into an older company might give one a purchase on the fabled country beyond the proclamation line. Another foothold might be obtained by surreptitiously disregarding the king's proclamation. George Washington certainly thought it foolish to remain idle. Anyone who "neglects the present opportunity of hunting out good lands and in some measure marking and distinguishing them for their own will never regain it," Washington told an old comrade in arms in 1767. Confidentially, he said, "I can never look upon that proclamation in any other light . . . than as a temporary expedient to quiet the minds of the Indians and [it] must fall of course in a few years especially when those Indians are consenting to our occupying their lands." Washington, with the aid of his friends living close to the frontier, would move "snugly" with "silent management" to mark out choice sections (he had his eyes on the upper Ohio River), on the gamble that policy would be changed, boundaries settled satisfactorily, and private deals with native tribes ratified by subsequent English or colonial legislation.

Henry, too, would not be restrained by an imaginary line drawn by a distant royal hand. He was building up his own set of connections in the western counties, men who could be counted upon to capitalize upon opportunities for quiet explorations and, later, for surveys and land sales to individual settlers. His sister Annie did marry the law clerk William Christian and settle with him over the mountains at the southern end of Virginia's great valley in Augusta County. Christian had served in the late war while still in his teens and proved an intrepid soldier and wilderness hand. Christian's sister had married another western soldier, an energetic Scotsman named William Fleming, who became adept at land deals and an eager business associate of Henry's. (In Virginia, a brother-in-law's brother-in-law was deemed a "connection" close enough to be considered kin.) Another of Henry's law clerks, Luke Bowyer, married Henry's sister Mary and settled in Augusta, and yet another Henry sister, Susannah, married Augusta's sheriff, Thomas Madison. In addition to forming the nucleus of a land company, these men would variously serve terms as burgesses and augment the strength of Henry's faction in the House.

In 1767, about the time Washington was putting his scheme for the Ohio in motion, Henry became active in a venture planned by Dr. Thomas Walker involving "lands lying on the Mississippi near its Junction with the Ohio." Walker was a physician from a long-established Tidewater family who had married into 15,000 acres in Albemarle and then headed the Loyal Company (1749), which received an 800,000-acre grant. He had important diplomatic connections and much experience in Indian trade and treaty affairs. Henry's half brother, John Syme, had married Dr. Walker's stepdaughter, so there was a connection, but Henry and Walker came together through their mutually shrewd appraisals of each other's power. Just as Henry had once attached himself to the county magnate Thomas Johnson in order to break into politics, so now he linked up with Walker as his entry into the land business. In both cases he chose well.

Walker had private knowledge of various efforts to conclude favorable treaties with the Indian tribes of the Ohio Valley, and in 1767 he moved to organize some adventurers in a far western scheme. Henry persuaded Walker to hire one of his connections, William Fleming, for a reconnaissance "jaunt." "Pardon me if I recommend to you a diary," Henry advised Fleming. "Even the trees, herbs grass stones hills etc. I think ought to be described," Henry suggested, in the belief that a well-kept, vividly detailed journal would be an effective advertisement later for settlers.

Talking about such a trip whetted Henry's appetite for both land and adventure. In the spring of 1768 he organized his own "jaunt" to reconnoiter the land he had acquired from John Shelton. The three thousand acres—described vaguely in parcels such as "1,400 acres on a branch of Clinch River called Mockison Creek" or "940 acres on the Middle Fork of Indian [Holston] River"—lay to the southwest, beyond the Virginia–North Carolina border.

Virginia claimed all of this beckoning region. When the Carolina border was first surveyed by William Byrd in 1728 he established its western terminus seventy-two miles beyond the point his associates thought necessary. A half century or more would pass before settlement pressed that far, they argued, but Byrd had a speculator's eye, and he knew what he wanted. The tide of population reached his benchmark in only twenty years. In 1749 Peter Jefferson surveyed the border westward to the mountain ridge south of present-day Abingdon; all the unexplored west-running watersheds beyond—the Holston, Clinch, Tennessee, and Kentucky rivers —presumably flowed through the vast domain Virginians claimed as their own.

Their claim, of course, rested upon patents and laws fashioned in Westminster and Williamsburg. The native tribes occupying the ground defined the boundary in practice, and in buying Shelton's land Henry knew the risk that treaties with the Cherokee might put the boundary east of his land. But Henry knew, too, that the treaties were only flimsy parchment, and the colonists had never honored them for very long. Since Thomas Walker served as the Virginia colony's delegate in many of the tribal conferences, Henry had some confidence that his speculative interests would be well tended. "After many contests and much altercation with the Indians, our own people, government here, and administration at home," Henry wrote a few years later, "an extension of territory was purchased from the Indians" and his lands taken into the Virginia colony.

The Henry party, including Patrick's brother William and brother-in-law William Christian, left for the southwestern frontier in the spring of 1768. They traveled up into Albemarle and reached west toward the Rockfish and Buffalo rivers, traversing the headwaters of the James and making their crossing of the Blue Ridge at Buford Gap, where Dr. Walker had often averred, "the ascent and descent is so easy that a Stranger would not know that he had crossed the Ridge." Following the Staunton River, they passed through the "Great Lick," now Roanoke, long a favorite feeding ground for deer, elk, and, in the old days, buffalo. Then they continued west into the lush meadows of the New River area where the Christian family had settled some years earlier. Here venison and turkey could be had with easy shooting, and the party diverted itself before setting out into the Holston country.

They were not trailblazers. The Indians had long ago found the easiest routes across the long, heavily timbered ridges that reached like fingers toward the Mississippi. Native hunting and trading parties had searched out the safest fords across the fast-moving streams—their waters as transparent as any men had ever seen and filled with shad, perch, and mullet—that tumbled southwest toward the wealth of Choctaw and Spaniard and the Gulf of Mexico beyond.

Narrow files of white families had freshened the path through these undulating valleys, letting their livestock graze the tall grasses, while their leaders dreamt of the lush grounds beyond the next ridge of rounded knobs. On his right hand Henry could point to the long ridge called Walker's Mountain; to his left there rose a rugged stretch called Iron Mountain, just about the highest, most impenetrable country they had yet seen. Between these densely wooded slopes, so often wrapped in the bluish haze at dawn and dusk, ran the beckoning trail their countrymen had already begun to call the "Wilderness Road."

Small settlements had dotted the Holston country for more than a decade, but the region was still wild—the community of "Wolf Hills" had not yet adopted the more civilized name of Abingdon—and periodically subject to Indian reprisals. (Another party that spring, led by the impetuous Josiah Martin, would establish an outpost on Powell's River near the Cumberland Gap, only to be routed by Indians before summer's end. They retreated to the safety of the Holston settlements, and Martin later became one of Patrick Henry's land agents in Kentucky.)

Passing through Wolf Hills the party moved southwest along the Holston and probably went as far as "the Long Island," where Indian hunters had long gathered. Walker's scouts, twenty years earlier, had seen young buffalo grazing there, along with a cluster of Indian bark houses and the skeletal remains of both hunters and their prey. Now the native dwellings were displaced by the whites' stockade, built in 1760 by William Byrd III's adventurers and named Fort Robinson in honor of the mighty Speaker. (In 1776 the outpost would be renamed Fort Patrick Henry.)

From the fort, Henry's group turned north, crossing the steep ridge into the Clinch River Valley, then working their way up the broad stream, with its fertile bottomlands and slopes of lofty hardwoods. They thrashed through underbrush of brambles, creeper, and the lovely mountain laurel in search of boundary markers for Shelton's tracts on Moccasin Creek and at a place known only as "Crabapple Orchard." They found nothing certain, but as they returned eastward toward the family outposts on New River, they could only marvel at the vastness, the beauty, and the princely wealth the country seemed to promise. The "third Virginia" would be a door into the Mississippi basin, and the Henry brothers, as much as anyone, would hold at least some of the keys.

It was a grand and distant region. The "Long Island" was as far from Louisa Court House as Louisa was from Philadelphia, yet what Henry had seen only increased his desire. He became involved in several ambitious ventures in the scramble to control the lush Ohio Valley. In December 1768 he joined prominent members of the Governor's Council as well as Thomas Jefferson, some of his Augusta County associates, William Henry, and William Christian in a scheme to patent fifty thousand acres on the eastern side of the Ohio River "precisely twenty miles below the mouth of New [Kanawha] River." This was in the rich, rolling, black-loamed country George Washington had glowingly assessed "for fertility of soil, pleasantness of clime, and other natural advantages . . . equal to any known tract of the universe of the same extent."

While dreaming of western riches, however, Henry kept his eye on the local land market as well. He had his Augusta contingent alerted to possibilities in that quarter, and he took a special interest in the long-anticipated sales of land that had belonged to the Robinson estate. Given Pendleton's reluctance to sue the late Speaker's friends for their unpaid loans, the repayment schedule promised to the House could not be met. In 1769 Henry served on the House committee that reviewed Pendleton's report that the estate could repay only five thousand pounds, and he shaped the House's curt reply: if the executors could not collect what was owed to Robinson, then they would have to liquidate the Speaker's estate within four months or else face lawsuits themselves.

In December 1769 the newspapers announced extensive estate sales—"in obedience to the direction of the House of Burgesses"—of the Robinson home plantation in King and Queen County and "all that exceeding valuable tract of land known by the name of Scotch Town, lying on New Found river in Hanover county, about sixteen miles above the courthouse."

This was news Patrick Henry had long wanted to hear. He had known of Scotchtown's preeminence all his life. The Chiswells had made it into the finest estate in upper Hanover, and Robinson had gained hold of it when he had married the feisty colonel's eldest daughter. Henry knew the advertisement did not exaggerate by claiming Scotchtown "remarkable for producing the finest sweet scented tobacco, which is eagerly sought after by cash purchasers, and therefore at all times commands the highest price." The soil, as Henry also knew, was "exceeding good for wheat," with stretches of low ground "that will suit for meadows." While much of the tract's three thousand acres remained woodland, the executors had up for sale three "plantations," outlying farms really, "cleared sufficient to work 20 or 30 hands, under good fences, with Negro quarters, tobacco houses, etc., all in order for cropping." Scotchtown's "oxen, horses, cattle, sheep, with the year's crop of corn and fodder, and all carts, ploughs, and working tools, belonging to the plantation" would be sold with the land, but as a separate venture the executors also announced the sale at Scotchtown of 250 "choice slaves," including many skilled craftsmen, gathered from Robinson's far-flung holdings.

Henry wanted the estate; he had his own complement of laborers. Operating through intermediaries Henry arranged to purchase nearly one thousand acres, including the manor house and the working farms, for about six hundred pounds, which his connections all considered a great bargain.

Scotchtown, named for the first Colonel Chiswell's dream of establishing a settlement with imported Scots laborers, lay in the hilly, northwestern corner of Hanover. Riding up from the courthouse one could feel the deeper swells that signaled the eventual lifting of the land toward the distant mountains; the wind seemed stronger and the air fresher than in the low-lying grounds of Pamunkey and Totopotomoy. To this salubrious place Patrick Henry brought his family in triumph. From the cramped rooms behind Shelton's Tavern and the modest homesteader's farmhouse on Roundabout Creek he had advanced at last to a spacious dwelling commensurate with his reputation.

The Scotchtown mansion, characteristically for Henry, was not a piece of fancywork. Indeed, it had a lumpish, barn-like look. The proportions appeared wrong because the house, long and rectangular with a vast hipped roof, had a one-storied facade while actually affording three floors of living space. The white clapboard house stood high enough on its brick foundations to permit ground-level windows for the earthen-floored rooms used for spinning and other handcrafts, food storage, and spare sleeping quarters. The main floor had eight good-sized rooms, four on each side of a spacious entry hall that ran the width of the building. Two massive chimneys, cleverly placed in the center of each four-room unit, permitted every room to have a corner fireplace, and each room, too, had at least one tall window. At the back of the hall a hidden stairway led to the enormous attic, ninety-four by thirty-six feet, spanning the entire house. Unpartitioned and lacking fireplaces, it served the swarm of children on rainy days and a mighty crowd of dancers on festive nights. In all, Scotchtown proved to be the kind of house people called interesting and well ordered, which meant that they did not find it beautiful. The furnishings looked plain, the heart-of-pine plank floors simple, with the only remarkable decorative touches being the beveled walnut doors and mantelpieces of black Italian marble in the parlor.

The house dominated a horseshoe-shaped courtyard, shaded by boxwoods and maples, around which stood the lesser buildings accommodating Henry's law office, the wash house, smithy and tanyard, and the roomy kitchen, which stood about fifty paces down a worn path from the corner dining room in the big house. Slave women presided over the large cookpots while black youngsters ran back and forth to serve the meals, clear the pewterware, and slop the pigs with table scrapings, having first appropriated the choicest morsels for themselves.

The Henry family settled into Scotchtown with enthusiasm. Their number was increased again by the births of Betsy in April 1769 and baby Edward in early 1771, making a total of six surviving children, shortly after the purchase of the new estate. The woods afforded rich hunting, the streams good fish, and for the first time a Henry plantation had its own mill, which stood about half a mile from the house on the New Found River and became a special haunt for the middle boys. Mount Brilliant lay only a short ride away, and Henry's youngest sisters, Betty and Sukey, joined his eldest daughter Patsy in the neighborhood social life. Mrs. John Henry wrote affectionately to her westernmost daughter Annie Christian of the clan's comings and goings. "Sallie Henry and Patsey is here," one letter ran. "They and your sisters have been to Deep Run to hear Mr. McRoberts [preach] today to their great satisfaction. Littel Edward is a fine child, I nursed him while they were gone." But, as always, the news from Mount Brilliant had a plaintive air: "It will not suit your sisters to visit you soon as we have not got a new chair yett nor hands for them."

Henry, too, moved readily back and forth between Scotchtown and Mount Brilliant, where he had to take an increasingly firm hand with his improvident father's affairs. However, his law practice no longer required him to ride the courthouse circuit without letup. In 1769 Henry won admission to the bar of the General Court in Williamsburg, which meant that he argued civil cases on appeal before the highest judges in the colony and took only the major criminal cases that came before them. Attorneys of the General Court did not, as a rule, take petty cases in the local courts, although this custom was not universally observed. Henry, therefore, dispensed advice by letter and spoke with the increasing number of clients who rode up to Scotchtown to obtain his counsel. He worked in a small clapboard cabin, only a few paces from the big house, built much like the Roundabout house with a dormered half story upstairs where his clerks might sleep. The nearest corner of the mansion had a separate doorway for travelers, who could take their ease at Henry's hunter's sideboard in a brick-floored hospitality room that well tolerated their muddy boots. Henry had the thrifty habit of regarding all his visitors as family members; that way, the local jest at Scotchtown still runs, "he didn't have to put but one kind of meat on the table."

Indeed, Henry's increasing prosperity led some to complain that he had an avaricious streak, but Henry enjoyed his reputation as a man of business. "He could buy or sell a horse or a Negro as well as anybody," a relative recalled, "and was peculiarly a judge of the value and quality of land." In the competitive and aggressive world of the commercial planter, these were complimentary words, although gentlemen of wealth wanted to be known as well for their benevolence and their public service. Even though Henry's assets never approached those of the Tidewater magnates or even his Piedmont friend Jefferson, he had the arriviste's desire to be recognized for what he had attained, and his associates soon learned that he was "better pleased to be flattered as to his wealth than as to his great talents."

Henry's commercial prospects, however, improved as his political standing grew, which reversed the more customary path in which power followed wealth. When he set off from Scotchtown in his new chaise, en route to Williamsburg for sessions of the assembly and the court where he planned to wear his fine new suit the color of peach blossoms, Henry might fancy himself a gentry magistrate in the mold his father once had tried to fit. Yet he knew that his strength and influence came from those who resented gentry privilege. In a very few years he had shown, in a contemporary's words, that "a new path" could be "opened to the temple of honor, besides that which led through the favor of the King." Now, as the pace of political crisis quickened, Henry began to turn that political power against the Crown itself.

CHAPTER 8

"Virtual Obedience"

News of the Stamp Act's repeal in May 1766 brought a brief period of rejoicing in Virginia, followed by many months of lingering resentment. The Virginians grumbled at London's attitude that they must express gratitude for the repeal. "All we hear from that side of the water," a Fairfax planter named George Mason complained, "is pray be a good boy for the future; do what your Papa and Mamma bid you, & hasten to return to them your most grateful Acknowledgements for condescending to let you keep what is your own; and then all your Acquaintance will love you, & praise you, & give you pretty things."

Given the prevalence of such mockery, Governor Fauquier felt obliged to admonish the House of Burgesses to remember its manners. At the outset of the tension-filled session of November 1766, in which the House first heard the extent of Robinson's abuse of the treasury funds, the governor solemnly advised the burgesses to make returns for "the many Acts of Kindness which you must acknowledge have been shewn to you" by "your Mother Country." "Your grievances have been redressed, the Act you thought oppressive repealed," he said, and "as an indulgent Parent has a right to expect a Return of Duty, Obedience, and Gratitude from her natural Children, she has a Right to claim the same for you, her political ones."

Unaware of how much his language confirmed the

planters' parodies, Fauquier found it "extraordinary" that the House declined to prepare a formal address of thanks. There was still "too much heat" in that body, he thought; it ordered a statue of the king raised in acknowledgment of repeal but showed what it really thought of that exercise by placing Patrick Henry, whose powerful vision of regicide had so provoked the late Speaker's wrath, upon the committee charged with formulating a suitable inscription.

Fauquier kept a sharp eye on the sullen burgesses, but the impetuous new politicians—Henry preeminent among them—had grown too crafty for him. "They have become so prudent as to have nothing appear on their Journals," Fauquier complained to London, "so that I am legally ignorant of what might drop in debate from some of the young, hot-headed, unexperienced Members."

The Virginians still groused because their fears of legislative despotism had not abated. Parliament, after all, had coupled repeal of the obnoxious stamp law with a declaration —a bill of right, some called it—that Parliament had authority to legislate for the colonies "in all cases whatsoever." A further declaration nullified any and all "resolutions, votes, orders, and proceedings" in the colonies "whereby the power and authority of the Parliament of Great Britain to make laws and statutes as aforesaid is denied or drawn into question." Resolutions like those Patrick Henry had advanced in Virginia had already done their work, of course, but no one knew what might come next. Another "experiment" like the Stamp Act, George Mason publicly warned a group of London merchants, "would produce a general Revolt in America," for having tasted "the sweets of liberty" in an abundant and prosperous country, the colonists had grown "impatient of restraint."

Such boastful talk struck some as shadow boxing, until the news from Britain in the summer of 1767 made crisis palpable again. Parliament had decided to extend the Grenville revenue program, which had led to the Stamp Act crisis. This time the architect was "Champagne" Charlie Townshend, the chancellor of the exchequer, whose debonair charm turned to insolence with drink. Townshend, trying to stay afloat in the tricky currents of cabinet politics, proposed that the colonies bear some portion of their civil maintenance by paying new duties on a long list of vital imports. Townshend conceded that such duties would not bring in more than a fraction of the true cost of administering and defending the colonies, but he wanted to make a point.

Parliament had heard the ungrateful noises coming from the colonies and did not much care for the sound. The Americans were an "irritable and umbrageous people" who needed to be taught a lesson. At New York, the War Department reported, the assembly was being niggling and vexatious about complying with General Gage's requests for military supplies in a way that brooked defiance of the Quartering Act. Other colonies were said to be amassing arms of their own, and one rumor had South Carolina declaring its independence.

Surely something had to be done. The Revenue Act levied duties on a list of enumerated articles, including paper, glass, painter's colors, and red and white lead. The Tea Act reorganized the affairs of the East India Company and imposed a mild tax of threepence per pound on tea reexported to the colonies. All these duties, payable in the hard-to-come-by sterling, would be collected at the American ports of entry and put into a fund earmarked for the salaries of the Crown's officers in the colonies. A companion act established a new board of customs commissioners and gave colonial courts the power to issue general writs of assistance, which allowed the king's men great breadth in the search for contraband. Another law had the effect of suspending the colonial legislature in New York until it complied with the Quartering Act.

Singling out New York, as it turned out, was Parliament's substitute for Grenville's angry and ill-considered proposal that every assemblyman in the colonies—and every member of the governor's councils, and the governors, too—formally subscribe to the Declaratory Act as a condition of holding office. Let 'em swear, Grenville contended, that "the colonies and plantations in America are, and of right ought to be, subordinate unto, and dependent upon, the imperial Crown and Parliament of Great Britain."

Although Parliament shied away from the proposed oath as both provocative and redundant, the Townshend program implicitly aimed at the same goal: securing colonial subordination to central authority. But Townshend thought he could secure responsible colonial government simply by insulating its administration from upstart legislatures and maintaining the revenue-collecting supremacy of central authority. The insouciant minister never realized how controversial his own measures would become, for the forty-two-year-old Townshend died of a seizure in September 1767, just as word of Parliament's actions was reaching North America.

Those colonists still smoldering over the outrages of the Stamp Act thus had their worst suspicions confirmed, barely a year after the repeal they were supposed to applaud. Over the next twelve months a horde of pamphleteers attacked the Townshend program from every possible standpoint. It violates the precedent of charters, said Richard Bland, and ought to be resisted like any other "invader" or "aggressor" who threatens the security of one's property. It is "a snare worthy of Nero," said the "Pennsylvania Farmer," to disguise taxes as trade regulation. The Townshend program is "like a bird sent out over the waters," the "Farmer" warned, "to discover, whether the waves that lately agitated this part of the world with such violence, are yet subsided." Another writer, styling himself "Monitor," said that the suspension of New York's assembly exposed the Caesarean tactic of divide and conquer. To the administration's insistence that all colonists enjoyed "virtual representation" in Parliament, "Monitor" had a sly, provocative answer. Virtual representation, he said, required only "virtual obedience." Richard Henry Lee called the Townshend Acts a "flaming sword" pointed at the people's liberties that had to be removed "by all means."

When Virginia joined Massachusetts in calling for a concerted petition from all the colonies, the ministry instructed colonial governors to dissolve any assembly that participated in so "flagitious [an] Attempt to disturb the public Peace" and "promote an unwarrantable combination."

The war of words intensified. A Massachusetts lawyer

named James Otis ridiculed the House of Commons as "a parcel of button-makers, pin-makers, horse jockeys, gamesters, pensioners, pimps, and whoremasters." Virginians spoke darkly about "aristocratic corruption" as the weakest part of the British constitution, and the newspapers reprinted Cromwell's attack on the Long Parliament: "Ye are a factious crew & enemies to all good government. . . . Go! get ye out! Make haste! ye venal slaves begone!"

The secretary of state, Lord Hillsborough, sent two fresh regiments to fractious Boston "to damp the spirit of insurrection" the ministry saw in the noisy street demonstrations there. Although the secretary worriedly told the king that "five or six ships of war and a body of marines" might be required "on very short notice" to suppress threatened disorder in Virginia, he decided first to try a more conciliatory approach.

The Crown had not yet named a replacement for the recently deceased Fauquier. Although the Virginians had generally referred to him as the governor, in technical point of fact Fauquier held the post of lieutenant governor, while the royal governor, Sir Jeffrey Amherst, remained in London and enjoyed the sinecure's fees. The planters had frequently complained that this long-settled practice affronted their dignity. Why not mollify the proud gentlemen, Hillsborough shrewdly reasoned, by sending a full governor of noble rank to Virginia? It would be an important gesture—assuring the nervous colonists of the ministry's respect and smoothing some of their ruffled feathers.

The cabinet agreed and, after some discreet maneuvering, settled upon a candidate: Norborne Berkeley, Lord Botetourt, an exceedingly affable but diligent country squire with excellent ties to the Bristol trading community so heavily engaged in colonial commerce.

Hillsborough had given Botetourt very careful and deliberate instructions to cultivate the leading Virginians and lead them from "their unwarrantable Claims and Pretensions." If the governor could not persuade them "to return to a becoming Sense of their Duty, founded upon just Ideas of the

Constitution," then he must act forcibly by dissolving any obstreperous assemblies and calling upon General Gage at Boston for the troops necessary to maintain order.

Botetourt's appointment flattered and excited the Virginians. The newspapers published His Lordship's pedigree, which contained a suitably long list of titles and even included a former Virginia governor, Sir William Berkeley, among the ancestral connections. Williamsburg's handful of versifiers busied themselves with welcoming odes, musicians readied festive airs, children made floral garlands, and a giddy public prepared to turn Botetourt's arrival into a stately, pastoral celebration worthy of one of Mr. Handel's operas.

As if on cue, clear skies and gentle zephyrs graced the welcoming ceremonies, which happily coincided with the autumn 1768 court session and Williamsburg's busy social season. The town was illuminated with candles at every window, and "all ranks of people vied with each other in testifying their gratitude and joy that a Nobleman of such distinguished merit and abilities" was "appointed to preside over, and live among them." One welcoming ode rhapsodized: "The peaceful olive branch on his brow he wears!/His listening ears will to your truths attend/And be your GUARDIAN, Governor, and FRIEND."

The new governor truly looked like a nobleman. He had a stately air about him, his handsome head carried elegantly upon a swanlike neck. Botetourt had large and luminous eyes, accented by arched brows and a high forehead. His thin lips habitually curled upward at the ends in a slight smile that might have seemed weak or supercilious were it not for the determined thrust of his jaw and shapely cleft chin. The man seemed genial and well spoken, but none could mistake the hint of iron in his character.

Until the governor's servants could sort the baggage and ready the palace, the "principal gentlemen" asked Botetourt to dine with them. The leaders liked him, for as a man of plentiful fortune and assured rank he embodied what they liked most about themselves. Like the Virginians Botetourt appeared cultured without being formally. educated, and he combined a generous and good-natured manner with a conscientious sense of duty that the Virginia elite thought essential to the patrician. After a week of wining and dining by Peyton Randolph, George Wythe, Robert Carter Nicholas, and other leading citizens, who of course invited those councilors and assemblymen who happened to be in town, the governor exclaimed, "I like their stile exceedingly."

Patrick Henry enjoyed the amiable suppers, but he did not drop his guard. Like Richard Henry Lee, Henry worried that Botetourt had put off a new session of the assembly until May. These shrewd politicians knew that the governor wanted time to exert his private influence, and they cautioned that the "general pleasure" given by "His Lordship's good sense, affability, and politeness" should not gull the public into thinking that the governor's "political opinions" would agree with those of Virginia. An anonymous pamphleteer spoke their minds in condemning those "fulsome panegyricks" addressed to Botetourt as "a curious species of lip-loyalty" unbecoming to free men.

Indeed, some disturbing intelligence had come to light. The good Botetourt, some said, had left England under a cloud of bankruptcy, having mismanaged some mining ventures in ways that left his partners bereft and his own reputation tarnished. As a court favorite he had been packed off to Virginia, while Lord Jeffrey Amherst was kicking up an awful row at having been eased from the post to make way for Botetourt.

The Virginians, having weathered the Robinson affair, could not become very exercised about murky financial maneuvers, but there was worse talk yet. Botetourt supposedly had royal instructions to lay the provocative Declaratory Act before the House of Burgesses. If he did the radicals—Henry, Lee, and the westerners—wanted to counter with a petition of colonial rights, but "the time-serving Men" counseled a dignified silence. R. H. Lee retorted that "silence in this case, must by all the world, be deemed a tacit giving up our Rights, and an acknowledgement that the British Parliament may at pleasure tax the unrepresented Americans."

The radical drumbeat continued through the waning months of winter and intensified in March, when news arrived that Parliament, relying upon an ancient statute from the time of Henry VIII, had ordered that colonists—especially the Boston protesters—being investigated on charges of treason should be brought to England for trial. The "axe" was now being "laid to the root of liberty," a pamphleteer styling himself "Atticus" charged on the eve of the assembly's session. Unconstitutional taxes had been levied, assemblies suspended, a standing army dispatched, the right to unite in petition inhibited, just complaints maligned as impudent efforts toward independence, and now, "Atticus" railed, the crowning insult: "statutes of treason are to be extended by construction, contrary to the known maxims of law and justice: which will render every man's life as insecure as his property already is." The "vilest ministerial arts," actuated by decadent venality, corruption, and ambition, he wrote, had provoked a crisis that "in a less loyal country" than America "would have infallibly produced . . . a civil war."

Such embittered talk had its effect on Lord Botetourt. Despite his confident demeanor, Botetourt was a fretful man who hated to give offense. "If the paper I write upon is improper," he wrote defensively in an early dispatch to Lord Hillsborough, "one line of direction to Mr. Conway my Agent in Beaufort Buildings, to send me a quantity of that sort you approve, will set that matter right." He liked the Virginia gentry he had met, but upon better acquaintance he had come to the grim conclusion that they would "never willingly submit to being taxed by the mother country; the reverse is their creed." Could he still lead them by "earnest persuasion," as His Majesty instructed, "to a becoming Sense of their Duty," or would he have the melancholy task of punishing those gentlemen who had befriended him?

Botetourt hoped to flatter the burgesses with pageantry. On the opening day of the session, Monday, May 8, 1769, Lord Botetourt, dressed in a coat of brilliant red cloth much embroidered with gold, rode from his palace to the Capitol in a kingly chariot emblazoned with Virginia's coat of arms.

(Word quickly spread that the coach, a gift to the governor from an uncle of George III, had been built for the monarch himself and had once borne the royal arms where Virginia's now stood.) The crowds cheered as if Botetourt were riding to Westminster for the ceremonial opening of Parliament itself.

The carriage horses stirred the most attention. Six cream-white animals, their silvery harnesses gleaming in the brilliant sunshine, drew the governor at a stately pace along the main street and into the Capitol yard, where Patrick Henry and the other burgesses waited. The gentlemen watched in astonishment as the finest horses ever seen in Virginia paraded before them. In the babble of excitement as the party surged into the building for the lengthy formalities, George Washington, who had come to town in a newly imported chariot of his own, could be heard vowing that someday he would have a team as fine.

More than one hundred members, virtually the entire House, took their oaths on that glittering morning. A good many, including Henry, had come to Williamsburg some days previously for court sessions, and much private talk had transpired about a united course of action should the governor, as anticipated, ask the House to endorse the Declaratory Act. No firm strategy having emerged, there was an edginess in the body that the astonishment created by Botetourt's resplendent procession masked but did not dispel. The burgesses went through the minuet of electing a Speaker—Peyton Randolph again, by acclamation—and then walked in a body upstairs to the Council Chamber, where Lord Botetourt, by custom, would approve their choice.

Randolph, in his own majestic dignity, stood before the brilliantly dressed governor and received his approbation. The ritual then called for the Speaker to "petition" the governor that the House "might enjoy" its "ancient rights and privileges" including freedom of speech and debate and exemption from arrest. Randolph had intoned those words on previous opening days, as had John Robinson for thirty years before him, but this day Randolph used a more dramatic phrase. According to the journal, "Mr. Speaker did, in the Name, and on Behalf of the House, lay Claim to all of their ancient Rights and Privileges." A subtle change, but in a gathering of lawyers, a significantly assertive one. Botetourt gave no sign that he noticed anything unusual and merely murmured the customary response that he should take care to defend them in all their just rights and privileges.

Then His Lordship delivered a signal of his own. He read, slowly and carefully, a short address that opened with flattering remarks about the ability of the assembly and went on to express His Majesty's "paternal Affection for all his Subjects in every Part of his Dominions, however remote from the seat of his Empire." The governor paused for a long time, then resumed his reading.

"Mr. Speaker, and Gentlemen of the House of Burgesses," he said, "I have nothing to ask, but that you consider well, and follow exactly, without Passion or Prejudice, the real Interests of those you have the Honour to represent; they are most certainly consistent with the Prosperity of Great-Britain, and so they will for ever be found, when pursued with Temper and Moderation."

The burgesses understood at once the conciliatory import of this statement. Botetourt would not formally place the Declaratory Act before the House. Most of the gentlemen recognized the courage that undergirded the governor's discretion, for it was common knowledge that Lord Botetourt's instruction had insisted that he do so. While the impressionable marveled that Botetourt's oratorical gestures resembled those of the king, others took comfort from the report that Botetourt had deliberately omitted the most astringent passages in the draft address supplied him in advance by the secretary of state.

Edmund Pendleton engineered a set of resolutions complimenting Botetourt, which he invited the young new burgess from Albemarle, Thomas Jefferson, to draft, in a shrewd bid to flatter the forty neophyte burgesses before hotheads like Henry could prejudice them against the leaders. Botetourt, in turn, sustained the harmonious mood by inviting the entire

House, in batches of fifty, to dinner at the palace, where the hospitable and convivial talk made it seem that, as Jefferson's address expressed it, "Wisdom and Benevolence will distinguish his Administration."

The formalities at last concluded, the House turned gratefully to the routine business of the session. Henry kept his posts on the two major committees and performed some services for the Hanover people who wanted the task of clearing the upper stretches of the Pamunkey River to become a public expense, or at least chargeable to all those using the warehouses along the upper river, rather than the lotholders alone.

Too many political grievances smoldered, however, for Henry to spend all his lobbying time on the Pamunkey. Although the governor had decided not to skirmish over the abstract statement of sovereignty, there remained the taxation quarrel, the dispatch of troops to Massachusetts, and the resurrection of the ancient statute allowing colonists to be transported to England for trial on charges of treason. The House must comment upon these matters, Henry and Lee insisted. If the governor meant to be as conciliatory as he seemed, perhaps some relief might be obtained; if his mildness was a deception, assertion of colonial rights would be even more necessary.

They quickly brought the House to a remarkably united position. There would be four resolutions: an affirmation, yet again, that the House possessed "the sole right" of imposing taxes upon Virginians; an assertion that the "undoubted" privilege of petitioning the Crown for redress of grievances carried with it the "lawful and expedient" right of seeking the concurrence of other colonies; an admonition that the transportation "to Places across the sea" of persons accused of treason or any other crime was "highly derogatory of the Rights of British subjects" to be tried before a jury of the vicinage and to produce witnesses in their defense; and, last, another "humble, dutiful, and loyal" address to the Crown asking that he "quiet the Minds" of the loyal subjects by removing these threats to their liberty.

When the committee reported these resolutions to the House, the burgesses immediately agreed to them "Nemine Contradicente," which literally means "no one speaking against" and politically means that although Hillsborough had wanted to tie up the hotheads in Massachusetts with the ominous old laws, even Peyton Randolph and Edmund Pendleton could feel the threat of the noose. The House further showed its spirit by repeating an action that had already caused offense; it ordered that the Speaker "transmit, without Delay" copies of the latest resolutions to the other colonial assemblies with requests for their concurrence.

More fireworks could be anticipated from the requisite address to the king, for in appointing a drafting committee Peyton Randolph pulled no punches. He set both Patrick Henry and Richard Henry Lee to the task, aided by a spirited Piedmonter, Thomson Mason, and restrained only by an intimate of the governor's, the courtly John Blair; treasurer Robert Carter Nicholas; and the Speaker's sluggish brother-in-law, Benjamin Harrison.

The committee did not need much time to voice its thoughts, for Henry and Lee had rehearsed the principal arguments in the debate. The House had made a dramatic shift in its position, ignoring the long-running quarrel with Parliament to concentrate instead—for the first time—directly upon a disagreement with the Crown itself. The new tack gave Patrick Henry another choice opportunity to demonstrate his talent for casting a complicated political issue in dramatic personal terms.

The draft of the address, presented to the House the very next morning, depicted the Virginians as aggrieved subjects, concerned that "their Loyalty hath been traduced" and filled with "Horror" at the idea that the inhabitants of America might be carried overseas for trial. In vivid phrases stamped with the directness of Henry's appeal to jurors rather than the convoluted formulas of previous petitions to the king, the address bemoaned "the Case of a wretched American, who, having incurred the Displeasure of any one in Power, is dragged from his native Home, and his dearest domestick

Connections, thrown into Prison . . . in Fetters amongst Strangers . . . Conveyed to a distant Land, where no Friend, no Relation, will alleviate his Distresses . . . and where no Witnesses can be found to testify his Innocence." Even when the anguished lament was read to the approving House in the suavely polished style of the chairman, John Blair, Jr., the influence of Henry could be heard.

Having completed the urgent political business, the House moved on to hear some private petitions on fish traps and parish infighting, but the burgesses' attention strayed from the clerk's table to the doorway. The governor had ordered the Council to convene at noon, and that could have only one likely meaning.

Indeed the clerk of the Council soon arrived with an urgent message.

"Mr. Speaker," he said, "The Governor commands the immediate Attendance of your House in the Council Chamber."

Led portentously by Peyton Randolph the House trooped up to the richly paneled, oval-shaped chamber where Botetourt and the councilors sat on ornate, thronelike chairs. His Lordship, dressed this day in a suit of plain scarlet, looked coldly at the burgesses and said:

"I have heard of your Resolves, and auger ill of their Effect: You have made it my Duty to dissolve you; and you are dissolved accordingly."

The love feast, it seemed, had ended.

Randolph bowed gravely, and the burgesses retreated politely from the chamber. Dissolution of the assembly, however, would not do away with the assertive assemblymen. Their resolves were already being set into type in the public press, and some of their number had begun to walk the half block up the main street toward Anthony Hay's tavern, formally known as the Raleigh, where by prearrangement the burgesses had agreed to reconvene informally in case the governor ended their official session.

Reports afterward conveyed the impression that "the late Representatives" immediately marched up to the tavern as a united and determined body, a veritable phalanx of decorously controlled indignation. In truth, gentlemen drifted in over the next hour or two, some first repairing to their town houses for dinner, others stopping at the taprooms to quench the legislator's traditionally powerful thirst, a few taking a quiet moment or two to ponder the wisdom or propriety of attending at all. The humid afternoon was well along, with rain clouds looming up from the river, before the eighty or ninety ex-burgesses found themselves ready to proceed.

Hay's establishment had the handsomest public rooms in town, far grander than anything Henry had known at Shelton's Tavern in Hanover or the other courthouse havens. The "late Representatives" commandeered the largest of several club rooms, the Apollo, a ballroom-sized chamber that opened out beyond the noisy bar and billiard parlor. (A companion room, for more private gatherings, cozily bore the name of Daphne, the nymph Apollo loved.) Apollo's room, with its six tall windows, generous expanse of powder-blue wainscoting, and gleaming heart pine floor, had a grander appearance than the Capitol chamber from which the burgesses had just been expelled, although the pink marble fireplace and the carved motto, HILARITAS SAPIENTIAE ET BONAE VITAE PROLES ("Jollity is the offspring of wisdom and good living"), supplied more frolicsome touches.

The mood of the gathering, despite its high edge of exhilaration, remained deliberative. Peyton Randolph now presided as "moderator," and a plan had already taken shape in many minds. The tactic would be a trade boycott and the form a solemn pact in which gentlemen pledged themselves to concerted political action to protect "social privileges founded in reason, guaranteed by the British constitution, and rendered sacred by a possession of two hundred years." Colonel George Washington, the muscular hero of the French and Indian War, had served ten years in the House in virtual silence, but now he found his voice. No one "should scruple, or hesitate a moment to use a-ms [sic] in defence of liberty," he had told his neighbor George Mason early in April. He continued to praise armed recourse, always adding, in a Virginia planter's approximation of French, the qualifier that arms should be "the denier resort." If the taciturn Washington, hitherto noted largely for his preoccupation with land speculation and fox hunting, had been stirred to advocate militant and united action, a shrewd observer like Henry could see at once that the center of political gravity had shifted markedly.

Washington's striking assertions won him a place with Henry and Lee on the drafting committee, which, after an evening's work, reported the text of an "Association" based on nonimportation agreements previously drawn up by merchants' groups in Philadelphia and Annapolis. The Virginia Association would "induce the good People of this Colony to be frugal in the Use and Consumption of British Manufactures" and pledge subscribers "by their own example" and "all other legal Ways and Means in their Power" to "promote and encourage Industry and Frugality, and discourage all Manner of Luxury and Extravagance." The Associators would be pledged to import none of the goods taxed by Parliament for the purpose of raising an American revenue, except a certain quantity of cheap paper, which, the committee realized, would be necessary for their continued political correspondence. Until the repeal of the revenue laws, moreover, Associators would abjure a list of British trade goods that ran on for several dozen lines and covered everything from hoes to silverplate and hair ribbons to saddles. Associators would also be asked to import no more slaves for the duration and purchase none imported by others, but here the committee proposed a cut-off date of November 1, 1769, as opposed to the first of September for the other commerce.

At the Apollo on Wednesday morning, May 17, the draft received hearty applause. "Starving their Trade and manufactures" will awaken "our Lordly Masters" to the necessity of recognizing our rights, the gentlemen told each other; no ministerial mandate can make us buy ten-pound coats when we prefer to warm ourselves by the fire of liberty in ten-shilling jackets.

With enthusiastic solemnity, each of the eighty-eight former burgesses pledged himself "upon his Word and

Honour" to the Association by stepping forward to sign the document. First, Randolph the Speaker, then Nicholas the treasurer, followed by the venerable scholar Richard Bland (the most senior member present). Tidewater planters and Piedmont lawyers rubbed shoulders as they leaned in toward the desk, old rivalries subsumed in a new gesture of unity. Archibald Cary, then Richard Henry Lee; Charles Carter, then George Washington; Carter Braxton, then Patrick Henry. The columns grew. Three-quarters of the new upland members signed, but only half of the new Tidewater burgesses came along. Pendleton had gone home early, and Benjamin Harrison and Landon Carter kept themselves aloof, but they were the only holdouts. It was a remarkable outpouring of resolve, and it was followed by lusty cheering and drinking.

"The King," someone cried, and the company raised glasses of punch. "The Queen and Royal Family" followed, and another round in honor of "His Excellency Lord Botetourt, and Prosperity to Virginia." The gentlemen drank to "a speedy and lasting Union between Great-Britain and her Colonies" and in the midst of general shouts for "constitutional British Liberty in America," they toasted some of their English allies, along with "the Farmer," "the Monitor," and their own Speaker and treasurer.

Then the gentlemen "retired," the minutes say, and most went off to dinner and a well-earned nap. George Washington, newly fired up with curiosity, stopped by the printing office on the way back to Mrs. Campbell's tavern to buy a copy of the Pennsylvania Farmer's Letters, but he fell asleep at eight that night before he had done much reading.

Patrick Henry left the Williamsburg session with much to ponder. Although he aspired to wealth, neither his law practice nor his farming had yet allowed him to import many of the commodities the Associators had pledged to forgo. While Washington was commissioning a handsome new chariot from the best London coach makers, Henry was buying a secondhand, two-wheeled riding chair (locally known as a chaise or shay) from one of his Winston cousins. He had no mercantile broker in Bristol or London, but rather sold his small tobacco crops through his half brother John Syme and purchased his necessary English goods through the local Scots merchants who were his clients and constituents.

The economic and social implications of the nonimportation campaign intrigued him, however. The loud praises of frugality and the accompanying denunciations of luxury and selfish indulgence among the wealthy suited his evangelical, antiaristocratic bent, while the appeal to home manufactures quickened his speculator's yearning to develop the outlying western region and promote a more diversified commerce for Virginia.

Every year merchant ships from Salem and Boston, Glasgow, Liverpool, and London crowded into the colony's rivers, Henry recognized, ready to take in barter the commodities whose culture the Virginians understood for the necessary goods they could not produce themselves. The outsiders carried away everything from tobacco and turpentine to beeswax and barrel staves and profited more than Virginia did from the exchange. If Virginia produced its own manufactured goods, there would be two important consequences. Virginians would be less dependent on imports and could improve both their bargaining position and their balance of trade. Even more attractive, Williamsburg and Alexandria could sell to the Kentucky and Ohio regions, as Glasgow and Salem now sold to Virginia. How this sparkling vision would reconcile greater economic independence with continued colonial political dependence Henry did not yet know.

If home manufacture posed new contradictions, in Henry's mind, it also held out the promise of easing an old conundrum. Talk of manufacturing and self-sufficiency implied the encouragement of artisans and craftsmen, which meant recruiting a new labor force of white immigrants to supplant the black workers brought in chains from Africa. The nonimportation movement engaged in much hand wringing about Virginia's excessive reliance upon tobacco as a cash commodity, and this gave those planters who were uneasy about the slave trade an opportunity to link an argument from conscience with the necessity for economic change. The Association barred only the importation of new slaves, however, saying nothing about the slave traffic within the colony.

As Henry rode up-country from Williamsburg these issues remained inchoate in his mind. He gave thought to planting less tobacco and more flax and wheat, as he had learned Washington (a shrewd planter with a gambler's instincts) had begun to do, but he mulled over the problem of making the colony attractive to artisans, and somewhere, in a quiet corner of his mind, he wondered whether he and his countrymen could possibly live without slaves.

"Don't you think the Virginians have behaved like men?" a Carolina planter wrote to a friend, as word of Virginia's resolves filtered out along the seaboard. "I fancy Lord Botetourt must by this time know that Titles, Burgundy, and a gilt coach will not be sufficient Inducements to bribe men out of their Liberties."

Virginians accepted praise as patriots, but as consumers they hedged their bets. Washington, for example, told his London merchants not to send him those articles expressly taxed by Parliament, but his invoices ignored the Association's ban on a number of luxury goods Parliament had not yet taxed. Other members of the gentry asked that their orders for party shoes and fancy hats be sent only "if the American Revenue Acts should be repealed before your ship comes out." Thomas Jefferson placed a contingent order for a clavichord, among other prohibited "fancy goods," but the controversy dragged on long enough for him to become "charmed" by a fortepiano and ask for one (with a case of solid mahogany and worthy enough to be a gift to a lady) to be shipped instead.

Such tentative ordering allowed even more than the usual room for confusion, and despite the high-minded resolves, the customs figures showed that imports to Virginia actually rose in the twelve months following adoption of the Association. While the northern colonies observed nonimportation with "religious punctuality" (the figures show a two-thirds decline for New York and Massachusetts), pamphleteers mourned

Virginia's fall from glory and warned that her weakness threatened the brave chain of union that "binds this new world from end to end."

Part of the trouble was practical. Unlike the northern seaboard towns, whose wharves and warehouses offered a focal point for protest and enforcement of the boycott, Virginia's commerce was far-flung along hundreds of Tidewater rivers, and the Association had made no arrangement for supervising the agreement. The more militant leaders began to talk about the formation of county committees to exact compliance from the merchants, as had been done so flamboyantly, and successfully, at the time of the Stamp Act business.

Political uncertainty, however, added to the practical difficulties. The whirligig of faction had brought new gentlemen into prominence at court and into power in the Commons, and by midsummer the Williamsburg papers purveyed rumors of impending repeal. Associators, of course, argued that this proved the effectiveness of the boycott, for it was widely known that colonial traders in Britain had bitterly complained of their injuries and had lobbied strenuously for repeal. The government also roused fierce opposition for its continued suppression of the radical editor John Wilkes, who was three times elected to Parliament and thrice denied his seat by the government majority on grounds that his character was too opprobrious and seditious. The London mobs who paraded for "Wilkes and Liberty" took up the colonial cause as part of the same constellation of constitutional issues. "The persons who wish to enslave America, would, if it lay in their power, enslave us," a linen draper said, and the colonists reciprocated by making the Wilkite cause their own. Virginians avidly followed events in their own newspapers and took each stroke against Wilkes as more evidence of the ministerial intent to suppress liberty. Piedmont farmers named new towns for Wilkes and the number 45 (the issue of Wilkes's paper suppressed by the Crown) took on patriotic significance.

With the government at home reeling from an unprecedented outpouring of public discontent, advocates of a conciliatory colonial policy did their best to get the revenue acts repealed. Meanwhile, in Virginia, Lord Botetourt indulged in uncharacteristic anger. Shortly after dissolving the assembly, the governor advised Lord Hillsborough, in a dispatch marked "Secret and Confidential," that "Opinions of the Independancy of the Legislature of the Colonies are grown to such a Height in this Country, that it becomes Great Britain, if ever she intends it, immediately to assert her Supremacy in a manner which may be felt, and to lose no more time in Declarations which irritate but do not decide." Now Hillsborough had to restrain the exasperated Botetourt. He instructed him to reconvene the assembly and resume his soothing efforts: "the King wishes that it may be possible for your Lordship to avoid coming to Extremities."

When the assembly reconvened in November 1769, Botetourt's opening address purred with conciliation. Henry, delayed by bad roads, missed the ceremony and only heard later that Botetourt had staked his reputation upon the promised repeal of the duties upon glass, paper, and colors, since those taxes had been laid "contrary to the true principles of commerce."

At second hand Botetourt's blend of honeyed words and gentlemanly fervor did not persuade Henry, although they captivated most of the burgesses who had heard them. Militant energy, already ebbing, drained away, and Henry, Jefferson, and Lee made little headway as they privately pointed out the threadbare nature of the compromise so suavely set before their colleagues. The obnoxious taxes would be repealed, but only as a commercial mistake, not as a recognition that Parliament had overstepped its authority in levying them. Indeed, the tax on tea would be retained, the ominous principle of the Declaratory Act still lurked behind it, and the threat of being transported across the sea for trial awaited those who might protest these matters. Even Botetourt's brave words, when studied carefully, amounted only to an assurance that the governor himself would labor for Virginia's "satisfaction." However welcome that statement might be, who could believe a distant governor might reverse the course of a ministry bent on tyranny?

The majority of burgesses, however, seemed ready for an accord. The governor should be trusted, they argued; indeed, Lord Botetourt had privately shown to Peyton Randolph some correspondence that convinced the Speaker of the ministry's sincerity. The established leaders replied to the governor's address with a document of surpassing sweetness, and the session proceeded uneventfully. At its close, just before Christmas, the Speaker and the burgesses feted Botetourt at a lavish ball. Not even the concerted appearance of a great many women in gowns of homespun (a direct statement of support for the Association) dimmed the lustrous spirit of confidence that had grown up between the once-spirited leaders and their immensely charming governor.

Not that Botetourt had ever spoken without foundation. Hillsborough subsequently chastised him for being too effusive in his statements to the burgesses, but the partial repeal Botetourt forecast in November did remain policy even when the ministry passed into Lord North's hands early in 1770. On March 5, 1770, Lord North asked a grudging Parliament to repeal most of the Townshend duties, and he hinted that he might well ask for removal of the tea tax as well, once matters could be arranged with the East India Company.

The two-month delay in receiving news from England, however, bedeviled the emerging truce. On the very day Lord North proposed repeal in London, an angry street fight in Boston between a waterfront crowd and a detachment of British regulars left five colonists dead and allowed the radicals in Massachusetts to broadcast reports of a "massacre" and portray the ministry once again as bloodstained tyrants.

Virginians read detailed accounts of the Boston affair in their newspapers by the first week of April, while the same editions carried London news of January and February. Alongside the Boston reports ran an account of the king's opening address to Parliament in January, in which His Majesty gravely declared that his endeavors to bring his American subjects back to "a true sense of lawful authority" had "not answered my [his] expectations," for "many persons" there "have embarked in measures highly unwarrantable and calculated to destroy the commercial connexion between them and the Mother country." The statement did not square with Botetourt's assurances and led popular leaders like Henry and Lee to suspect "some state trick, that plain honesty cannot easily penetrate."

News of the partial repeal did not come until the end of April, and by that time anxiety had warmed a Virginia effort to revive the boycott. The Associators wrangled throughout the month of May about amendments that would provide more consistent enforcement, but Henry and Lee had to contend with a rear-guard effort led by Pendleton and Nicholas to resume importation as a gesture of gratitude "to meet the Parliament half." Now would be the time to return to the quiet diplomacy of the past, they argued, rather than continuing the noisy parade of patriotism which had more show than substance. Angrier men like Henry ridiculed the idea that "going our half" meant surrendering first principles. America must work for her own salvation, the radicals argued, and put no trust in great men—either in Williamsburg or in London—for giving her relief from any motive but necessity.

Although the protesters achieved a mildly strengthened Association by mid-June, the prime architects had begun to think that only a unified continent-wide effort would stand a chance of success. Out of frustration with Virginia's laxness and the ease with which Botetourt had moved into command, the popular leaders now insisted that "lovers of liberty" in every province ought to maintain a private correspondence in order to exchange both information and counsel until each assembly created a committee for more public communication. Lee had already taken the initiative by writing to John Dickinson, the wealthy Philadelphia lawyer who had roused public opinion as "the Pennsylvania Farmer," when an unusual opportunity arose for Henry, who disliked stating political strategy on paper, to undertake a bit of personal reconnaissance.

Henry became a plenipotentiary. The House appointed him and Richard Bland as Virginia's commissioners to an intercolonial conference on the Indian trade, scheduled to convene in New York City on July 10, 1770. As an aspiring land magnate Henry had closely followed recent treaty negotiations with the Cherokee, and Bland's unrivaled knowledge of the law would be an asset in any effort to draw up intercolonial trading rules. The House knew, of course, that it was sending abroad two preeminent defenders of colonial rights, the impulsive and aggressive Henry paired with the more temperate but equally staunch Bland, who had first entered the House of Burgesses in 1742, when Henry was only six years old.

Henry left Williamsburg a week before the session ended to make preparations for the journey, his first beyond Virginia. On July 1, on his way to New York, he stopped at Mount Brilliant, where his father surprised him by repaying one of the innumerable small loans the son had made to him.

The trip to New York could be expected to take a week or more. Riding on horseback, accompanied only by a man-servant and a minimum of baggage, a traveler in summertime could cover about forty or fifty miles a day, unless delayed by ferry crossings or the long boat passage from Annapolis across Chesapeake Bay. Travel in Maryland left most Virginians feeling smugly superior. The land across the Potomac struck them as at best "indifferent" or "sorry," and the little capital Annapolis proved inferior to Williamsburg, with uneven, hilly streets, a dilapidated church, and a new Capitol that still lacked its dome. Once on the eastern shore, however, moving steadily northeastward into the Delaware counties of Pennsylvania, their discerning farmers' eyes would be opened to changing uses of the land. Broad level fields, well fenced and well cultivated, appeared given over to various crops of grain, grown—as could be learned quickly in conversation—on a rotation system still considered unusual in Virginia. Meadows of timothy and clover, punctuated by large stands of timber, gave an air of prosperity, confirmed for travelers by the abundance of hay, oats, and corn set out for horses during stops at the public houses. Numerous and neat houses, with fewer mansions than in the Chesapeake and fewer distinctions in rank among the people, contributed to the hearty impression of well-being. The quiet panorama of prosperous small-scale farming and thriving trade prevailed all the way to Philadelphia, whose thirty thousand inhabitants made it the largest city in the colonies. Well-laid-out streets (both paved and illuminated), long wharves piled high with barrels of flour and immense quantities of shingles and other forest products, a profusion of shops, a higgledy-piggledy mixture of brick and wooden houses, and the great gabble of accents and dialects produced by the tide of Scotch-Irish and German immigrants running through Pennsylvania all made Philadelphia seem as grand as the fabled London neither Henry nor Bland had ever seen.

If the Virginia commissioners sought out their Pennsylvania confreres, or endeavored to call upon the eminent lover of liberty John Dickinson, no record survives. They would have looked around a bit, swapped news in the famous coffee-houses along the market street, and made arrangements to continue their journey the remaining ninety miles to New York. It would take them two days to cross the pleasant Jersey countryside and ferry Raritan and New York bays, whether they rode their own horses or arranged to board them in favor of the "flying stage waggon" that many travelers preferred.

The city of New York occupied the southern tip of a large island whose wooded hillsides reached as far upriver as one could see. A small fort, with stone-faced bastions and a row of cannon, guarded both the entrance to the North (or Hudson's) River and the preferred anchorage on the eastern channel, which led toward Long Island Sound. A half dozen church steeples, the round dome of the city hall, and a thicket of ships' masts made a crowded skyline that anticipated the busy city with a population twenty times that of Virginia's capital village.

From the ferry landing at Whitehall Slip, sandwiched between the battery and the East River docks, the travelers were pitched at once into a cobweb of streets, irregularly laid out and badly paved with open drains running down the centers, and a congeries of indifferently built houses in which stone, brick, and wood were fashioned in a mélange of old

Dutch and contemporary English styles. Only on the west side of town, where residential streets turned at right angles off a spacious tree-lined promenade called "the Broad Way," would the Virginians see stately town houses and a straight-forward plan that might remind them of Williamsburg.

Henry had walked into a donnybrook without parallel in his Virginia experience. The nonimportation agreement had collapsed, and the broad coalition that had formed in opposition to the Stamp and Townshend acts had now fractured into two groups, one composed of merchants and other well-to-do gentlemen eager to resume trade now that partial repeal had come, the other a pugnacious set of waterfront workers and artisans led by "the Wilkes of America," Alexander McDougall, who insisted upon continuing a loud opposition to parliamentary taxation.

The city buzzed with bitter and self-righteous argument. That very day a merchants' group had placed pouches filled with orders aboard the royal mail ship *Earl of Halifax* bound for London on the next tide, while angry "Liberty Boys" roamed the streets denouncing the high-toned merchants for their selfishness.

Even a brief stroll up "the Broad Way" revealed the tensions, with the majestic liberty pole and the statue of the king each fenced off against vandals and the angry factions headquartered in taverns less than a block apart.

Henry met with Alexander McDougall at the Liberty Boys' "Hampden Hall" and found a man much like himself. The son of a Scottish immigrant, McDougall had Henry's broad face and firm chin and, like the Virginian, communicated a sense of clarity and vehemence held under tight control. McDougall had made his own way into the commercial community, first as a privateer and then as ship's captain and broker, and along with John Lamb and Isaac Sears—also self-made men who had earned their reputations at sea—McDougall had a large following among the New York populace. Indeed, he had become the Liberty Boys' hero earlier in the spring, when he published a pamphlet roasting New York's governor and assembly for pusillanimous acquiescence to the revenue laws. For this literary attack McDougall had spent eighty days in jail on charges of sedition. (Forty-five friends had visited him on his forty-fifth day of confinement in order to press the parallel of John Wilkes.)

The merchants had secretly decided to resume imports, McDougall told Henry, even before conducting a poll of the city over the previous weekend. Although the commercial gentlemen had loudly condemned the popular party for creating turbulence, McDougall related with some passion the story of how the merchants had intimidated the voters and connived with city officials to block the Liberty Boys' parade protesting the resumption of trade in advance of the other colonies. Plainly nonimportation had lost its political power in New York, as indeed it had waned in Virginia. In meeting at a time of declining political fortune, McDougall and Henry realized the immense importance of concerted action in the future; each man reinforced the other's conviction that although the resistance to the revenue acts was collapsing from exhaustion, any further oppressions—and they were sure that there would be some—would be met by firm and zealous resistance.

The trade conference that had brought Henry and Bland to New York never took place. On July 11 Governor Colden wrote apologetically from his country home in Flushing that he had learned on July 6 (too late to alert the Virginians) that Pennsylvania had decided not to participate and that Quebec's commissioners found travel too inconvenient in the present season. Shrewd politicians like Henry and Bland understood that beneath these pallid excuses lay a higher-up decision to undermine any intercolonial gathering, but having gathered intelligence on their own unofficial mission, they went through the lame charade of meeting the next morning, July 12, with the three New York commissioners in the rooms of the chamber of commerce on Wall Street. After signing a brief statement of their readiness to meet another time, the Virginians left the city immediately for an unusually rapid trip to Virginia, for they arrived back in Williamsburg a scant seven days later, on July 18, and filed for expenses amounting to nearly seventy-five pounds.

Henry returned to Virginia with a new appreciation of its relative unanimity and a vivid impression of how class differences sharpened the politics of resistance. Although not as devoted to the mystique of the House of Burgesses as the veteran Bland, Henry had made the assembly his forum for protest. New Yorkers like McDougall, however, had lost confidence in their own assembly and felt that it was dominated by wealthy interests willing to make accommodations with Parliament in order to preserve their own power. The radical party had taken to the streets instead.

Virginia, too, seemed ready to put aside the gauntlet, not so much because the well-to-do had come to fear popular excess (for, unlike New York, the aristocratic element had directed the protest without many allies in the streets) as because Lord Botetourt had so well succeeded in his mission of regaining the political trust of the ruling magnates.

In October 1770, however, while Henry was attending the General Court in Williamsburg, Lord Botetourt suddenly took ill and died. Grieving and shaken, many of the well-connected burgesses extolled the late governor as the instrument of their dawning happiness and predicted a resurgence of ministerial tyranny in the face of this untimely loss. They retold the stories of His Lordship's generosity and understanding, the perfect ease with which he joined in front-porch singing of a summer's evening, and the redoubtable firmness he brought to the pledge of repeal.

On Friday, October 19, Williamsburg witnessed the most elaborate funeral in its history. The bells in the Capitol, the college, and the church began their melancholy tolling at one o'clock, and two hours later, in the waning autumn light, a solemn procession accompanied the governor's body on its final journey from the palace. The town's militiamen, augmented by companies from York and James City, lined the greensward between the mansion and the parish church. Peyton Randolph and Richard Bland of the House joined members of the Council as pallbearers, and behind the hearse walked "His Excellency's servants, in deep mourning," the clergy, the professors of the college, the city officials, the gentlemen of the law, and the clerk of the court, all wearing white hatbands and gloves and walking two by two in a prescribed order that reached deep into medieval memory. A large company of unranked townspeople followed the chief mourners into the church. The lead coffin, covered with crimson velvet, was adorned with silver handles and a silver nameplate. Many wept over it as the organist played a funeral anthem and the minister rendered a sad discourse. Following the service the procession resumed, in the same order, and escorted the hearse to the college chapel at the western end of town, where the coffin was laid in the Randolph family vault while awaiting transport to England, the militia firing three volleys during the interment.

Eulogized as a noble figure of active and exemplary virtue, Botetourt earned among the Virginians a reputation that he never quite achieved at home and that they had never expected from an agent of the present embattled ministry. As they turned away from the crypt most public men felt bereft of a powerful friend; only a few of the impetuous young lawyers quietly thought that perhaps fate had removed a charming obstacle from liberty's path.

CHAPTER 9

"The New Boanerges"

The quietus with Parliament seemed to aggravate quarrelsomeness among Virginians. They argued about whether planters along the James and Rappahannock rivers ought to receive the same rate of compensation for tobacco washed away in the great flood of July 1771, and they argued about whether Shockoe's or Rocket's warehouse ought to be allowed to move to choice higher ground on Richmond Hill. Arguments broke out about the organization of the courts, the licensing of tobacco inspectors, the right of civil authorities to punish a dissolute clergyman, and the aesthetic merits of the steeple added to Bruton Parish Church in Williamsburg, a wooden octagonal affair that struck some as more appropriate to a Moroccan pigeon house. Such grumbling bespoke more than social crankiness, for Virginia was undergoing a profound religious change, and the ensuing controversy allowed Patrick Henry to consolidate further his reputation as the champion of the common folk.

In the late 1760s another evangelical revival swept across the Virginia countryside. Like the Presbyterian upheaval of Henry's youth, the new awakening began in cabins and houses, as itinerant Baptist preachers spread their message from family to family. When the ranks of the converted swelled, the revival moved outdoors, with assemblies in the meadows and the river bottoms and congregations holding meetings in barns and tobacco sheds. The Baptists drew folks with a vociferous style of preaching that went beyond the word into shouts and drones, thunderous hand clapping, and the ecstatic twisting and jerking of the body itself. The emotional rituals of the new sect, which included fervent handclasps and kisses along with baptism by total immersion, turned congregations into communities, and the great springtime association camp meetings drew several thousand together in a swelling social fellowship.

The ecstatic revival had to endure the gentry's scorn and the magistrates' persecution, for the Baptist movement posed a severe challenge to established ways. Itinerant preachers (heeding no call but their own) mocked all episcopal order, and separate Baptist congregations (independent even from one another) dissolved traditional parish bounds. The revival, moreover, drew its strength from the lower orders—the poor, the landless, and the unlettered—who cut their hair like Puritan roundheads, disdained the fine dress and frolicsome ways in which the gentry displayed their power, and called each other brother and sister in a nurturing, egalitarian fellowship that threatened an end to their long-settled dependence upon the squirearchy.

The evangelicals seemed as threatening as the Anabaptists of old, and the specter of peasant uprisings and religious revolt gained special force from the Baptists' willingness to include slaves in their communion. "We are verging fast towards republicanism and puritanism," prominent citizens complained, and (writing under a nom de plume) the attorney general lamented that Baptist preaching induced many to "forsake their Church and the cheerful innocent Society of their Friends and Families, and turn sour, gloomy, severe, and censorious. . . . Wives are drawn from their Husbands, Children from their Parents, and Slaves from the Obedience of their Masters. Thus the very Heartstrings of those little Societies which form the greater are torn in Sunder, and all their Peace destroyed."

In county after county, especially across Henry's Piedmont, where the itinerants found mightily responsive listeners, the authorities jailed preachers and countenanced violent reprisals against them. In June 1768 the sheriff of Spotsylvania

County jailed a quartet of preachers for forty days. When an itinerant named John Ireland, jailed in neighboring Culpepper, tried to preach from his cell, ruffians rode up "at a gallop" to disperse the faithful. The "poor negroes" attending were "stripped and subjected to stripes," Ireland lamented, and he was threatened with "being shut up in total darkness if ever I presumed to preach to the people again." On other occasions in Culpepper, Ireland was nearly suffocated by smoke and sulfurous gas, and "miscreants" mocked the evangelicals' version of baptism, Ireland said, when they climbed upon a table while he preached "and made their water in my face."

In Caroline, where Edmund Pendleton presided over the local bench, the authorities proved especially severe. The minister of the parish personally accosted the Baptist preacher John Waller in July 1771, roughly tumbling the leaves of his hymnbook with the butt end of a riding whip, which the parson then shoved into the preacher's mouth when he attempted to pray. Waller was "violently jerked off the stage" by the clerk of the court and dragged, head beating "against the ground, sometimes up, sometimes down," to the sheriff standing nearby, who "gave him something not much less than twenty lashes" and then, after some "abominable ill language" departed with parson and clerk. Waller, "in a gore of blood," "went back singing praise to God, mounted the stage and preached with a great deal of liberty."

The spectacle of persecution extended to twenty-eight counties as the revival spread and the number of separate Baptist congregations climbed from six to sixty in less than a decade. Legal proceedings against the itinerants usually took the form of civil complaints such as disturbing the peace or vagrancy, which emphasized how much the authorities feared the Baptists' challenge to the social order. The revivalists retorted that the civil charges concealed the magistrates' intention of regulating religious matters and infringing their rights of conscience.

The Baptists chronicled the martyrdom of their preachers, recording scores of incidents in which their evangelists were "pulled down while preaching," "dragged out amidst clenched fists," "pelted with apples and stones," "commanded to take a dram or be whipped," "brutally assaulted by a mob," "arrested, abused, and released," and—over and over again— "jailed for preaching." Their suffering became a watchword, a testament of faith, but coupled with it went the story of the one stalwart friend the Baptists had among Virginia politicians, the celebrated lawyer Patrick Henry.

Henry, it was said, rode fifty miles out of his way to volunteer his services to the Baptists jailed in Spotsylvania. He walked into the courtroom on the day of trial and, hearing the charge of disturbing the peace read aloud, asked to see the indictment.

"Did I hear it distinctly, or was it a mistake of my own?" he is supposed to have said. "Did I hear an expression, as of a crime, that these men, whom your worships are about to try for misdemeanor, are charged with,—with—what?,—preaching the Gospel of the Son of God?"

The lawyer paused, exploiting the silence as only he could. He held the paper high in the air and slowly waved it three times around his head. Then, with face and arms raised toward heaven, Henry simply said, "Great God!" and again, "Great God!" and, once more, "Preaching the gospel of the Son of God—Great God!" The prosecution, the story concludes, could make no rejoinder, and the case had to be dropped.

The dissenters celebrated Henry as their Robin Hood. The most frequently told story concerned an itinerant preacher, John Weatherford, who had been imprisoned for five months in Chesterfield County, where the presiding magistrate was Henry's rival burgess Archibald Cary. Henry, it was said, successfully obtained an order of release, but the jailer refused to let Weatherford out until the preacher paid the costs of his long confinement. Weatherford had no money and remained in prison some weeks longer until the jailer one day announced that an anonymous friend had paid Weatherford's fees so that the preacher could go free. Only later did Weatherford learn that Patrick Henry had been his secret benefactor.

Henry's emergence as the gentleman-protector of dissenters seems a mixture of intuition and calculation. Evangelical sympathies ran deep in Henry's family. His wife, his mother, and his sisters all found refreshment by attending "preaching," and the Winston side of the family had joined the once-reviled but now respectable Presbyterians. Before assisting the Baptists, Henry had helped the Society of Friends with its legislative exemption from military service and earned Quaker accolades as "a man of great moderation." He had an instinctive appreciation of the rights of conscience and a healthy respect for the assertive individualism that gave energy to the revival. Although most of the Baptists did not own land and thus could not vote, Henry sensed their potential power, not only by their growing number in Louisa and Hanover counties but in the course of western settlement. That his long-standing political rivals like Pendleton, Cary, and the Randolphs took a more repressive position undoubtedly heightened Henry's own willingness to link himself with popular insurgency.

From the gentry's standpoint, however, aid to the schismatics amounted to demagoguery, the fomenting of social rebellion under the false banner of liberty of conscience. In their minds they could apply to Henry himself the popular sarcastic jibe that an "Anabaptist Preacher" could be brewed in two days' time by taking "the Herbs of Hypocrisy and Ambition," two drams of "the Spirit of Pride," "a Pint of Self-Conceitedness," and four pounds of "the roots of Stubbornness and Obstinacy" and blending them in "the Mortar of Vain-Glory, with the Pestle of Contradiction."

The Baptist challenge led Virginia's political leaders into a long and confused debate on the subject of religious toleration. No fixed starting point could be ascertained, since neither the House of Burgesses nor the General Court could say with certainty that the Act of Toleration, passed in the first year of the reign of William and Mary as part of the settlement ending Parliament's quarrel with the Stuarts, fully applied to Virginia. Most public gentlemen favored some kind of "toleration to scrupulous consciences," as Attorney General John Randolph put it, but Randolph spoke for the conservative majority when he insisted that the legislature (by the burgesses' own laws or by application of the 1689 Toleration Act) had the power to fix the limits of toleration with "a due Regard for the Public Peace." "The private Opinions of Men are not the Objects of Law or Government," Randolph declared. "While they keep those to themselves, they may enjoy them without Interruption from the civil Magistrate. But if they go about publickly preaching and inculcating their Errors, raising Factions tending to disturb the publick Peace, or utter Doctrines which in their Nature are subversive of all Religion or Morality," they deserve punishment. The fundamental problem, Randolph warned the Anabaptists, stemmed from their disregard of legislative authority. "You must not make *yourselves* your own Judges of what is fit to be done," Randolph said.

To the Baptists, however, who could not bear the idea of giving even their own ministers or congregations power over each other, the idea of legislative supremacy was anathema. It was "intolerable," one group complained, "for one set of men to make application to another set of men (cap in hand) and in the most humble posture, ask their consent and allowance, to worship the God that made them."

This nascent democracy appealed to Patrick Henry, who advocated what he called "a general Toleration of religion" as enlightened social policy. He extolled the right of private judgment and believed that the promise of "the free exercise of religion" had attracted great numbers of European immigrants to the northern colonies. With the impressions of his trip to New York still fresh (and his hopes for extensive western settlement in Virginia still green), Henry argued that religious toleration had helped make Pennsylvania lands rise to "five times the value of ours." "A Dutch, Irish, or Scotch emigrant finds there his religion, his priest, his language, his manners, and everything but that poverty and oppression he left at home," Henry said. With characteristic disregard for the conventional wisdom Henry insisted that most Virginians had only a "trifling" concern for religion, but "when we suppose that the poorer sort of European emigrants set as light by it, we are greatly mistaken." If Virginia wanted to import the pietistic European artisans, be they Lutherans or Quakers, who could lead the colony into prosperous manufactures, then, he said, "a general toleration of religion appears to me the best means of peopling our country."

Henry agitated the issue in the House of Burgesses by pressing for clarification of dissenters' rights under the famous Act of Toleration, but year after year Robert Carter Nicholas, the chairman of the committee on religion, forestalled any action as imprudent and precipitate. Then, in 1772, after the terrible attack upon John Waller and the other Baptists in Caroline County the previous summer, Henry found some support in an unexpected quarter, the pulpit of the Williamsburg church.

A new young minister, the Reverend Samuel Henley, newly arrived at the college and filled with the latitudinarian ideas of a popular group of English divines, conducted a service at Bruton Parish Church expressly for members of the House on March 1, 1772. Mr. Henley chose a provocative topic, "The Distinct Claims of Government and Religion," and he shocked a good many burgesses by implying that suppression of the Baptists lay beyond the legislature's purview. "Is *every* State infallible in the doctrines it imposes?" Henley asked. If not, "how dreadful" might be the condition of dissenters who were "forced to receive" teachings they did not regard as gospel. In Henley's view the burgesses were no better than agents of the Inquisition for insisting upon legislative control of religion.

No previous minister had the temerity to address the burgesses so boldly, and within a year the Speaker and the treasurer, both vestrymen of Bruton Parish, denied Henley its rectorship and sent him packing from the college as well. Meanwhile, stung by Henley's denunciation of legislative bigotry, they felt obliged to allay "the spirit of persecution" by supporting a bill that would have explicitly applied the old Act of Toleration to Virginia.

In committee, however, Henry changed the terms of the debate. "It was represented," Nicholas recalled, "that there were some dissenters in the upper Parts of the Country, who could not conform to the English toleration, as by that they were obliged to subscribe to the [39] Articles of our Church, which, in Conscience, they could not do." While Henry argued in committee that the toleration bill had to be made more general, a newspaper article, widely believed to come from Henley's pen, also argued that "Revolutions in Opinion" had rendered the once-admirable statute obsolete. Instead of insisting that dissenting ministers swear fealty to Anglican doctrine in order to obtain licenses, the writer urged that toleration simply be extended to all who would subscribe to a belief in a supreme being, God's government of the universe, and the obligations of morality. In this way "the peace of society" would be secured; moreover, "fresh inhabitants will be urged to settle amongst us, manufactures flourish, and the value of our lands be daily encreased," the letter concluded in words directly echoing Henry's position.

Nicholas was furious. He hated being addressed from the outside on matters pending before the committee, and he complained that people like Henley were too much in the grip of "ill-digested Notions of modern Refinements" and too much "borne on the Tide of Popularity." Nicholas took the view that it would be enough to avoid "every Species of Persecution." There was no need, he thought, to "give a general Invitation to every People under the Sun to come and inhabit with us," while asking only the most trifling profession of Christian belief. He warned Henry and his clerical ally Henley that setting so little store by church doctrine would lead to "a babel" of religious voices, sever the "friendly and amiable Alliance between Church and State," and lead to serious social disorder. Everything would be set at large if the government allowed freedom of judgment to people incapable of reasoning on complicated matters. "Look 'round the World, when you are thinking of the rights of private judgment, and consider who make up the far greater Part of its inhabitants," Nicholas warned. Could they decide questions of theology?—or politics? he could have added. "You might as well expect them to compute an eclipse."

For all his fulmination, however, Nicholas had little recourse. Like all the other burgesses he opposed efforts to strengthen the church by appointing a bishop in Virginia, which the House saw as inevitably threatening local legislative prerogatives. Forswearing authentic central control and affirming, however indistinctly, the rights of conscience led nowhere but toward the general toleration Henry advocated. For his part, Henry was a latitudinarian who saw the ethical principles of religion as an important element in a political society that was learning to control itself. The Baptist congregations imposed voluntary restrictions on their members' behavior, as did the Quakers and others, and it appeared that various communions might peaceably coexist in a secular society bound together in a political rather than a religious contract.

Nicholas gave in and agreed to Henry's bill proposing: "all his Majesty's Protestant Subjects dissenting from the Church of England, within this Dominion, shall have and enjoy the full and free Exercise of their Religion, without Molestation or Danger of incurring any Penalty whatsoever." Having agreed to making toleration "more extensive here than it was in England" by asking dissenting ministers to swear only to "the truth of Scriptures," Nicholas then proposed a troublesome list of local restrictions on the building of meetinghouses, the hours of services, gatherings in private homes, and the baptism of slaves without their masters' written permission.

Now Henry and his supporters on the committee had to "doubt the Propriety" of such limitations and express "their Apprehensions that these might give Uneasiness to some of the Dissenters." Nicholas's provisions amounted to a subtle discrimination that inhibited the free exercise promised by the bill.

The result was a standoff. The House passed the bill on second reading but then postponed final action and instead ordered it printed and circulated so that "the whole Country might have an Opportunity of considering it more maturely."

Neither side gained a clear victory. The legal position of

the dissenters remained unchanged, but the "jangle and disputation" had enhanced the moral claims for religious liberty and led in practice to a diminution of attacks upon the Baptists. In the short run Nicholas outfoxed Henry by adding the crippling restrictions, but by securing a referral for further public discussion Henry underscored the growing political necessity of reckoning with popular feeling. No one, it seemed, wanted a toleration bill that could not be enforced. The weakening of traditional social bonds frightened some Virginians and confounded others. Patrick Henry had an unusual talent for recognizing new social forces and adapting the political process to accommodate them, but not even Henry had developed a fully realized solution for the perplexing question of how modern religious diversity might be squared with the ancient assumption that the general welfare required an alliance between church and state.

In working out his ideas about the free exercise of religion, moreover, Henry kept stumbling over the question of slavery. Much of the hostility toward the Baptists originated in fears that the religious revival would foment disorder among the slaves. An advocate of toleration faced the dilemma of either insisting upon the rights of conscience for the blacks and thus further undermining the rationale of slavery or reassuring whites on this point and thus further sanctioning a system many gentlemen recognized as morally embarrassing, if not shameful. Like most Virginians Henry tried to wish away the peculiar institution and regarded toleration as a panacea, a means of attracting white immigrants from Europe as a new labor force. He once sat down to write a pamphlet advocating a general toleration, but mournful reflections upon slavery broke into paragraphs devoted to other points of argument, and he eventually had to put the botched draft aside. "Is there a man so degenerate as to wish to see his country the gloomy retreat of slaves?" he asked, rhetorically, and answered, "No; while we may, let us people our lands with men who secure our internal peace, and make us respectable abroad; who will contribute [word obliterated] influence and establish in posterity the benefit of the British Constitution."

Leading Virginians looked both west and east for a solution to the slavery question. They magically assumed that only yeoman farmers would settle the third Virginia beyond the mountains, forgetting that they had brought the once-boundless tracts of the second Virginia into prosperous cultivation by the gang labor of slaves. They also inveighed mightily against the inhumanity of the Atlantic slave trade, blaming it entirely upon grasping British merchants. A few days after completing action on the toleration bill in March 1772, the House of Burgesses agreed to petition the Crown to "check so very pernicious a Commerce," which they insisted "greatly retards the Settlement of the Colonies, with more useful Inhabitants, and may, in Time, have the most destructive Influence." The protest may have been heartfelt, and not simply another political blow in the struggle against English commercial domination. However, slave imports had declined over the decades in Virginia as the black population increased naturally to comprise nearly half of the colony's population of 500,000 by 1773. A cutback on African imports actually enhanced the value of Virginia-born slaves, and no member of the House proposed that the unsavory trade be restrained within the colony itself. Slave auctions took place within the shadow of the Capitol, on the front steps of the burgesses' favorite tavern, and in the courthouse yards of every county.

Patrick Henry bought and sold his share of slaves, and fears of slave uprisings filled his neighborhood as they did every other. People in Hanover still spoke of the bloody Christmas of 1769 when a group of slaves held their overseer hostage at Bowler Cocke's plantation, only a few miles from Scotchtown. Forty Negroes assembled in a barn fought furiously against the party of whites come to rescue the steward, until the desperate battle ended with three slaves shot to death and five others wounded by broadswords.

As a man of "great moderation," however, Henry found himself importuned by people of conscience to speak out against slavery. The Quakers, especially, conducted a vigorous campaign not only against the slave trade but against slaveholders within their society and in their mild but tenacious fashion urged their example upon others. Henry had come to know a wealthy Quaker planter named Robert Pleasants during the struggle to secure the Friends exemptions from militia fines, and the two men had earnest conversations over the years.

Pleasants was a fatherly sort, fourteen years older than Henry, who lived not too far from Scotchtown at Curles' Neck on the upper James River. As head of the tiny Virginia Abolition Society, Pleasants put himself beyond reproach by emancipating his own slaves and rehiring them as paid laborers instead, a sterling example which, the gossip ran, cost him at least three thousand pounds. He also tried to advance the issue in the autumn of 1772 by sending prominent Virginians a notable series of essays against the slave trade by the French-born Philadelphia Quaker Anthony Benezet.

Henry, whose correspondence tended to be hasty, terse, and impersonal, responded on January 18, 1773, with an unusually long and reflective letter. In expressing his thanks for the volume, Henry registered bafflement at the way religion and slavery coexisted in Virginia. "It is not a little Surprising that Christianity, whose chief excellence consists in softning the human heart, in cherishing & improving its finer Feelings, should encourage a Practice so totally repugnant to the first Impression of right & wrong," Henry wrote. "What adds to the wonder," he continued, "is that this Abominable Practice has been introduced in the most enlightened Ages. . . . [An era that] boasts of high Improvements in the Arts, Sciences, & refined Morality [has] brought into general use & guarded by many Laws, a Species of Violence & Tyranny, which our more rude & barbarous, but more honest Ancestors detested."

Equally "amazing," Henry said, was that such an evil should exist in Virginia, "a Country above all others fond of Liberty." Yet, even here, he wrote, at a time "when the Rights of Humanity are defined & understood with precision . . . we find Men, professing a Religion the most humane, mild, meek, gentle & generous; adopting a Principle as repugnant to humanity as it is inconsistant with the Bible and destructive to Liberty."

"Every thinking honest Man rejects it in Speculation, how few in Practice from conscienscious Motives?" Henry remarked as a preliminary to praising the Quakers for "their noble Effort to abolish Slavery." "It is equally calculated," Henry said, "to promote moral & political Good," and while "the World in general has denied your People a share of its honours . . . the Wise [will extend] a just Tribute of virtuous Praise, for your Practice of a train of Virtues among which your disagreement to Slavery will be principally ranked."

The implicit comparison with Pleasants humbled Henry. "Would any one believe that I am Master of Slaves of my own purchase!" Henry exclaimed. "I am drawn along by the general inconvenience of living without them, I will not, I cannot justify it." Having spoken thus far with heartfelt, even astonishing simplicity, Henry found himself apologizing in a more elevated, stylized tone. "However culpable my conduct," Henry said, "I will so far pay my devoir to Virtue, as to own the excellence and rectitude of her Precepts, & to lament my want of conforming to them."

As in his other musings on slavery, Henry tried to summon optimism. "I believe a time will come when an opportunity will be offered to abolish this lamentable Evil," he assured Pleasants. "Every thing we can do is to improve it, if it happens in our day; if not, let us transmit to our descendants together with our Slaves, a pity for their unhappy Lot, & an abhorrence for Slavery. If we cannot reduce this wished for Reformation to practice," Henry declared, "let us treat the unhappy victims with lenity, it is the furthest advance we can make toward Justice."

"I exhort you to persevere in so worthy a resolution," Henry concluded, gratuitously pointing out that some of "your People" are "lukewarm" and that many Virginians, including clergymen protected by law, have heaped the resolutions of the Quaker meeting with "redicule and contempt." Yet, Henry said, "silent Meetings (the scoff of reverend doctors) have done that which learned & elaborate Preaching could not effect, so much preferable are the genuine dictates of Conscience & a steady attention to its feelings above the teachings of those Men who pretend to have found a better Guide." Having circled the argument and returned to his starting point, Henry broke off abruptly, saying, "I know not where to stop; I could say many things on this Subject; a serious review of which gives a gloomy perspective to future times."

It was an extraordinary performance, as compelling as any of Henry's speeches, and filled with a similar blending of the forthright and the facile that left his audience moved yet wondering just what he had actually said. The letter reveals the intuitive sympathy Henry had with the "natural religion" of the dissenters and the passion he could bring to denunciation of hypocrisy. There is also a streak of stubbornness, in which the exposure of contradiction somehow masks his own refusal to yield. Just as he shared the dissenters' outlook without leaving the Anglican church, he agreed fully with Pleasants while refusing to change his own behavior. Henry remembered the genteel poverty of his youth too keenly to undergo the "inconvenience" of untangling himself from the slaveholding gentry, and as a parvenu he had dynastic and landed dreams that precluded any thought of emancipating slaves at his death. He was a man skilled at political gesture, brave in defiance of convention, but on the question of slavery he would follow the common path of least resistance and, like his contemporaries, only squirm in private agony about what he knew to be a public wrong.

The pensive mood of January deepened a few weeks later with the death of Henry's father. The family gathered at Mount Brilliant, draped in black bombazine, to bury the old colonel. His brother, the aging parson, read the service, and in the next few days Patrick and his brother William, still wearing their black buckles of mourning, as executors tried to settle their father's estate. There was pitifully little, and it seemed best for their mother to give up Mount Brilliant and, with her unmarried daughters, join Patrick's family at Scotchtown. The senior Mrs. Henry could regard her move as an errand of mercy, however, for her daughter-in-law, Patrick's wife Sallie, was not well. Rather melancholic since the birth of little Edward eighteen months earlier, Sallie had grown more peculiar lately and, though hardly anyone wanted to say so openly, seemed in danger of losing her mind. The family remained extremely guarded about Sallie's condition, which opened the door to rumors while making it impossible for posterity to discern the truth.

On the snowy first day of March 1773, Henry returned to Williamsburg for a special session of the general assembly. Within a fortnight he had engineered a stinging rebuke to the governor, embarrassed the old leadership of the House, and forced them into supporting new measures for rousing against Parliament what the genteel called "a spirit of opposition" and radicals like Henry now insisted should be called by the "proper name" of "self-defence."

The summons for the early session had not specified the cause. Not until Henry and his fellow burgesses crowded into the Capitol on the chilly, blustery morning of March 4 did they learn that a serious outbreak of counterfeiting threatened to swamp completely the colony's barely credible system of paper money. The new royal governor, Lord Dunmore, wanted the House to enact legislation to shore up the public credit. Thanks to the quick action of the treasurer and the cooperation of an informer, the ring of fifteen persons including the under sheriff and other substantial citizens in Pittsylvania had been smashed and the suspected felons jailed in Williamsburg awaiting trial.

Henry became suspicious. Had there been no proceedings in the county courts first? Was this another Chiswell case in which favoritism in the capital would protect wrongdoing among the well-to-do? Henry's irritation grew when Nicholas and Pendleton brought in an address thanking the governor for his prompt action in dealing with the mischief. The House approved the address, but Henry asked that the body go into a committee of the whole for further discussion.

The story then came out. Dunmore thought that ordering the suspects named by the informer to appear in Pittsylvania County court for examination would be "ineffectual," since they might easily flee over the border into the Carolina hinterland. The governor consulted with Nicholas and both Randolphs, who all countenanced Dunmore's proposal that in his capacity as chief justice he order the suspects seized and brought under armed guard directly to the capital. The five accused men were then questioned informally in the Governor's Palace by Peyton Randolph, who advised that one clearly innocent man be released and the others jailed until trial.

Such zealous law enforcement by the governor with the private concurrence of members of the House riled Henry and his allies. They saw in it not so much echoes of the Chiswell affair, after all, but rather an alarming parallel to the long-standing threat that colonial agitators might be transported to England for trial. If the governor could order men dragged under guard to Williamsburg, what would prevent him from sending them on to London, with or without the Speaker's connivance?

These were not idle questions, for after two years of relative quiet, the quarrel with Parliament had become aggravated once again on this very point of distant and despotic legal proceedings. The previous June a royal customs ship, the *Gaspée*, had run aground on the coast of Rhode Island. During the night five or six boatloads of colonists swarmed over the ship, shot its commander in the backside, and, after putting the crew ashore, torched the ship. Vigorous enforcement of taxes the colonists regarded as unconstitutional had soured relations with Crown officials even after the collapse of nonimportation, but the attack on the *Gaspée* came as a shock. The home government appointed a royal commission to investigate the incident and granted it power to send suspects back to England for trial, which revived the threat of "transportation" for treason, the ominous issue that had triggered the protests and Association of 1769.

Henry had composed Virginia's protest then, and now he saw the chance to bring the point closer to home. He and Richard Bland insisted that the House undertake a complete investigation of the Pittsylvania case, and on Saturday,

March 6, Henry led a delegation to Dunmore requesting a complete statement of the proceedings by which the suspects had been "apprehended, examined, and committed."

This was Henry's first confrontation with the new governor. Dunmore was not a "courtier" or "a man of parade" in the Botetourt mold but rather a hearty Scotsman—not unlike Henry himself—bluff and athletic, who made no bones about his desire to reap a fortune in western lands. He had laid the groundwork for this during his brief tenure as governor of New York in 1770–71, and he reportedly had launched into a drunken soliloquy in front of his councilors when informed that he would be going to Virginia to succeed the late Lord Botetourt. "Damn Virginia—did I ever seek it? Why is it forced upon me?" Dunmore stormed. "I asked for New York—New York I took, and they have robbed me of it without my consent."

His reputation as a "very goodnatured Jolly Fellow who loves his Bottle" preceded Dunmore to Virginia, along with tales of midnight sorties in which the governor and his drunken companions would sally forth to play pranks on their fellows, once clipping the tails of the chief justice's carriage horses and smashing his coach to splinters. The conviviality might have appealed to the Virginians, however, had it not been accompanied by the haughtiness typical of "great Folks bred in the pride of Life & us'd to implicit Obedience from their inferiors." Dunmore kept himself aloof and refused even to keep an office hour for the conduct of public business, until some gentlemen of the bar remonstrated with him in a stormy session.

Dunmore, however, dropped his hauteur and realized that the Virginia gentlemen, who fancied themselves noblemen without titles, shared his tastes and his adventurous ways. He moderated his behavior, and with his skilled horsemanship, his large collection of arms, his impressive wine cellar, and his clear commitment to a liberal land policy Dunmore reached an accommodation with the established leaders of the colony.

Henry now served notice that coziness had its limits.

Dunmore checked his temper and promptly delivered a statement, which Henry made the basis for hearings before the House. For two days he made Randolph and Nicholas squirm as their participation in an executive assault upon constitutional liberties became all too clear.

Yet Henry proceeded with unusual care and restraint. At the conclusion of the investigation, he and Bland proposed a resolution which thanked the governor for his vigorous efforts while observing: "as the proceedings in this Case, tho' rendered necessary from the particular nature of it, are nevertheless, in the Opinion of the House, different from the usual Mode . . . the House therefore humbly entreat his Excellency, that they may not in future be drawn into Consequence or Example." The resolution thus protested the action without actually censuring anyone, and the House, with some division, accepted it.

Henry, however, had not yet finished with Randolph and Nicholas. That night, Thursday, March 11, he caucused in a private club room at the Raleigh with Richard Henry Lee, his brother Francis Lightfoot Lee, Thomas Jefferson, and his brother-in-law Dabney Carr. The threat posed by the *Gaspée* inquiry had to be met directly, and the group felt that the time had come for coordinated actions with the other colonies. Yet they still wanted to preserve a patriotic coalition in the House and proceed with as much unanimity as possible. While the "old and leading members" had not yet arrived at "the point of forwardness and zeal" that would allow them to endorse the violent destruction of His Majesty's vessel, they smarted from Henry's censures on the Pittsylvania case and did want to reestablish their credentials as defenders of constitutional liberties. Henry had them boxed in.

The Raleigh group worked late into the night on a series of resolutions that tactfully avoided mention of the *Gaspée* incident and referred only to "disturbing . . . rumors and reports of proceedings, tending to deprive [the colonies] of their ancient, legal, and constitutional rights." They would ask the House to form "a standing committee of correspondence and inquiry . . . whose business it shall be, to obtain the most early and authentic intelligence of all such acts and resolutions of the British Parliament, or proceedings of administration, as may . . . affect the British colonies in America . . . and to keep up and maintain a communication with our sister colonies, respecting these important considerations." In a brilliant final stroke, they decided not to leave the composition of the committee to the Speaker's discretion, but named eleven persons in the proposed resolution; they boldly nominated themselves, added Bland and Pendleton for balance, and then sugar-coated the list by placing the names of Peyton Randolph and Robert Carter Nicholas at its head. It was a nomination no patriot could decline, and after some debate on Friday, March 12, the House accepted the group's plan. Emboldened, the radicals successfully tacked on another resolution directing that the new committee should "without delay, inform themselves particularly of the principles and authority, on which was constituted a court of inquiry, said to have been lately held in Rhode Island, with powers to transport persons accused of offenses committed in America, to places beyond the seas, to be tried."

On Monday, March 15, however, yet another raw and cloudy day, the Speaker (newly designated as the patriotic head of the committee of correspondence) had to stand before the governor and present the resolutions that obliquely censured the conduct of both of them in the Pittsylvania case. "The duty we owe our constituents obliges us, My Lord, to be as attentive to the safety of the innocent as we are desirous of punishing the Guilty," Randolph read with as much grace as he could muster; "and we apprehend, that a doubtful construction and various execution of Criminal Law does greatly endanger the safety of innocent Men."

Dunmore replied stoutly that he had acted "with the greatest Caution" and with the "advice and assistance of Gentlemen, in whose Judgement, Candour, and Integrity I could confide." He thought the court would uphold the method as proper, but if it were found "amiss" he would not repeat it.

The governor then declared that since the House had completed its business, he would sign the various bills and adjourn the session. Dunmore said nothing about the creation of the committee of correspondence. Technically the resolution pertained only to the internal organization of the House and did not require the governor's assent, and politically Dunmore decided to regard the matter as an instance of "ill humour" too insignificant to notice. The governor, at his paternalistic worst, seemed indirectly to admonish the burgesses in his closing homily, in which he recommended that the burgesses "use your endeavours, in your several Counties, to abolish that Spirit of Gaming, which I am afraid but too generally prevails among the People, and to substitute in its place a love of Agriculture, and attention to their private Affairs, by which you will render a most essential Service to them and to your Country." The governor nodded and looked severe. With the customary bowing, and more than a few sly grins, the burgesses withdrew.

Henry had cut quite a figure at the session: bold, skilled, and eloquent. A young college student, St. George Tucker, who observed Henry in the House and in the court sessions that followed, recalled his striking visage: long and thin, with thick, dark eyebrows that made his blue-gray eyes seem black and penetrating, and a grave look relieved only by a half smile that signaled his dissent more effectively than a cascade of satirical remarks. He never took on the melodious air, the pleasant manner, and the studied gesture considered the hallmarks of public oratory, and Tucker was initially quite disappointed when Henry was first pointed out to him as the most powerful voice in the House. Watching intently from the gallery Tucker thought Pendleton far more graceful and Richard Henry Lee, whose very striking profile gave him the authentic Roman look, more mellifluent and more gifted at embellishment and gesture than Henry, who remained as severe-looking as any country preacher.

"You would swear he had never uttered or laughed at a joke," Tucker recalled. "In short, in debate either at the bar or elsewhere, his manner was so earnest and impressive, united with a contraction or knitting of his brows which appeared habitual, as to give his countenance a severity sometimes bordering upon the appearance of anger or contempt suppressed, while his language and gesture exhibited nothing but what was perfectly decorous. He was emphatic, without vehemence or declamation; animated, but never boisterous; nervous, without recourse to intemperate language; and clear, though not always methodical."

Virginians eager to get a good look at the celebrated Henry crowded into the gallery, itself a recent addition to the House chamber—and a sign of the growing power of public opinion. William Roane, a burgess from Essex County, "always came home in raptures" about Henry, Roane's son Spencer recalled. "That a plain man, of ordinary though respected family, should beard the aristocracy [gratified] my father's Whig principles," Roane said, and he "considered Henry as the organ of the great body of the people [and] the instrument by whom the big-wigs were to be thrown down." The senior Roane brought his son and his Scotch tutor up to Williamsburg especially to hear Henry speak, and the family ever afterward cherished the story of how tutor Bradfute became so transfixed by Henry that he "unconsciously squirted tobacco juice from the gallery onto the heads of the members" and nearly fell from the balcony into the House.

The affectionate enthusiasm of ordinary people who sensed a connection with Henry set him apart, even from the other radical leaders, and gave him an extraordinary personal celebrity. "His imagination painted to the soul," Edmund Randolph wrote, and "a pronunciation which might disgust in a drawing room" gave Henry "access to the hearts of a popular assembly." One admirer spoke for many when, referring to the names Christ had given the disciples (Mark 3:17), he called Henry the new "Boanerges," "a son of Thunder." "In religious matters" his sympathy for the persecuted dissenters made him "a saint," but that evangelical enthusiasm, as the established leaders had learned to their discomfort, could make him "the very Devil in Politicks."

Part Three

1774-
1776

CHAPTER 10

"Hurrying to an Alarming Crisis"

Henry's increasing boldness signaled a shift in the public mood. Instead of denouncing Parliament's right to tax, people denied Parliament's power to govern. Consoling visions of reconciliation gave way to stout talk about separation and, sotto voce, the specter of armed resistance, if necessary.

In October 1773 a Pennsylvanian styling himself "Hampden" urged the House of Burgesses to rename itself the "Parliament of Virginia," since "names have an influence upon things." "You possess all the Powers of a British Parliament over your own Colony," Hampden declared; you owe the Parliament at Westminister only the affection due "your elder Sister."

In November another patriot published a "Plan of Union" that would resolve the dispute. Assemble "a Congress of American States . . . as soon as possible," he said, to "draw up a BILL of RIGHTS, and publish it to the World; choose an Ambassadour to reside at the British Court, to act for the united Colonies . . . and bring the two Countries to a right Understanding." That Great Britain continues "to insult and alienate the growing millions who inhabit this Country" is glaring foolishness, this writer declared, for "No People that ever trod the Stage of the World have had so glorious a Prospect as now rises before the Americans."

At "Squire" Richard Lee's annual New Year's ball (1774) in northern Virginia, while a great assembly danced minuets, jigs, and reels to the music of two violins and a French horn and the rustle of the ladies' silks, the side rooms filled with "Vociferators" noisily toasting "the sons of America." Groups of "six, eight, ten & more" gentlemen "would put their Heads near together and roar 'Liberty Songs,'" sounding out their boast as "The Lords, the Lords, the Lords, the Lords of North America."

Along with the continuing threat of being transported overseas for political offenses, the colonists still faced the imposition of taxes. In the latest move, the ministry had encouraged the East India Company to sell large cargoes of tea at bargain prices through favored consignees in the major American seaports. The system recalled the luckless stamp distributorships, and colonial agitators took this as a further sign that the new tea policy showed yet again the "ministerial plot" to trick Americans into paying the nominal but—to their minds—unconstitutional duty that remained.

The company would be "a Cat's Paw," the Virginians heard from friends in London, for the government's effort to establish the tax. Although Virginians fulminated against the tea tax and extolled the virtues of sassafras and other native herbs, they remained on the fringe of the anti-tea activity. The colony had no major seaport, and no Virginia broker received the company's new patronage. Lacking physical targets of their own, Virginians could only follow the doings elsewhere.

The late January newspapers brought news that the tea distributors had, under threat of public obloquy and mob action, renounced their posts in Charleston, Philadelphia, and New York (where Henry's friend Alexander McDougall led the newly revived Liberty Boys); no ships had arrived yet in New York, but in Philadelphia the river pilots—cheered by shoreline crowds—refused to conduct the tea-laden ships up the Delaware. Only in Boston, where the consignees included the royal governor's sons, had the protest movement met intractable opposition. Although the owner of the tea ship had bowed to the wishes of a massed town meeting and agreed to turn his vessel toward London with the tea still on board, the governor held fast and would not issue the special customs clearances necessary for refused cargoes. After waiting all afternoon in the rain to hear the governor's decision, the meeting of several thousand adjourned, and a delegation, the Virginians read in their gazette, "repaired to Griffin's Wharf, where the Tea Vessels lay, proceeded to fix Tackles, and hoisted the Tea upon Deck, cut the Chests to Pieces, and threw the Tea over the Side." They carefully disposed of 342 chests of tea while taking care, the dispatch from Boston emphasized, to prevent looting or damage to the other cargo on board.

Although the Boston "tea party" seemed likely to result in the overseas prosecutions the radicals had long feared, the incident provoked little comment, either public or private, from the Virginians. Henry found himself in the unusual position of having no clear strategy for advancing the protest.

On the first Monday in May, Henry arrived in Williamsburg for the spring assembly session. The Capitol yard crackled with an extraordinary late frost, and, like his colleagues, Henry looked at the ground with despairing thoughts of his blighted crops back home. The political picture seemed no brighter as Henry went upstairs to attend his first meeting of the committee of correspondence he had helped to create the year before.

In typical fashion he had set a scheme in motion and then let it gather momentum without his direct participation. While the colonies had all endorsed Virginia's scheme for coordinating their protests, no one yet knew what should be done, or whether the committees could do it.

Looking around the committee room, Patrick Henry had reason to wonder just how forward his own colleagues might be. There was old Dick Bland, stooped and wrinkled at sixty-four, his eyes failing so badly he could hardly read the correspondence, much less the ancient works that made him Virginia's preeminent authority on the constitution. The chairman, Peyton Randolph, ten years younger than Bland, had come a long way since he had raged at Henry's resolutions in 1765, but the portly, dignified, and profoundly cautious Randolph had proved himself more capable of taming protests initiated by others than taking the lead himself. Facile Edmund Pendleton, at fifty-two still the handsomest man in the House, took dim views of both protests and Patrick Henry. Pendleton could be expected to use his formidable powers as a legal technician to complicate matters unnecessarily. Robert Carter Nicholas, short and balding, could hardly match Pendleton in looks but was every bit his equal in pedantic controversy. However, the grave Nicholas, bred in the bosom of piety, brought industry and learning to his contentious manner and conceivably might prove more aggressive in a new political cause than Randolph or Pendleton. The two other men, nearing fifty like Nicholas, would never be radicals: Benjamin Harrison, the Speaker's brother-in-law, gave every impression of being a complacent country gentleman—corpulent, ribald, red-faced, and lazy—while Dudley Diggs, a cipher who had signed neither Association and who hardly ever spoke in committee, gave no impression at all.

Henry, just three weeks short of his thirty-eighth birthday, could only count upon the two other younger members of the committee, forty-year-old Richard Henry Lee and thirty-one-year-old Thomas Jefferson. Tall and spare, his gaunt visage dominated by a beaklike nose, "Ritt" Lee communicated a bold and hortatory energy that made him both hard to avoid and hard to like. Jefferson, not yet arrived from Albemarle, was more diffident, even shy, but Henry and Lee hoped that his brilliant intellect would overmatch Pendleton and persuade Bland to accept the political consequences of the old scholar's own forays into the doctrine of natural rights.

On May 6, however, not even Henry and Lee knew what they wanted the committee to do. Their colleagues did not all share the view that the tea had met, in Lee's words, "a well deserved fate," and it did not appear likely that the Virginians could mobilize a new round of protest on the tea issue alone. Lee had privately written to Samuel Adams in Boston hoping for news of more "tyrannic proceedings of Administration" and hinting that a rousing public communication from the Massachusetts committee to the Virginia committee, timed to arrive while the burgesses met, might generate support for some new measures.

Lacking news from Britain and a fresh signal from Boston, Henry and Lee could only temporize. They decided at least to enlarge the forum by suggesting that the committee's accumulated papers be referred to the entire House, and later that day the burgesses agreed to consider them in a fortnight. They also tried to close the colony's courts by stalling passage of the necessary legislation establishing fees, but the ploy riled Pendleton and did not succeed.

Two days later the desultory mood broke when an express from Fincastle County reported three or four skirmishes with the Shawnee, and a long petition from 587 settlers on the Ohio River complained of imminent danger from both Indians and the rival government of Pennsylvania, which had briefly arrested a Virginia magistrate (and land agent) in a flare-up of an ancient border dispute. The House, in a great show of apparent unity, urged Governor Dunmore to fix a temporary line with Pennsylvania and use his full powers, as vested by the assembly, to protect the western borders from Indian attack. Yet the House would not accede to the governor's request for the raising of a regular army; the county militias would be adequate, Dunmore was told, for no burgess at this critical juncture in imperial affairs wanted to put troops under the governor's direct control.

In the midst of the frontier war scare came equally frightening news from overseas. The home government's reaction to the tea protests could not be more hostile, correspondents reported from London. Dr. Franklin, the esteemed scholar, entrepreneur, and colonial agent for Pennsylvania had suffered extraordinary abuse from the solicitor general before thirty or forty privy lords "purposely invited as to a Bull-Baiting." The colonies would, in all likelihood, be declared "in open rebellion," and "coercive" measures should be expected. The predictions sounded frightfully wild. It was "whispered" that Massachusetts would forfeit its charter, that other colonial governments would be "new modelled," that a fleet of fourteen ships of the line would blockade the major ports "to bring the Americans back to their duty" and enforce the revenue act "in its full and literal Extent."

The fretful and uncertain mood, heightened by a violent hailstorm on the fourteenth, intensified further as day after day went by without the usual post rider with letters and newspapers from the northern towns. Had the fleet arrived? Had all correspondence been embargoed? No one knew, but the arrival of a ship from London early in the week of May 16 brought shocking confirmation of the prior reports. Parliament had decided that "dangerous commotions and insurrections" in Boston had rendered trade and customs collection unsafe, and therefore no commerce would be allowed in or out of the port (under pain of forfeiture of both goods and vessels and criminal penalties for wharfingers who aided and abetted trade) until His Majesty pleased to restore it.

The news struck Williamsburg like "a shock of Electricity," with "astonishment, indignation, and concern" giving way to fury when the *Gazette* (on May 19) gave new credence to the rumor that "a Sloop of War" had sailed from Plymouth in mid-March "for Boston, with Orders to bring to England, in Irons, Messrs. Hancock, Row, Adams, and McIntosh." The last named, the *Gazette* reported gravely, had "been very active among the lower Order of People, the others among the higher."

The radicals had their thunderbolt, and they began to storm. Private intelligence from London, they said, confirmed the view that the ministry intended the Boston Port Bill as an example for the other colonies "whenever they shall dare to assert their Rights" but thought it "prudent to begin with one Colony first."

Henry and Lee passed around a fresh letter from Lee's brother Arthur in London reporting that Lord North had contemptuously told the House of Commons that "he would not listen to the complaint of America till she was at his Feet." Members of Parliament, others said, spoke with dark jollity of sending "Gunpowder Tea" to the colonies, to be taken "with a little Smack of British Spirit."

Yet another story assiduously circulated by the radicals described Lord Hillsborough's supposed tête-à-tête with the king. His Lordship spoke cleverly "of some American Turkies he some time ago had from Virginia; that having neglected clipping their Wings, in proper Time, they had now got such high Notions of their Freedom and Liberty that they constantly roosted on the highest Trees in his Park" and he couldn't get the better of them "unless he levied war, and subdued them by Arms." (Ah yes, went the radicals' retort, but if he destroyed the birds, he'd no longer have their eggs for puddings.)

For all the anger and alarm, the radicals could not make much headway on specific measures, and for lack of a plan, they had to put off the scheduled report from the committee of correspondence for another week. They talked heatedly and floated ideas about a trade boycott, court closures, and an immediate call for a continent-wide congress, but the old leaders of the House hung back. Even a conservative like Edmund Pendleton denounced the Port Bill, although he did so on the characteristically narrow ground that Parliament should not be executing a summary judgment in what was manifestly a civil case involving recovery for property damages sustained by a private company. But the conservatives wanted to keep the growing flames of protest "smothered" (Pendleton's word) until the burgesses had completed the "public business." This laudable purpose had some subterfuge behind it, since a number of important bills had languished in committee for nearly three weeks without action, and no one seems suddenly to have expected their passage.

The radicals, meanwhile, tried to come up with a scheme for breaking the unexpected stalemate. Their caucus became an open secret, for when the Fairfax planter George Mason arrived in Williamsburg on Sunday, May 22, to pursue some land grant business (impossible in the atmosphere of crisis), he quickly learned that measures in response to "the Boston affair" were being "prepared with a great deal of privacy, and by very few members, of whom Patrick Henry" was "the principal." The "gentlemen concerned" (who included

Ritt Lee, his brother Frank, and Thomas Jefferson) admitted Mason, a sharp-witted advocate of nonimportation, to a meeting of their circle. On Monday evening, May 23, they had boldly convened in the Council Chamber of the Capitol because, Jefferson said later, they needed to use the library.

The group wanted to head off yet another round of petitions to London, which was all that Randolph, Pendleton, and the other moderates would countenance. Henry and his allies wanted action. They would denounce the "invasion" of Boston but also call for an immediate general congress to formulate a ban on exports as well as imports. Lee started sketching a resolution, leaving blanks only for the names of Virginia's deputies and the location of the meeting. To soften up the opposition, however, and rally public opinion throughout the colony, they wanted to reach beyond the burgesses, as Henry had done in 1765 with his Stamp Act resolves. With Henry's genius for converting popular feelings into political ammunition driving them, the caucus hit upon the masterful idea of appointing a general day of fasting and prayer. The rising generation did not remember, as Henry so vividly did, how Samuel Davies had roused patriotic fervor against the French in 1755, and some new solemnity would be a novel and striking way of sounding the alarm.

Pulling the copious volumes of Rushworth's *Historical Collections* from the library shelves, Henry, Lee, and Jefferson "rummaged" in "the revolutionary precedents and forms" of the antiroyalist Puritans and "cooked up a resolution, somewhat modernizing their phrases," Jefferson recalled. Their text expressed the House's alarm at "the hostile invasion" of Boston in their "Sister Colony of Massachusetts Bay" and urged that the first day of June (the date on which Boston's commerce would be stopped by an "armed force") "be set apart by the Members of this House as a Day of Fasting, Humiliation, and Prayer, devoutly to implore the divine Interposition for averting the heavy Calamity, which threatens Destruction to our civil Rights, and the Evils of civil War."

Under guise of a call to prayer they had written a political broadside, and the House might well reject it as transparently cynical were Henry, Lee, or Jefferson—none noted for his piety—to introduce it. With the high-spirited inspiration that sometimes graces late meetings, they conceived the evening's most brilliant stroke: ask Bob Nicholas to introduce it. The treasurer possessed, in Jefferson's words, a "grave and religious character more in unison with the tone of our resolution," and if the call came from this pious, powerful, and cautious officer no one could make serious opposition. With the fasting idea approved, they could go on with the rest of their program.

Early the next morning, Tuesday, May 24, Henry and others called upon Nicholas and secured his cooperation. The treasurer introduced the measure that very day. The House accepted the text without change and ordered that the members would march on June 1 in a body with the Speaker and the mace to the parish church where prayers would be read.

There was "not above one Dissentient appearing amongst near an Hundred Members," Nicholas said later, but a good many burgesses did grumble privately, arguing that there should have been proper petitions, drawn in decent language, instead of this "scheme calculated to *inflame* and excite an *enthusiastic* Zeal in the Minds of the People, under a Cloak of Religion."

Henry spoke powerfully in the House. "Your passions are no longer your own when he addresses them," Mason exclaimed after hearing Henry, but decided that "his eloquence is the smallest part of his merit." So able, so virtuous, so adept in his popular command, Henry "is the first man upon this continent," Mason concluded, and he went around town saying that Henry's talents would "have put him at the head" of the "glorious" Roman republic.

The radicals made sure that Clementina Rind, the printer, made up a great batch of copies of the resolution, and they went about town helping the burgesses organize relays of express riders to carry the call into their respective counties.

The fast day scheme proved to be the radicals' only victory that week. When the House convened on Thursday, May 26, the order of the day called for the twice-postponed report from the committee of correspondence. Lee had the radicals' propositions in his pocket. Unsure of their reception and under great pressure from the old leaders, who repeated their insistence that the public business should be completed before risking a dissolution, the radicals agreed to another week's postponement. The remainder of the morning saw a succession of private petitions and minor bills parade across the calendar; none of the major pending legislation—on court fees, the militia, and the tobacco tax bill—came up.

In midmorning Lord Dunmore sent an unexpected message to the House. When the burgesses faced the governor in the Council Chamber, he held up the printed broadside that decreed the day of fasting. This paper, he said, is "conceived in such Terms as reflect highly upon his Majesty and the Parliament of Great Britain, which makes it necessary for me to dissolve you; and you are dissolved accordingly."

"As usual," Jefferson muttered, as the burgesses trooped back to their own chamber to gather their papers and ponder their next move, which led straight to the Apollo Room of the Raleigh and another meeting of the Association. Meanwhile, capital gossips circulated word that the attorney general, Peyton Randolph's brother John, had "traitorously informed" the governor that the solemnity of a public fast was intended to prepare the popular mind for other resolutions likely to inflame the whole country. A prompt dissolution, the governor let it be known, was intended to forestall acts that might rouse the mother country's indignation.

Whether Henry and Lee could have persuaded the House to accept their proposition for an immediate congress remains an open question. They did not have much luck in the unofficial meeting at the Raleigh on Friday, May 27, which diluted Lee's draft resolutions until their substance disappeared. The newest Association, signed by eighty-nine former burgesses, decried the "heavy hand of power" lifted against North America and denounced the Boston Port Bill as a violent and arbitrary deprivation of property. It proposed a boycott on tea and all other East India Company goods but went no further toward a cessation of trade. While recognizing that the attack upon Massachusetts "threatens ruin to the rights of all," the meeting did not call for an immediate congress, but proposed only that the committee of correspondence "communicate" the idea of holding an annual intercolonial meeting "on those general measures which the united interests of America may from time to time require."

Henry and Lee considered this formulation "much too feeble." "The dirty Ministerial Stomach is daily ejecting its foul contents upon us," Lee fumed; we need "the friendly streams of information and advice [from an immediate congress] . . . to wash away the impurity." But the Randolphs and the Pendletons insisted that an unofficial body like the Associators lacked the power to appoint deputies. Such delicacy at a time of "immense danger" left Henry infuriated. He signed the tepid document and went home.

On the ride up to Scotchtown Henry could see that the woods still looked like winter after the unseasonable frost and hail; the peach orchards stood ruined, and livestock grazed the blasted fields of wheat and rye and peas. Everywhere people talked with alarm about the Boston crisis. The mood mixed determination with despair: we won't allow ourselves to be sacrificed "piecemeals," people said, "but God knows what will become of us."

On June 1 bells rang across Virginia, the churchyards filled with gentlemen dressed in mourning, and the day of fasting concentrated popular attention upon the political crisis. Not until the solemn day had passed did Henry learn that he had missed an exciting political turnabout in the capital. He received a printed letter from Williamsburg, signed by Peyton Randolph as "moderator" of the Association and by two dozen former burgesses, inviting all the members of the Association (that is, the recently dissolved House) to meet in Williamsburg on the first of August in order to consider a trade embargo against Britain!

"We flatter ourselves it is unnecessary to multiply Words to induce your Compliance with this Invitation," Randolph's message concluded. "Things seem to be hurrying to an alarming Crisis and demand the speedy, united Councils of all those who have a Regard for the common Cause."

Henry's experience in 1765 should have taught him the folly of quitting Williamsburg abruptly. It turned out, as Henry heard the story later, that on Sunday morning, May 29, an express rider hurried to Peyton Randolph's house near the palace green and delivered a bundle of documents that sent the normally phlegmatic Speaker into frenzied activity. The packet contained three letters in a chain of correspondence that had begun sixteen days earlier in Boston. From that beleaguered port Samuel Adams had written the fervent plea Lee had sought nearly a month before. The town, Adams said, could not believe that it would "now be left to struggle alone," and its inhabitants wanted the other colonies to resolve jointly to stop all imports and exports to Great Britain until repeal of the Port Bill. Should the others hold back, the Bostonians said, "fraud, power and the most odious oppression will rise tryumphant over right, justice, social happiness, and freedom." The other letters in the bundle contained comments from other towns through which the express rider had passed with Boston's appeal: Philadelphia wanted more time to think about the merits of an embargo versus a general convention, but Annapolis heartily endorsed a trade boycott and urged, moreover, that the courts be closed to British creditors and trade be broken off with those colonies who failed to go along with the protest. Randolph recognized immediately that events had made irrelevant the cautious statement he had signed two days earlier.

Within twenty-four hours Randolph's servants had rounded up about two dozen burgesses from the nearby counties and a few, like Jefferson, who had not yet gone too far up the road toward home. The hastily assembled handful recognized that their Association of the previous Friday would have to be "enlarged" to ban imports. Since they divided sharply on the question of suspending exports, however, they called a larger, more representative meeting for August so that the gentlemen might "have an Opportunity of collecting the Sense of their respective Counties."

The pressure of public opinion outside the colony had moved Henry's colleagues more forcibly than he had succeeded in doing, yet the dispatch from Williamsburg made plain that a fundamental division over tactics still existed. Henry, along with Lee, Mason, and Nicholas, advocated a strenuous program of opposition that embraced a complete embargo on trade, a moratorium on the payment of debts in Britain, and a cessation of the local courts (justified by the lapsing of the fee bill). Peyton Randolph and Pendleton, however, would countenance only a nonimportation scheme, although they were willing to consider prohibiting exports in a year's time if the crisis were not resolved. Neither side expressed much interest in a continental congress.

Henry recognized at once that "collecting the sense of the counties," as the dispatch put it, afforded the radicals an opportunity to rouse public opinion in advance of the August 1 meeting. George Mason, who like Henry had left Williamsburg seething at the timidity of the May 27 Association, immediately drafted resolutions for Prince William County insisting that the counties ("the fountain of power") take "proper and salutary measures" since "the late representatives have not fallen upon means sufficiently efficacious to secure to us the enjoyment of our civil rights and liberties."

The county mobilization took various forms. Churches collected foodstuffs for the relief of Boston, and prominent gentlemen tried to awe the populace with grand gestures of subscription. The dissenting ministers preached indefatigably on the sweetness of liberty, and parish rectors fashioned suitable discourses upon newly apt texts, such as I Samuel 4:9, "Be strong, and quit yourselves like men." Rowdy groups in the taverns roared liberty songs, drank innumerable toasts on intricate variations of the theme, and formed impromptu juries to condemn Lord North's corruption and treason. Up in Frederick County the Sons of Liberty burned an effigy of General Gage that looked "grim as Pluto & deformed as Vulcan."

Fresh alarms quickened the public mood. By mid-June the newspapers confirmed that Parliament had altered the

Massachusetts charter by giving the new military governor unprecedented power over the judiciary and the town meetings. Worse yet, a new "Murder Act" signaled rising despotism by providing that Crown officials or soldiers accused of murder in the course of suppressing riots or collecting revenues might be returned to Britain for trial. Unconfirmed reports held that Parliament would soon allow military commanders to quarter troops in private homes and would clamp down yet again on western land grants. Mrs. Rind gave extraordinary prominence in her gazette to a notice from London, signed "Truth," that warned: "It may be relied on, as a fact . . . that all the colony assemblies will be annihilated" and the cabinet intended "to take away from every colony the right of representation."

Meanwhile Virginians staged a pageant of representation on an unprecedented scale. In county after county "freeholders and inhabitants" gathered at their courthouses to instruct their representatives about the August 1 meeting. The resolutions, for the most part, derived heavily from those previously published or circulated privately from one place to another. (Richard Henry Lee's resolves for Westmoreland turned up a few weeks later as Frank Lee's proposal for Richmond, while Richard Bland's propositions for Prince George found their way into New Kent and Nansemond.)

While the county resolutions differed in their tactical recommendations, all insisted upon the colony's right to tax itself, denounced the "ministerial design" against liberty, expressed a willingness to undertake united action with the other colonies, and declared that "the cause of the Town of Boston is the common Cause of all the American Colonies." About half the meetings felt obliged to preface their statements with professions of loyalty to His Majesty, but none pressed the point so carefully as the freeholders in Edmund Pendleton's Caroline County, who declared that anyone who jeopardized the union between colony and parent either by "attempting to deprive the Colonists of their just Rights on the one hand, or to effect their Independence, on the other" should be deemed an "Enemy to the whole Community."

Other counties sought to proscribe as "infamous" those who objected to associated protest or recommended that "large committees of respectable Men" be formed to prevent breaches in the united front.

In Patrick Henry's Hanover the inhabitants staged an impressive ceremony at the courthouse. Henry and his half brother John Syme, the county's burgesses, stood in front of the large assembly to receive its thanks for "patriotick, faithful, and spirited Conduct." One of the magistrates then read an address containing the freeholders' sentiments about the August 1 meeting and the measures "most likely to effect our Deliverance from the Evils" now looming. The address employed the vigorous, highly personal language that so characterized Henry's own style; "we are freemen," it declared, who regard the right to tax ourselves as "the great Badge of Freedom." Parliament is "trampling" upon that right, and now "the arm of power . . . is stretched forth against us," which fills "our minds with anxiety" and makes us "read our intended Doom" in the "detestable" acts directed first toward Massachusetts.

"The Sphere of Life in which we move hath not afforded us Lights sufficient to determine, with Certainty, concerning those Things from which the Troubles of Boston originated," the freemen confessed. But the destruction of the tea, warranted or no, was now beside the point, for "the united Wisdom and Fortitude of America" must be "collected for its Defence."

The style and tone reflect Henry's leadership, yet the meeting's specific instructions reveal disagreements. Hanover's freemen, regarding a withholding of exports as a last resort, would only endorse a nonimportation scheme, and they ignored entirely Henry's proposals to close the courts and to stop actions for debts. They did, however, follow Henry's lead in condemning the slave trade as "most dangerous to Virtue," and they wished "to see it totally discouraged." Asserting that Virginia's loyalty to the Crown could not be doubted, the freemen declared their "ardent desire" to live under "the genuine unaltered Constitution of England" and prayed that those "Wretches who affirm that we desire the contrary feel the Punishment due to Falsehood and Villainy."

The courthouse meetings and addresses sought "to feel how the pulse of the common people beat," but the spectacle of "the greatest men in the colony encouraging the common people" to express any opinion, especially views hostile to government, offended a good many gentlemen of affairs. Aristocrats jibed that law-breaking demagogues had caused the crisis and pitched a peaceful colony into distress. The attorney general, John Randolph, spoke for the conservatives in a July 1774 appeal to the "rational part" of the public, rather than "the ignorant vulgar," whom he considered "as unfit to judge of the Modes, as they are unable to manage the Reins, of Government." In a thinly veiled attack on Patrick Henry, Randolph ridiculed the idea of calling someone a patriot "because he enjoys the Acclamations of the People. The Populace, from Freak, or Interest, are ever ready to elevate their Leader to the Pinnacle of Fame; and Experience informs us, that they are as ready to pull him down. . . . Those who are running the Race of Popularity, whilst they are the greatest Sticklers for the Liberty of others, are themselves the most abject Slaves in Politicks."

True patriotism, Randolph said, consisted not in pursuing the will of "noisy constituents" but in upholding the "due poise" of the "vast political Body"—the famous equilibrium of king, lords, and commons—ordained by the constitution. If the colonists repudiate the destruction of the tea, resume law-abiding ways, and "apply ourselves quietly to the Cultivation of our Soil," Parliament will surely heed a petition "prepared in a language suited to the Ears of Princes" to reopen the port of Boston and restore peaceful relations. Most of all, Randolph enjoined against the exercise of passion and emphasized that the "publick Happiness" depended upon keeping "Gentlemen of Ability and Fortune" in the assembly instead of empowering "Men who can be no great Losers in the general Wreck of the Constitution."

Courthouse orators like Henry regarded the conservative

charges as a calumny. To open the eyes of the people is not seditious, they argued, but an act of duty and righteousness. Opposition to measures that subvert the constitution is no new doctrine in the history of England, they insisted, and they buttressed patriotic history with classical and biblical quotations that justified popular resistance to tyranny.

The protesters also mocked the conservatives' faith in an uncorrupted constitution. The "ministerial plot" stemmed directly from the bribery that undermined traditional virtue and filled Parliament with fawning nabobs. So long as a corrupt ministry controlled the House of Commons with its tools and placemen while excluding popular champions like John Wilkes, the radicals warned, there could be no hope for repeal.

Even the moderate Virginia burgesses, typified by George Washington, had lost confidence in the ordinary processes of government. Washington rejected Randolph's suggestion of another humble petition as hopeless: "Does it not appear, as clear as the sun in its meridian brightness, that there is a regular, systematic plan formed to fix the right and practice of taxation upon us?" For Washington, as for Henry, the question had come down to whether the colonists had reached "the last extremity."

"A deeper tone broke forth" in 1774, recalled young Edmund Randolph, the attorney general's son and the Speaker's nephew. For the first time "deep and pervading popular sentiment" became a political force of unprecedented power, and while his father refused to concede its legitimacy, Edmund Randolph recognized its significance. In the young man's admiring view, no man in Virginia exceeded Henry in bringing that opinion to life. His powerful eloquence did not create public sentiment where none existed, Randolph emphasized, but no man knew better how to rouse common feeling into action. Henry so deftly applied the "torch of opposition" that no one had to burden himself with "deep research into the ancient treasures of political learning." "It was enough to feel, to remember some general maxims." Henry moved people because he knew how to make "grand impressions in the defense of liberty," a talent that, in the excited young patriot's mind, seemed unrivaled in "the Western world."

The August 1 meeting, Henry realized, would defy Lord Dunmore by reconvening the dissolved assembly in an unofficial emergency session. Lord Dunmore understood this too and, citing the frontier Indian crisis, suddenly tried to confuse the issue by calling elections for a new assembly to meet August 11. Dunmore's move was a snare, the radicals believed, for should they put off the Association meeting on August 1, surely the governor would find a pretext for postponing the new assembly to autumn or winter. Peyton Randolph skillfully trumped the governor by announcing that any new burgesses elected for August 11 would be welcomed at the meeting of former burgesses on August 1. Word went out privately that the counties ought to reelect the incumbent burgesses and advise them to be in the capital by the beginning of August.

Dunmore then took the time-honored high road to popularity. He decided to take personal command of the war against the Indians. Upon leaving Williamsburg in mid-July, he ordered the assembly meeting postponed until November and declared that he would proceed to Fort Pitt at the forks of the Ohio in order to negotiate a peace treaty. His orders to the frontier county militia commanders, however, left no doubt that he wanted them to regulate matters by "Striking Such a Stroke as might prove decisive" before the conference.

The governor's martial expedition to the West had Henry's full approval. He had family connections in the frontier counties, of course, and his brothers-in-law played prominent roles in the campaign against the Indians, but Henry, like Washington, also had a speculator's interest in the potential gains from Dunmore's war. Indeed, Henry and Washington had jointly hired a surveying party to explore and claim sections for them all summer in Ohio and Kentucky. The governor, who had already pleased the Virginians by making exceedingly generous interpretations of London's restrictions on land grants (including the issuing of provisional warrants against the day London might ease the stringent rules supposedly in force), thus appeared to be doing the colonial leaders a very good turn, just when the imperial quarrel had turned most sour and alarming.

With Dunmore off in Pittsburgh, the August 1 meeting began in the giddy atmosphere of boys playing at school while their headmaster is absent. More than one hundred men—the largest crowd since Botetourt's resplendent opening—had come in, and that number did not include some of Henry's heartiest western friends, whose preoccupation with the Indian troubles kept them on the far side of the Blue Ridge. Stout talk about the frontier riflemen led on to bold assertions of how well the colonists might do in combat against British regulars. If there were to be a continental congress, men said, it ought to meet in one of the country towns, like Winchester, Frederick, or Lancaster, so that the "expert riflemen" of the interior might repel any "unwelcome visitors" dispatched by General Gage.

George Washington, who had arrived in a coach drawn by the same gorgeous horses that Lord Botetourt had once employed to dazzle the Virginians, spoke grimly about marching a company of men at his own expense to relieve poor Boston. George Mason's brother Thomson, so nearsighted that on hunting trips he shot at stumps more frequently than ducks, nonetheless looked ahead to a spirited colonial victory in war and loudly ticked off the advantages Americans would have in fighting on their home ground. Even on a sultry August forenoon the talk of war could send shivers down the spine, and nearly every avowal of determination, every proud boast, ended with the despairing sigh, "Heaven only knows where these tumults will end."

The deputies did not meet in the clubby rooms of the Raleigh but set up informally in the Capitol itself, where solemn portraits of King George and Queen Charlotte stared down at them from the walls of the burgesses' chamber. They placed Peyton Randolph in the great oak Speaker's chair but referred to him as the "moderator," a word that came out of the self-governing traditions of the Scotch Presbyterians. The meeting, while technically called by signatories of the May 27 Association, had become an unofficial session of the House. Both members and public alike had started calling it "the convention," another term with Presbyterian roots that evoked memories of the Glorious Revolution of 1689 when an ad hoc meeting convened by leaders of the House outside the regular channels became a surrogate Parliament, passed the famous Bill of Rights, and summoned William of Orange to the throne. The gentlemen meeting in the Virginia town named for that obliging sovereign had no such grandiose ambition, but they did see themselves as heirs to the constitutional principles of the Whigs who had made William king: government by compact, government exercised in balanced forms, and government that protected life and property by observing due procedures when they need be commandeered.

The Williamsburg convention declared that it had gathered, on its own recognizance as it were, because "hasty dissolutions" had deprived the people of their accustomed mode for expressing grievances. The convention believed that government had lost its equilibrium and that the constitutional compact stood in jeopardy, but the members differed substantially about remedies. The moderates wanted to exert just enough pressure on sympathetic Britons (especially the merchants) to force a change of ministries at the next parliamentary election. The more militant thought that only forceful action in America would convince the ministry to devise a constitutional remedy that would end the dispute by recognizing the colonial legislatures' autonomy in money matters and protecting the colonists' rights of free speech and assembly. Henry—along with the Lees, the Masons, and Jefferson—believed in a stout demonstration of strength. Although they still hoped that a trade embargo would be adequate, they now realized that a display of "virtue" entailed the risk of civil war with Britain. Talk of unity within the colonies, therefore, could not be idle chatter. The radicals would push, but they would temper their demands in order to preserve the political alliance.

On the opening day, however, no one was ready to give. The convention could only agree that a general congress of deputies from all the colonies "assemble as quickly as the nature of their situations will admit." The meeting should consider effective means of "so operating on the commercial connection" with Britain as to secure redress for Boston, an end to "arbitrary taxation," and a restoration of "harmony and Union." The convention could do no less—the county resolutions all strongly favored such a meeting, as did the other colonies—but the convention could not yet do more.

Each side saw the congress in a different tactical light. The cautious preferred it as an alternative to a complete trade embargo and a possible brake on the headlong pace of affairs, while the more aggressive saw the proposed meeting as a means for both countering what they regarded as the divide-and-conquer tactics of the ministry and putting pressure on the recalcitrant elements in the provinces.

Between Tuesday and Friday the convention took no formal action but kept itself busy in committee debate on two related papers: revision of the May 27 Association and instructions for Virginia's yet-to-be-chosen deputies to the general congress. The draftsmen shuffled the documents back and forth in search of political compromise. A point that proved contentious in the Association might find a more comfortable home in the instructions, and those who complained about omissions in one statement could be mollified with promises about the other.

The resolves from the various counties gave the delegates a myriad of proposals. About half favored a cessation of both imports and exports, while the advocates of non-importation had long lists of possible exceptions, ranging from spices and medicine to books, cotton cloth, and tools. Although Henry and his allies fought hard for a ban on exports, they could only secure a promise to refrain from exports in a year's time, after the tobacco crop presently ripening in the fields could be safely harvested and sold. Those who favored nonimportation alone, however, agreed to make the boycott simple and comprehensive. Only the purchase of medicines would be permitted, and a separate clause would be added, much to Henry's satisfaction, barring the importation and purchase of slaves. Nonimportation would begin on November 1 (the earliest practicable date, although the radicals had argued for a more immediate one) and would last until the "redress of all such American grievances as may be defined at . . . the General Congress."

This formulation, while a nod in the direction of unity, concealed another profound difference. The radicals wanted to denounce the "ministerial plot" to deprive the colonies of liberty; the moderates did not want to antagonize Britain when they could avoid it. The most they would agree to in the text of the Association proved to be a compressed sentence (every clause a compromise) asserting "that the present unhappy Situation of our Affairs is chiefly occasioned by certain ill advised Regulations, as well of our Trade as [of] internal Polity, introduced by several unconstitutional Acts of the British Parliament, and, at length, attempted to be enforced by the Hand of Power."

Yet another quarrel erupted over enforcement. The radicals wanted the Association generally supervised by county committees that would search out violators, investigate the circumstances, and enact ceremonies of either apology or obloquy. The convention would only pledge to deal with those merchants who signed the Association and would use the committees principally to ensure that merchants did not raise prices to take advantage of scarcity. Denunciation of persons "inimical to the community" would be reserved for those who violated the ban on exports in the summer of 1775. Even though most of the county courts had suspended operations owing to the lack of a fee bill, the convention would not accept a radical plank calling for a cessation of civil actions on behalf of British creditors, Pendleton leading opposition to the measure as dishonorable and an invitation to anarchy.

In response to the claims of Henry and the others that their sister colonies favored more stringent measures, the moderates agreed to a catchall clause committing the Virginia Association to "all such Alterations or Additions, assented to by the Delegates for this Colony [at the general congress], as they judge it necessary to adopt." This clause sounded high-minded but contained some ambiguity. Would Virginia go along with whatever the congress decided or only with those measures its delegates favored? If the congress, like the convention, strove for unanimity, all might be well, but if the Virginians found themselves on the losing side of a divided question, would they feel obliged to recommend it to the Association upon returning home?

The separate controversy over instructions to the delegates failed to clarify the point, since they forbade acquiescence in an earlier date for nonexportation but advised cooperation in other measures judged proper by "the Majority" of the congress. But the instructions also charged the delegates with expressing the colony's allegiance to the king and its desire for "a constitutional Connexion with Great Britain." The moderate temper, maintained over a week's debate, only gave way in the last two paragraphs of the instructions to a tirade against General Gage's proclamation proscribing town meetings in Massachusetts as treasonable. Enforcement of such "an alarming process" would "justify Resistance and Reprisal," although the instructions failed to say by whom.

Much would depend upon the character of the Virginia delegation, and Friday morning, August 5, the convention proceeded to ballot. Henry tied with Washington for second place with 104 votes, while Peyton Randolph led with 107. Ritt Lee stood fourth at 102, with Pendleton just behind at 100. The Speaker's brother-in-law Benjamin Harrison had 94 votes, and Bland 90 to complete the delegation. Henry and Lee looked quickly around; the delegation mirrored the divisions in the convention. Pendleton, Harrison, and Randolph would present problems, but they could probably count on Bland (if he were well enough to travel). That put three against three, leaving Washington to be a swing vote within the delegation. He had sounded firm enough, except on the question of halting collections for debt, and he had worked with Mason on Fairfax County's resolutions, far more stringent than the convention's. Yet Washington generally held back in debate and kept his own counsel.

On Saturday morning, with rain showers making eddying scratches in the dusty streets, the convention came to a close. The deputies each stepped forward to sign the Association, with the congressional delegation given pride of place. Finally, the convention agreed that each county would contribute fifteen pounds toward the one thousand pounds judged necessary for the expenses of the delegates, who, it was now learned, would be going to Philadelphia to meet with representatives of the other colonies on the first Monday of September.

Amid the general bonhomie that followed a hard week's debate and excited importunings from the college students and townspeople who had filled the galleries each day, Washington approached Henry with an invitation. Stop over at Mount Vernon on the way north, Washington proposed, and we can ride to Philadelphia together. Henry accepted without hesitation.

CHAPTER 11

"The Present Measures Lead to War"

Henry hoped to have Washington's ear all to himself on the long ride to Philadelphia, but he ended up having to share the cautious soldier with Pendleton, whose plantation in Caroline lay squarely on Henry's path to Mount Vernon. Courtesy dictated that the rivals travel together, and they quietly obliged, arriving at Washington's estate on the afternoon of Tuesday, August 30. The day was "exceeding hot," with a dry little wind blowing up from the south. The mansion house had a disheveled, lopsided appearance, owing to the new wing under construction, and the veranda—with a commanding view of the Potomac—lacked its usual freshening river breeze.

Virginians, however, would be hospitable in the most adverse circumstances, and Washington showed off his dogs, his stables, and his crops in customary style and presided with grace over a comfortably laden table. His neighbor, George Mason, who had so admired Henry's leadership in May, rode over from nearby Gunston Hall to meet the delegates and, since the talk ran late, stayed the night with them. After a hearty noon meal, the horsemen made ready; Washington had decided against the carriage. They would ride themselves, each accompanied by a black bodyservant, who would see to the baggage and extra horses. Martha Washington, who had kinfolk among Henry's neighbors in Hanover, stood "like a Spartan mother" in the doorway as they rode off and pointedly enjoined Pendleton to stand as firm as she knew her husband would.

A poetaster in that week's newspaper offered a more lyrical sendoff to the delegates, who "shine more conspicuous in the common cause/So strictly pious, in support of laws." "Say to what better end was HENRY born?/Why should persuasive speech his lips adorn?," the versifier asked, and answered, "But that our most inveterate foes/May learn, Virginia wants not Ciceroes."

The trio set a hard pace, crossing the Potomac by ferry and advancing halfway to Annapolis by dusk. The next morning they rode nine miles in the dawning light before stopping for breakfast and completed the long boat passage across Chesapeake Bay that same evening. The horses, however, didn't come over until the next afternoon, which meant that the delegates got only fourteen miles farther. They lodged Friday evening at the aspiring inland port of New Town on Chester, in the heart of Maryland's wheat country, where the local people boasted of mill runs choked with yellow perch and travelers from Virginia were apt to say that they could smell the phenomenon long before seeing it. On Saturday they crossed the head of the peninsula and arrived at Newcastle on the Delaware, about forty miles short of Philadelphia. On Sunday morning they followed the river road, muttering at its sorry state but admiring the neat stone bridges that eased passage over the numerous creeks. After a noon meal in Chester, they made good time over the gradually improving road, and by midafternoon they stood on a flatbed ferry, being hauled across the narrow Schuylkill River with a set of ropes and pulleys. Three more miles along a broad highway lined with stately manor houses brought them into the heart of Philadelphia, and guided by cheering crowds of Liberty Boys, the Virginians made their way through the crowded streets to Smith's New Tavern, where increasing numbers of delegates had gathered each day to get acquainted and swap thoughts on how the Congress might proceed.

Richard Henry Lee, who had arrived with Randolph three days earlier, met the latecomers at the tavern and even before they had brushed the dust from their clothes began to tell them of the worthy gentlemen he had already met and the "high" views most had espoused. (Lee had made his mark, too, as a "masterly man," and he relished the flattering attention of those who sang his praises as "as true a trout as ever swam, as staunch a hound as ever ran.") During a boisterous supper, marked by numerous toasts to wisdom, unanimity, and firmness, many more gentlemen than Henry could possibly remember pressed forward to introduce themselves, and he felt the confused pleasures of celebrity even as he struggled to learn just what had gone on before his arrival.

Later that evening, comfortably lodged with Lee at his brother-in-law's nearby town house, Henry got a full report. Lee had spent much time with the Boston leader, Samuel Adams, and his cousin John Adams, a country lawyer with a formidable mind and a shrewd sense of politics, and, in three days of earnest conversation the delegates formed the most glowing impressions of one another. The Massachusetts men had won general praise for their moderate and obliging manner, while the other Virginia men had spoken with more spirit than they had ever displayed at home. Colonel Harrison had gone around saying he would have come to the Congress on foot if necessary, and Randolph and Bland had conducted themselves in a bold, forward style that had awed the other delegates. The stout Virginia talk had assuaged the lingering resentment of the Massachusetts men, who felt that if Virginia had only moved decisively in May they might have organized a trade boycott without going to the risk and bother of the Congress.

Once seen as a moderate alternative to more belligerent action, the Congress now presented an unprecedented opportunity to rally all the colonies behind a firm program. The copies of the *Pennsylvania Journal* strewn about the tavern vividly symbolized this hope in its new front-page banner depicting the colonies as a segmented rattlesnake poised above the slogan "Unite or Die." Yet the adulation directed toward the worthy delegates could be misleading, for Congress had its detractors, too. Pamphleteers denounced the congressmen as "imposters in patriotism" and "quacks in politics" who would intimidate "the well-meaning deluded multitude" with the "passions and language of a common Town Meeting." How dared the Congress, "like some foreign imperial power," to "sit in judgment on the decrees of a British legislature," one critic fumed, while another wondered "whether some degree of respect be not always due from inferiors to superiors & especially from children to parents?"

Henry had heard such talk at each unfolding chapter in the decade-long crisis. It did not faze him, but he would have to take into account that such sentiments extended to the very doorstep of the Congress. The delegates had arrived in the midst of a fierce dispute among the Pennsylvanians themselves, and Lee and the Adamses, Henry learned, could not but get involved. Working in concert with the radical leaders of the Philadelphia committee, they had cooked up a plan that would presumably win friends for the Congress while strengthening the hand of the local committee.

As Henry already knew from the summer's correspondence, the Philadelphia committee, an uneasy coalition of well-to-do merchants and ordinary mechanics, had encountered much opposition from the provincial assembly. Its Speaker, a wealthy Quaker merchant named Joseph Galloway, had kept the most respected radical leaders, John Dickinson (the author of the "Farmer's" letters) and Charles Thomson, out of the delegation to Congress. Galloway wanted Congress to meet in the Pennsylvania State House, while the committee had offered use of its private meeting place, a hall recently built by the Carpenters Company, an organization of master builders in the city. Adams and Lee had lobbied strenuously for Carpenters' Hall, and although when Congress convened on the morrow it would look at both situations, the choice had already been made. The delegates would impress the populace by accepting the Carpenters' offer; Virginia's part in the scheme would be rewarded by the appointment of Peyton Randolph to the chair, and the Philadelphia radicals would gain entry to the debates by inviting Charles Thomson to become secretary of the Congress. It was an intricate design, perhaps too bold for an untried group and an untested alliance, but one thought necessary to prevent the Congress from meeting under the roof of those who had opposed its existence.

Promptly at ten o'clock the next morning, Monday, September 5, Henry joined the other delegates milling about in the club rooms of the New Tavern. A cheer went up when someone realized that their number amounted to the glorious Wilkite sum of forty-five, and they swung out into the street in a lively march that took them two blocks west across the Dock Creek bridge, past an odoriferous tanning yard, and up narrow Whalebone Alley to the Carpenters' Hall courtyard.

The hall, a trim, two-story brick building in the shape of a cross with decorative gables and pediments on all four sides, looked like a comfortable county courthouse unfortunately squeezed onto a narrow city lot. The delegates walked up a series of stone steps into a long entry hall, which still smelled faintly of plaster and wood shavings, and the committeemen, including the building's designer Robert Smith, proudly opened the wooden doors to the east room, a large rectangle twenty by thirty feet, where the morning sun made the heartpine floor gleam, comfortable Windsor chairs stood arranged in an inviting semicircle, and a large fireplace stood swept, cold, and superfluous in the muggy September heat. Ascending the curving stairs to the floor above, the delegates saw a convenient committee room and a chamber tenanted by the Library Company of Philadelphia, whose collection stood shelved securely behind grill-worked doors.

Downstairs again in the east room, Henry stood in awed silence as the Lee-Adams plan unfolded. Thomas Lynch, a wealthy South Carolinian whose plain hair and homespun dress could not conceal "more Force in his very appearance than most powdered Folks carry in their Conversation" stepped forward to propose formally that Congress now sit in it. James Duane, an elegantly dressed New York lawyer with a sly, surveying eye complained, but Lynch's motion received a shout of approval. The delegates took their seats. Then Lynch nominated Peyton Randolph as presiding officer, and with applause filling the room, the stout, majestic Virginian (who "seems designed by Nature, for the Business," a Connecticut delegate mused) assumed his accustomed post before the most unorthodox assembly of his career. Randolph nodded to Lynch, who completed the previously agreed-upon program by proposing that Charles Thomson, a merchant "highly esteemed by the people of Philadelphia," be appointed secretary. Much to Galloway's mortification his rival quickly entered the hall. Thomson was a hard-driving, self-made Presbyterian merchant who had a knack for advancing himself without alienating his superiors, and in Thomson's grave, determined mien Henry could sense at once a kindred spirit.

Randolph then called upon each delegation to produce its commission, a tedious procedure during which men leaned forward to catch the names and craned their necks around the room to identify the various delegates. In an undertone of conversation they shared hastily gathered information about occupations and connections as the roll call proceeded from north to south.

At its conclusion, the New Yorker Duane tried to seize the initiative by proposing that a committee be appointed to formulate rules for the Congress. John Adams, earnest and precise, asked Duane for an example of a rule he thought necessary, and Duane answered "the mode of voting." Should Congress proceed by "the Majority of Voices of its Members," by a unit rule in which each colony would cast a single vote to be determined by a majority within the delegation, or by some proportional system according to "the interests" of each colony?

Silence greeted Duane's enumeration of the alternatives. After only a few hours of existence, the Congress had stumbled onto the vexing question best calculated to undermine its hoped-for unity. Men looked around uncomfortably, for this was one issue the informal managers had not settled ahead of time.

Always ready to lead an improvised charge, Henry took the floor. Dressed in a suit of parson's gray and wearing a plain, unpowdered wig, Henry favorably reminded Charles

Thomson of a Presbyterian minister "used to haranguing the people." With his habitual stoop and chin thrust forward Henry looked older than his thirty-eight years; "now in full life, perhaps near fifty," one delegate guessed.

The Virginian began disarmingly, as was his custom, in low tones that foretold none of the dramatic brilliance that lay in store. He introduced the humble example of a man in distressed circumstances who turned to his friends for advice: "one would propose one thing, and another a different one, whilst perhaps a third would think of something better suited to his unhappy circumstance, which he would embrace, and think no more of the rejected schemes." Henry turned this little scene into an argument for free and candid debate within the convention, while maintaining public silence until a course of action be agreed to. Although, he said, "this was the first general Congress that had ever happened," they were likely to have occasion for more and therefore ought to establish their precedents carefully.

Then Henry threw his thunderbolt. It would be a "great Injustice, if a little Colony should have the same Weight in the Councils of America, as a great one." Let a committee determine some method of proportional voting.

Major John Sullivan, a strapping young New Hampshireman, would not let this pass. "A little Colony has its All at Stake as well as a great one," he said, and in the ensuing hubbub the chair diplomatically entertained a motion to adjourn until Tuesday morning at ten o'clock.

Henry's bold assertion marked him as a political maverick. The tide of conversation in the taverns and at the dinner tables where delegates gathered ran strongly toward questions of the colonial relationship to Parliament, but Henry impulsively asked the delegates to consider their relationship to one another. For all the talk of unity, the deputies had only the most nodding acquaintance with the other provinces and deep suspicions about one another. They might drink toasts to "American" liberty, but in their hearts the delegates considered themselves ambassadors from separate countries, tribal emissaries sent, like their Saxon ancestors, to a "grand Wittenagemoot," in which differences must be respected. Old John Rutledge of South Carolina had already started grumbling about the leveling spirit of the New Englanders, and the Virginians could hardly forget that their western kinsmen were at that very moment embroiled in a triangular border struggle with heathen Shawnee and land-hungry Pennsylvanians. Congregationalists from Massachusetts regarded the pietistic Quakers as heretics, and Virginia's Benjamin Harrison had loudly and ungallantly proclaimed Philadelphia's women to be remarkably hard-faced and sour.

The Virginians' high talk and powerful swagger had awed the other delegates. Next to the Virginians the Bostonians are "mere milktoasts," a Philadelphian said, and another delegate exclaimed that "more Sensible, fine fellows you'd Never Wish to See." Henry's bid for proportional representation sought to translate this magnetism into votes, and by creating an unexpected stir (indeed, a diversion) on the opening day, Henry succeeded in concentrating attention upon himself. "[He is] the compleatest Speaker I ever heard," a Connecticut delegate marveled to his wife, "but in a Letter I can give You no Idea of the Music of his Voice, or the highwrought, yet Natural elegance of his Stile, & Manner."

When debate opened on Tuesday morning, Henry had all eyes upon him. He began with the startling insistence that parliamentary oppression had reduced the colonies to a state of nature. "All Government is dissolved," he said grandly, and then he drove the point home with a series of hammer blows.

"Fleets and armies and the present State of Things shew that Government is dissolved," he said.

"Where are your landmarks? your Boundaries of Colonies?" Henry asked, implicitly reminding the delegates of the repeated assertion that the attack upon Massachusetts was an attack upon all.

"The distinctions between Virginians, Pennsylvanians, New Yorkers, and New Englanders are no more," he said, coloring the argument in his intensely personal way with the flamboyant declaration, "I am not a Virginian, but an American."

Wiping the slate clear of artificial distinctions based on geography, Henry urged proportional representation as a matter of popular justice. If future generations are to applaud our proceedings, Henry argued, it will be because we honored "one of the great Duties of the democratical Part of the Constitution to keep itself pure" and did not become ensnared in the "great mischief" of unequal representation. "That part of North America which was once Massachusetts Bay, and that Part which was once Virginia, ought to be considered as having a Weight," Henry said, for people would complain if "10,000 Virginians have not outweighed 1000 others."

It would indeed be unjust, Henry's colleague Benjamin Harrison insisted, and forsaking Henry's lofty ground, declared that "if such a disrespect should be put upon his Countrymen we should never see them at another Convention."

Henry frequently made bold assertions without bothering about their consequences. If he really intended to transform the hastily convened Congress into a representative governing body, he had moved too soon. John Jay, a suave young lawyer from New York, praised Virginia's "Virtue, Spirit, and Abilities" and admitted that Henry's argument would have force, "could I suppose that We came to frame an American Constitution, instead of endeavoring to correct the faults in an old one." But Jay could not agree that the government had reached the point of dissolution. "The Measure of arbitrary Power is not full," he said calmly, "and I think it must run over, before We undertake to frame a new Constitution."

Even passionate John Adams, whose patience had long since run out, did not want to divert attention from Massachusetts' plight by a volatile argument over the less pressing issue of representation. (Privately he thought that recording votes by colonies rather than individuals might create a greater appearance of unity.) Admitting the abstract principle, he argued, only increased the perplexities, for the meeting lacked enough accurate information about each colony's population and trade to assign a ratio. "It will not do in such Case, to take each other's Words," Adams said. "It ought to be ascertained by authentic Evidence, from Records."

If by authenticity was meant "attestations of officers of the Crown," Henry replied, he would agree that such accounts could not be had. Yet it was clear, to him at least, that "All America is all thrown into one Mass" and that, without insisting upon "the Minutiae of Rectitude," all "freemen ought to be represented according to their Numbers." When one of the Carolinians, however, urged that "a compound of Numbers and Property should determine the Weight of the Colonies," Henry bluntly suggested that slaves "be thrown out of the Question."

He had tried to summon nationalistic spirit as an indirect lever for expanding provincial power, and he had clearly failed. When Lee reiterated John Adams's theme that insufficient materials precluded a fair determination, and when Dick Bland lent his quavering voice to the same proposition and reminded the body that "the question is whether the Rights and Liberties of America shall be contended for, or given up to arbitrary Power," Henry realized that he had gone too far. As an experienced lawyer he knew when to back away from an argument jurors would not accept, and now he raised his hands graciously and said, "I will submit. I am determined to submit if I am overruled."

In short order the Congress approved a motion that each colony would have one vote. To meet Henry's argument that this not be taken as binding precedent, however, the journal soothingly noted that Congress was not "possess'd of, or at present able to procure proper materials for ascertaining the importance of each Colony."

The ink had barely dried on this calm resolve when a messenger burst into the room with the alarming news that Boston had been bombarded. The Massachusetts men turned pale, and everyone rushed out into the street. People gathered in sorrowing knots on street corners to hear various pieces of the story. General Gage had tried to seize gunpowder from a magazine in Cambridge, and six inhabitants had died in the ensuing skirmish! The countryside clear over to Connecticut had risen up in arms! The naval fleet in the harbor had shelled the town! In "utmost confusion" rumors of cannonade at Boston spread, and throughout the city muffled bells began to toll in mourning.

The panic gradually subsided. The message was garbled; the riders had brought it in less than seventy-two hours; it came from an irregular source; the people would have to endure the "cruel suspense" until more reliable information arrived. It took most of the afternoon for the delegates to collect their emotions and reassemble in their chamber, now deep in shadow. They gravely moved on to a brief consideration of rules, including a vow to keep their proceedings secret until ready to "publish the whole," and then decided to facilitate their work by establishing two committees, one to state the rights and grievances of the colonies, and the other to examine the various restrictions on trade and manufacture.

With the Boston affair on everyone's mind, Thomas Cushing (the Speaker of the Massachusetts House) moved that the next morning's session be opened with prayers. Something about Cushing—his belligerent jaw or his sardonic look —annoyed the patrician Jay and the planter Rutledge, who thought they detected unseemly "Enthusiasm and Cant" in the proposal. Private devotions would be more efficacious, they reasoned, because the members were "so divided in religious Sentiments" that formal worship would only aggravate their differences.

Samuel Adams, his round face wreathed in a halo of sweet reasonableness, arose "and said he was no bigot," his cousin John recounted, "and could hear a Prayer from [any] Gentleman of Piety and Virtue, who was at the same Time a Friend to his Country." The elder Adams went on to say that although "a stranger in Philadelphia," he had heard that an Episcopal clergyman, Mr. Jacob Duché, "deserved that Character" and hoped that Congress might invite him to read prayers on the morrow. Much soothed, the delegates agreed.

Henry had already employed the day of fasting as an engine of political mobilization, but neither he nor Samuel

Adams, a strategist without parallel, realized how brilliant a stroke this invitation would prove. The next morning, with the mournful bells still tolling and an air of dreadful catastrophe hanging over the city, the Reverend Duché read the morning's collect, a text from the Thirty-fifth Psalm so apt that everyone felt the finger of Providence had pointed to it:

> Plead my cause, O Lord, with them that strive with me and fight against them that fight against me.
> Take hold of shield and buckler and stand up for mine help.
> Draw out also the spear and stop the way against them that persecute me; Say unto my soul, "I am thy salvation."
> Let them be confounded and put to shame that seek after my soul. Let them be turned back and brought to confusion that devise my hurt.
> Let them be as chaff before the wind and let the angel of the Lord chase them.
> Let their way be dark and slippery, and let the angel of the Lord persecute them.

This lamentation had the cadence and the emotion of Henry's most moving efforts, and the clergyman heightened its power (much as Henry would have) with an extemporaneous prayer —for America, for the Congress, for Massachusetts Bay, and especially for poor, beleaguered Boston—that John Adams later called "as pertinent, as affectionate, as sublime, as devout, as I have ever heard offered up to Heaven." It "filled the bosom of every Man present" with fervor and ardor and thus, Adams and the other radicals realized at once, had a "very good Effect . . . on the Sentiments of People here."

Following the ecclesiastical fireworks, the meeting considered the appointment of its working committees. Henry's theatrics of the previous day made him suddenly unpredictable and lost him a seat on the grand committee charged with stating rights and grievances. The Virginians deputized Lee and Pendleton. In the interest of building a united front this was a shrewd choice, though Bland was the delegation's undisputed expert on constitutional matters. They gave Henry Virginia's seat on the second committee, charged with inquiring into the system of commercial regulations.

This assignment did not prove taxing. The committee met several times and, as instructed, reviewed all the regulations restricting trade and manufacturing in the colonies. Implicit in the committee's charge lay the idea of challenging Britain's commercial dominance, an idea that rested well with Henry, whose thoughts on the conditions necessary for development of western lands had led him to appreciate the ideas of home manufactures and free trade. Henry's committee report, a review of the British regulatory system reaching back to the Navigation Acts of the mid-seventeenth century, did not take long to prepare, but it quickly became irrelevant.

The committee on colonial rights had become stalemated over an abstract statement because the members could not agree whether Great Britain had any right whatsoever to regulate trade. Yet with the situation at Boston growing ever more urgent (the rumored cannonade had not taken place, but Gage had confiscated some provincial ammunition) and the continent waiting anxiously for tactical recommendations, the committee had to move. It ducked the larger questions of imperial regulation of trade by proposing simply that the Congress confine itself "at present, to the consideration of such rights only as have been infringed by acts of the British parliament since the year 1763, postponing the further consideration of the general state of American rights to a future day."

Henry went along with this oblique formula. Never one to insist upon abstractions at the expense of practical results, he favored anything that would expedite business. No one in Congress, it seemed, countenanced "submission," but like the Virginia burgesses, the delegates in Philadelphia had varying degrees of confidence in the home government's willingness to respond to colonial protest.

The news from London, as indicated by extracts from

letters reprinted in the Philadelphia papers, hardly supported optimism. While some writers predicted success for a trade embargo, others reported an ominous rise in contempt and ridicule. The colonists are called "thieves, pirates, and rebels," it was said. Your resolutions will be seen "as very inoffensive and as the mere ebullitions of a set of angry men," another correspondent advised; the ministry will "laugh" at the Congress and has already determined not to receive any of its petitions. Still others reported that Philadelphia's port would soon be closed and Pennsylvania's charter revoked; that furthermore, thirty thousand Roman Catholics would be armed in Quebec to march into the Protestant colonies at the first sign of trouble.

The Quebec Act seemed an especially troubling sign of growing absolutism. All territory north of the Ohio River would be annexed to Canada, which would continue to be ruled by an appointed council and governor. An unrepresentative government combined with a large Catholic population raised the specter of the late Stuarts all over again. A large crowd of Wilkites in London had hurled the old "No Popery" slogan against George III as he rode to Westminster to assent to the Quebec Bill, the newspapers said, but the king "bronzed it out" in a manner that reminded the letter writer of the contempt shown by James II, who once aboard his ship of exile "let a fart to show how much he despised" the people. The Quebec Bill confirmed the overall ministerial design, yet another writer warned, for it was intended "to keep the other colonies in awe, by extending a chain of forts through the new province on the rear of the old."

The Quebec Bill indeed alarmed the delegates, and virtually all were willing to add it to the growing list of grievances. Yet the grim reports from London could not shake most gentlemen's conviction that a united stand—and a trade embargo—would force the home government to reconsider "the ruinous system of colony administration" that had led to the crisis.

For Henry, as for the Adamses whose hometown smoldered on the verge of war, the time for genteel remonstrance had ended. The real task of the Congress, Henry now thought, would be to mobilize public opinion and prepare for war. The boycott might be necessary to cement unanimity in the colonies, he believed, but he lacked any conviction that it would accomplish its intended purposes overseas. That thousands of men had streamed across New England to defend Boston from the rumored bombardment led Henry to believe that public opinion would countenance more militant preparations. Lee, too, thought that such demonstrations of strength might do more than trade policy to soften the ministry's heart and lead it to a prudent reversal.

It would take quite an effort to bring most of the delegates to that harsh view. As representatives of obstreperous Boston, John and Samuel Adams felt obliged to check their militancy in public, while Henry and Lee gave theirs free rein. No wonder that the quartet became firm friends as they worked their way through the innumerable dinner parties and tavern conferences by which "Fifty Gentlemen . . . all Strangers" overcame their skittish suspicions and got acquainted with one another's "Tempers, Views, Characters, and Designs."

Committee work took up the mornings, but the delegates followed the practice of "the Southern gentlemen" in conducting no business after an ample "dinner" in midafternoon. The leisurely pace irked some of the New Englanders. "We shall sett a long while," a Rhode Islander groused, but the eastern delegates curbed their impatience and realized that their alliance with the South had to be rooted in the camaraderie of social relationships.

Philadelphia lionized the delegates, and the opening weeks of the Congress turned into a dignified roundelay of dinner parties, city rambles, and riding parties into the countryside. "The gentlemen of the City are entertaining the Gentlemen of the Congress every day by parcels," a Delaware man wrote home, and John Adams confessed to his diary the menu of each evening's "most sinfull Feast." Commercial connections, family ties, and emerging political friendships gave practical shape to each day's invitations, with whole delegations going by turns to the mayor's, the councilors', and the chief justice's, along with more private gatherings at the country homes of the leading merchants and attorneys. The conversation ran heavily to political subjects, of course, along with an exchange of curiosities and tedious comparisons of the laws and customs of the bar in the different provinces.

The social whirl enabled the delegates to test one another's tempers and to get a feeling for the bedrock of character that underlay the brave words most seemed willing to utter. Over the turtle steaks, luscious melons, and fine wines the delegates convinced each other of their probity and commitment. "The Members of the Congress are such choice Characters," John Adams reassured his wife, "that no Danger can happen to Us, which will not involve the whole Continent, in Universal Desolation, and in that Case who would wish to live?" The feasting turned into a public pageant of unity on September 16 when the leading merchants of Philadelphia honored the delegates with "a grand entertainment" at the state house attended by nearly five hundred people including "genteel strangers" from every province on the continent. There was "a plenty of everything eatable, & drinkable, & no scarcity of good Humor and diversion," and rumor assessed the cost at nearly a thousand pounds. Music and a discharge of cannon punctuated dozens of toasts in which delegates offered uplifting sentiments ("a Happy Reconciliation . . . on a constitutional Ground") and low comedy ("May the Cloud that hangs over Great Britain and the colonies burst only on the Heads of the present ministry").

The local people had never seen their town so crowded. Philadelphia had become "another Cairo," aswarm with politicians and land jobbers as well as merchants, people said. Most of the delegates kept an enterprising eye out for business, and speculative proposals multiplied along with the political pamphlets. Henry had an excellent entry into Philadelphia's commercial society, for his friend Robert Pleasants had given him generous letters of introduction to the most prominent Quaker merchants, including the city's mayor, William Fisher, and the leading Indian trader Israel Pemberton. Henry accepted the special hospitality accorded him as a champion of Virginia's Quakers and listened politely to homilies on moderation while pursuing his own western land interests with circumspect enthusiasm. Speculators wooed him with shares in their ambitious, often untenable claims, all of which he refused. Henry did some courting of land agents himself, spending a cozy private breakfast with the wealthy merchant, Thomas Wharton, who headed a group interested in securing an Ohio Valley land grant extensive enough to form the separate colony of Vandalia. The two men probed each other for information, and Henry left Wharton with the impression that the Virginian would be willing to offer a legal opinion that would validate private purchases of land from the Indians as a means of getting round the Crown's restrictions. Wharton did not know that Henry had hopes of making a "snug little purchase" of Cherokee lands in the Kentucky country beyond the Cumberland Gap. Yet Wharton guessed something when Henry casually asked, "Do you know where a gentleman can buy some Indian goods?"

"It's not possible you mean to enter the Indian trade at this period," Wharton protested.

"The wish-world is my hobby horse," Henry said with a laugh, and he left the old merchant tantalized by the Virginian's intentions.

Later that day Henry joined the other Virginia delegates for dinner at the elegant home of Pennsylvania's chief justice, Benjamin Chew. The company, which included John Adams and the other Massachusetts men, mingled amiably in the richly furnished rooms. Justice Chew had Virginia connections, especially among Mr. Pendleton's dear friends the Madisons. One of his nephews had served with Colonel Washington and had some bounty land warrants in the Ohio country. Talk swirled for a time about Ohio and Vandalia, but when the parade of jellies, sweetmeats, whipped syllabub, floating islands, fools, and trifles finally ended, Henry, Adams, and Lee found themselves equally exasperated with the tedious pace Congress had followed. "Slow as snails," Adams complained, as they reviewed the alternatives still before them, while drinking Madeira at the chief justice's and adjourning later for talk at Adams's lodgings that lasted until midnight.

They saw three classes of action: proposals by petition, which might range from appeals to the king to sending ambassadors from the Congress with various peace proposals, such as an offer to raise money (say £200,000) in the colonies as a contribution to the royal navy; commercial struggle, which embraced both the support of manufactures at home and a refusal to engage in overseas trade with Great Britain; and preparations for war, which bluntly meant raising arms and ensuring that every province had its militia at full strength and well drilled.

While Henry and Lee, especially, felt the urgency of military preparations, they realized that most of the delegates had not yet arrived at that antagonistic pitch. If they could gain quick endorsement of the economic boycott, however, they would achieve a tactical base from which to press their military program and prevent any retreat toward the amorphous comfort of petitions.

With newfound resolve Henry and the others brought the flagging Congress back to legislative vigor. By Wednesday, September 28, Congress voted a nonimportation agreement, and by Friday the thirtieth came to an agreement on nonexportation as well. The New Englanders pushed for an immediate ban, but Henry could take little part in these debates, hamstrung as he was by the Virginia convention's instruction to refrain from a boycott on exports for at least another year. In the unaccustomed role of laggard, he tried to conciliate those fretful delegates who worried about even an immediate cessation of imports. Why not postpone nonimportation from November to December, Henry suggested successfully; "We don't mean to hurt even our Rascalls—if We have any."

Henry took a more vigorous role in beating down the effort made by Joseph Galloway, the conservative Speaker of the Pennsylvania House, to sidetrack debate from the suspension of commerce to negotiation through petition. Galloway pressed hard for his pet scheme, the creation of an American Parliament, but Henry ridiculed it at every turn. He wouldn't consent, he said, to indirect representation, nor would he want to "liberate our Constituents from a corrupt House of Parliament" only to "throw them into the Arms of an American Legislature that may be bribed" by the aristocratic London politicians who avow "in the Face of the World" that bribery is a part of their system of government. Then Henry took the opportunity of alluding to his own committee's sidetracked report. "Before we are obliged to pay taxes" levied by an American version of Parliament, "let us be as free as they are" in Britain. "Let us have our Trade open with all the World," Henry declared, turning the debate back to the divisive issue of trade regulation and increasing Galloway's suspicion that Henry and his ilk really aimed at "total Independency."

Galloway's plan was tabled, but at the week's end his conservative group tried to dominate the proceedings again with a proposition that a "loyal address" be prepared entreating His Majesty's "gracious interposition for the removal of . . . the grievances that alarm and distress his faithful subjects in North-America." The radicals countered, first by having Lee, Henry, and John Adams named to the drafting committee, and second by creating a debater's free-for-all with a welter of amendments purporting to "instruct" the draftsmen.

The loudest fight took place over Lee's motion that Congress recommend to the colonies "that a militia be forthwith appointed and well disciplined And that they be well provided with Ammunition and Proper Arms." Lee argued that since the oppressive revenue acts were held to be for the defense of the colonies, North America could relieve the mother country of that unreasonable expense by showing that the continent was "able, willing, and . . . determined to Protect Defend and Secure itself."

Rutledge of South Carolina immediately attacked Lee's motion as "out of line" and "in degree, a Declaration of War." Virginia's Benjamin Harrison also recoiled, saying, "It will tend only to irritate, whereas Our Business is to reconcile."

Henry then took the floor. He favored the motion, he said, because "a preparation for Warr is Necessary to obtain peace." "America is not Now in a State of Peace," he insisted. "All the Bulwarks of our Safety, of Our Constitution, are thrown down, and we are Now in a State of Nature."

What if the planned boycott fails, Henry asked, and exploited the fateful silence for as long as he dared. "In that case," he answered, "Arms are Necessary." He paused again and added: "if then, it is Necessary Now" to make ready.

Henry had heard "high" talk for weeks from the delegates, and it was evident that no gentleman wanted poor Boston to submit. Yet talk out of doors seemed to run ahead of what the Congress would countenance. Henry had to persuade the delegates that the continent was on a collision course. "The present measures lead to war," he kept insisting, by which he meant not only the ministry's oppressive acts but what the delegates had already committed themselves to do. The boycott must be tried, but if it did not obtain redress, would Congress then backtrack and submit?

With all the fervor he could summon Henry charged the delegates to look at the consequences without blinking. "Arms are a Resource to which we shall be forced," he insisted; "a Resource afforded Us by God & Nature."

"Why in the Name of both are We to hesitate providing them Now whilst in Our power?" he asked, posing a debater's challenge with a stare every bit as uncomfortable as the glare Preacher Davies had directed at the sinners in his congregation.

The speech brought substantive debate to a full stop. The opposition initiated a long wrangle over procedure, which Henry countered zealously at every turn. Eventually, though, the moderates who considered Henry and Lee "impolitic" rallied and successfully watered down the motion by putting all talk about the militia in the subjunctive mode. The resolution passed unanimously, although Lee was so disgusted that, within the delegation, he voted in the negative. Among the Virginians, Lee and Henry were a highly vocal minority; they had not made much headway with George Washington, who pursued a vigorous social schedule and cultivated his reputation for cool courage by saying nothing in debate.

For several more days Congress wrangled over possible instructions to the drafting committee. Tempers flared, and Henry fought bitterly with the conservative phalanx of Jay, Rutledge, and Galloway. John Adams sourly remarked that they were seeing "art and address" worthy of "a conclave of Cardinals at the Election of a Pope," and one evening, dining privately with Adams, Henry vehemently expressed his "horrid opinion" of their opponents. "Their system he says would ruin the Cause of America," Adams wrote in his diary. "[Henry] is very impatient to see such Fellows and not be at Liberty to describe them in their true colours."

With tempers fraying, Adams had to remind Henry of the importance of unanimity in the Congress. This was no shibboleth. For better or worse, the Congress had emerged as the most influential engine yet for pushing colonial opinion, and they could not afford to let the Galloways and Jays wreck its usefulness, especially—from Adams's view—when Boston could not survive prolonged crisis without continental aid.

Boston! The name proved a potent rallying cry but evoked fear and anger, too. Congress regarded Boston with great ambivalence. Many delegates thought that the better sort had allowed the mob to take over the town and pitch it into provocative disorders such as the destruction of the tea. While Boston's punishment had become America's cause, many feared that aggressive action by the Bostonians would plunge the continent into war. The Massachusetts delegates, while maintaining a moderate air, tried hard to convince their colleagues that the mother country had virtually declared war upon the town already and that only heroic restraint by the citizenry had prevented bloodshed. They wanted Congress to sanction an offensive move, either the establishment of a provisional government or armed resistance. Only Henry and Lee, however, seemed to have grasped this point, for the rest of the Congress seemed to counsel nothing more than temperance and fortitude. An excess of zeal, the conservatives maintained, might ruin the cause.

When word came that General Gage had taken steps to make Boston a "garrison town" by fortifying its surrounding hills and entrenching the narrow neck of land connecting the port with the countryside, Samuel Adams prepared a draft letter from the Congress to General Gage that bluntly threatened bloodshed and civil war if he persisted in the plan to cut off Boston. Some of the conservative, petition-minded delegates countered with the suggestion that Congress dissociate itself from Boston and leave Massachusetts to its own discretion. (Later John Adams said he was sorry he hadn't called their bluff.) However, the great majority favored a toned-down letter to Gage urging him to refrain from any provocative action while Congress, as guardian of continental liberty, endeavored to restore "a good understanding with our parent state." To both General Gage and the Boston committee Congress, in effect, had the same message: do nothing to aggravate hostilities further.

Henry took scant part in the Boston debate, once the temper of Congress became clear. In his view stalemate was no solution. By refusing to countenance military preparation Congress was allowing the initiative to pass to Parliament. The newspapers contained rumors that the principal defenders of American rights would soon be "brought over" to England for "inquiries into their conduct" and each week brought fresh reports of troops embarking from British ports for undisclosed destinations.

Unlike most of his colleagues, Henry had no expectation that the trade boycott would work or that the ministry would prove conciliatory. War would break out before the colonies were adequately prepared and public opinion had accepted what Henry now regarded as inevitable. Henry privately tried to reassure the Adamses that the continent would support a Massachusetts resort to arms, so long as it was understood as an act of self-defense, and the Massachusetts delegates unofficially counseled their friends back home to gather ammunition and hold themselves at the ready. "But let them avoid War, if possible," John Adams told his wife, underscoring "if possible" in a way that left no doubt he did not advocate heroic restraint.

By October 12 Congress had completed an outline of its policy. There would be a continental association, pledging colonists to a trade boycott and recommending that local committees be elected in every county, city, and town to enforce it. There would be a "bill of rights," a grand statement in the best Whig tradition that simultaneously would articulate cherished principles and give instances of their violation. Even the cautious delegates favored this bill of rights, which underplayed the problem of taxation in favor of the constitutional abuses inherent in the acts against Boston and couched the provocative question of trade regulation in highly ambiguous langauge. There would be addresses to the king and to the inhabitants of Great Britain but, significantly, none to Parliament. Appeals would go out, however, to the North American colonies—Georgia, East and West Florida, Nova Scotia—that had not yet sent representatives to Congress. Boston would be praised for its resistance and exhorted to remain peaceful. And the Congress would convene again on May 10, 1775, should the situation still warrant.

Once the policy crystallized, however, it still took an additional two weeks for the documents embodying the program to take final shape, and most delegates chafed at the "nibbling and quibbling" required to achieve a satisfactory expression of the unanimity all professed to cherish.

Henry helped only perfunctorily. Responsible for drafting the petition to the king, Henry completed the assignment with little enthusiasm or fuss. He pieced together eight dutiful paragraphs, one of which tried to resurrect a portion of Lee's rejected motion on the militia, and another which borrowed heavily from the dramatic petition against overseas trials he had written for the House of Burgesses in 1769. The draft did contain touches of Henry's oratorical stamp—the ability to cast abstract issues in highly personal terms. "Drive us not to despair," he implored; "urge us not to the last extremity." "Compell us not . . . to that Situation in which All is Gloom & Horror," he reiterated, trying to insinuate the threat of war disfavored by his colleagues.

Congress rejected Henry's draft as unsuitable. John Dickinson (who had caucused with Adams and Lee even before his nomination to Congress in mid-October) prepared a new version—longer, more elaborate, less dramatic and threatening—which the delegates preferred. Henry did not seem put out; he read Dickinson's draft carefully and accepted its terms, smoothing and clarifying at least one paragraph that retained some of the asperity objected to in his own effort.

On October 20 the delegates lined up in Carpenters' Hall to sign the Association and then retired to the City Tavern for "a very Elegant Entertainment" offered by a newly elected, far more radical Pennsylvania assembly. Amid the music and dancing—and the self-congratulatory farewells that poured forth although the business of Congress would not be completed for almost another week—even the Quakers joined in the prayerful toast, "May the Sword of the Parent never be Stain'd with the Blood of her Children."

In a private farewell Henry confided less pacific opinions to John Adams. The two men—so different in talent and temperament yet alike in their strategic vision—had come to admire each other greatly during their six weeks' service. Adams listened sympathetically one night as Henry spoke simply about his lack of formal education and the hard family circumstances that had left him "struggling through life" on his own since the age of fifteen. Henry admired Adams's intellectual breadth and political patience. More than most delegates he understood the self-control the Massachusetts men had imposed upon themselves in the interest of gaining continental support for the dangerously tense position their province occupied.

Neither man thought the Association, petitions, and declarations of the Congress would melt the ministry's heart. Adams understood them as necessary to "cement the union of the colonies" but felt certain they "would be but waste paper in England." Henry agreed that they "would be totally lost upon the government" but felt that they might make "some impression" among the English people. Henry had no illusions that the American cause could be won in the English newspapers, however, for he was convinced that corruption made the British government impervious to popular will. He now wondered if his own congress sufficiently appreciated popular feeling in the colony. Did the gentlemen of substance truly lag behind the country people, or would the issues need further dramatization before the leading Whigs could count upon a general determination to fight? Congress never put the question in this fashion, but to Henry's way of thinking it was the most crucial of all.

Massachusetts, at least, stood ready to fight, and Henry knew it. Adams allowed Henry to read a confidential letter from Joseph Hawley, a western Massachusetts leader who shared Henry's and Adams's belief that Congress should have devised a plan for military preparation. While it would be "madness to commence hostilities before we have a sure plan," Hawley wrote, war would surely be necessary to protect "free government." "We must fight," Hawley concluded. "It is now or never that we must assert our liberty."

"By God, I am of that man's mind," Henry burst out with "an energy and vehemence" that Adams never forgot. Henry's agreement was so complete and so emotional that Adams regarded Henry's expression as a "sacred oath, upon a very great occasion." Henry proved the only man in Congress who, Adams thought, appeared "sensible of the precipice, or rather, the pinnacle on which he stood, and had candor and courage enough to acknowledge it."

Shortly after Henry's passionate meeting with Adams he left for Virginia to attend the pending session of the House. He had to ride home with men who did not share his views. Randolph, Pendleton, Harrison, and Bland all retained hope that reconciliation would come; they had left their proxies with Colonel Washington for the final work on several documents. Henry, however, left his proxy with Richard Henry Lee, the only Virginian who shared his mind on the need for immediate military preparation.

Virginia's Cicero had not had an easy time in Philadelphia. Henry had found himself on the political fringe of the convention, and his powerful oratory had worked no magic, largely because the convention remained cut off from the public opinion from which Henry's words drew their deepest strength. As Henry rode home, the slogan "we must fight" drummed a tattoo in his mind, and he quickened at the prospect of showing the world that "Altho' our belligerent pow'rs are new/[Virginia] has Scipios and Caesars too."

CHAPTER 12

"The Busy Voice of Preparation"

An anxious family waited at Scotchtown. The "sickly season" had touched the people—black and white—with fever, though the children had remained well. Henry's widowed mother, his sister Annie Christian, and her children had left the western country for protection in Hanover while William Christian fought in Dunmore's expedition against the Indians, but Mrs. Henry's mind remained uneasy. "I assure you We have our lowland troubles and fears with respect to Great Britain," she wrote to a family connection in Botetourt on October 15, 1774. "Perhaps our good God may bring us out of these many evils, which threaten us not only from the mountains but from the seas," she said. "My son Patrick has gone to Philadelphia near seven weeks," she added, but "as the affairs are kept with great secrecy," no one yet knew what the Congress would advise.

Mrs. Henry kept silent about Scotchtown's worst affliction, but in an accompanying note Annie Christian complained, "My brother Pat is not returned from Philadelphia yet his Wife is extremely ill." The details, however, proved "too much to write." Sallie Henry's despondency had left her helpless, unable to care for herself and subject to fits of lunacy. Sometimes she had to be put in "a strait-dress" and confined to a ground-level workroom; the family set a black woman to nurse and guard her. Word went round the neighborhood that a crazy woman was kept in a dungeon at Scotchtown, talk later embroidered into a tradition that "Pahtrick" himself passed food to his afflicted wife through a trapdoor in the front hallway.

Henry returned at the end of October to a household in tragic disarray. His very presence comforted his mother and sister, and he did what little he could for poor Sallie. Henry addressed himself to plantation business, preparing for the shortages the Association's embargo would surely entail. He learned that Annie had dispatched their brother Billy to Williamsburg with the maps of Ohio land the Henrys and their brother-in-law hoped to claim, and she had tried to remedy defects in the papers of some of their Hanover partners. Her industry distracted her from worrying about her husband's fate with the frontier army.

By mid-November, however, Scotchtown's gloom lifted with the news that the militia had dealt a great blow to the Indians and that Colonel Christian had suffered no harm. Colonel William Preston, the Fincastle County leader associated in a number of Henry's land projects, relayed a message from Christian that the militia had defeated a Shawnee attack at Point Pleasant, where the Great Kanawha River joined the Ohio. Dunmore, already farther downstream in hopes of parley with other tribes, would be joined by choice troops from Colonel Lewis's command, while Christian's group entrenched at Point Pleasant.

A week after this happy news reached Scotchtown, Colonel Christian himself arrived, still bronzed and worn from the long campaign. Christian's column had, after all, marched to join Dunmore at the Indian Towns, but an express stopped them en route. The defeat at "the Point" had persuaded the Shawnee to make peace, they were told, and Dunmore had concluded a treaty with all the northwest tribes. Some of the Fincastle backwoodsmen, still bent on reprisals, could hardly contain their anger at the sudden peace, and Colonel Lewis felt obliged to post extra guards around His Lordship's tent until tempers cooled.

The great victory, while sparing the Henry family, had cost Virginia more than seventy lives. The Shawnee had fought bravely and furiously, Christian said, but they required several hundred tomahawks to cut saplings enough to carry off their wounded. Christian recounted the battle to the menfolk in exuberantly gory detail and laughingly told how the red men had shouted curses to the Virginians and mocked the militia's fife calls with the taunt, "Don't you whistle now." Christian thought the Indians would honor the treaty, which required them to return prisoners, renounce war on the settlements, and refrain from roaming or hunting south of the Ohio.

The martial fervor stirred by the Point Pleasant triumph played neatly into Henry's intended political campaign. With Christian at his side, he rallied the Hanover militia at Merry Oaks, a popular tavern a few miles south of the courthouse on the Richmond road. Young men, especially, turned out to hear "a very animated speech" from Henry, in which he reiterated his firm belief that the time had come to make military preparations. Henry urged the formation of a volunteer company—an expeditionary force—that would choose its own officers as soon as a sufficient number enrolled. Before Henry's tocsin had completely faded into the chill autumn air, a sizable group of men had lined up to enlist.

Henry could be a very subtle agitator. In private circles he built support by appearing to share secrets. Meeting with some prominent neighbor gentlemen at Colonel Samuel Overton's one evening to talk over the work of the Congress, he held out no hope for reconciliation. Great Britain "*will* drive us to extremities," he said in response to the anxious questions posed by his host. Then Henry looked around the room, as if to assure himself of the company's reliability, and went on in a confidential tone. "No accommodation will take place— hostilities will *soon* commence—and a desperate and bloody touch it will be."

Asked if he believed that the colonies could successfully oppose Great Britain's fleets and armies, Henry replied candidly that he doubted it could be done—"*alone.*" Then he grew animated and jumped from his chair, shouting, "But where is France? Where is Spain? Where is Holland? . . . Do you suppose they will stand by, idle and indifferent spectators? . . . Will Louis the Sixteenth be asleep all this while? Believe me, *no*." The talk of rival European powers injecting themselves into the looming civil war left the company startled. Had talk at Philadelphia really gone so far as to contemplate foreign alliances? Henry implied as much, neglecting to say that others had raised European intervention as a dreadful specter that would propel Great Britain toward reconciliation.

Henry had made his reputation by voicing what others thought but feared to say. "Our Patrick," said a gruff, hard-drinking planter, can "certainly be very uncivil" in his challenge to genteel assumptions. He is "in these times a very useful man, a notable American, very stern & steady in his country's cause & yet at the same time such a fool that I verily believe it w'd puzzle even a king to buy him off." To countless admirers Henry projected an innocent righteousness that, for all its power, made them feel protective of him. Had they known the difficulties he had experienced in making headway in Congress, they would have sympathized with him as a prophet among casuists. While some of the radicals, like John Adams or Thomas Jefferson, fortified their spirits that winter with inquiries into the constitutional underpinnings of resistance, Henry refreshed himself with the confidence born of knowing that he spoke what his countrymen felt. Congress, with its eyes upon London, had tempered its program and had shied away from Henry's more aggressive stance. Yet his own impulse, he soon learned, closely matched the public mood. His countrymen regarded the Congress's statements as a signal for the very militancy most delegates had feared precipitate.

Very little word had filtered back to Virginia during the Congress. Old Landon Carter had heard "through the key-hole" that only the aristocratic New Yorkers were proving balky and that the Massachusetts men had "a great Character." A Mr. Adams's wife had written, during the war scare, that she hoped they would all die rather than live under a "tyrannick Government." "A fine woman this," Carter went around saying, "if the letter was not made for her."

Most Virginians learned what the Congress had done at the end of October when the gazettes published the session's proceedings and major documents. The Association closely followed the Virginia statement of August and occasioned much satisfaction, as did the Bill of Rights and Grievances. At courthouse after courthouse public reading of these documents turned into vivid tableaux of resistance. The crowds listened to the stern measures and solemnly pledged acceptance by "the *sacred ties of virtue, honour, and love to their country*." Then they congratulated Virginia's delegates for their brave work, elected committees of inspection, and—although the Association said nothing on the point—made plans to give the local militia new vitality. "The busy voice of preparation echoes through every settlement," a Chesapeake visitor wrote with some alarm. A young Englishman named Nicholas Cresswell, newly arrived in Virginia to scout western land, heard the king cursed on the streets of Alexandria and saw its militiamen shoot at an effigy of Lord North. "They are all liberty-mad," he thought.

The committee system proved the Congress's boldest stroke. It brought the resistance campaign into the heart of every community by creating an elected body independent of the Crown administration and fully committed to the continental cause. This transfer of authority occurred implicitly in most places, but several county meetings pledged openly that the resolutions of "the AMERICAN CONTINENTAL CONGRESS" would be "the *sole rule of their conduct*, in all matters respecting their *present political engagements*." One farmer put the matter even more succinctly by altering a posted proclamation to read "God Dam the King."

Twenty-two Virginia counties formed committees by the end of 1774, and nearly thirty more followed early in the new year. Many county magistrates and other established leaders served on the committees, which lent the quasi-legal bodies some prestige and protection. The committees gained further popular authority by opening a large number of new seats, thus becoming a moderately democratic doorway into politics for men newly roused to civic participation. More than one thousand freeholders served on Virginia's committees; in Hanover, as elsewhere, the membership proved equally divided between those accustomed to public office, such as Henry's half brother John Syme, Jr., and Colonel Overton, and newcomers, including two Presbyterians who had served on the jury in the Parsons' Cause a dozen years earlier and several freeholders of modest circumstances. (The technique of creating broad local participation meant that, overall, the colonies had put forward nearly seven thousand "leaders" in a few months, a formidable number for royal authority to suppress. Renewed rumors of blacklists and arrests, however, undoubtedly sprang up as an effort to intimidate and retard the popular upsurge.)

The committees asserted jurisdiction over both commerce and public opinion, which they exercised with the zeal of political evangelists. They supervised mercantile dealings and patrolled the river wharves in efforts to control smuggling; they auctioned seized goods and directed the proceeds to relief of Boston; they tried cases of price gouging and policed instances of gaming and other profligacy that violated the Spartan virtue required by the Association. They also interrogated those accused of holding opinions "inimical to liberty" and ostracized or held up to ridicule those who failed to apologize.

The ceremonies of recantation closely resembled the evangelical religious revivals in which sinners came forward to give public witness of their conversion experiences. A Hanover man named Malcolm Hart stood in committee to apologize for saying that "a little Gold properly distributed among the populace" would show the real value of American virtue. Another critic, Paul Thilman, apologized for the "unguarded Heat and Passion" he displayed when others had questioned his attempts "to stir up a Party" of opposition to the committee. Thilman promised henceforth to adhere "most strictly and religiously" to the Association.

In some cases bad-tempered or cantankerous individuals found their intemperate behavior no longer indulged. A man in Fredericksburg had to apologize for saying, "Can't the poor dogs pay their own expenses?" when asked to contribute to a fund for the delegates to Congress. A merchant in Caroline, under the "unsupportable weight of publick Censure and publick hatred," recanted the contumacious act of having pushed a young Negro forward at the courthouse ceremony saying, "Piss Jack, turn about my Boy and sign."

It was the coldest winter anyone could remember, with very sharp frosts and air so chill that spittle froze before it hit the ground. Inside homes and taverns, however, heated arguments raged, for despite the claims of unanimity Virginians still disagreed. The widening breach alarmed people of cautious temperament, and even some of those who believed in the constitutional rights of the colonies had grave difficulty accepting the growing power of the ad hoc committees. The committees censured the disrespectful in order to enhance their authority, and people not yet converted to the cause of resistance charged the committees with encouraging mob rule.

Peyton Randolph advised "the gentlest measures" in bringing "miscreants" to "a sense of their misconduct." The committees, Randolph said, "should take care not to exceed the powers . . . intended to be given them. . . ." Randolph hoped that "rigorous methods" would be used only so that "the public shall not suffer [from] obstinate opposition." In his genteel way, Randolph had become a revolutionary. The Speaker regarded the committees as a legitimate means of emergency self-government, but the governor saw their very existence as an instance of mob rule. When London heard from Dunmore that self-styled committees of safety enforced the edicts of a so-called congress, the colonial secretary declared himself "at a loss for words to express the criminality" of such steps.

Recoiling from the reports of crowds wielding tar brushes and militia companies exercising in the fields, American critics charged that the "Presbyterian rascals" in Congress had sounded the "trumpet of sedition" and had cursed the colonists with bullying committees that smacked of "the popish inquisition." More than one dissident grumbled that he'd rather be ruled by one tyrant three thousand miles away than three thousand tyrants not a mile away. "There is an Enthusiasm in politics, like that which religious notions inspire, that drives Men on with an unusual Impetuosity," one pamphleteer complained, and another grumbled that "to public speakers alone is the government of our country now completely committed . . . the orators of our committees & subcommittees, like those in higher spheres, *prevail with their tongues.*"

In Alexandria the ambitious Nicholas Cresswell felt "obliged to act the hypocrite"; since the committee there turns miscreants "over to the mob-ility [*sic*] to punish as they think proper, and it is seldom that they come off without tarring and feathering. It is as much as a person's life is worth to speak disrespectfully of the Congress," Cresswell concluded, and he resolved to avoid committee censure by appearing "a little Whigified."

The abusive old party terms "Whig" and "Tory" came back into circulation. By styling themselves "Whigs," the defenders of colonial rights identified themselves with the "revolution-principles" of 1689. This legacy, as transmitted through the writings of Sydney, Locke, and Harrington, as well as the Bill of Rights itself, rested upon the compact theory of government. According to this theory, men are created equal and concede authority to government to protect the public good. Kings are neither divine nor invincible, but rather ministers of the people, and if they abuse their authority, the people may (in John Adams's restatement) "resume it, & place it in other hands, or keep it themselves, whenever it is made use of to oppress them." England had gained by resisting the Stuarts, just as the Romans had gained by resisting Tarquin and the Low Countries had profited by resisting Philip of Spain.

The appeal to the Whig tradition also gave a constitutional sanction to militia preparation, for Whig principle regarded a standing army as a grave threat to liberty. Standing armies meant taxation and patronage, both sources of government corruption. A standing army could become a Praetorian guard, owing its allegiance to the ruler and removed from the body of the people. The employment of professional soldiers, moreover, gave a mercenary cast to society and showed that citizens had become too selfish to defend themselves. This moral sloth, this slackened will, made people ripe for the tyranny that concentrated power would inevitably bring. The citizen soldiers who took up arms at their country's call—and returned to private stations when the emergency passed—should be regarded as the great bulwark of the commonwealth, for their power derived from the people. The colonial Whigs justified their turn toward arms in the winter of 1774–75 not only as a measure of self-defense but as a constitutional remedy, a legitimate means for restoring balance to a political system made dizzy by an oppressive Parliament and Crown.

At the end of December 1774, Henry learned that Maryland's provincial congress had resolved that "a well regulated militia, composed of the gentlemen, freeholders, and other freemen, is the natural strength and only stable security of a free govt." Drawing upon the facetious arguments R. H. Lee had used in Congress—that a militia would relieve Great Britain of expense, obviate the necessity of taxation, and render a standing army "(ever dangerous to liberty)" unnecessary—the Marylanders urged that all male inhabitants between the ages of sixteen and fifty be formed into militia companies, armed, well drilled, and "in readiness to act on any emergency."

The militia law in Virginia had lapsed, but the county committees had followed Henry's lead in calling for the formation of volunteer companies to serve under committee direction. In mid-January, however, the Fairfax County committee, at the urging of George Mason and George Washington, used the language of the Maryland resolution to order all able-bodied men to serve in a countywide militia. The committee pushed its authority further by levying a three-shilling tax to be used for the purchase of ammunition and asked the sheriff—an appointee of the royal governor!—to collect it.

Along with news of this bold stroke, Henry received a

letter from Silas Deane in Connecticut that described the "respectable footing" being attained by the militia in all the New England provinces. All the officers had resigned their commissions from the governor, and the companies had chosen new ones themselves. The companies had drafted one-third of the whole to hold themselves in readiness "with Arms, Ammunition, a good Horse, and ten days provision . . . to march at a Minutes Warning." Deane thought twenty or thirty thousand men could thus be assembled at Boston "in Two Days time." Deane expressed great interest in the news of Virginia's "decisive" victory on the Ohio and renewed discussion of the plan to settle Connecticut men on Henry's Ohio lands. Having conversed extensively with Henry while at the Congress, Deane knew that they shared the view that "another Tier . . . of Colonies settled back of Us" would make America "invincible, though the united Powers of the whole World should attack Us." Our descendants, Deane had prophesied, "will give Law, not to North & South America alone, but to the World if they please. This will, & must be the most independent Country on the Globe."

Martial sentiments also came in from the western counties, whose volunteers had won the Point Pleasant encounter. From Fincastle, William Christian, now head of that frontier county's committee, brought a passionate address of "real, though unpolished sentiments" that pledged a fight to the death before a surrender of liberty. The men of Botetourt, meanwhile, declared that they stood "prepared for every Contingency," for "when the honest man of Boston, who has broke no law, has his property wrested from him, the hunter on the Allegheny must take alarm." The frontier spirit stirred Whigs in Piedmont and Tidewater. Fincastle alone would furnish one thousand riflemen, people said, and joined by the other western counties would produce "the most formidable light infantry in the world." The frontiersmen were amazingly hardy and quick, and so dexterous with their rifles that "every shot is fatal." Not one "wishes a distance less than 200 yards on a larger object than an Orange," said Richard Henry Lee, whose carelessness in shooting had cost him three fingers.

By mid-February Virginia looked anxiously to the next

colony convention, which Peyton Randolph had called for March 20, ostensibly to elect delegates for the May Congress but, as everyone knew, to address "other purposes of public security." Upon his return from the Ohio country in December Lord Dunmore had refused to call the assembly into session and later postponed the session until May, at the earliest. With Dunmore in Williamsburg realizing that the powers of his government stood enfeebled and disregarded ("There is not a justice of the peace . . . that acts, except as a committee man," the governor fumed), Randolph prudently ordered the convention to gather upriver in Richmond.

The Hanover committee elected its customary delegates —Henry and Syme—on February 18, but because the turnout of freeholders was small, they adjourned for several weeks before drafting instructions. Although the documents are silent on the matter, it appears that Henry did not attend on the eighteenth because his afflicted wife had died a week or so before. At the end, people said, she had developed a "strong antipathy" to her husband and children and retreated into an unfathomable world of her own. The grieving Henry could not summon a gentleman's stoicism and, the family physician said, pityingly described himself as "a distraught old man."

Somehow Henry gathered himself for the March convention. Richmond offered little to a crowd of visiting politicians. No more than a trading village of six hundred souls at the head of James River navigation, it had two or three taverns, an unprepossessing courthouse, a modest frame church, and several mercantile establishments—wharves, tobacco warehouses, stables—belonging to firms in Glasgow, sprawled across the point of land where Shockoe's Creek spilled into the river. The town's promoters had annexed the hilly region west of the creek, but so far Richmond had not prospered enough to grow in that direction.

Although the town's founder, William Byrd II, had expected Richmond to engross the vast trade of the backcountry, it had not yet come into its own; oceangoing vessels still anchored a few miles south in the deep channel at Warwick, which had aspirations of its own, and a considerable traffic in coal and lead passed through Manchester on the south shore. Richmond's few business streets ran parallel to the river at the bottom of a fairly steep hill, with houses straggling up the bluff. Henry's friend Colonel Thomas Marshall, a tall and rugged planter who had worked his own way up in the world, liked to say that the Scotch factors' houses looked as if "the poor Caledonians had brought them over on their backs, the weaker of whom were glad to stop at the bottom of the hill, others a little stronger proceeded higher, while a few of the stoutest and boldest reached the summit."

The view from the hilltop had inspired Byrd to name his town after Richmond-on-Thames, and he had donated two lots at the crest for the Henrico Parish Church. A spare wooden building with a peaked roof and squat belfry, the town church proved the only place in Richmond large enough to house the one hundred or more delegates expected for the convention. About seventy-five climbed the hill for the brief opening session on Monday morning, March 20, 1775. After a weekend of heavy frost and chill northern winds, the breeze had shifted, and the men mingled in the churchyard enjoying the warmth of a lowering spring day, with southerly freshets blowing up from the river and the roar of the falls (actually seven miles of rapids) sounding like a distant echo of the conversation and hubbub.

Henry knew most of the delegates. Three-quarters had served with him in the House of Burgesses or the August convention. The Richmond meeting had also drawn a number of western delegates unable to attend the previous session because of the looming war. Henry had close ties among them as well, including the pugnacious Lutheran minister Peter Muhlenberg, who represented the German settlers of the Shenandoah Valley. Henry also could count upon Thomas Jefferson and the four Lees—the Whig leader Richard Henry and his levelheaded brother Frank, along with their cousins, the boisterous "Squire" Richard Lee and his stodgy brother Henry. Paul Carrington, Henry's ally in the Stamp Act fight ten years earlier, was there, also a grave widower, but now more cautious than his friend from Hanover. Henry had worked up the famous Stamp Act resolves with old John Fleming of Cumberland; now his son William held his seat and joined the Henry camp. Henry's uncle Anthony Winston also attended and caused a stir by bringing along his indentured servant, a hulking six-and-a-half-foot giant named Peter Francisco. The young man contributed to the feisty mood by hoisting two tavern troublemakers aloft and banging them against each other until they begged for mercy.

The rest of the delegates ranged from elderly Richard Bland, who wore a green eyeshade to protect his failing eyes from the glare, to blond, handsome Henry Tazewell, the twenty-two-year-old scion of an old tidewater family. The old leaders of the House—Randolph, Pendleton, and Nicholas—came, of course, and a sizable military contingent attended as well. Colonel Andrew Lewis, who had commanded the troops at Point Pleasant, was a delegate, along with other veterans of the campaign including William Christian. The delegate from Fairfax, Colonel George Washington, had stopped at Dumfries to review the Independent Company on his way to Richmond, and Washington's second in command in the Monongahela campaign two decades earlier, Adam Stephen, joined him again as a delegate from the mountainous region north of Winchester. Still rugged at fifty-four and as much a braggart as ever, Stephen went around saying that he'd heard that Lord North was threatening to punish Virginia as if it were a schoolboy to be thrashed with a brine-soaked switch. His Lordship may have "a Rod in piss for Virginia," Stephen chortled, but let him just come here and "I would make the meanest American I know, piss upon him."

The belligerent mood suited Henry's purpose. Rumors flew that he would press the convention to assume the regular functions of government by levying taxes and commissioning magistrates to reopen the courts. Not even Massachusetts had gone that far, although Richard Henry Lee had the latest news from Samuel Adams about the successful manner in which their provincial congress had mobilized a large militia force. Boston remained tense, Adams had said, and they expected General Gage to strike a blow against the provincials at any moment. Britain had authorized action against all the congressional leaders, Lee believed, and the recent parliamentary elections had returned Lord North's government with undiminished power. The king's harsh speech at the opening of the new Parliament proved yet again, the Whigs thought, that the ministry would not respond to colonial petitions. Peyton Randolph had heard two disquieting reports. One held that "we are to be treated as rebels and Enemies without any ceremony," and the other raised the hope of repeal on condition "that we pay for the tea and acknowledge the superiority of Parliament." "What is meant by superiority must be properly defined," Randolph declared, "otherwise they may as well pursue their old plan."

On Thursday, March 23, after the convention had concluded two days of approving discussion on the work of the Congress, Henry made his move. The weather had turned cloudy and chilly, with the raw bite of impending snow. Yet when the delegates had crowded into the pewboxes on both sides of the narrow aisle and filled the newly built alcove on the north side, the church windows had to be opened in order to relieve the stifling and oppressive atmosphere.

Henry proposed "that this Colony be immediately put into a posture of Defence" and a committee draft a plan "for embodying, arming, and disciplining such a Number of Men as may be sufficient for that purpose." "A well-regulated Militia composed of Gentlemen and Yeomen is the natural Strength and only Security of a free Government," Henry's resolution began, echoing the words of the Maryland and Fairfax County statements made earlier in the winter. Yet Virginia's militia laws had expired. "The known Remissness of Government in calling us together in a Legislative Capacity," Henry's preamble emphasized, "renders it too insecure in this time of Danger and Distress to rely that Opportunity will be given of renewing them in General Assembly, or making any provision to secure our inestimable Rights & Liberties from those further Violations with which they are threatened."

So that was Henry's rumored plan. Cleverly put forward on the tactical subject of military preparation, it presumed that the convention would—of necessity—act as a government. Richard Henry Lee jumped to second the motion, and a fierce debate ensued. Pendleton, Bland, and Harrison, repeating the arguments rehearsed at Philadelphia, insisted that the time to arm had not yet arrived. Pendleton predicted that Britain would neither repeal the acts nor attempt to execute them by force but would try colonial endurance in a long, drawn-out commercial struggle for which patient fortitude would be the best defense. Nicholas declared that the motion pushed too far; all he intended was "to have error rectified & not to alter or destroy the constitution."

Henry had heard enough. He rose to defend his motion by delivering a sermon on "the illusions of hope." He conceded that it was natural to "shut our eyes against a painful truth" but urged that "wise men engaged in a great and arduous struggle for liberty" not "be of the number of those, who having eyes, see not, and having ears, hear not, the things which so nearly concern their temporal salvation." *He* was willing to face the truth, however anguished, and, knowing the worst, make provision for it.

Instead of the illusions of hope, Henry urged the convention to guide itself by "the lamp of experience." Calmly and solemnly he reviewed the course of the dispute with Great Britain and condemned the rising tone of violence and arrogance with which the colonial petitions and remonstrances had been greeted. Now a "martial array" was dispatched to force them into submission. After all this, Henry said, "we indulge the fond hope of peace and reconciliation . . . in vain."

"There is no longer any room for hope," Henry said. "If we wish to be free, we must fight!—I repeat it, sir, we must fight! An appeal to arms and to the God of Hosts, is all that is left us."

The words sounded "as the doom of Fate," one listener remembered, and the effect was as profound as if the convention had seen the handwriting on the wall of Belshazzar's

palace. "Henry was his pure self," Edmund Randolph said
later, speaking with "his native fire," yet resembling Saint
Paul calling upon the Athenians to turn away from the
worship of false gods.

Henry's voice intensified, and his gestures broadened. No
relief could be obtained from the king, who had become "a
Tyrant, a fool, a puppet, & a tool to the ministry." Nor could
hope be vested any longer in the British people. There were
"no Englishmen, no Scots, no Britons," but only "a set of
wretches sunk in luxury" who had "lost their natural courage"
and "could not look the brave Americans in the face."

He turned aside the contention that the colonies were
still too weak to risk a war against the formidable power of
Great Britain. "Shall we gather strength by irresolution and
inaction?" he asked. "Shall we acquire the effective means of
resistance . . . by hugging the delusive phantom of Hope until
our enemies shall have bound us hand and foot?"

Henry insisted that the colonists no longer had a choice.
"Gentlemen may cry peace, peace, but there is no peace,"
he said. It would not be much longer before "the clash of
resounding arms" would be heard at Boston. War was inevitable, Henry declared, and in a rising voice he welcomed it.

"Let it come!!" Henry said. He let the words float in
the air for a long time, and when the silence grew nearly
unbearable, he made them echo. "Let it come!!"

From the depth of his political frustration and his private
grief Henry summoned a voice and a histrionic strength that
surpassed his own expectations. "What is it that [these]
gentlemen wish?" he taunted as he slumped into an attitude
of helplessness, head bowed and wrists crossed as if manacled.
"Is life so dear, or peace so sweet, as to be purchased at the
price of chains and slavery?

"Forbid it, Almighty God!" he said in a prayerful shout,
as he raised his head and arms toward the high ceiling of the
church. "I know not what course others may take," he said,
meeting with a fixed stare the eyes of the old burgesses who
opposed him, as they had ten years earlier, "but as for me—
give me liberty, or give me death."

He had paused, arms flung outward, as the word "liberty" rang out in the hushed sanctuary; then he smote his breast with an imaginary dagger in the perfect embodiment of heroic Roman virtue. He stood "with all the calm dignity of Cato of Utica," St. George Tucker thought. Another listener, also remembering the story of the Roman who had martyred himself rather than submit to Caesar's tyranny, thought Henry embodied Cato's "unconquerable spirit" and spoke with "the awful cadence of a hero's dirge, fearless of death and victorious in death."

The convention sat in silence for several minutes, for Henry had called them to the bar of judgment, not roused them into military frenzy. With an evangelical emphasis upon personal choice, Henry presented the delegates "a question of awful moment" in which, he said, holding back would be "an act of disloyalty to the majesty of Heaven." Although he conjured up in some minds the lesson of Cato, who preferred suicide to slavery, Henry's posture of "liberty or death" also raised the prospect of revolutionary immortality, of making war against tyranny and, if necessary, sacrificing oneself in a noble cause. Outside the east window, just a few feet from Henry's pew, an ardent young man from Cumberland (already enlisted in a militia company) had hung on every word, and when the speech was done, he sighed, "Let me be buried at this spot!"

At length debate resumed, with R. H. Lee advocating passage in his "frothy," "artificial" style, although, under the spell of Henry's biblical cadences, even Lee managed a scriptural reminder that the race was not to the swift, nor the battle to the strong, but that those were doubly armed whose cause was just. Jefferson also argued "closely, profoundly, and warmly" in support of Henry's motion. The old guard condescendingly tried to amend the motion to read, "Resolved . . . *as the opinion of this Convention*, that This Colony *ought to be* put in a posture of defence &c . . ." As an advisory statement, this might preclude the appointment of a committee and the risky assumption of governing powers. A new voice, however, belonging to a portly young merchant from Yorktown, Thomas Nelson—whose father, grandfather, uncle, and brother had all served in Crown-appointed posts —shocked the moderates, as Henry had not, into realizing how far militancy had spread. As a militia commander, Nelson ardently declared, he would not obey an order that forbade him from repelling an invading army at the water's edge.

Henry's motion passed by a margin of five votes, and Peyton Randolph, pointing down from the reading desk in the tall, canopied pulpit, named Henry chairman of the committee to produce a militia plan. He would be joined by R. H. Lee, Jefferson, Colonels Lewis, Stephen, Christian, and Washington—all representing the majority—and Pendleton, Nicholas, and Harrison for the minority.

The militants already had a plan in their pockets and submitted it (in Jefferson's hand), with committee approval, the very next morning. It called upon the counties to form "one or more volunteer Companies of Infantry and Troops of Horse," "and be in constant training and Readiness to act on any Emergency." The infantry companies, each to have sixty-eight men, would wear "hunting shirts" and carry tomahawks as well as rifles. The plan did not provide for the election of officers or the issuing of commissions, so it remained more a call for volunteers than the creation of an army. The proposal, however, did "recommend" that the county committees collect "from their constituents" by any acceptable method enough money to supply "half a pound of Gunpowder, one pound of Lead, necessary Flints and Cartridge paper, for every titheable person in their County" and that "each Individual" pay a proportionate share of the money. The resolution did not explicitly call for the levy of taxes, but the moderates still tried to delete this clause as objectionable. Henry "flattened their ardor" by threatening more radical resolves that would be "no less than the taking of government into [the convention's] hands." Henry would urge that the convention issue new commissions, appoint its own judges, and reop̱___ the courts, but when the moderates droppe___ ___ion to his defense plan, Henry went alc ___ ___ reaffirming that the courts would stay cl ___ e ended.

Henry's committee report passed unanimously, after which the convention—much to R. H. Lee's horror—resolved to thank Lord Dunmore for his "truly noble, wise and spirited Conduct" on the frontier. Henry and Jefferson countered this praise with a resolution protesting Dunmore's revision of the rules on the granting of western land. The western soldiers received tribute, too, although the convention did nothing but promise "ample satisfaction . . . so soon as Opportunity permits" for the combat pay Henry's Hanover instructions had asked him to pursue.

One important piece of business remained. In the election for delegates to the next Continental Congress, Henry received 105 votes, one less than George Washington and two less than Peyton Randolph. R. H. Lee had 104, Pendleton 100, and Harrison and Bland, 94 and 90. The radicals scored a slight advance when Jefferson was named Randolph's alternate, should the Speaker's deteriorating health not permit such arduous service.

When Henry rode off to Scotchtown on March 27, he could count the convention as a great success. His legislative and rhetorical skills had achieved in Richmond what he could not obtain at Philadelphia: the commitment to armed resistance that the most ardent Whigs now believed indispensable. "You never heard anything more infamously insolent than P. Henry's speech," a Tory merchant in Norfolk reported to his superior in Glasgow. "He could not have been more completely scurrilous if he had been possessed of John Wilkes's vocabulary," the merchant added in an unintended compliment that any Whig would cherish.

Buoyant with success and spoiling for a fight, Henry carried the banner of "Liberty or Death" back into Hanover. "This creature is so infatuated," the Tory merchant heard, "that he goes about praying and preaching amongst the common people." Henry anticipated the advice then en route to Virginia's Whigs from Samuel Adams in Boston. "This is not a Time for us to relax our Measure," Adams said. "Let us like prudent Generals improve upon our success and push for perfect political freedom."

CHAPTER 13

"A Man of Desperate Circumstances"

In mid-April express riders galloped through the greening upland counties with startling news from Williamsburg. A detachment of royal marines, under orders from Lord Dunmore to proceed in the dark of the night, had stealthily removed a large quantity of gunpowder from the public magazine.

An alarmed and angry crowd, beating drums and bearing arms, confronted the governor later in the morning on Friday, April 21. He would talk only with the mayor and the Speaker, and only after they persuaded the independent company to stand at a distance during the colloquy. His Lordship suavely explained that, having had private information about a brewing slave uprising, he thought it prudent, as a trustee of the public safety, to remove the powder to a safe location. Should the citizens desire it returned on some other occasion of need, it might be accomplished in half an hour's time. As governor he would not accede to any request until fury abated and public order was restored.

The crowd knew Dunmore was lying and adamantly refused to disperse until Peyton Randolph and Robert Carter Nicholas, insisting that nothing could be gained by aggravating the governor further, refused to countenance an armed confrontation and persuaded people to go home. They could reconvene later in the day to draft a proper statement of protest. More zealous members of the independent company, however, rode out to neighboring counties in an appeal for reinforcements.

Parties from the counties adjacent to the capital marched into town over the weekend, drilled smartly for a time on the palace green, and promised to return again when the outlying country had responded. By Monday, April 24, the news had spread as far up as Fredericksburg, one hundred miles away, where the Independent Company, already assembled for drill, voted to send new relays of messengers to Colonel Washington's Fairfax Company and the frontier riflemen. The call was clear: join them by Saturday, April 29, for a march upon Williamsburg to recover the powder and secure the magazine. This "first public insult" could not be "tamely submitted to" without prejudicing the common cause and encouraging the governor "to commit more violence" against the colonial ammunition supply. In Hanover and Caroline, counties that lay along the route between Fredericksburg and the capital, the independent companies held themselves in readiness to join the angry procession.

To secure the latest intelligence, three horsemen from Fredericksburg raced to Williamsburg in less than twenty-four hours, where they encountered a rider from Patrick Henry's Hanover group on a similar errand. The town had stayed calm, but it did not take the couriers long to hear about Lord Dunmore's anger. If so much as "a grain of Powder was burnt" at himself or his officers, the governor had stormed, then "by the living God" he would free the slaves and reduce the city to ashes. He had two hundred muskets loaded in the palace, and he'd take the field with them if the Fredericksburg marchers came below Ruffin's Ferry. This was the governor's message: "He had once fought for the Virginians, and by GOD, he would let them see that he could fight against them."

Peyton Randolph took a soothing, genteel view of the situation. "The Governor considers his Honor as at Stake," Randolph explained. "He thinks that he acted for the best and will not be *compell'd* to what we have abundant Reason to believe he would cheerfully do, were he left to himself."

Randolph thanked the up-country men for their proffered assistance but urged that "matters may be quieted for the present at least." Lord Dunmore had given "private assurances" to "several gentlemen" that the powder would be returned, and Randolph could see "no hazard or even inconvenience" in allowing Dunmore to save face. "Violent measures," Randolph feared, "may produce effects, which God only knows the consequences of."

The riders took a letter from Randolph embodying these views back to Fredericksburg the very next day, along with the news that the Speaker would be setting out shortly thereafter for the Congress at Philadelphia and would happily meet the independent companies in each county along the way. (As Lord Dunmore had proclaimed the appointment of delegates "unwarrantable" and ordered the county magistrates "to use their utmost endeavors" to restrain "such an unjustifiable Proceeding," Randolph was not averse to a military escort on his way north.)

Arriving back in Fredericksburg on Friday, April 28, the riders found more than one thousand men assembled from fourteen companies. Roaring with indignation and brimful of the confidence induced by a month of twice-weekly drilling, the volunteers awaited their signal. They wore the popular Virginia uniform: a tough canvas hunting shirt decorated with fringe about the shoulders or waist and emblazoned with Henry's slogan "Liberty or Death." Never had the town seen such a crowd, "every Man Rich & poor with their hunting shrts Belts and Tomahawke fixed off in the best manner." To more than one Tory "the Shirt men" looked like "a band of assassins."

Randolph's message led to a three-day "Council of War." While some officers warned that accepting private assurances about the governor's good intentions offered no security whatsoever, others accepted Randolph's logic and advised that the troops disperse. The debate grew more heated and complicated by another express—this time from the north— which brought extremely fragmentary news about a battle between British regulars and provincial troops outside Boston. By Sunday, April 30, more dispatches confirmed the story: General Gage had sent a detachment to the outlying towns of Lexington and Concord to seize ammunition and arrest leaders of the provincial congress, but militiamen had thwarted the attempt on April 19 and harassed the regulars all the way back to Boston.

News of the skirmishes in Massachusetts had a sobering effect in Fredericksburg. Amid stout cries of "God Save The Liberties of America," the Fredericksburg contingent advised temporary dispersal and a renewed pledge "to be in readiness, at a moment's warning, to re-assemble, and, by force of arms to defend the laws, the liberty, and rights of this, or any sister colony, from unjust and wicked invasion." On "the third day [Monday, May 1] in the evening, we were all draw'd up in ranks and discharged," one volunteer told his brother, adding with the foot soldier's traditional bewilderment, "some promise of the governor's delivery of the Powder."

Fredericksburg sent expresses to acquaint the surrounding counties with its vote, but the news did not sit well. The Albemarle and Orange County contingents decided to advance anyway, while the Caroline men decided to wait until they talked directly with Peyton Randolph. In Hanover, Henry inspired a wholesale rejection of Randolph's appeal.

Henry had greeted the news of Dunmore's seizure of the powder with elation. It would rally the apathetic and rout the cautious, Henry thought. "Tell them of the robbery of the magazine, and that the next step will be to disarm them, and they will be ready to fly to arms to defend themselves," Henry predicted. The news from Boston gave new vigor to his view.

The ministry clearly intended war, and the fighting at Lexington had spilled its first blood. Henry knew that Massachusetts would continue to fight back and that the other colonies would be called upon for support. No matter what the governor told the Speaker, the removal of the powder could only be understood as part of the administration's plan to subdue the colonies. Dunmore would have to be checked before he arrested Virginia's leaders or staged another raid of his own.

No one could seriously believe that Dunmore would ever return what he had taken, Henry argued. The best course would be to make some reprisal upon the king's property sufficient to replace the powder, which might well be needed to defend Boston today or Norfolk tomorrow. Henry wanted to lead a counterattack that would show Virginia's mettle and embarrass the governor; as always, he judged that popular opinion favored such a course. Lodging at the tavern across from Hanover Court House on the evening of May 1, a North Carolina delegate bound for Philadelphia heard nothing but talk of "1500 men being under Arms to proceed to Williamsburg" to "Oblige" Lord Dunmore to make restitution for the powder.

The next morning, May 2, Henry outlined his plan to the Hanover committee, which met all day to consider it in the straggling little river town of Newcastle, laid out with such ambitious hope forty years earlier by Henry's father. In the late afternoon, having secured the committee's backing, Henry, with his customary passion, addressed the volunteers waiting in the street. Cheering his insistence that they march on Williamsburg to demand satisfaction of the governor, the company immediately elected Henry its commander and ceremoniously "invested" him with a "Hunting Shirt." Then they awaited orders.

Henry asked for sixteen volunteers to accompany his trusted friend Parke Goodall on a delicate night mission. Goodall's party left as soon as it formed, with sealed orders to be opened en route, while the remaining volunteers rounded up stragglers for the march to Williamsburg.

With Henry in the lead, the column of one hundred or more men marched that afternoon to Park's Spring and set out at dawn the next morning, May 3, for a spirited march through the Pamunkey lowlands. They moved vigorously, their rifle barrels and tomahawk blades glinting in the morning sun, their voices charging the air with liberty songs and patriotic exhortations in the neighborhoods they passed. Recruits joined in from King William across the river, and when the marchers passed through New Kent Court House at midday they cheered the county committee's vote that the inhabitants ready their arms for the emergency. In the afternoon they clumped across the causeway that bridged the marshy ground below Ruffin's Ferry, followed the Pamunkey until it flowed into the broad reaches of the York River, and then went a few miles farther on the high road toward Williamsburg.

At Duncastle's Ordinary, a popular tavern about twelve miles from the capital, Henry called a halt. The troopers, "all well accoutred" and with "a very martial appearance," bivouacked in the yards and took refreshment from the innkeeper. At Duncastle's Henry expected to rendezvous with the Goodall party. He had ordered it to cross the Pamunkey and Mattaponi by night and surround the baronial residence of Richard Corbin, the king's receiver general. The soldiers would demand payment for the powder from the king's quitrents, and should Corbin refuse, Goodall had orders to take the gentleman into custody and bring him directly to Henry.

While awaiting word from Goodall, Henry broadcast news of his encampment and sent an express to Yorktown, advising the committee and company there to be on guard lest Lord Dunmore try either to secure reinforcements from the Fowey, a man-of-war moored offshore, or to retreat toward the vessel himself. Henry also received messages from the capital. The governor had convened his council that morning and issued a proclamation denouncing "the rapid recurrence to arms" and the unjustified defiance of legitimate executive power. He had threatened the Williamsburg magistrates with the town's destruction if they did not succeed in putting a stop to the march and vowed again that he would put muskets in the hands of his slaves in order to defend the palace. Henry sent the messengers back to the capital with a request that Treasurer Nicholas provide a valuation of the missing stores.

Then Carter Braxton rode into camp. He had come down from Caroline County, where the day before he had stood with Pendleton and Harrison, listening to the "good old Speaker" convince the militia company to restrain itself from marching to Williamsburg. Instead, the company went in the opposite direction, escorting the three Philadelphia-bound delegates as far as the Potomac River ferry. Braxton hoped "on the strength of that precedent" to get Henry to reverse his own course.

Henry, the insurgent popular leader, stared at Braxton, a contemporary in age but his antithesis in nearly every way. Blond, blue-eyed, and elegant, with "refined manners" acquired on a long sojourn in England, Braxton had one of the finest pedigrees and easiest fortunes in Virginia, derived from his grandfather, the fabulously wealthy "King" Carter. Braxton had one manor house on the Pamunkey, but when he married Elizabeth Corbin, daughter of the receiver general who was Henry's present quarry, Braxton built a second mansion downstream, and the couple whirled with "considerable splendor" from one to the other in pursuit of fashionable diversion.

Henry defended his demand for reprisal and grew even more determined to proceed as Braxton, with aristocratic hauteur, combined praise for Henry's zeal with genteel contempt for the unseemly resort to mobbish action. Henry would not turn back; the insult was too grave, the need to dramatize the cause too pressing. Dunmore's raid had demonstrated the wisdom of the Whigs' shift in concentration from constitutional abstractions to the necessity of self-defense, and Henry would not miss so glaring an opportunity to drive the point home. In light of the new crisis in Massachusetts, moreover, any hope of averting a larger-scale war lay in demonstrating the Americans' fighting strength to the ministry. The other delegates might ignore him and ride off to the pressing business of Philadelphia (Randolph and Harrison had steered clear of Hanover on their way to join Pendleton), but Henry would not turn his back on Virginia in this crisis. Popular sentiment favored action, and Henry would provide it; no ardent Whig could defer, at this late date, to the claims of executive authority.

In the gathering darkness Henry and Braxton remained at loggerheads. Then Goodall arrived, with neither receipt nor receiver general. His men had surrounded the Corbin mansion as instructed but learned at daybreak that the officer had spent the night in the capital. Henry resolved to resume the march at dawn, but then another messenger rode in from Williamsburg. Corbin had capitulated and sent £330 in bills of exchange drawn on a London mercantile house as restitution.

Henry refused to accept Corbin's paper, even though Braxton tendered his own endorsement. Surprised and "much mortified," Braxton asked Henry why he "should be refused as indorser for so small a sum." With cool reserve Henry let Braxton know that he doubted "his political attachments, not his ability to pay." If Lord Dunmore decamped to his warship, he might well take all the Crown officers and their connections, Henry said pointedly, and then the paper would be worthless. Henry said he would only accept as endorser "any responsible character of known attachment" to the Whig cause.

Braxton swallowed his pride and rode off to Williamsburg. He found cannon drawn up on the palace green and the governor railing against Henry. He was "a man of desperate circumstances" who had "excited a Spirit of Revolt among the People for many years past" and now attempted to extort money by physical threat. Yet Dunmore made a new threat of his own: if Henry entered Williamsburg, the governor would order his warship, the Fowey, to shell Yorktown and reduce it to ashes. Braxton conferred with the council president, Thomas Nelson, as well as with Corbin and the treasurer, who was outraged at Henry's breach of civility. But the elderly Nelson, whose Yorktown mansion stood directly in Dunmore's threatened line of fire, agreed to underwrite Corbin's bill and volunteered to ride out with Braxton to vouch for the money in front of Henry.

At Duncastle's the sun had just come up and Henry and his legion stood ready to march when Braxton and Nelson rode in, prepared to meet the demand for restitution. Henry accepted their assurances and put the proposition to the company, which "judged [it] satisfactory." Henry took the bill of exchange and gravely wrote out a receipt to Corbin for £330 "as a compensation for the gunpowder lately taken out of the public magazine by the governor's order; which money I promise to convey to the Virginia delegates at the general congress, to be, under their direction, laid out in gunpowder for the colony's use." The delegates would arrange for storage until the next colony convention, Henry directed, "unless it shall be necessary, in the meantime, to use the same in the defence of this colony." Henry signed the document boldly, with his seconds in command as witnesses.

Braxton accepted the receipt and then waited anxiously while the company debated its next step. Since the reprisal would "amply" replace the powder and the cost of transporting it, the men could consider the major part of their mission accomplished, but the Hanover committee had also charged them with protecting the public treasury from retaliatory injury by the governor. Henry had better write a letter to the treasurer offering their services as guards.

"The affair of the powder is now settled," Henry began, "so as to produce satisfaction to me, and I earnestly wish to the colony in general." If the treasurer apprehended any danger, "a sufficient guard is at your service" to escort the funds to a safer place. "I beg the return of the bearer may be instant, because the men wish to know the destination."

Braxton took this unanticipated communiqué back to town. The treasurer, who had fumed all week at the hotheads who had frantically spurned reason and refused to respect the governor's decent intentions, coldly declined the offer as neither necessary nor proper. Nicholas, indeed, believed that the governor—acting for the king—had a right to remove the powder, which, in his view, belonged to the administration. As "a friend to order" Nicholas deplored "the leaven of discontent" that had tried to precipitate a crisis.

Henry's company held different views on the origins of the conflict, but they "judged it best to return home" and await "the farther directions of the general congress, or colony convention." They paraded triumphantly and, once more in Hanover, met detachments from Albemarle and Orange, four nights out and hurrying to join forces. Henry explained the favorable outcome of the expedition and nobly thanked the newcomers for their spirited offer of assistance. The Florentine immigrant, Philip Mazzei, deeply admired Henry's courage and direct mode of address. He looked straight into the faces of the two Tuscan farmers who worked for Mazzei and spoke so warmly that, even without translation, "the eloquent expression on [one Tuscan's] face indicated that at that moment he would not have swapped places with a great lord."

While his Hanover neighbors cheered Henry, Lord Dunmore officially denounced him as a rebel. "A certain Patrick Henry . . . and a Number of deluded Followers, have taken up Arms . . . marched out of their County, encamped, and put themselves in a Posture of War . . . excit[ed] the People to join in these outrageous and rebellious Practices . . . in open Defiance of Law and Government," Dunmore proclaimed on May 6. He charged "all Persons . . . not to aid, abet, or give Countenance to, the said Patrick Henry, or any other Persons concerned in such unwarrantable Combinations . . . which Designs must, otherwise, inevitably involve the whole Country in the most direful Calamity, as they will call for the Vengeance of offended Majesty and the insulted Laws, to be exerted here, to vindicate the constitutional Authority of Government." Dunmore's proclamation stopped short of branding Henry an outlaw. It was both a rhetorical exercise and a bill of particulars for the attainder proceedings he knew the ministry had contemplated.

Dunmore's harsh words did not faze Henry, who made sure that his carefully composed receipt and a full endorsement of his conduct by the Hanover committee soon reached the newspapers. His admirers in neighboring counties—Louisa,

Albemarle, Orange, Culpepper, and Caroline—all prepared resolutions of gratitude within a few days, and these, too, kept lessons of the reprisal fresh in Virginians' minds. Up in Albemarle, Jefferson, who had stayed aloof from the military upsurge, described to his former teacher, William Small, now in London, the "phrenzy of revenge" that had "seized all ranks of people." Jefferson railed against the governor's "incendiary" tactics. The administration had deluded itself into thinking that "a few hotheaded demagogues" had raised the "whole ferment," when actually "the utmost efforts of the more intelligent people [had been] exerted to moderate the almost ungovernable fury of the people."

Henry invariably followed an episode of public action with an interval of private withdrawal, but affairs now moved too quickly to permit such indulgence. He did brood about his critics in Tidewater, however, and temporarily surrendered to self-doubt and the fear that he had gone too far. Just before leaving for Philadelphia Henry implored his friend Frank Lee to defend him in the Virginia convention if "some gentlemen from below" tried to "condemn the measure and misrepresent my conduct." He had "designedly" referred to the convention any question about the propriety of the money figure chosen, lest he be charged with "presuming too much," and he hoped that his countrymen supported "the Moderation and Justice of the proceeding." Henry expressed great annoyance with his opponents' contention that the powder belonged to the king. That was "a quibble," he insisted; the Virginians' taxes had purchased it, and public funds had built the magazine. The king had no right to turn "conveniences necessary for our defence into . . . engines for our destruction."

"I chose to be active in making the Reprisal" against the governor's "Trespass," for the sake of "the public Tranquility, as well as of Justice," Henry wrote, adding that "the hostilities to the Northward would have justified much greater Reprisals." These he "chose to decline" since the Congress would soon meet to face the question of a continental war.

On May 11 a large contingent of Hanover volunteers, headed by Parke Goodall, rode up to Scotchtown to escort Henry on the first leg of his journey to Philadelphia. The procession moved slowly because of the "great number of Addresses & Resolutions . . . sent after him by express Riders & which he frequently halted upon the Road to read and answer." Volunteers clad in hunting shirts joined the escort as it passed through King William and Caroline counties. In Port Royal, at the Rappahannock ferry crossing, Henry received a salute from an Orange County deputy, a short, pale young man named James Madison, Jr., whose father headed their county committee. Henry beamed with pleasure as the nervous youth read his county's address of "cordial thanks" and heard its resolve to oppose in convention any attempt to order the money returned. "We take this occasion," Madison concluded, "also to give it as our opinion, that the blow struck in the Massachusetts government is a hostile attack on this and every other colony, and a sufficient warrant to use violence and reprisal, in all cases where it may be expedient for our security and welfare."

Henry immediately wrote a short reply to the committee assuring it "that nothing called us forth upon that Occasion, but Zeal for the public Good." Then he added cannily that "I can discover nothing improper for the public Eye" in the message and "The Gentm. who are now so kind as to escort me wish it (together with similar Votes of three other Cotys. recd. today) to be printed."

Madison, meanwhile, asked Henry to deliver a hastily written note to his dear Princeton friend, Billy Bradford, whose father served as the Whigs' favorite printer in Philadelphia. In the letter Madison described the reprisal from Henry's point of view and declared that while the other Virginia delegates might disapprove (even Washington and R. H. Lee, Madison believed, had counseled against the Fredericksburg march), Henry's action had "gained him great honor in the most spirited parts of the Country." "The gentlemen below," however, "whose property will be exposed in case of a civil war in this Colony were extremely alarmed lest Government should be provoked to make reprisals." Some of them, Madison added, displayed "a pusillanimity little comporting with their professions or the name of Virginian."

The large contingent crossed the river, amid fanfares from fife and drum, and crossed the neck of land to Mrs. Hooe's ferry on the Potomac. There the company gave Henry more salutes and repeated huzzahs. Mrs. Hooe offered hospitable entertainment and provided, at her expense, boats and hands for the crossing. Only a small detachment accompanied the patriot across the Potomac, for they could hear the fifes and see the brightly colored coats of the Maryland volunteers lined up on the beach, waiting to provide the next link in a display of homage and protection that would reach all the way to Philadelphia.

That city breathed an extraordinary "Martial Spirit." "They have 28 Companies Compleat which make near 2000 Men who March out to the Common & go thro their Exercises twice a Day regularly," a North Carolina delegate marveled. "Scarce any thing but Warlike Musick is to be heard in the Streets." Even the Quakers were "carried away," John Adams said approvingly; "Uniforms, and Regimentals are as thick as Bees." Delegates shopping for drums, fifes, and colors for their companies back home found supplies exhausted and tent makers running up prices for officers' shelters and marquees.

"The Drum & Fife are hourly sounding," Connecticut's Silas Deane wrote to his wife, "& my brainpan, is this moment echoing, to the beat, parading under my Window." Disappointed not to find his friend Henry in Congress, Deane thrilled to the news of Henry's exploit and immediately exaggerated it: "The Southern Colonies are also all in Arms," he told his wife, and conjectured that America had "one hundred thousand [troops] ready to take the field."

Every morning at five the delegates could watch the Philadelphia companies drill. The volunteers wore coats of dark homespun, tufts of bucktail fur decorated their caps, and the word "Liberty" blazed in large white letters on their cartouche boxes. Rifle companies from the backcountry had camped on the edge of the city. Every afternoon, when Congress adjourned, the delegates joined large crowds of spectators at "the groves," watching these "shirt men" take target practice with knives and tomahawks.

On the morning (May 18) that Henry took his seat, Congress learned that a small party of New England men had captured Fort Ticonderoga "without drawing one drop of blood." This conquest at the head of Lake Champlain would protect New York from an attack out of Quebec and, not incidentally, gave Congress two hundred cannon and a large quantity of powder. With the Tory party in New York dislodged from its control of the assembly, that colony now could organize itself against a possible British landing in the city. Yet George Washington, attending the debates in his old French and Indian War uniform, remained cautious about New York's commitment. "As I never entertained a very high opinion of your sudden Repentences, I will suspend my opinion till the arrival of the Troops there," he said.

Other cautious delegates, including the New Yorkers and the North Carolinians, worried about the pace of events and the giddy license released by the martial activity. "Men Women & Children feel the patriotick glow," said William Hooper, "& think every man in a state of Reprobation beyond the power of heavenly mercy to forgive, who is not willing to meet death rather than concede a tittle of the congress creed."

But what was the Congress creed? Henry had walked into a meeting still feeling its way. With the significant exception of Joseph Galloway, who had lost favor in Pennsylvania and fallen into Tory apostasy, most of the first session's delegates had returned. This time, however, Congress had taken on enough legislative dignity to assemble two blocks west of Carpenters' Hall in the Pennsylvania State House, an imposing red-brick hall with a tower handsomely decorated yet so rotted that the city fathers had forbidden the ringing of its bell.

The militants had picked up strength, and Henry's insistence upon armed defense, provocative in October, had become watchword in May. Even Pennsylvania's John Dickinson, who had emerged as the principal spokesman for caution, acknowledged that "the answer to our petition is written in blood." He now concurred in measures that would prepare the continent for war but pressed the view that a new diplomatic effort could not hurt. The radicals insisted, however, that since the war had begun, the colonies could not secure their rights by anything less than a military victory. For the better part of two weeks Congress pulled and hauled at the question, with Dickinson—supported by Jay and Duane of New York and by Virginia's Pendleton—advocating a petition and a diplomatic mission that the radicals regarded as abject. Henry could barely contain his anger. "The Bill of Rights must never be receded from," he insisted. Henry, along with Lee, the Adamses, and the other radicals, had abandoned dreams of reconciliation for the wildly surging hopes of revolution.

But Henry, whose actions had irrevocably declared him independent of royal authority, did not have much influence in Congress. Henry's rashness, Philadelphia Quakers told each other, had "lost him the Confidence and Esteem of most sensible moderate men." His Virginia colleagues regarded Henry with circumspection. Pendleton recommended that they put aside "approbation or censure of the Hanover March," since "the Variety of Opinions . . . makes it prudent to have it Agitated as little as may be, less difference of Sentiment should be wrought into dissentions, very injurious to the common cause." The delegates thought Congress should not "meddle" with the disposition of the money Henry had obtained from Corbin, and they referred it to the Virginia convention. Of course, Pendleton said, "Mr. Henry need not doubt a firm & united protection from all, should any Attempt be made to give serious effect to [Dunmore's proclamation] which I consider at present as Waste Paper, or a mere Subject of Ridicule."

Henry's presence helped remind the Congress of the angry state of public opinion beyond its doors, and delegates from other provinces expressed their admiration for him. "I am not at all sorry that the pent up flame has broke out," said a Maryland delegate to whom Henry delivered letters, adding that the gunpowder controversy in Virginia "will rouze and unite better than all the Arguments & Oratory in the World." But Henry played little role in carving out the compromise resolutions of May 26 that put an end to the tedious debate. These embraced both a program of military mobilization and a petition to the king "not incompatible with a just regard for the undoubted rights and true interests of these colonies."

Henry, impatient with the delays in Congress, took a prudent measure of his own. He decided to get inoculated against smallpox. Reports of an epidemic grew daily, and the "distemper" was rumored "extremely thick" in all parts of town. Inoculation, while not a routine public health practice, had acquired a safe and respectable reputation among the gentry. Philadelphia had not had much smallpox the previous fall, and Henry had put off the matter, but with the number of cases rising daily and the prospect of a slow session that might last throughout the summer, Henry made a discreet withdrawal from Congress. Inoculation required several weeks of seclusion while the patient went through a mild case of the disease induced by laying a thread infected with smallpox into a small incision in the arm. Pain in the back and knees, alternating fits of shivers and fevers, general languor, and the arrival of a modest number of pocks characterized the distemper. John Adams, who had undergone an elaborate "cure" prior to inoculation in 1764, testified loudly to the benignity of his own case, and Henry's ran its course in about two and a half weeks.

Henry returned to a Congress preoccupied with military affairs. On June 8 the delegates attended a field day in which three battalions of soldiers—two thousand men— marched in review. An array of uniforms—homespun coats, hunting shirts, proper green-and-buff infantryman's jackets with crossed leather straps accentuating muscular shoulders—excited the populace, who cheered the "wonderful Phenomenon" of a suddenly formed army of light infantry, grenadiers, riflemen, light horse, and a formidable squadron of artillery.

Duly inspired, the delegates accelerated their pace and between June 10 and 16 enacted a series of measures that created a Continental Army. Fifteen thousand soldiers would be raised—two-thirds to be stationed in Massachusetts, the remainder in New York—and two million dollars in continental currency would be issued to pay and provide for the army. Congress approved a governing set of articles of war and on June 15 appointed Virginia's George Washington as commander in chief of the fledgling Continental Army.

Henry assisted Washington in the assumption of command. The general left for Boston with a host of questions about military organization unresolved and gave Henry the task of procuring answers from Congress. They dealt primarily with the numbers of subordinate officers, the issuance of commissions, and allowances for aides-de-camp, all of which Henry arranged to Washington's satisfaction.

Given Henry's interest in western land, it was inevitable that he become involved in the sensitive question of Indian affairs. Congress feared that the ministry would spare no endeavor to stir up the frontier tribes against the colonists, and Henry served on a committee charged with formulating a program for "securing and preserving the friendship of the Indian Nations." The committee recommended an intensive round of treaty making and suggested that the frontier be divided into three districts with commissioners appointed for each. Henry, Franklin, and the astute Pennsylvania lawyer James Wilson would head the delegation for the Pennsylvania-Virginia section of the frontier, a diplomatic post that, not incidentally, might provide a commissioner with information useful in his own speculative ventures.

The ubiquitous land jobbers regarded Henry as more influential in Congress than he really was, and Henry allowed himself to be courted by rival claimants for the large Ohio

Valley tracts. To protect themselves as the gulf widened between Britain and America, Thomas Wharton's Vandalia group wanted Henry to get Congress to validate private treaty purchases from the Indians, a legal position Henry had already defended as proper to both Wharton and Lord Dunmore. Wharton also had enlisted Dr. Franklin's services, and both Wilson and Franklin had accepted shares in the Vandalia scheme. Dr. Franklin showed Henry a draft for a plan of colonial confederation that would give Congress jurisdiction over the creation of new western territories and confirm prior purchases of Indian lands while forswearing such thereafter. Henry approved the idea, but Congress did not get around to the matter before adjournment.

Congress had more cheering news at the end of June. The forces in Massachusetts had withstood two great charges by British regulars before giving ground on Bunker Hill in Charlestown. They had killed five hundred regulars, including Major Pitcairn, who had commanded the redcoats at Lexington, and wounded nearly a thousand more. Such valor should rebuke the boastful jibes Dr. Franklin had often heard in London that a thousand grenadiers could go through America "and geld all the Males, partly by force and partly by a little coaxing."

Henry had little to do with the completion of various documents that consumed most of July. The petition to the king, a declaration of the reasons for taking up arms, and appeals to the inhabitants of Britain and Canada all received close, interminable scrutiny. "[America] is like a large Fleet sailing under Convoy," John Adams sighed. "The fleetest sailors must wait for the dullest and slowest." Even so, the radicals fumed. By now, they thought, Congress should have fashioned a formal confederation and defensive alliance among the colonies, raised a navy and opened American ports to free trade, advised the colonies to fashion their own internal governments, arrested all Tories, and then opened the door to negotiation. "Is all this extravagant? Is it wild?" John Adams asked, and he answered his own question with an insistence that it was the "soundest policy." "Powder and artillery are the most efficacious, sure, and infallible conciliatory measures we can adopt."

The radical agenda would have to wait until the next session, after the delegates had had more opportunity to judge the public mood. The moderate Virginians needed firsthand acquaintance with the fast-moving events in their province. Lord Dunmore had convened the assembly in early June, but after another skirmish over arms in the magazine, the governor had fled Williamsburg for the safety of a man-of-war. The Hanover men, under the leadership of Henry's brother-in-law Samuel Meredith, marched with other upland companies to guard the capital and nearly captured the governor, who was making a surreptitious visit to his farm outside town. With the royal government collapsed, a new convention had convened in Richmond on July 17, and it would undoubtedly assume de facto the burden of governing the colony and supervising its defense. Henry and the other delegates suggested from Philadelphia that the convention send a delegation to Washington's command post in Massachusetts to learn what they could from that "military school," but toward the end of July Henry grew too impatient to advise from a distance. With Congress winding down, Henry set off for the convention at Richmond, hoping to take command of Virginia's defense. "Make yourselves sheep," he had heard Dr. Franklin say, "and the wolves will eat you." Just before leaving Philadelphia he expressed to General Washington his earnest wish that "many Virginians might see service." "In the Fluctuation of things," Henry wrote with barely concealed ambition, "our Country may have occasion for great military Exertions."

CHAPTER 14

"From the Senate to the Field"

The call came soon enough. Henry entered the Richmond convention on August 9, 1775, and learned that four days earlier the fractious assembly had elected him colonel of the First Virginia Regiment. He had sent word from Philadelphia that he desired a command, but his friends had secured the post only after a spirited, intensely partisan contest.

The convention had not managed its business well. Unlike the previous meetings, which took positions and issued manifestos, this session faced an array of practical tasks that would have staggered even a united, more fully committed assembly. It had to raise an army for immediate service, reestablish the militia on a sound legal footing, and ready about one-fifth of it for the field at a minute's notice. It also had to incorporate the hastily organized independent companies into the military plan, provide arms and ammunition, and finance the war effort out of an economy dislocated and strapped by the trade embargo.

This agenda proved "hard duty," said Henry's friend George Mason, attending his first convention as delegate from Fairfax. Mason, a man of formidable intellect and frail digestion, took the lead on the committee charged with formulating the military plan. The group met for several hours in the cool of the morning and again in the evening, after lengthy convention sessions that consumed most of the day. These sessions exasperated Mason and left him feeling faint and disgusted. "Partys & Factions," Mason grumbled, "ran so high that we frequently had no other Way of preventing improper Measures but by Procrastination, urging the previous Question, and giving men time to reflect."

Other obstreperous delegates drew Mason's wrath as "Bablers." "We are of as many different opinions as we are men . . . [and] are undoing one day what we did the day before," another "greatly disgusted" delegate said. Peyton Randolph, feeble and inattentive in the chair, seemed unable to expedite the business, and he was not much helped by the stubborn pedantry of Robert Carter Nicholas, in charge of the leading committee. The delegates sputtered about the details of war-making because they still had not accepted the political consequences of war.

For three weeks the convention drifted. It argued about whether the colony should raise four thousand, three thousand, or one thousand troops and whether the convention should choose a general commanding officer or allow direction of the army to rest with the senior regimental colonel. If there is to be a commander in chief, "it is considered that the Contest will lye between [the junior Thomas] Nelson and Henry," a delegate reported.

When the vote came on August 5 the opposition charged that Henry "was very unfit to be at the head of troops" since he had no acquaintance with "the art of war . . . and no knowledge of military discipline." Henry's friends countered with praise for their candidate's patriotism and boldness, especially in the gunpowder reprisal. That impetuous business, however, still rankled the lowland gentlemen. They now distrusted Henry because he no longer seemed constrained by their ethic; he had grown too "popular" and could no longer be counted on to play even by the political rules he had, over the decade, helped to redefine. They rallied to the candidacy of Colonel Hugh Mercer, a French and Indian War veteran from Fredericksburg who, as company leader there in May, had restrained the angry contingent of marchers at Peyton Randolph's request. But as a Scot Mercer was subject to the bitter animosity Virginians felt toward the Scotch merchants who had generally spurned the Association and remained what one Tory cryptically described as "Sgnik Sdneirf."

On the first ballot, however, "a great push" for Mercer gave him a one-vote edge over Henry, forty-one to forty, with eight votes going to Nelson, whose soft manners, portly frame, and asthmatic lungs made him the most improbable choice of all. In the runoff Henry picked up enough of Nelson's votes to win by a small majority. "We have chosen our Commander in Chief Pat. Henry," Robert W. Carter told his father, Landon, although technically the election had selected only the colonel of the First Regiment. Pendleton's young protégé, William Woodford, ended up with command of the Second Regiment, and the doting lawyer returned from Philadelphia with a "tent and marquie" of "very genteel fine Duck" for his favorite.

As a commander, "Paterick Henery [is] a very improper person, in my humble opinion, & indeed in that of the generality of the Gentlemen here. But he was chosen by a Party merely thro opposition to a Scotchman," a high-toned young man wrote to a patrician friend in Williamsburg. "However we have this consolation," predicted the writer, "that should troops be sent against us the Continental Congress, or Genl Washington will set some experienced officer over him."

The imbroglio did not end with the election. When Henry arrived in convention on August 9 he did not shrink from bringing lurking resentment to the surface. He informed the convention that he had "purchased a ton wt. of Gunpowder which is now at Baltimore, with the money he got from old Corbin," R. W. Carter told his father. "I imagine it will occasion great altercation and perhaps some battles, as some are too warm. I wish it had never been thought of again, but it seems Braxton insisted when he carried him the money, that the Convention should determine it." Although Carter disliked the prospect of Henry as field commander, he did not want to impugn his patriotism by raking old coals. "I really fear insulting him, as he is very popular & I know his principles," Carter said.

Henry's friends had spent the summer defending his leadership of the gunpowder reprisal against a steady murmur of criticism. The people of Frederick County hoped that Henry "knows *us* better than to suppose any proclamated distinctions, respecting the property of the powder, can ever make us condemn activities so worthily achieved, or forsake the achievers." Others forced John Randolph, the King's Attorney, who was contemplating an extended visit to England, to deny that he had called Henry a common robber. One writer retold the episode in a mock-biblical style, depicting "a certain Patrick, of the tribe of the Hanoverians, a man full of wisdom and knowledge, and beloved by the people" rising up against the oppressive "Rehoboam" and obtaining "shekels of gold" from a palsied and grasping officer.

While the convention had spent nearly a month fashioning military plans that everyone regarded as necessary, some delegates could not bring themselves to accept the powder Henry had purchased. It would somehow taint them with militancy or, worse, demagoguery. After a long debate, the convention voted to send for the powder in Baltimore but to ask the congressional delegation to determine its use. Since the returning delegates had referred the business to the convention and a new slate had not yet been chosen, this dodge exemplified the shilly-shallying behavior that gave George Mason stomach pains.

The convention labored for two weeks more. With the "weighty Members" returned from Philadelphia and Randolph retired from the chair to nurse his health, the pace quickened. As a legislature unauthorized by existing law the convention shied away from calling its proposals statutes but devised the term "ordinance" as a suitably formal alternative. "Every Ordinance goes through all the Formalities of a Bill in the House of Burgesses," Mason explained, and "in every respect wears the Face of Law." Henry assisted in the passage of the ordinance dividing the colony into military districts for the purpose of raising both regular and reserve troops. He took the lead in shaping the convention's favorable response to a Baptist petition requesting that dissenters be allowed to preach to their brethren in military service. He also helped to draft the ordinance creating a "committee of safety" as an executive body to superintend the war effort and ensure civilian control of the military. Henry believed in the principle, but when the convention chose Pendleton as president of the committee, Henry knew at once that their old quarrels would continue into the new offices.

Henry hoped that George Mason would succeed him in Congress, but the reluctant Mason—a widower who considered himself "both father and mother" to nine young children—resisted all the considerable pressure that Henry, Jefferson, and Lee mustered. These ardent Whigs wanted a man of Mason's firmness and skill because they knew that Congress would have to confront the issues of foreign trade and a formal union of the colonies before much longer; indeed, they had copies of Franklin's proposed Articles of Confederation with them and showed them quietly around to their most trustworthy colleagues. Lord Dunmore got wind of "artful" talk among "the knowing ones," and Robert W. Carter, despite his boredom and fatigue, saw "the necessity for honest men being Conventioneers, as many deep Schemes appear to me to be laid which tend in my opinion toward the ruin of our [British] Constitution." When Mason remained adamant and declined nomination in a heartrending convention speech, the Whigs turned to Frank Lee and secured his election over the conservative Carter Braxton by a single vote.

Braxton, for his part, waited until the tag end of the convention to strike back at Henry by proposing that since only fifteen half barrels of powder could be proved missing from the magazine, no more than £112 of the £330 Henry had "forced" from Corbin be retained as replacement cost. Henry had enough strength in the convention to tone down the extortionist slurs that still gave pleasure to his opponents, but the last-ditch maneuver revealed Henry's vulnerability. As a popular hero he had acquired aristocratic enemies, who feared both the direction of his leadership and its chances for success. With Braxton joining Pendleton on the committee of safety, Colonel Henry would likely face a political battle nearly as severe as any devilment Lord Dunmore might have in store.

Henry sought a military command with the same direct-ness and presumption that had transformed him from a tavern keeper to an attorney. He had conviction, he had confidence, and he had an uncommon ability to inspire and persuade. He also had an evangelical combativeness that, in common with most patriots, he believed would confer special advantages upon the Americans in a political holy war. "The riseing world shall sing of us a thousand Years to Come/And tell our Childrens Children the wonders we have Done," ran one regimental song that owed more to the hymnal than to tradi-tional barracks bravado.

Henry had done much to make the cause seem glorious, and he fully believed that he had standing enough to lead a war that would be voluntary, virtuous, enthusiastic, and short. In convention his critics laughed up their sleeves when a sup-porter innocently said that he was satisfied because Henry would never have solicited a command had he not thought himself qualified. But this anonymous delegate expressed the common view that in the choice of commanders force of character counted more than training. "In the beginning of a War . . . where the martial Spirit is but just awakened and the People are unaccustomed to arms, it may be proper and neces-sary for such popular Orators as Henry . . . to assume a military Character," John Adams declared. Yet even if he were a good soldier, Adams thought, Henry would be a better statesman: "Henrys Principles and Systems are . . . conformable to mine."

But the issue of experience could be exaggerated. Few men in the colonies had fought against well-drilled European regular troops, and even fewer had served as officers in the British corps. Washington and the other veterans of Brad-dock's wilderness campaign had learned about problems of supply and the fearful rigors of warfare, but, twenty years later, some of the lessons could be only dimly remembered.

Certain of his ability to learn quickly, Henry approached military command more with a speculator's daring than with a cadet's ardor. Frustrated in Congress, he gambled that the chief Virginia command would give him new influence and power. Unlike his colleagues among the Whigs—Lee, Adams, and Jefferson—whose minds had raced ahead to the excitement of shaping new governments, Henry preferred an immediate challenge to a theoretical one. For a full year he had pressed the necessity of armed defense, and now honor, ambition, and his dramatic political style all led him to the theater of war. But the regular army would be different from an improvised march of volunteers, and if the conservatives suspected him as a popular leader, they feared him even more as a potential Caesar in a hunting shirt.

Henry formally took up his military office on September 18, 1775. Standing before the committee of safety, which had convened for a week-long meeting in Hanover Town, Henry swore to be "faithful and true to the colony and dominion of Virginia," to defend "the just rights of America," and to disband his troops when so ordered by the convention. Then Pendleton handed him a parchment commission signed by the nine members present. It declared that the convention had designated him "colonel of the first regiment of regulars, and commander in chief of all the forces to be raised for the protection and defence of this colony," and it empowered him to "resist and repel all hostile invasions, and quell and suppress any insurrections which may be made or attempted against the peace and safety of this his majesty's colony and dominion." He would serve "during the pleasure of the Convention, and no longer," and he would "pay due obedience to all orders and instructions . . . from the Convention or Committee of Safety." The committee authorized a two months' advance of pay (at twenty-five shillings a day, this came to seventy-five pounds). They held long discussions about recruiting and supplies and the best means of keeping Dunmore's offshore raiders at bay. Then Henry departed for Williamsburg.

The volunteer companies that had restlessly guarded the capital all summer marched out in force to meet Henry and escort him to town. They "paid him every mark of respect and distinction in their power," and Henry addressed himself to the formidable task of creating a unified command out of the miscellaneous crowd of independent gentlemen and new recruits that surged rambunctiously about him. Henry ordered that a regular encampment be established on the broad plain beyond the college and set up procedures for receiving and victualing new companies as they arrived.

Henry's popularity gave a great boost to the recruiters, as they roamed the new military districts offering twenty-shilling bounties to all free men "at least five feet four inches high, healthy, strong-made & well limbed, not deaf or subject to fits." Spirits ran high. So many riflemen insisted upon going in one company that the officer asked recruits to fire at a nose-shaped target nailed to a tree at 150 yards. The first forty men to fire had blown the nose to flinders, people said, and by the time the company was filled, the target board was shredded, too. In Alexandria, Nicholas Cresswell found "the people . . . ripe for a revolt, nothing but curses and imprecations against England, her Fleets, armies, aand friends. The King is publicly cursed and rebellion rears her horrid head."

Yet target practice and raucous shouts could not make an army. As the feisty companies marched into Williamsburg, Henry had to meld them into a unified fighting force. The only model people knew—the British army—held itself together by Draconic discipline, meted out by aristocratic officers to the vagrant poor who filled the ranks. The Whigs, by contrast, prided themselves on the virtuous quality of American volunteers. They believed that native idealism and frontier hardiness could prevail against the British war machine and, in the beginning anyway, thought the mutual cooperation demonstrated in local committee work would give adequate strength to their army.

Even so, a concern for fundamentals underlay Henry's orders. No one really knew the routine of a military day, and the troops had to be taught what the drumbeats signaled. Junior officers had to be endlessly reminded of their responsibility for their troops' cleanliness and health. "A particular Observance of Orders is Expected from the Officers and Soldiers for their own Safety," Henry said repeatedly, "and publick Good Demands strict Discipline." Recognizing that "some irregularity" had to be expected from "young Recruits," Henry insisted that laxness be corrected as soon as possible. "The Health of the Soldiers Greatly Depends on the Cleanliness of the Camp," he had to explain. "The Tents, Streets, and Entrenchments are to be Clean, the Necessary Houses are to be cleaned once in two days, and the Camp Swept once every day."

Until enough tents and straw could be found, some troops slept out in the open, while some officers casually found rooms in town. Quartermasters worked "in a Frett" to round up wagons and teams, cloth, beef, pork, flour, shovels, kettles, and canteens. Henry had to ask again and again for officers to provide lists of the cloth needed to make haversacks and shot pouches. He found such "repetition of Orders . . . very Painful."

A shroud of wood smoke from the cooking fires enveloped "college camp" much of the time. The sentries chattered loudly on duty, and stragglers roamed the camp long after retreat had sounded. Soldiers wandered off without leave to shoot ducks, sport with women, bedevil the college professors, or lounge annoyingly about the town. Henry had to declare numerous times: "It is expected that the Officers will Remain in Camp Constantly as possible, in order to Exert their Un-remitted Endeavors to preserve Order and Decorum & pro-mote Discipline." The officers also had to be reminded to see to the men's health. The tents had to be kept dried, and bodies and clothes washed. The brave hunting shirts readily bred lice, and those afflicted used applications of lard to quell the itch. Since country men, unaccustomed to crowds, recognized no need to modify their customary ways of "easing them-selves" wherever nature called, the camp stank powerfully of excrement. "The men are again forbidden to ease themselves, Except at the Necessary Holes, & those to be covered once in two Days," Henry had to remind the camp.

The companies spent one hour each day learning "the usual exercise," the repetitive drilling by which troops learned to advance and retreat, fire and reload, while maintaining fixed position in rank and file. Unarmed men practiced marching and borrowed weapons for instruction in the drill. The un-trained volunteers who had camped all summer at Waller's

Orchard east of town had to be taught in small squads and then integrated into "the Grand Squade" as they became competent. No one expected fresh troops to attain the fearsome precision of the British regulars, but even with a simplified system of commands, the companies remained ragged. Henry ordered that three hours a day be spent "in Learning the Discipline of Woods Fighting," which pleased the western riflemen and which gave William Christian, now Henry's second in command, an opportunity to apply the lessons of the Point Pleasant campaign.

The logistics of military supply caused endless vexation. Muskets had to be inventoried and repaired, and soldiers had to make do with the firing pieces they had brought from home until the committee could issue something better. Powder horns had to be found and powder distributed, but the men had to make their own shot bags before they could draw buckshot, cartridges, lead, and flints. The work went slowly. On October 21, a month after taking command, Henry urged "that the Officers . . . by their Diligence Surmount every Obstacle in Getting each Soldier fixed with a powder horn & Shot Bag. This order has often been Repeated," he said. It took several weeks for the companies to make reports on the state of their equipment, and at the end of October Henry issued a general order instructing the captains and subalterns to read aloud at roll call "all such orders . . . which Concern the Soldiers & Explain such parts of them as Relate to their Conduct, so that none may Pleade Ignorance."

These halting preparations took place in a capital made jittery by rumors that Lord Dunmore's tiny squadron of vessels would soon be reinforced by frigates dispatched from Boston. Henry regularly sent out detachments of riflemen to reconnoiter the creeks and maintain patrols at the ferry landings, but the neighborhood remained quiet. Except for a quick stab at Hampton, which was repulsed by a detachment of Culpepper riflemen, Dunmore concentrated his raids on the southern side of the James in the vicinity of Norfolk. Dunmore had armed some runaway slaves and, rumor went, had begun to seize property and slaves from "rebel" sympathizers. As a port town, Norfolk harbored a good many Toryish merchants, and it seemed likely that Dunmore might take the town and make it his new capital and base of operations.

With more than eight hundred regulars in his command by late October, Henry felt the time had come to press Dunmore by moving to defend Norfolk. He spoke with the committee of safety, which deliberated for several days before issuing its orders. Henry would remain in the rear while Woodford led an expeditionary force to Norfolk with broad orders "to be attentive to the force and motions of the enemy, and act offensively or defensively, as your prudence may direct for the good of the common cause."

The committee of safety, working with only six of its eleven members in Williamsburg, had bypassed its commander in chief to give the war's first prized assignment to the protégé of the committee's presiding officer. (Woodford's company marched to drum, fife, and colors presented as Pendleton's gift.) Henry had no friends on the committee, since illness kept both George Mason and Thomas Ludwell Lee away, and he had two powerful antagonists in Pendleton and Carter Braxton. Richard Bland had grown old and feeble, and Dudley Diggs carried no more weight than he had on the old committee of correspondence. Only the committee vice-president, Jefferson's young friend John Page, an aristocrat like Braxton but the only member of the Governor's Council who was Whiggish enough to rebuke Dunmore's seizure of the powder, had much regard for Henry.

Partisanship on the committee reached into the army as well. Henry felt obliged to admonish the officers in each regiment to show "the same Regard and Respect" to their counterparts in the other regiment that they extended to their own. "This is done," Henry said, "to abolish all party Distinctions." However, meeting without Henry, a group of his regimental officers complained to the committee that the imminent departure of the Second Regiment would leave the capital too thinly defended. The committee took umbrage at this "mark of Suspicion" upon its judgment, and in a stern letter to Henry from John Page pronounced as "irregular" and "extraordinary" a "Council of Officers, if it may be called so" that would presume to meet without either its commander or officers from the rival regiment.

As the expedition made ready, Virginia heard the sad news that Peyton Randolph had died of apoplexy on October 22 while attending the Congress in Philadelphia. Hailed more than once as "the father of his country," Randolph's death came as a sobering reminder that the Whigs had committed themselves to mortal struggle. Henry ordered that all officers "immediately provide themselves with Crape and go in mourning for . . . our late worthy & Patriotic Speaker."

Then more grim news arrived. On November 7 Lord Dunmore declared martial law and "raised the royal standard," which meant that all who would not bear arms for the king now might be indicted as traitors and rebels and be liable to forfeit life and property for their crimes. Dunmore also declared that all slaves belonging to rebels would be freed if they fought for the king. In Norfolk a rump council, alarmed by rumors that Patrick Henry was advancing with five hundred shirt men to burn their town, swore allegiance to the Crown and petitioned Lord Dunmore to land and protect them. The emboldened Tory merchants in Norfolk cursed the provincial troops as "lawless banditti" and mockingly declared their sorrow that Peyton Randolph had not lived long enough to be hanged.

Woodford ferried his advance companies across the James in mid-November, while Henry obeyed his orders to put his troops in winter quarters, using "the Capitol & other such Houses" as seemed necessary. The committee recessed briefly, and Pendleton went off to the mountains "for a little bracing up." In his absence Henry took the liberty of advising the counties of Dunmore's proclamation, which he termed "fatal to the publick Safety." Henry recommended "early and unremitting Attention to the Government of the SLAVES" in order to counteract Dunmore's offer of freedom: "Constant, and well directed Patrols seem indispensably necessary."

(Dunmore had lived in Virginia long enough to understand how the force of arms held the institution of slavery in place. His stark threat of slave insurrection roused the Whigs to the furious indignation of men hoist on their own petard. The planters doubled their internal defenses and industriously propagated tales of Dunmore's cynical duplicity. People said that the governor would leave the aged and infirm behind and ship the blacks who fought for him off to the West Indies when he had no more need of them. Even those who had tried to stay out of the political contest would "resent the pointing of a dagger to their Throats through the hands of their Slaves," Archibald Cary predicted to R. H. Lee; Dunmore had now "involved his friends as well as others in the general danger.")

All through November Colonel Henry waited to hear from Woodford but received no reports. Woodford informed John Page on November 26 of his progress toward Norfolk and the situation of forces there, and he casually asked Page to convey the news to Henry, if he had returned to town from a reported visit home. Henry let this slight pass, but when another ten days went by without a direct report from Woodford—and with a new session of the convention ready to convene in Williamsburg—he could bear the snub no longer.

On December 6 he dispatched a special messenger to Woodford with a polite note. "Not hearing of any dispatch from you for a long time, I can no longer forbear sending to know your situation, and what has occurred," Colonel Henry wrote. "Every one, as well as myself, is vastly anxious to hear how all stands with you. . . . But I wish to know your situation particularly, with that of the enemy, that the whole may be laid before the convention now here. The number and designs of the enemy, as you have collected it, might open some prospects to us, that might enable us to form some diversion in your favour."

Woodford, it turned out, had addressed four reports that week to Edmund Pendleton, now the presiding officer of the convention, in which he described a standoff at Great Bridge, where a causeway spanned the marshy Elizabeth River on the main road to Norfolk. Dunmore had built a fort on the Norfolk side and manned this "hogpen" (as the Virginians called it) with several hundred Negroes and Tories. Woodford had entrenched his troops in opposition but did not feel he had enough men for an attack. Pendleton had advised him to take few risks and wait for the reinforcements reportedly coming from North Carolina. Woodford, however, requested that "the greatest part of the first regiment" be sent to him, if the defense of Williamsburg permitted.

On December 7 Woodford answered Henry's express by referring him to the letters previously written to the convention, "which no doubt they will communicate to you, as commanding officer of the troops at Williamsburg." In this casually insubordinate way Woodford indicated that, while at Norfolk, he would not recognize Henry as his commander in chief. "When sent to command a separate and distinct body of troops, under the immediate instructions of the committee of safety—whenever that body or the honourable convention is sitting, I look upon it as my indispensable duty to address my intelligence to them, as the supreme power in this colony." While pledging harmony, Woodford went on to complain about the pitiable condition of his troops "situate in mud and mire" and supplied only slowly and shabbily from the capital. "Most of those arms I received the other day from Williamsburg are rather to be considered as lumber, than fit to be put in men's hands, in the face of any enemy," Woodford told Henry, in language harsher than any he directed to the committee.

Woodford's deliberate slap infuriated Henry. He complained to the committee of safety, only to find that Pendleton fully supported Woodford with a complicated legal argument. Pendleton found several ambiguities in Henry's hastily drawn commission and discovered a clause in the defense ordinance that gave to the committee ultimate control over troops marched to different parts of the colony. In Pendleton's view Henry had no clear title as chief commander. Henry did not dispute the committee's final authority but insisted that the commonly recognized order of command should be observed. When the committee remained indifferent to his complaint, Henry threatened to take the matter directly to the convention.

An old friend of Henry's, the respected Fredericksburg

attorney Joseph Jones, intervened. Jones advised Henry "to treat the business with caution and temper, as a difference at this critical moment between our troops would be attended with the most fatal consequences." Jones sympathized with Henry's sense of "ill-treatment" and convinced him that Woodford would submit to a "just and reasonable solution." After all, Jones pointed out, Woodford had agreed to defer to Colonel Howe, who had arrived at Great Bridge with his North Carolina troops. Howe held continental rank, which gave him precedence, and Woodford had heeded Pendleton's advice not to allow the common cause to be "interrupted by Punctilios of no real consequence." But Pendleton had encouraged Woodford's insubordination to Henry, and Pendleton had raised the dispute to a constitutional plane. It now required the convention's determination, Henry insisted. Jones asked for more time and wrote to Woodford, tactfully suggesting that Woodford's correspondence be directed through Henry. To Woodford, Jones emphasized that the problem might be short-lived, since plans were under way to integrate the Virginia regulars into the Continental Army.

News from Great Bridge made it impolitic for Henry to lodge his protest with the convention. Dunmore's troops had rashly charged out of the hogpen on the morning of December 9 in an ill-timed attack on the Virginians' camp. Woodford's troops repulsed the charge, killing its leader, Captain Fordyce, and seventeen regulars, while sustaining no serious injuries themselves. The British abandoned the fort the next day, and Woodford (joined by the Carolina men) stood poised to regain Norfolk. Great Bridge "was a second Bunker's Hill, in miniature," Woodford exulted, "with this difference, that we kept our post."

Woodford's victory aggravated Henry's sense of insult, but now he could say nothing against the man without appearing to be spiteful. With Henry's friend Joseph Jones added to the committee of safety, a face-saving compromise emerged. The committee resolved, unanimously, "that Colonel Woodford, although acting under a separate and detached command, ought to correspond with Colonel Henry, and make returns to him at proper times, of the state and condition of the forces under his command; and also that he is subject to his orders, when the convention, or the committee of safety, is not sitting, but that while either of those bodies are sitting, he is to receive his orders from one of them."

The mild rebuke to Woodford, however, could not mask the diminution of Henry's power. He would be the titular commander in chief, but in practical terms he would not have direction of any regiment except his own, so long as Virginia governed itself with its present machinery. Either the convention or its executive arm, the committee, would always be in session. The committee regarded the compromise as an interim solution, for it fully expected Congress to name a new "general officer" if, as expected, the six newly authorized Virginia regiments were taken into the Continental Army. Pendleton told Woodford that the committee would not "intermeddle" in that matter, "lest it should be thought propriety requires our calling or rather recommending our present First Officer to that station. Believe me Sir The unlucky step of calling that Gentleman from our Councils where he was useful, into the Field in an Important Station, the duties of which he must in the nature of things, be an entire stranger to, has given me many an anxious and uneasy moment." Yet Henry had "done nothing worthy of degradation and must keep his Rank," Pendleton admitted, although he believed it cost Virginia "the Service of some able officers, whose Honor and former Ranks will not suffer them to Act under him."

Henry realized that he would get no further in the military, and he waited for a propitious time to resign. On a routine inspection of the defenses at Hampton, he had the good fortune of directing privateers to capture two merchant ships intended for Dunmore. The raid netted a large quantity of precious salt and gave Henry's command a modest achievement. He reported the affair to Pendleton in terse, correct dispatches but declined to appear before the committee personally, claiming "an indisposition."

On New Year's Day 1776 a skirmish between Woodford's regiment, now encamped in Norfolk, and Dunmore's offshore batteries led to the shelling of the town. Three days of looting and burning ensued, in which the restive Virginians wildly participated, although Woodford concealed this from the convention and allowed Norfolk's destruction to be blamed entirely upon Dunmore. The governor's fleet, each ship crammed with Tory refugees from Norfolk, tried to sustain itself by foraging raids upon the eastern shore until the much-rumored reinforcements might arrive. Meanwhile, Dunmore tried the diversion of using Richard Corbin as an emissary for "peace talks" with the committee.

In this lull, toward the end of February, Henry resigned. Congress had taken six of the nine proposed Virginia regiments into its army, and Henry was offered a continental commission as colonel of the First Regiment. He had no chance at the brigadiership, which went, justifiably enough, to Andrew Lewis, the hero of Point Pleasant. Given the opposition to Henry in Virginia, his friends in Congress could not afford to press his case, and Washington, too, thought that Henry ought to step aside. "I think my countrymen made a capital mistake, when they took Henry out of the Senate to place him in the field," Washington wrote; "and pity it is that he does not see this, and remove every difficulty by a voluntary resignation."

Henry did not go quietly. His officers put on mourning bands and begged their "father and General" to stay, although they applauded his "spirited resentment to the most glaring indignity." At a tearful farewell dinner at the Raleigh, Henry thanked them for their "spirit, alacrity, and zeal" and closed tenderly by saying, "I leave the service, but I leave my heart with you." A "tumultuous" crowd of soldiers interrupted the ceremonies to demand their discharges, too, "declaring their unwillingness to serve under any other commander." Henry had to spend the rest of the night going from one barracks to the next with William Christian persuading the troops to remain on service. "His honor alone was concerned," Henry insisted, and he promised that "although he was prevented from serving his country in a military capacity, yet his utmost abilities would ever be exerted for the real interest of the United Colonies."

The soldiers "reluctantly acquiesced," although Henry's resignation made what Pendleton sourly called "a noise in the Country" for a few weeks afterward. Ninety officers, including many from Woodford's regiment, signed an address in praise of Henry's leadership against the oppression "your eloquence first . . . taught [us] to resent, and your resolution led forward to resist." They hoped that he would continue in public service and urged him to disregard the manner in which "the envious undermine an established reputation." Henry's opponents minimized his departure as a fit of pique at being passed over for continental promotion; he had lost "the fringe of Commander in chief," Pendleton scoffed, and would lose the "Headquarters Trimmings" too.

But a militia captain in Williamsburg said everyone knew Henry's resignation was "occasioned principally by his not being treated with that politeness which he had a right to expect from the committee of safety." "An Honest Farmer" also saw through the attacks and told the *Gazette* that "envy sought to bury in obscurity his martial talents" and "fettered" Henry "with only an empty title" and "the mere echo of authority."

More than any other Virginian, Henry embodied resistance to tyranny and the political change that now verged on revolution. Yet personality alone would not carry the struggle forward. The colony quickly found that it could not maintain its own army; the war would require more central, even professional direction, for the ideal of the virtuous armed citizen would not be adequate in a protracted continental struggle. The colony also required a stronger set of institutions than the makeshift committee system; the struggle over Henry's command demonstrated that the leaders had reached the limit of improvised political cooperation. Henry had badly miscalculated, for his military post, rather than enhancing his voice, had put him on the defensive and hobbled his influence. He had excelled in political mobilization, and it would be in the political forum that he would reclaim his reputation as "the able statesman, the soldier's father, the best of citizens, and liberty's dear friend."

CHAPTER 15

"I Own Myself a Democrat"

"The time *hath found us*," a pamphlet entitled *Common Sense* announced in January 1776. Offering "nothing more than simple facts, plain arguments, and common sense," this writer fashioned the most compelling argument yet made for continental independence. Henry, along with a hundred thousand other readers, thrilled to find his deepest thoughts expressed in print. "The period of debate is closed," *Common Sense* emphasized; "a new era for politics is struck." "Arms as the last resource decide the contest," and the hopes we entertained before "the commencement of hostilities" (at Lexington in April 1775) are now as "useless" as last year's almanacs.

Yet the war had settled into stalemate almost as soon as it had begun. Washington's raw continental forces had kept General Gage besieged in Boston, but Congress's hope for the quick military conquest of Quebec had ended in retreat. In March 1776, Gage, too, retreated—to the British base at Halifax, Nova Scotia—but the American command fully expected him to return as part of the major British force expected by the summer.

In the spring of 1776 the continental battle remained a political one. *Common Sense* fired the imaginations of the committed by joining the issues of independence and democratic government. The pamphlet's argument rested upon the natural ability of all people to reason and think for themselves. On that foundation, which reached deep into the dissenting traditions of both evangelical religion and Whig politics, the writer boldly attacked the idea of monarchy as tyrannical and unnecessary. Kings did nothing more than give away jobs and make war, he wrote: "Of more worth is one honest man to society, and in the sight of God, than all the crowned ruffians who ever lived." *Common Sense* mocked the idea of the "divine right" of kings, irreverently described William the Conqueror as a "French bastard" who had mobbed the English throne with his "armed banditti," and castigated George III as "the royal brute of Britain."

Having stripped the mystique from royalty, the pamphlet insisted, "A government of our own is our natural right," and it emphasized that simple representative assemblies elected under law would be adequate government for a virtuous, republican people like the Americans. Anything short of independence and republican government would be "patchwork" that only "leaves the sword to our children." "There is something very absurd in supposing a continent to be perpetually governed by an island," the writer argued, for just as nature made satellites smaller than planets, so did nature indicate that England belongs to Europe and "America to itself." The American cause, *Common Sense* prophesied, would become the cause of freedom itself. "Every spot of the Old World is overrun with oppression . . . O! ye that love mankind," the writer pleaded, "prepare in time an asylum for liberty. . . . the birthday of a new world is at hand, and a race of men, perhaps as numerous as all Europe contains, are to receive their portion of freedom from the events of a few months."

Common Sense made "a great noise" in Virginia, the Tory Nicholas Cresswell reported; "Nothing but Independence will go down. The very Devil is in the people." He regarded the pamphlet as "one of the vilest things that ever was published to the world. Full of false representations, lies, calumny, and treason, whose principles are to subvert all Kingly Governments and erect an Independent Republic. I believe the writer to be some Yankey Presbyterian, Member of the Congress."

From Boston, where he was still holding the British regulàrs under siege, the Congress's "generalissimo" predicted: "The sound doctrine and unanswerable reasoning contained in the pamphlet 'Common Sense' will not leave numbers at a loss to decide upon the propriety of a separation." Washington's aides proved even more emphatic. "Shall we never leave off debating and *boldly declare independence?* That and only that will make us act with spirit and vigor."

Within the Congress, however, *Common Sense* did not prevail. The Adamses and the Lees pushed hard for three points: a declaration of independence, a formal organization of the colonies into a defensive league or confederation, and a commercial alliance with a foreign power (preferably France) in order to obtain vitally needed supplies. Without such steps, they argued, Congress could not successfully prosecute the war it had realized it must fight. Yet, as Henry's ally Thomas Nelson, Jr., wrote to Virginia's John Page, these issues "have been but gently touched upon. . . . Independence, Confederation & foreign alliances are as formidable to some of the Congress, I fear to a majority, as an apparition to a weak enervated Woman. . . . Would you think that we have some among us, who still expect honorable proposals from [the] administration." Styling himself "an infidel in Politicks," Nelson added the flourish, "Away with such squeamishness say I."

The excitable Page, who tended to side with Henry and Lee politically, worried that the favorable consequences of independence, especially a boost in morale and the possibility of foreign aid, would be realized too late. "Our Army is but a handful of raw undisciplined Troops indifferently armed, wretchedly clothed, & without Tents or Blankets," he told R. H. Lee. Worse yet, "Our People [are] discontent at Henry's resignation," others annoyed that troops are moved from their counties, and some timid souls lulled into "a Stupid Security" by "the Tales" of impending peace talks. The committee of safety had moved too cautiously, Page thought, and had not adequately worked to procure salt and gunpowder or mobilize troops in the best positions. "God knows what will be the consequence of a vigorous Push made by a Fleet or 6 or 7 regiments!"

General Charles Lee, the land-hungry, eccentric English soldier of fortune whom Congress had assigned to oversee the military effort in the southern colonies, shared Page's view about the committee of safety. The members, Lee insisted, had dealt too gently with Virginia's Tories and had laid the colony open to mischief by their indecisiveness. With the exception of Thomas Lee and Page, the general found the committee "desperately infected with th[e] epidemical malady"—timidity. Lee had acquired an Indian wife during the French and Indian War along with a Mohawk nickname that translated as "boiling water," and he had no patience with the political politesse of the Virginia elite. "From Pendleton, Bland, the Treasurer & Co *libera nos Domine*," Lee prayed. Bland doddered along calling the author of *Common Sense* "a blockhead and ignoramas" for some minor mistakes in his biblical references, and Pendleton on the question of independence "talked or rather stammered nonsense that would have disgraced the lips of an old midwife drunk with Bohea tea and gin."

Yet the argument for independence made rapid headway. Echoing *Common Sense*, a writer in the *Gazette* argued that even before the political crisis the colonies had already reached the point "when independence would have become a natural event, and dependence a political absurdity." Independence could be justified as "a means of conducting [the war] successfully," the writer said, but he maintained that the colonists already exercised a practical independence through the functioning system of committees, conventions, and Congress. To deny that independence was the goal resembled "more the dark guilt of rebellion than the manly candour of a righteous resistance."

In the countryside the advocates of independence predominated, and the spring elections for delegates to the next convention produced a great ferment. Several Piedmont counties instructed their delegates to push for independence and bid His Britannic Majesty "a good Night forever." The mobilization had brought many more participants into politics, and the field of candidates grew larger. Many experienced delegates, on both sides of the question, felt "much pushed" to retain their seats, and in the rush of spirited contests "many new ones got in." Thomas Lee urged his brother R. H. Lee to come back from Philadelphia for the convention: "You will find there a noble spirit, worthy to be cherish'd, which if not regulated & directed by a skillful hand, may dissipate in idle fume, or be blasted by the arts of sly timidity."

Patrick Henry had no difficulty winning a place in the convention, and when Lee knew that he could not leave Philadelphia with the crucial issues still undecided in Congress he turned to Henry for aid. "I am well pleased to hear that you are going into Convention," Lee told Henry, "and I hope your powers will be fully exerted in securing the peace and happiness of our country, by the adoption of a wise and free government." The Whigs in Congress, Lee emphasized, needed a strong signal from Virginia for independence. This would rouse Congress from the "fatal lethargy" bred by "Tory machinations" and the "feebleness, folly and interested views" of the middle colonies. Lee insisted that the time had arrived for "taking up government immediately" or else riding "the high road to Anarchy." Setting up a new government would both preserve society and "set an example" for the laggard colonies. "When this is done," Lee advised, "give peremptory instructions to your [congressional] Delegates" to declare independence and seek foreign alliances. (Lee and Henry both hoped that a firm Whig could be found to replace Virginia's newest delegate, Carter Braxton, whom Pendleton and Nicholas had dispatched precisely to retard the move toward independence.)

"Ages yet unborn, and millions existing at present," Lee told Henry, "may rue or bless" the work of the impending Virginia convention. Quoting Shakespeare—"There is a Tide in the Affairs of Men. . . ."—he implored Henry to join "in leading our countrymen to embrace the present flowing tide, which promises fair to waft us into the harbor of safety, happiness, liberty and virtue."

The Whigs in Congress hoped, with the help of leaders at home, to extricate themselves from a political dilemma. "Those who wish delay, and want nothing done, say let the people in the Colonies begin, we must not go before them," Lee said, "Tho' they well know the language in the Country to be, Let the Congress advise." "We continue still between Hawk and Buzzard," John Adams complained to his lieutenants in Massachusetts.

Henry understood what was needed, although he told Lee and Adams that he hoped Congress would not declare independence without having laid firm groundwork for the French alliance ("which with me is everything") and formally organized the colonies, at least loosely, in an "offensive and defensive" confederacy. Don't attempt "a minute arrangement of things," Henry advised, for that may "split and divide." "The adjustment of Representation, and other lesser matters, may be postponed without injury," said Henry, who, eighteen months earlier had pitched the first Congress into a premature argument on the subject.

Adams replied that in theory the most "natural" sequence would be to set up new governments in each colony, then define the limits of a continental confederation, then declare the independence of "the confederated sovereign states," and, finally, to make treaties with foreign powers. "But," said Adams, "I fear we cannot proceed systematically, and that we shall be obliged to declare ourselves independent States before we confederate, and indeed before all the colonies have established their governments." Since it was "pretty clear" that all these measures would occur in short order, Adams concluded, "it may not perhaps be of much importance which is done first."

When Henry came down to Williamsburg in early May for the convention, he mulled over the question of strategic priorities with the irascible General Charles Lee, who held "the highest opinion" of Henry's "liberal way of thinking." Lee assured Henry of something that his friends in Philadelphia feared to put in writing: Congress had already established a secret negotiation with France and dispatched Henry's friend Silas Deane to Bordeaux and Paris to make commercial connections. Lee also reminded Henry that "the spirit of the people" cried out for independence, "except a very few in these lower parts of Virginia whose little blood has been suck'd out by musketoes." "The military in particular, men and officers, are outrageous on the subject," Lee said, and need that political spur to the war effort.

Henry had a resolution for independence ready when the convention met in the Capitol on May 6, but it took him more than a week to get it discussed. Previous conventions had become habituated to tedium and delay, and since 50 of the 126 delegates were novices, it took even longer than usual for the meeting to settle into a productive routine.

Pendleton again presided. Henry's friends had proposed Thomas Ludwell Lee as an alternative, but Henry himself did not want to cause a ruckus over personalities and did not contest Pendleton's election. Pendleton regarded the vote as an expression of confidence in his leadership; in his opening remarks the president enumerated an agenda—military arrangements, loyalty oaths, bounties for salt production—that pointedly ignored the question of independence and only hinted at the idea of forming a permanent government. "Permit me to recommend calmness Unanimity and Diligence as the most likely means of bringing [the convention] to a happy and prosperous issue," Pendleton said.

In appointing the standing committees, however, Pendleton shrewdly bid for the allegiance of the new delegates. Instead of loading the committees with the usual crowd of Tidewater magnates, Pendleton appointed a few old hands, including Henry, and then took the unorthodox step of moving alphabetically down the roster of counties to fill the positions. This resulted in much greater representation for the western counties and, not coincidentally, won Pendleton a number of new friends.

After a week of reviewing contested elections, approving troop deployments, and sorting an accumulated bundle of private petitions for relief from the distresses of war, the convention finally reached the crucial point on Tuesday, May 14. Thomas Nelson, Jr., introduced the resolution Henry had drafted. The preamble denounced the king as a "tyrant instead of [a] protector" and charged that Britain's war measures—including arming frontier Indians and rousing slaves to insurrection—showed its disposition to "crush" the colonies, not conciliate them. The resolution therefore declared Virginians "absolved of our allegiance to the crown" and "obliged by the eternal laws of self-preservation to pursue such measures as may conduce to the good and happiness of the united colonies." "The only honourable means under Heaven of obtaining that happiness" would be "an immediate, clear, and full Declaration of Independency," and Henry's text "enjoined" Virginia's delegates in Congress "in the strongest and most positive manner" to pursue that goal.

Nelson urged passage with the argument that the Americans could not return from war "with the cordiality of subjects." He made a quiet speech, and when Henry rose to second the measure, he started in the same vein. He spoke of the "critical" subject in a curious, noncommittal way, insisting (as Edmund Randolph recalled) that "a cause which put at stake the lives and fortunes of the people should appear to be their own act, and that he ought not to place upon the responsibility of his eloquence a revolution of which the people might be wearied after the present stimulus should cease to operate." At length, however, he put aside his diffidence and urged the convention to "cut the knot" in his rousing, evangelical fashion. He likened "the spirit of the people" to "a pillar of fire" which, despite the darkness of the present situation, would lead the colonies to "the promised land."

A long day's debate ensued. Robert Carter Nicholas rehearsed all the arguments for delay: the inexperience of the army, the difficulty of obtaining supplies, the uncertainty of receiving foreign aid, the likelihood of the continent's tearing itself apart with internal quarrels stemming from different conceptions of government and conflicting land claims. Nicholas insisted that he had a duty to say these things and believed that he was not alone in doubting America's competence at this juncture. He went on and on, Jack Washington (the general's brother) complained, "saying a great deal, prov[ing] nothing."

Another complication came from competing resolutions that called more explicitly than Henry's did for a new Virginia government but fudged the question of continental independence. Sorting out the merits and defects of each text, while fending off Nicholas's attacks, wearied everyone. Jack Washington thought that if Nicholas "had held his tongue" the various draftsmen might have quietly "compared notes" and agreed on a single proposal.

Eventually Edmund Pendleton himself produced a composite, which the convention considered on Wednesday morning, May 15, 1776. Pendleton softened Henry's preamble with language emphasizing how slowly and unwillingly the colonies had come to the alternative of separation. Unlike Henry's draft, Pendleton's substitute did not explicitly or immediately absolve Virginians of allegiance to the Crown, yet it concisely accomplished all the necessary political consequences. It ordered a declaration of rights and a plan of government prepared for Virginia and instructed Virginia's delegates in Congress to propose a declaration of independence and to assent to measures for forming foreign alliances and a confederation of the colonies.

A "very full house"—the journal expressly noted 112 members present—voted unanimously for the resolution. Nicholas and the few other opponents did not want "to contradict the general Voyce" by asking for a roll call vote and sat quietly amid the general roar. Henry found the new preamble "not quite so pointed as I could wish," but, he told John Adams, "I put up with it . . . for the sake of unanimity." Mason thought the preamble "tedious" and "rather timid." Jack Washington agreed that "it might have been better done," being "not so full as some would have wished" but told R. H. Lee that he hoped the resolution might "answer the purpose." Tom Lee told his brother that although the resolve lacked "that peremptory & decided air" he desired, the resolves gave "infinite joy to the people." "The principles of [*Common Sense*] now stalked in triumph," Edmund Randolph wrote, "under the sanction of the most extensive, richest, and most commanding colony in America."

An impromptu celebration took place. Delegates streamed out of the chamber into the yard to watch the Union Jack "struck from the Capitol and a [red-and-white-striped] Continental hoisted in its room." Bells tolled, amid the discharge of artillery and small arms, and the troops paraded before the townspeople. The celebration continued into the following day, when the resolution was read aloud in a formal ceremony at the soldiers' encampment. The committee of safety served "refreshment" to the troops, and the company drank toasts "to the American independent states," "to the Grand Congress," and "to General Washington, and victory to the American arms." That night all the inhabitants of Williamsburg put candles in their windows for a general "illumination" and other "demonstrations of joy." On Friday, May 17, however, solemnity reigned, as the colony observed the day of fasting decreed some time previously and popularly known as "Congress Sunday." Henry marched in procession with his colleagues from the Capitol to the parish church, where the convention's chaplain preached an inspiring sermon on the text "Be not afraid, nor yet dismayed, by reason of this great multitude; for the battle is not yours, but God's."

In the ensuing "grand work of forming a constitution," Henry told R. H. Lee, he anticipated no diminution of struggle because "too great a bias to Aristocracy prevails among the opulent." "My most esteemed republican form has many and powerful enemies," Henry told John Adams, and Henry's ally Thomas Ludwell Lee made the complaint explicit: "A certain Junto," or "set of aristocrats, for we have such monsters here . . . exert themselves against every measure of sense & spirit."

Henry and his friends perceived that their cautious opponents wanted a new government that conformed as closely as possible to the much-admired British constitution, with its traditional social balance among king, lords, and commons. Henry's old nemesis Carter Braxton used it as his model in recommending a plan to the convention that avoided "the restless spirit of innovation" and "all the tumult and riot incident to simple democracy." Braxton wanted very much to continue English government as Virginia had known it before the crisis; he suggested an assembly elected every third year, a council chosen for life by the assembly, and a governor to serve on good behavior and embody the monarchic dignity necessary for good order. Pendleton agreed with Braxton, declaring that "a democracy, considered as *referring determinations*, either legislative or executive, TO THE PEOPLE AT LARGE, is the worst form [of government] imaginable. Of all others, I own, I prefer the true English constitution, which consists of a proper combination of the principles of honor, virtue, and fear."

For Whigs like Henry, however, the British constitution had ceased to be an object of veneration. Two-thirds of the government in the hands of a hereditary king and propertied nobles no longer seemed glorious, and the "phantom" of the British constitution reflected in the colonial arrangement of assembly, council, and royal governor had not sufficiently protected liberty. Henry suspected that the advocates of the old British constitution would endeavor to create a role for hereditary privilege and, perhaps, even limited monarchy in the new governments. When Braxton wrote, "We ought to adopt and perfect that system, which England has suffered to be so grossly abused," Henry pounced in anger. "I suspect his whiggism," Henry said, denouncing "the whole performance" as "an affront and disgrace to this country."

Braxton regarded independence as "a delusive Bait" because it concealed "the hook" of "purely democratical" governments incompatible with the equilibrium of the British constitution. New England wanted "to throw off all Subjection & embrace their darling Democracy," Braxton said.

Henry, however, wished he had Sam and John Adams with him in convention "so to form our portrait of government, that a kindred with New England may be discerned in it. If all your excellencies cannot be preserved," Henry told John Adams, "yet I hope to retain so much of the likeness, that posterity shall pronounce us descended from the same stock." To Henry's enthusiasm, Adams responded with an exuberance of his own. "The dons, the bashaws, the grandees, the patricians, the sachems, the nabobs, call them by what name you please, sigh and groan, and fret, and sometimes stamp, and foam, and curse, but all in vain," he wrote to his Virginia friend. "The decree is gone forth, and it cannot be recalled, that a more equal liberty than has prevailed in other parts of the earth, must be established in America," Adams wrote, and "the insolent domination" of "a very few, opulent, monopolizing families" will be "brought down nearer to the confines of reason and moderation."

Henry had come to prominence as the antagonist of entrenched oligarchic power, and his sympathy for dissenting religion suggested a kinship for what was widely regarded as the "leveling" spirit of New England congregationalism. New England's towns enjoyed a much more open and independent government than Virginia's self-perpetuating county and vestry system, which was challenged by the upsurge of popular politics Henry had inspired. Conservatives like Braxton frankly abhorred the New England spirit, partly because it was more antagonistic (at least in theory) to aristocratic accumulation of wealth and power and partly because it rebuked the plantation society's foundation in the coercive power a minority of whites held over a majority of black slaves. In looking to New England as their ideal, Virginians like Henry (and Lee) perhaps yearned for a society not cursed by slavery, but in practice they realized that Virginia would compromise the republican principle.

When Henry told R. H. Lee, "I own myself a Democrat on the plan of our admired friend J. Adams," he meant that he favored the principles of representative government, founded on popular consent, directed in the interests of the commonweal, refreshed by annual elections, circumscribed in its powers by written constitutions, and operated in accordance with the rule of law rather than prerogative or privilege. These Whigs shared a sense of possibility and exhilaration that, in Adams's words, would be envied by "the greatest lawgivers of antiquity." "No Colony, which shall assume a Government under the People, will give it up," Adams said.

"There is something very unnatural and odious in a Government 1000 Leagues off. An whole government of our own Choice, managed by Persons whom We love, revere, and can confide in, has charms in it for which Men will fight."

The rapturous excitement of founding a new form of government could not be diluted by the compromises they would obviously have to make. "It is certain in Theory, that the only moral Foundation of Government is the Consent of the People," Adams wrote. "But to what an Extent Shall We carry this Principle?" Chastised by his wife to "remember the ladies in your new code of laws," Adams could turn aside her complaint with domestic wit. In principle, however, he realized that democratic theory gave a political voice to "old and young, male and female, as well as rich and poor." Like Henry and Lee, he believed that property holding might be diffused widely enough to afford most men the vote, but he justified the practical exclusion of youths, women, the destitute, and slaves on the grounds that they were too dependent on others (parents, husbands, warders, masters) to act as equal members in the political community.

These ardent Whigs recognized that the resistance movement necessitated a coalition with the lower orders, and they accepted the political participation of leather-aproned artisans and mechanics in a way that aristocrats like Virginia's Braxton or New York's proprietary landlords could not. Braxton warned that democratic politics would lead to "all the mischiefs" of "sumptuary" and "agrarian Laws" that mandated plainness in dress and "an equal division of property." New York's Gouverneur Morris spoke more bluntly. "The mob begins to think and reason," he said. "Poor reptiles! It is with them a spring morning; they are struggling to cast off their winter's slough, they bask in the sunshine, ere noon, they will bite, depend on it."

In building their coalition, the Whigs counted on their own ability to lead. John Adams's fears would be eased by the firm regard the Boston "mob" had for his cousin Samuel, and Henry of course held firm control of the moderately insurgent lower orders in Virginia. The propertyless mass in

Virginia, however, consisted largely of slaves, and Henry's antagonists there—first Dunmore, then Nicholas and Pendleton—tried to brake his efforts by forcibly reminding him of this contradiction.

Henry served on the committee charged with formulating the declaration of rights that would serve "as the basis and foundation of government," but his friends George Mason and Thomas Lee generated the draft upon which the convention worked. That the Virginians regarded a bill of rights as the cornerstone of government emphasizes both the power of their Whig tradition and the long decade of opposition to governmental encroachment. Unlike the famous English bill of 1689, Virginia's declaration did not settle grievances against an existing power. Rather, it enunciated broad precepts that should govern the exercise of any power and laid specific prohibitions against the government now in formation.

The proposed bill made no reference to English statutes or colonial charters but spoke the revolutionaries' language of natural rights. "All men are born equally free and independent," it began, and it went on to insist that power was derived from the people, who had the right to "reform, alter, or abolish" governments that fail to meet their purposes. Election of representatives ought to be free and regular, and the people could be bound only by laws to which their representatives had consented. The bill emphasized that public officers could serve only limited terms, that no office could be hereditary, that legislative and judicial powers must be separate, and that the military must be subordinate to the civil government, with no standing armies maintained in peacetime. The bill of rights affirmed the "sacred" right of trial by jury, forbade the granting of general search warrants "unsupported by evidence," and insisted that as "one of the great bulwarks of liberty . . . freedom of the press" could not be restrained. The bill also contained guarantees of fundamental liberties in criminal prosecutions—notice of the accusation, a speedy trial by a jury of the neighborhood, the right to confront witnesses and examine evidence, a protection against being compelled to give evidence against oneself, and the bedrock principle of "due process" that "no man be deprived of his liberty except by the law of the land, or the judgment of his peers." Finally, the proposed bill extended "the fullest toleration in the exercise of religion" and declared that the "blessing of liberty" could only be preserved by "a firm adherence to justice, moderation, temperance, frugality, and virtue, and by frequent recurrence to fundamental principle."

When the committee's proposed text came before the convention on May 29, 1776 (Henry's fortieth birthday), Robert Carter Nicholas raised such bitter objection to the first article that the convention remained "stumbling at the threshold" for several weeks. "We find such difficulty in laying the foundation stone that I very much fear for that Temple to liberty which was proposed to be erected thereon," Thomas Lee wrote. The first article read:

> *That all men are born equally free and independent, and have certain inherent natural rights, of which they cannot, by any compact, deprive or divest their posterity; among which are, the enjoyment of life and liberty, with the means of acquiring and possessing property, and pursuing and obtaining happiness and safety.*

Nicholas concentrated his objections upon the first clause. The democratic implications disturbed him; he also feared that the assertion of equality "in a fundamental act" would "have the effect of abolishing" the condition of chattel slavery so fundamental to Virginia's way of life. To let the proposition stand would create "civil convulsion," either from the slaves or from licentious, propertyless whites who would demand an equality of wealth.

Henry and his ardent Whig allies denounced Nicholas and the "junto" of aristocrats for advancing "a number of absurd, or unmeaning alterations" and retarding business "by a thousand masterly fetches & stratagems." The Whigs insisted that the convention not get mired in what Henry once derided as "the minutiae of rectitude." They said, confidently, that "with arms in our hands, asserting the general rights of man," they not be too "restricted" in the "delineation" of them. It was a truthful but lame answer, and Thomas Lee morosely admitted to his brother: "We are quite overpowered by the maneuver & heartily wish the congress would send us another General Lee from the Northward." (R. H. Lee would indeed hurry to Williamsburg as soon as he—on June 7—moved in Congress the resolutions of independence mandated by Virginia. Congress, still not ready, tabled them until July 1 but ordered a committee to draft a declaration on the assumption that they would then be approved.)

Work on the Virginia bill of rights had to be postponed for a week while the committee sought so "to vary the language, as not to involve the necessity of emancipating the slaves." They needed some way of blunting the implication of equal birth without repudiating the claim of natural rights. Pendleton, an expert at drawing fine distinctions, came up with an acceptable formula: "All men are by nature equally free and independent," he suggested, but enjoy their "certain rights" only "when they enter into a state of society." Since the slaves were not "part of the society to which the declaration applied," no promise could be inferred, and those already possessed of political power could control when the excluded might enter. Having at last limped over the threshold, the convention completed work on the document with relative dispatch.

Henry took the lead on two important matters. The committee's draft contained a mildly worded statement that laws defining crimes "in retrospect" and punishing offenses "committed before the existence of such laws" were "generally oppressive and ought to be avoided." Henry understood the danger of attainders and other ex post facto laws, but he nonetheless urged that this clause be dropped. The convention thus far had done little to inhibit Tories; a band of Crown Loyalists near Norfolk had staged violent raiding parties on Dunmore's behalf, and Henry did not want to bar their eventual arrest and punishment. Mason believed that "the great law of necessity" would prevail in such a case, but the convention went along with Henry's motion to delete.

Henry also urged changes in the proposed article on religion. In the committee's draft it read:

> *That religion, or the duty which we owe to our* CREATOR, *and the manner of discharging it, can be directed only by reason and conviction, not by force or violence; and therefore, that all men should enjoy the fullest toleration in the exercise of religion, according to the dictates of conscience, unpunished and unrestrained by the magistrate, unless, under colour of religion, any man disturb the peace, the happiness, or safety of society. And that it is the mutual duty of all to practice Christian forbearance, love, and charity, towards each other.*

Henry, having defended the rights of dissenters for so many years, knew that they had passed the point of being grateful for the privilege of "toleration" and insisted upon the "right" of complete religious liberty. The much-contested religion bill of 1772—tabled by the House but published for general comment—had, thanks to Henry, contained the pledge that dissenters would "have and enjoy the full and free Exercise of their Religion, without Molestation and Danger of incurring any Penalty whatsoever." He now saw the opportunity of redeeming this sidetracked promise in the new bill of rights.

Henry had a talented ally in one of the new young delegates, James Madison. This fresh-faced, diminutive twenty-six-year-old from Orange County had fervently expressed his admiration for Henry at Port Royal in the aftermath of the gunpowder march, and now in convention Madison sought Henry's leadership on the issue of religious liberty. Educated at the Presbyterians' College of New Jersey (Princeton), Madison had an intellectual grounding in the dissenting tradition and had for several years doubted the wisdom of religious establishments. The persecution of the Baptists in Orange and neighboring Culpepper shocked him, and when he returned from Princeton to his father's "obscure corner" of the Virginia Piedmont, the attacks on dissenters proved the one issue capable of rousing him from a torpid, self-pitying depression. The "diabolical Hell conceived principle of persecution," Madison wrote, "vexes me the most of any thing whatever," and "I have squabbled and scolded abused and ridiculed so long about it . . . that I am without common patience."

Madison, too, saw opportunity in the pending bill of rights. Scratching upon his printed copy of the bill, he altered the "toleration" clause to read, "all men are equally entitled to enjoy the free exercise of religion, according to the dictates of conscience . . . unless the preservation of equal liberty and the existence of the State are manifestly indangered." The invocation to "Christian duty" he left unchanged.

Edmund Randolph recalled later that Henry sponsored the free exercise amendment on the floor. As a new delegate, with a shy, retiring manner and a weak voice, Madison had asked his admired leader's assistance. Randolph also remembered that the opposition (as in 1772) charged that "unfettering the exercise of religion" would be a prelude "to an attack on the Established Church," but Henry "disclaimed such an object." The convention, in a burst of liberality that must have startled the sponsors, improved the Henry-Madison amendment by striking the qualifying proviso, so that the document simply proclaimed that "all men are equally entitled to the free exercise of religion, according to the dictates of conscience."

The Declaration of Rights "made by the representatives of the good people of Virginia, assembled in full and free Convention," received final approval, *nemine contradicente*, on June 12, 1776. Edmund Randolph, the late Speaker's nephew and, with Madison, one of the youngest delegates present, said that the document had two purposes: that the legislature "should not . . . violate any of those canons" and that "in all the revolutions of time, of human opinion, and of government, a perpetual standard should be erected, around which the people might rally and by a notorious record be forever admonished to be watchful, firm, and virtuous."

The convention next turned to the "plan of government." Young Edmund Randolph, on behalf of Jefferson, who was preoccupied in Philadelphia with drafting Congress's proposed declaration, made a profound objection. No permanent constitution should be made until the people could elect deputies especially charged for that purpose, Jefferson believed; the convention would be acting as any ordinary legislature and not enacting a fundamental law beyond the reach of ordinary process. Henry thought, and both Pendleton and Mason shared his view, that if the convention had the authority to declare the colony independent, it had the power to pursue the consequent obligation of forming a new government. If the convention drew back from this act of political sovereignty, the leaders argued, it might cast doubt upon the validity of their act of separation.

Randolph withered. Although Jefferson would not concede the point, he did dispatch a lengthy draft to the convention, which when added to Mason's proposal and the many pamphlets and suggestions floating about town, gave the committee the task of sorting what Mason described as "heterogenious, jarring & unintelligible Ingredients." During the middle weeks of June, while the committee labored on a composite plan, Henry served on innumerable small committees of legislative detail, ranging from choosing the location of the military hospital to frontier defense plans, the rating of paper money, and the temporary administration of justice. He played only a small role in shaping the constitution and certainly made no effort to turn Virginia's institutions into a recognizably Yankee mold.

The plan, nonetheless, did owe a great deal to John Adams's little pamphlet on government, which Henry had "read with great pleasure" and circulated among his friends. Adams had worked up a short essay at the behest of Lee and other Whigs in Congress in order to show that the transition to independent government might not be as difficult as some feared. Adams insisted, "There is no good government but what is Republican," by which he meant a government founded on consent and directed in the interests of the commonweal.

Adams admired the spirited manner in which *Common Sense* had evoked this republican ideal, and he was flattered when people suspected him to be its author. Eventually it became known, however, that an English dissenter named Thomas Paine, recently arrived in Philadelphia, had written the popular pamphlet, and in *Thoughts on Government* Adams expressed his disagreement with it on points of republican "Architecture." Paine had proposed a single representative assembly, with a large number of delegates annually elected, as an adequate government. Adams regarded this scheme as too naive and dangerous. A single assembly, he warned, might become as whimsical as a single individual or as despotic as the "long Parliament." A second chamber, elected by the first, with an equal voice in legislation, would provide some check on excessive power. A governor, annually elected by the two houses (or by the electorate), would provide another check, especially if he were given a legislative veto—but none "of those badges of domination called prerogatives." Annual election and rotation in office should be vital precepts, but Adams thought executive and judicial officers might be either appointed by the governor (subject to confirmation) or, in a more "popular" government, by one or both houses of the assembly.

Architecture, however, had to be subordinated to spirit. The "new-modelled" Virginia government embodied republican principles and in some respects had a decidedly popular tone, yet for the present it seemed amenable to control by the established leadership. Adams had cautioned that at first "it will be safest to proceed in all established modes to which the people have been familiarized by habit." Thus Virginia's Declaration of Rights held that "all men, having sufficient evidence of permanent common interest with, and attachment to the community, have the right of suffrage," and the constitution provided that voting rights "shall remain as exercised at present." This ambiguous formula meant that the existing, relatively mild property qualifications remained in force, along with the customary inclusion (in many counties) of tenants on long-term leases. Jefferson's draft, however, would have broadened the suffrage considerably more in principle by admitting all municipal taxpayers. Jefferson also would have undermined the property requirement by granting a head-right in fifty unsettled western acres to any landless white man. However, in the hotly contested atmosphere of the convention the drafting committee, Mason and Henry included, did not try to press so fundamental a reform immediately.

Virginia's constitution proved more "popular" than Adams or Henry anticipated in that both houses of the legislature were to be elected directly by the people. But the convention refused to meddle with the existing county system and maintained representation on a geographical basis; Jefferson's draft had proposed the more equitable principle of proportional representation based on population. The convention briefly considered modifying the oligarchic character of the county court system by requiring the governor to appoint justices of the peace from a list of nominees twice as long as the number of places to be filled. In the end, however, the county courts remained self-perpetuating, since the justices were still allowed to name their own successors.

The new government proved "very much of the democratic kind" in that it provided a firm foundation for legislative power. Assemblies would be elected and would meet each year, in accordance with the Whig maxim "Where annual elections end, there slavery begins." The executive, moreover, would be only a vestigial royal governor, shorn of prerogatives and deprived of a veto. Henry strenuously contested this decision in convention, following Adams's argument that otherwise the governor (or "the Administrator," as Jefferson wanted the officer to be styled) would be a dependent instead of coordinate power, unable to "interpose on a vehement impulse or ferment" in the legislature. This was the cautious Whig speaking, distrustful of concentrated power in any agency, not the practical exponent of popular sovereignty.

On June 29, following the adoption of the "plan of government," the convention chose the new commonwealth's first governor. Thomas Nelson, Sr., the aristocratic president of the council, who under the old order of things would have served as acting governor after Dunmore's departure, proved the conservatives' nominee. Other than his brief appearance at Duncastle's Ordinary, Nelson had taken no part in the Revolution. This recommended him to Pendleton, who thought it unbecoming "for those who pushed on the revolution to get into the first offices."

The radicals disagreed, insisting that they would "cut a pretty figure" by giving the office "to a man who was no Whig." They nominated Henry, who received sixty votes to Nelson's forty-five. His election underscored the popular character of the Revolution, and there was a certain poetry in Henry becoming Dunmore's successor as the head of an independent state. The convention intended to reward Henry and endow the commonwealth with his prestige, yet he would assume an office stripped of Dunmore's power and regarded with suspicion even by his friends.

Henry promptly accepted the office in a gracious address that bore no hint that the office might be a dubious honor. "I lament my want of talents," Henry said, but pledged his "unwearied endeavours to secure the freedom and happiness of our common country." He would rely upon "the known wisdom and virtue" of the House "to supply my defects and give permanency and success to that system of Government which you have formed." The task—"to secure equal liberty and advance happiness"—had urgency both for themselves and posterity, Henry concluded; "from the events of this war, the lasting happiness or misery of a great proportion of the human species will finally result."

Henry had written his message with a shaking hand. He had come down with the malarial fever and ague so prevalent in Williamsburg in the "sickly" summer months, and his condition worsened daily. He did not attend the last week of the convention, and upon adjournment on July 5, the governor-elect was reported near death. The next morning, with Henry still "very ill," John Page, one of the councilors-elect, had a dreadful thought. "If he should die before we have qualified and chosen a [Council] President [to act as lieutenant governor] the Country will be without any head [and] every Thing must be in confusion."

Harassed by at least fifteen requests for some kind of business while he scrawled a plaintive note to his friend Jefferson, Page felt the uncomfortable burden of office descending upon him. He scurried to find the four council members necessary, and they went immediately to Henry's rooms. From his sickbed Henry feebly raised his hand and swore to execute his office "without favor, affection, or partiality." Henry swore to "support, maintain, and defend the Commonwealth of Virginia, & the Constitution of the same, & protect the people thereof in the secure enjoyment of all their rights, franchises, and privileges." The oath went on and on. He promised to "endeavor that the laws and ordinances of the Commonwealth be duly observed, & that law and justice, in mercy, be executed in all judgments." Finally, the oath required him to promise that he would "peaceably and quietly resign the government" at the conclusion of his elected term.

"So help me God," Henry said. It was then his turn to read similar oaths to the council members. In that torpid sickroom an anxious group of men quietly inaugurated the new government of Virginia. Until the convention reassembled as the new legislature in October, their responsibility would be comprehensive and urgent, but they left the chamber not knowing whether Henry, their leader and embodiment of the revolutionary Whig spirit, would meet them again in this world.

Part
Four

1776-
1789

CHAPTER 16

"A Thousand Things to Mend, to Begin"

"We shall now see what we shall see," groused the aristocratic Landon Carter when he heard that Patrick Henry would be the commonwealth's first governor. This choice of "the multitude" carried a "destructive tendency," Carter believed, and he rejoiced a few weeks later when a neighbor brought the simultaneous news that the former governor, Lord Dunmore, had fled his island hideout under shelling of Virginia batteries, while the new governor, Henry, had died up-country. "We ought to look on those two joined as . . . glorious events . . . Particularly favourable by the hand of Providence."

Carter's ugly talk derived from both fear and jealousy. He shared his nephew Carter Braxton's view that Henry sought a demagogic popularity and would throw Virginia into the arms of New England's levelers. But Carter, who had served many years in the House of Burgesses while Henry was a youth, writhed at the "absurdity" of giving Henry credit for the Stamp Act resistance. Carter pedantically insisted that his own resolutions of 1764 had given "the first breath for liberty in America." How typical of Henry's villainy, Carter thought, to accept applause from the crowd for an achievement not his own.

Most Virginians, however, knew that Henry had inspired not simply a petition but a vast popular movement, and they understood his election as their crowning triumph. While the governor recuperated at Scotchtown in July and August, thus dashing Carter's regard for Providence, congratulatory messages came in from all quarters. The addresses from two newly significant and self-conscious constituencies —religious dissenters and soldiers—gave Henry special satisfaction. A Baptist meeting in nearby Louisa sent a message of "unspeakable pleasure" to Scotchtown. "As a religious community, we have nothing to ask of you," the church brethren said. "Your constant attachment to the glorious cause of liberty and the rights of conscience, leaves us no room to doubt of your Excellency's favorable regards." Henry replied at once with a promise that he would always endeavor "to guard the rights of all my fellow-citizens from encroachment." He expressed hope that the once-heated religious disputes would be forgotten and "Christian charity, forbearance, and love . . . unite all different persuasions as brethren who must perish or triumph together."

The First and Second Virginia Regiments declared that "once happy under your military command, we hope for more extensive blessings from your civil administration." Recognizing that "His Excellency" now had "the support of a young empire" in his trust, the soldiers pledged to maintain Henry's "authority as chief magistrate" and hailed the day "when freedom and equal rights, established by the voice of the people, shall prevail through the land." (In a separate note to the newspapers Colonel Woodford of the Second Regiment insisted that "justice" required public knowledge that he had not subscribed to the address, which was "not presented as containing the sentiments of the colonel, but of the officers and their men.")

Henry ignored this latest slight from his old rival in composing a cordial response. "The remembrance of my former connexion with you shall ever be dear to me," he said. Henry pledged to establish a government "in every part of which the genius of equal liberty breathes her blessed influence." He praised the regiments for their "patriot virtue" and looked forward to honoring them as "the triumphant deliverers of America."

By mid-August Henry had recovered sufficiently from the malarial attack to walk and ride near Scotchtown, although he did not venture as far as either Hanover Court House or Richmond for the joyous public readings of the Declaration of Independence, which took place on August court days throughout the commonwealth to "universal" satisfaction. More gratifying news followed: the entire First Regiment had reenlisted and would be joining General Washington to defend New York against General Howe's long-anticipated British invasion.

While Henry recuperated, he suddenly had to make a decision about another crucial theater: the Kentucky frontier. On a steamy August afternoon a tall, athletic young backwoodsman turned up on Henry's doorstep with an urgent political message. His name was George Rogers Clark, and he represented a contingent of Virginians who had recently settled the lush grasslands of central Kentucky. Clark had grown up in neighboring Caroline County and in 1772, at the age of twenty, had surveyed Ohio River lands for his father's friends. Two years later, the boundlessly energetic Clark had captained militiamen in Dunmore's campaign against the Shawnee, then headed west with other veterans to take up tracts near Harrodsburg, on the Kentucky River in the middle of the vast territory seemingly pacified by Dunmore's victory.

With shrewd eyes, shaggy red hair, and a long chin that gave a bullying thrust to his relentless manner, Clark stood before Henry as the latest incarnation of Virginia's westward drive. Clark told the governor that the Kentuckians feared the collapse of Dunmore's 1774 treaty. The tribes northwest of the Ohio, once pledged to neutrality, now seemed poised for renewed attacks, which Clark blamed on the intrigues of British agents in the region. With this growing menace on Kentucky's northern flank added to the warfare already begun by the disgruntled Cherokee to the south, the future of the beckoning country suddenly seemed grim. Were the Indians to drive the settlers back over the Cumberland Gap, Virginia's backcountry door would be shut, and, even worse, the redskins and redcoats might unite for an attack upon central Virginia from the west.

Clark wanted Henry to commit the commonwealth to

Kentucky's defense. If the governor would provide the ammunition, Clark would head west to organize an army of shirt men to keep the northwestern Indians at bay. Henry understood that Clark's proposition carried immense political consequences. Although Clark had occasionally worked for a syndicate of Virginia speculators, in the swirl of Kentucky politics he represented a rebellious group of squatters who challenged the vast proprietorship over Kentucky asserted by a Carolina syndicate headed by Judge Richard Henderson. Henderson's Transylvania Company had courted Henry for years, and it claimed Kentucky on the authority of a private purchase from the Cherokee—a venture Henry had once contemplated for himself and a style of acquisition Henry considered legal. But the Virginia convention would not recognize Transylvania's claim to set up a proprietary government, and it prohibited such private purchases in the new Virginia constitution. To counter Henderson's bid for recognition from Virginia the Harrodsburg settlers had sent Clark to Williamsburg with a petition that he be seated as their delegate in Virginia's convention, but Clark endured a harrowing journey over the mountains and arrived only after the convention adjourned.

If Henry accepted Clark's proposition, he would promote the Kentucky yeomen's attachment to Virginia while protecting the commonwealth's border. But siding with Clark would signal his break with not only Henderson and Transylvania but the other large companies seeking to dominate the west through the validation of private purchases. When Richard Henry Lee warned Henry that his legal opinion (endorsing the Vandalia claim) for Wharton had caused murmurings in Philadelphia, Henry flatly replied that he had given an opinion only "as a lawyer"; "notwithstanding solicitations from every great land company to the West, I've refused to join them."

Yet Henry had not lost his interest in land. Sitting under the trees at Scotchtown he listened raptly as Clark celebrated Kentucky's canebrakes and clover, its huge flocks of turkey and grouse, and the game that frequented the abundant salt licks. Crossing the mountains might be "divilish ruff," but once in Kentucky, the saying went, it was like being in a garden where there was no forbidden fruit. Clark also expressed the antagonism his friends at Harrodsburg felt toward the presumptuous Henderson, whose aristocratic bias had generated popular ill will among the North Carolina Piedmonters and who now wanted to charge Kentucky settlers quitrents and other feudal dues. Henry realized that the Revolution had come to Kentucky, too. If Virginians wanted to gain ground there, the commonwealth needed Clark. In this raw, unlettered, ambitious young man Henry sensed not only a kindred boldness but possibly a valuable new land partner for himself. He and Clark shook hands on the deal; the young giant would organize the defense, and Virginia would organize a government in Kentucky.

Henry sent Clark off to Williamsburg with a letter to the council requesting that it give Clark five hundred pounds of gunpowder. The council concurred with the governor's intention but demurred at the cost of transporting the twenty-five kegs of ammunition overland to Fort Pitt, where Clark would then float them down the Ohio to his outposts. The council pointed out that the Kentuckians were still "a detached people not yet united to Virginia." If the assembly in October did not seat Clark as a delegate, would he personally be accountable for the transportation costs? Clark had a short fuse, and he angrily left Williamsburg declaring that "if a Cuntry is not worth protecting it is not worth claiming." The council, fearful that Clark might take Kentucky's business somewhere else, relented and sent a messenger to catch Clark with the news that the powder would be shipped at Virginia's expense.

Such a caviling spirit in the capital emphasized the need for Henry's presence. John Page, the lieutenant governor, wanted Henry in Williamsburg to relieve him of the press of petty detail that had devolved upon him during the governor's illness. While the constitution had but vaguely sketched the governor's obligation "to exercise the Executive powers of government," the convention had passed an ordinance conferring upon the governor (with the advice of the council) the broad administrative powers previously vested in the committee of safety. The grant would run only until the next session of the assembly, but it turned the modestly conceived "executive" into the agency at least temporarily responsible for managing the war effort. On Tuesday, September 17, Henry took his seat at the oval council table on the second floor of the Capitol. In that handsomely paneled chamber, two years earlier, Henry's caucus of ardent Whigs had drafted the fast day resolution to protest the Boston Port Bill. From that chamber Henry had walked many times after hearing the assembly summarily dissolved by a royal governor seated on the grandly carved mahogany throne Henry now occupied. Yet Henry would have to direct the fortunes of his commonwealth by inspiration, not sanction. His ascendancy symbolized the revolution that had taken place, but while authority had shifted from Crown to people, power had turned from the governor to the assembly. Henry could neither convene nor adjourn the legislature, nor could he veto its actions.

Henry thanked the five councilors who had doggedly attended to business all summer. They seemed a complaisant group, unlikely to oppose Henry and completely devoid of "the spice of the old aristocracy" that had hobbled the committee of safety and so vexed General Charles Lee. The former council president, the senior Thomas Nelson, and his fabulously wealthy compatriot Charles Carter had declined to serve on the new council, which Jefferson had already disparaged as the fifth wheel on the wagon.

The morning's agenda proved long and tedious. Henry had to review warrants for expenditures made by a host of military officers for tents, kettles, hunting shirts, blankets, recruiting bounties, and powder horns. Each invoice and bill had to be examined, the sum approved, and the account properly recorded. Other claimants wanted adjustments in pay or needed commissions signed. A merchant named Matthew Phripp came in to complain that he should not be stigmatized because his hired ship's captain violated instructions by sailing to the interdicted port of Bermuda. Henry Lee, a young captain of dragoons, requested an order for clothing for the troop of horses he intended to recruit in Stafford County. The commissary needed a written authorization to deliver four hundred pounds of bacon to the schooner *Hornet* as part of a state-sponsored trading expedition to the French and Dutch West Indies in pursuit of salt, woolens, medicines, ammunition, and other necessities. The council recorded action on three dozen items that day, each consuming—in a society that loved both rambling talk and precise accounts—an astonishing amount of time.

In addition to the work of virtually daily council meetings, as governor Henry heard the private importunings of the discontent and the ambitious, who wanted either to circumvent the council or to rely upon the governor's interest with it. Henry also had to draft the letters, proclamations, and orders issuing from council decisions and make sure that his clerk copied and dispatched them correctly. As always, executing policies necessitated a host of subordinate decisions by the administrator.

Virginia lawyers and planters never seemed to complain about the press of their daily work. It generally afforded both variety and a fair amount of time in the saddle, and one dealt by and large with a familiar circle of clients, overseers, and laborers. Government in wartime—with the need to tend to a multiplicity of matters, to cope with an unusual volume of paperwork, and to deal with numerous strangers on anxious and urgent matters—set one to groaning from the outset. "From morning till night I have not a minute from business," Henry lamented. "I wish it may all do, for there are a thousand things to mend, to begin."

Virginia had three wars to fight. The commonwealth had its obligations to the continental cause, but every dispatch of men or matériel to General Washington had to be weighed in light of Virginia's need to defend its own frontiers: the porous eastern coastline that a handful of British warships could readily penetrate and the long mountain valleys so easily enfiladed by angry Indians. Yet the commonwealth had no overall plan and could only react to emergencies. John Page had long advocated an aggressive mobilization within Virginia; Dunmore could have been driven off months earlier, Page insisted, and Norfolk would have been spared the torch. But Virginia could not afford to keep the militia on full pay and rations except during an emergency, and poor farm families did not want to spare their able-bodied men for longer than absolutely necessary.

With three Virginia battalions rushing off to join Washington at New York, the situation at Williamsburg seemed precarious. Within ten days of Henry's assumption of leadership, the council had ordered twenty-six companies of militiamen to the capital as a replacement force, and Henry offered a good swatch of the palace grounds as a barracks site. (When Landon Carter heard of this, he immediately complained to George Washington that Henry had taken on presumptuous "dignity" and surrounded himself with a palace guard. Next, fumed Carter, the capital would be moved to Hanover and renamed "Henry-town.")

Although a visiting Frenchman addressed Henry as "Son Altesse Royale" and state papers styled him as "His Excellency," the local people called him simply "the governor." The question of titles vexed the revolutionaries. The gentry's instinctive desire to preserve old habits of deference, when combined with a wish to confer respectful legitimacy upon the new institutions, encouraged the liberal use of "honorable" and "excellency." Yet the most vigorous republicans regarded these "tinsel epithets" as unbecoming, pompous cant. "If I should sometimes address . . . you without the Excellency tacked on," General Charles Lee told Henry, "you must not esteem it a mark of personal or official disrespect, but the reverse."

The decline of ceremony appeared most noticeable when the legislature convened in early October 1776. The new assembly, to the delighted eyes of one republican farmer, appeared "not quite so well dressed, nor so politely educated, nor so highly born as some Assemblies I have formerly seen. . . . They are plain and of consequence less disguised . . . less intriguing, more sincere," and thus fit to be "the People's men." These delegates took their places in the burgesses' former chamber, elected Pendleton their Speaker, appointed committees, and proceeded to conduct business as if nothing extraordinary had happened. Yet as governor, Henry had no official role to play. He mounted no splendid opening ceremony, as Botetourt used to do, nor did Henry stand augustly in the Council Chamber, in the name of overseas authority, to approve the choice of Speaker, grant the house its privileges, and exchange purling words of welcome with its leaders.

In these first months, no branch of government wished to seem presumptuous. Henry deferentially referred letters from Congress to the assembly before answering them, and the assembly, even when countermanding executive actions, did so in a gravely courteous manner that evoked no antagonism. (The House did send the twenty-six militia companies back home, regarding the mobilization as both premature and expensive.)

Henry took no part in the formation of a legislative program. That task fell to Assemblyman Thomas Jefferson, who, from his quarters in George Wythe's house a few doors down from the palace, drafted bills for the creation of county government in Kentucky, for the abolition of feudal land tenures, and for releasing dissenters from the obligation of paying taxes to the Episcopal church. Illness curbed any inclination Henry may have had to lobby privately on these questions, and "the low state of his health" forced the governor to go up-country for three weeks at the height of the session.

Henry returned to a capital cloaked in black. Richard Bland, who had served in every assembly and convention since 1743, had dropped dead in the street. While mourning one old patriot, Williamsburg buried another. Peyton Randolph's remains had come home from Philadelphia, and the entire town, led by the governor and the assembly, marched behind the hearse to the Randolph family's vault in the college chapel, where the late Speaker was eulogized one last time as the father of his country.

In this somber atmosphere Henry had more grim news to face. Washington had lost New York; the British, now overrunning New Jersey, seemed poised to take Philadelphia, and Congress might have to adjourn to Baltimore. An express brought reports that "upwards of one hundred Sail of the Enemy's Ships have moved from New York and are Steering Southwardly." Anticipating an invasion of Virginia, Henry immediately mobilized the militia in the counties athwart the entrance to Chesapeake Bay, again called up reinforcements to Williamsburg and Hampton, and ordered a ton of ammunition sent to Portsmouth. Henry's previous discretion with the assembly now paid dividends, for the House "highly" approved his prompt actions and formally assured "the Governour of the entire confidence we place in him."

Henry shrewdly chose this moment to accomplish some administrative changes. He sought greater authority for the commissary's office and worked out a system that delegated responsibility for military purchases to a subcommittee of councilors. He requested more clerical help and proposed simplified accounting procedures that would relieve the council of its daily, tedious reckoning with treasury warrants.

Although the southern movement of Howe's fleet proved a feint (its real objective being Newport, Rhode Island), the sense of beleaguerment did not ease. Virginia urgently dispatched more cavalry and ammunition to Washington's hardpressed troops in New Jersey. (If the present recruiting drive fails, the general emphasized, "the game is pretty well up.") Meanwhile, Henry shored up the militia in Virginia's northwestern counties in anticipation of Indian attacks, and he issued a touching statewide appeal for clothing and blankets. Surely "our worthy Countrymen will spare from their Beds" the protection every soldier has a right "to expect from the Humanity of those for whom he is to fight," Henry wrote to every county lieutenant. "Send what Blankets you get to me," he added.

With the frontier uncertain and the Continental Army facing its gravest crisis yet, the assembly could not adjourn without granting Henry interim powers for coping with a military emergency. "The present imminent danger . . . calls for the utmost exertion of our strength," the House resolved, and it declared that "the usual forms of government should be suspended during a limited time, for the more speedy execution of . . . measures to repel the invasion of the enemy." This language, hastily drawn up by George Mason, appeared on second thought to be an invitation to dictatorship, and instead of the phrase "the usual forms . . . be suspended" the state Senate substituted the more circumscribed and accurate phrase, "additional powers be given to the Governor and Council." Henry would, until the assembly met again, have power to requisition more soldiers, to call forth troops in conjunction with other states, and to provide for their pay, with the assembly pledged to make up any deficiency at its next session. This extraordinary grant over the purse strings —a departure from "the constitutions of government"— should not be "drawn into precedent," the law insisted, "being in this instance founded on the most evident and urgent necessity."

In his new office Henry had earned, all over again, the people's trust. Henry worked all through Christmas week on military preparation, and shortly after New Year's heard the cheering news that Washington had crossed the Delaware on Christmas Night to surprise a mercenary force at Trenton and start a drive that would push the British back across New Jersey. "Our people . . . are firm & not to be shaken," Henry wrote confidently to R. H. Lee on January 9. "I am endeavoring at vigorous measures," he said; "I trust the honor of our arms will be retrieved."

Two months later, however, an exasperated Henry told Lee that despite "every possible method" the state had not yet filled its quota of troops. "I've sent expresses twice to each colonel, & besides have had public advertisements repeatedly in the papers," Henry said, but the recruiters seemed slow, even "remiss." He could exhort, but he could not order, since "in the opinion of most people the executive of this country can exercise no command" over continental officers. "Can you tell us nothing from France?" Henry asked with an impatience edged with despair.

To General Washington, Henry addressed apologies for the deficiency and delay. Georgia and Carolina, allowed to recruit in the state for a few months, had drawn off more men than anticipated, and the western campaign pinned others close to home. The "terrors" of the smallpox and malicious talk from deserters also dampened enthusiasm for enlistment. Would the general, Henry asked, entertain an interim plan of meeting the quota with short-term volunteers drawn out of the militia?

"No," Washington replied, with asperity. Transient troops are "uneasy, impatient of command . . . generally assume the privilege of not only thinking, but doing as they please," and spend much of their alloted time in "marching to and from camp." Washington wanted enlistments, for three years or the duration, and advised Henry to meet the quota "by coercive methods" if necessary. Henry heard the voice of command, and in May the governor successfully urged the assembly to authorize drafts from the able-bodied militia.

Henry also worked hard at the acquisition of supplies. He dispatched Virginia's infant navy—five doughty ships named *Congress, Liberty, Defiance, Scorpion,* and *Hornet*—on expeditions to the French and Dutch West Indies, where they traded state-purchased tobacco for salt and gunpowder. He initiated more ambitious commercial ventures in France and Holland and designated R. H. Lee's brother William as Virginia's agent in "Nantz" and Bordeaux. "Great exertions are made here to import & fabricate," Henry declared, and he took special pride in the small-arms-and-munitions factory established near Fredericksburg. He also admonished the public against the selfish practice of engrossing foreign goods and country produce in order to drive up prices, and threatened to use powers of impressment and confiscation in order to obtain war matériel in a manner that forestalled profiteering.

Henry had a keen head for business and hated to pay more than he had to for anything. When the scion of the well-regarded Tucker family, young St. George Tucker, called upon the governor to request reimbursement for services connected with the purchase of indigo in Charleston, he received rough handling. The governor kept him waiting two hours and then brusquely reviewed the papers without offering the gentleman a chair. Instead of the remarks of gratitude Tucker confidently anticipated, he heard Henry complain at the high price and grumble that the young man had made the purchase in too much hurry. Tucker remained indignant for years.

In reviewing plans for a defensive expedition to Kentucky, Henry urged the leaders to conduct it "on the cheapest Terms Circumstances will allow." If they made some allowance for hunting "wild meat" along the way, Henry suggested, they could reduce both the cost of food and the number of pack horses necessary to carry it. "The Necessity of Frugality," the governor explained, arises "from the great Extent & Variety of Military operations that all together bring on monstrous Expense to the State."

Henry found the frontier situation especially delicate. William Christian had led an expedition that subdued most of the Cherokee towns on the upper Tennessee River without bloodshed and arranged for a great treaty conference at the Holston River's old Fort Robinson, which the men now called Fort Patrick Henry. But Christian reported that one rebellious Cherokee leader, Dragging Canoe, had retreated with hundreds of followers deep into the hinterland, where he intrigued with British agents and the riled-up Shawnee. If this Cherokee group made common cause with the Ohio River tribes, the entire frontier could still be ablaze. Henry had to caution the northwestern frontier to hold itself in readiness yet give no cause to attack. If their Indian allies demanded protection from the Shawnee, Henry ordered it provided: "If the Indians chuse to come into our settlements for Shelter, make them Welcome, & share with them all your ammunition. . . . Any Injury done them, is done to us while they are faithful," Henry explained. "In one word, support protect defend & cherish them in every Respect to the utmost."

Annie Christian communicated privately with her brother, the governor. She had intended to come down from the mountains with her husband, "but our Family & cares increase so fast, that God knows when I shall be able to take another journey." Indeed, Mr. Christian "is so much abroad that I am more confined on that account." Could brother Pat assist in "the great favor" of seeing that Mr. Christian left the public service long enough to "get his affairs brought into some better way than at present"? His stay at home might yet "save a whole family from ruin," she urged, with apologies for troubling Henry on "any domestic business."

Henry did not mind, for he had domestic business of his own. He told Christian to spend the summer at home in New River building the new house sister Annie so desperately needed and to scout the neighborhood for another estate. Henry wanted to sell Scotchtown, he explained, for its painful memories of Sallie made the place intolerable to him. He could not think of renewing family life there when his term of office expired.

Family life? Two years had passed since the death of his wife, and with his health recovered and the affairs of the commonwealth in tolerable order, the governor had started courting again. On his trips up to Scotchtown, he frequently stopped to visit the Dandridge family. Nathaniel Dandridge, an old friend and client, was married to a daughter of Governor Spotswood; their son had served in Henry's regiment and now had joined the staff of General Washington, whose wife, Martha, was Nat Dandridge's niece.

There were four attractive daughters in the family. Henry soon paid his addresses to Dorothea, a dark-eyed, dark-haired young woman of twenty-two, the same age as Henry's newly married daughter Patsy. Neighborhood gossip held that "Dolly" had fancied an impecunious young sailor named John Paul Jones, then visiting cousins on a nearby plantation, but her father dashed her hopes in favor of the more glorious match with the governor. Colonel Dandridge gave twelve slaves and some Hanover land as dowry, and the wedding took place October 9, 1777, the first marriage for a generation in either family not celebrated by the governor's uncle, the Reverend Patrick Henry, Sr., who had died several months earlier. The Dandridge and Winston clans, however, joined the festivities with the exception of one of the bride's Spotswood aunts, who had turned Tory. She had not spoken to the rest of the family for years but rather stayed at home "and enjoy[ed] her own thoughts," as Dolly's mother put it.

Henry wanted to retire to the mountains; indeed, he had offered to trade all his Ohio River lands for any tract near the Christians, but his brother-in-law wouldn't hear of such a swap. "I can't think of your parting with it, unless to your own children upon the approach of your Matrimonial affair," Christian advised. If nothing suitable turned up, Christian said, "you shall have this one I live on, & I will be your near neighbor at Town, or go to my James River land, so that you may lay out your Accounts as soon as you please for making preparations to move your estate."

Despite Christian's generosity, Henry could not move immediately. In May the assembly had reelected him, without opposition, to another term as governor, and in late summer the state had undergone another invasion scare. The Henrys hurried back to the capital after their wedding, and so he brought his bride home to the palace her grandfather had built.

Under its competent and vivacious young mistress the old house regained some of its splendor. Botetourt's and Dunmore's elegant furniture had long since gone back to England, but the 1776 convention had authorized expenditure of one thousand pounds to fit the building with enough beds, chairs, and tables for family use. Skilled slave carpenters, masons, and plasterers had added a new fireplace and remodeled the entry hall and reception area from a plan sketched by Jefferson. Even though soldiers still camped on the lawn, the palace lost the rough atmosphere of the officer's mess that had marked Henry's widowerhood.

With the governor's daughter and sister also in residence while their husbands fought in the war, and the young offspring of several families running about, the domestic circle familiar to Henry from his youth—the peerless male surrounded by admiring women and a shadowing cluster of servants—had reconstituted itself. It would steadily grow. Dolly gave birth to their first daughter, also named Dorothea, the following August and delivered a second girl, Sarah, two years later. Five sons followed in the next decade; in the twenty-two years of her marriage Dorothea Henry would bear eleven children. "The cradle began to rock in his household when Patrick was eighteen, and it was still rocking when he died at sixty-three," his sister Elizabeth remarked sourly. (She quarreled with her brother on a number of issues, especially his unwillingness to act upon the abhorrence of slavery they both felt; in her later years, after achieving renown as a Methodist evangelist, Elizabeth Henry Russell manumitted the slaves she had inherited from her father and husbands.)

Shortly after Henry and his new wife arrived in Williamsburg, they learned that General Burgoyne's entire army, pushing south from Canada to divide the Northeast, had met fierce resistance from the Continentals and surrendered at Saratoga. It was a decisive victory, which Henry confidently expected would achieve his long-desired hope of securing French aid in the American cause. On October 30 the capital held a feu de joie to celebrate the victory at Saratoga. The cheering and saluting began at three in the afternoon, and Governor Henry expressed his "hearty congratulations" by ordering a gill of rum issued to every soldier marching in the grand parade.

The war, however, was far from over. Washington had lost two engagements with Howe's forces outside Philadelphia and retreated into winter quarters at Valley Forge while the British occupied the city. Another winter and spring mobilization would be required to replenish the army, and with the Northeast secure, the fighting would in all likelihood concentrate increasingly in the South and West. Recruiting would be even more difficult, for the exuberant martial spirit of 1775 had inevitably dissipated as the horrors of the battlefield became known. In the shocked words of an army private who fought under Washington at Brandywine Creek, the war meant "Cannons Roaring muskets Cracking Drums Beating Bumbs Flying all Round, men a-dying, woundeds Horred Groans"; it "would Greave the Heardiest of Hearts to See Such a Dollful Sight as this, to see our Fellow Creators Slain in Such a manner as this."

Saratoga came to wear this somber aspect for Henry. His twenty-year-old son John, an artillery captain, had distinguished himself in the fighting, then walked among the American dead, lingering over the bodies of men he had known. Then he drew his own sword, broke it to pieces, and grieved inconsolably. After a melancholy winter, John Henry resigned his commission; the governor had to dispatch money and a servant to New Jersey to fetch the poor boy home.

The military and diplomatic significance of Saratoga led Henry to take a good look at the map. He yearned for an equally decisive stroke in the southern theater, and he mulled over ways a connection with Spain might check the British in the Mississippi Valley. Acting on his own initiative, and confiding only in R. H. Lee, Henry made overtures to the Spanish governors at Havana and New Orleans. Ostensibly he wrote about trading connections. European goods could be loaded at those ports by Virginia's agents and sneaked through the tricky North Carolina coast, or they could be shipped up the Mississippi. Henry would venture to set up a post at the mouth of the Ohio to receive Spanish shipments. "I suppose I need not inform your Excellency," Henry told each of the Spanish governors, "that these states are now free and independent, capable of forming alliances and of making treaties." Describing a "mutually beneficial connection," Henry painted a lively portrait of Virginia's hemp, flax, shingles, pork, flour, and tobacco passing through the "free port" of New Orleans, where French and Dutch ships might take off what Spain herself did not want. Henry also dangled the prospect of Spain's recovering the British-held outposts at Pensacola and St. Augustine and thus securing the Atlantic trade as well. If these overtures drew favorable interest, Henry next intended to take up the question of a Spanish loan

to Virginia, but he told Lee, "Keep it close, and mention it to
no one."

Henry's grand design for the Mississippi Valley suddenly
gained a military dimension when the Kentucky fighter
George Rogers Clark turned up in December with a tantaliz-
ing proposition. Meeting privately with the governor, Clark
broached the idea of an expedition into the Illinois country
where the British had taken over the old French garrisons at
Vincennes and Kaskaskia. Clark had already sent trusted
scouts to spy out the situation. Kaskaskia, which lay thirty
leagues north of the Ohio's junction with the Mississippi,
contained about one hundred French and English families,
who conducted an extensive trade both with the Indians and
the Spanish at New Orleans. The stone fort had about ten
thousand pounds of powder and several cannon, but not a
single guard.

The place could be taken very easily, Clark told Henry,
and sensing the governor's excitement, he sketched out a plan.
Clark could quickly raise three hundred men in Kentucky and
float them, with forty days' provisions, down the Ohio to the
Wabash River. There would be only a short five-mile march
to the town. This could be accomplished at night without
detection. Although the inhabitants regarded the Americans
as "notorious rebels," Clark did not think they would offer
much resistance. If they ran to the fort, they would lose their
provisions in the town; and if they tried to defend the town,
Clark would grab the fort and threaten to burn it down and
leave their unprotected families to starve.

"I could be in full possession of the country by next
April," Clark promised. If Virginia held Kaskaskia, "it would
fling the command of the two great rivers into our hands,
which would enable us to get supplies of goods from the
Spaniards, and to carry on a trade with the Indians . . . [that]
might perhaps . . . keep them our friends."

Henry tried not to show his excitement. Kaskaskia would
be the Ohio post he desired, the key to the Spanish trade,
and a taunt, from an unexpected quarter, at the king's domain
in Canada. Although Clark pointed out that control of
Kaskaskia would cut off some flow of provisions to Fort

Detroit, the paramount British outpost in the Northwest, he kept silent about his dream of launching an attack on Detroit from Kaskaskia and the intermediate post at Vincennes. Clark feared that Henry would dismiss the scheme as too wild and too expensive, for surely Detroit could not be taken with fewer than five times the men Clark thought adequate for the Illinois project. Yet Henry could read the map as well as Clark and draw his own conclusions about what might become possible. "Great things have been affected [*sic*] by a few men well conducted," Clark said solemnly.

Henry questioned Clark closely. Sending a party so far off would be a daring risk, the governor said; did Clark have any plan of retreat in mind? Such an expedition could only succeed under a cloak of secrecy; could Clark recruit men without telling them of the hazards ahead? The assembly was in session, Henry explained, and he had no emergency powers to set this venture in motion without its consent. Yet it would be "dangerous" to discuss it publicly, because word would spread through the frontier "and probably the first prisoner taken by the Indians would give the alarm which would end in the certain destruction of the party." These were all worrisome questions, Henry explained, and he would have to think them through before making any commitment.

Clark waited in Williamsburg for several weeks while Henry quietly set the project in motion. He had earnest private consultations with Jefferson and Mason, in town for the assembly session, and they urged that George Wythe, who had become Speaker of the House when Pendleton crippled himself severely in a riding accident, be taken into confidence as well. Henry also wanted advice from R. H. Lee, then taking a brief holiday from Congress at his Westmoreland estate, and although he thought it "cruel to deny" Lee his "little repose," the governor summoned his old ally to Williamsburg for a confidential talk.

These gentlemen all shared Henry's favorable view. They agreed that the assembly might be asked simply to permit Clark to raise additional companies for the defense of Kentucky. The governor would accordingly issue public instructions to Clark for that purpose, but he would draft a second set of more explicit, confidential orders to be approved by the council alone. Jefferson, Mason, and Wythe would give Clark a private letter (to be used in recruiting) that described the expedition as a reprisal against Indians and promised three hundred acres of any conquered land to each volunteer.

On Friday, January 2, 1778, Henry skillfully went through the routine of securing the council's agreement to "set on foot the Expedition against Kaskasky with as little Delay and as much Secrecy as possible." The governor presented a draft of the secret orders for Clark, and the council endorsed them. Henry gave Clark authority to recruit 350 men as Virginia militiamen for an attack on Kaskaskia. "If the White Inhabitants at that post and the Neighborhood will give undoubted Evidence of their Attachment to this State (for it is certain they live within its Limits) . . . Let them be treated as fellow Citizens & their persons & property duly secured," Henry said. Otherwise, "these people must feel the miseries of war." Cannon and ammunition seized should be used to fortify the desired post at the mouth of the Ohio with "the fairest prospects being opened to the Dominions of both France and Spain."

The next day Henry presented the orders to Clark along with the commonwealth's voucher for twelve hundred pounds in expense money. The two men also shook hands on their private partnership for "taking a body of Land" in what Clark liked to call "the French country." Henry reviewed the plan with the hulking young soldier, looked him straight in the eye, and, as Clark recalled, said that "he did not wish [that] an implicit attention to his instructions should prevent my executing any thing that would manifestly tend to the good of the public." Clark nodded. The Kentuckian would "set forward Cloathed with all the authority I wished." Later Henry would write Clark that his operations "should not be confin'd to the Fort and Settlement at the place mention'd . . . but that you proceed to the Enemy's settlements above or across, as you may find it proper." In his youth Henry had been a patient angler, but never before had he sent someone else to do his fishing—and in so vast a stream.

The Kaskaskia project had all "the éclat" Henry longed for, and after Clark's departure the governor set a secondary scheme in motion by dispatching twenty-eight men to scout the vicinity of New Orleans. The expedition's leader would confer with the Spanish governor about the planned Virginia trading post. "Describe to that Gentleman the real Strength and Situation of Virginia the Progress of the War & whatever else he may wish to know of the American Confederacy," Henry said. He also enclosed a personal letter to the governor that repeated his sketch of a commercial alliance but went on to broach the subject of a loan. "Naturally your Excellency will desire to know what I have to give you as compensation for these loans," Henry said, and he answered his own question by enumerating as possibilities "the thanks of this free and independent country, trade in one or all of its rich products, and the friendship of its brave inhabitants." "Ignorant at the present time which of these things Your Excellency prefers," Henry loftily added, "I offer them so that you may select those which are most pleasing to Your Excellency and the Spanish Nation." (Henry sent a duplicate letter to New Orleans by ship, the captain of which was ordered to throw the packet overboard if he saw "a certainty of being taken.")

With the western expedition launched, Henry returned his full attention to impending disaster in the East. The congressional machinery for supplying the army had come to a standstill, owing to poor management, a shortage of funds, and a diminution of spirit. From his winter headquarters at Valley Forge, General Washington implored the states to assist the army. In November 1777 he had urged that a "moderate assessment" be made in every county for clothing and blankets. Henry promptly requested the assembly to call upon Virginians to contribute one pair of shoes or gloves for each soldier raised in their county, and when the assembly complied, Henry publicly proclaimed it "of so important a Nature to the Welfare of our Soldiery, and consequently to the grand Interests of America, that I cannot too warmly press it upon the Attention of the good People of this State." Using his emergency powers of impressment, Governor

Henry ordered fifteen thousand pounds of woolens seized for continental use, and he managed, by early December, to fill nine wagons with other necessaries for the supply of the Virginia regiments with Washington.

The general expressed immense gratitude but coupled his thanks with renewed pleas for help. The army "must inevitably . . . Starve, dissolve, or disperse," Washington warned, unless adequate supplies could be gained. "I assure you Sir," he told Henry, "it is not easy to give you a just and accurate Idea of the sufferings of the Troops at large." The public would scarce believe it, but on December 23, a field return showed "not less than 2898 men unfit for duty by reason of their being barefoot and otherwise naked." A few weeks later Washington had to tell Henry: "We have experienced little less than a famine in Camp and have had much cause to dread a general mutiny and dispersion."

The failures of the commissariat made Henry angrier than he had been since Lord Dunmore expropriated the gunpowder. The governor quickly ascertained that eight or ten thousand hogs and "several thousand fine Beeves" might be had in the Shenandoah counties of Virginia that lay across the Susquehanna Valley from Washington's camp at Valley Forge. When the congressional deputy would not send a purchasing agent to the area immediately, the exasperated Henry did it himself. He hired three "gentlemen of character" and advanced them enough cash to buy ten thousand pounds of beef and pork and drive it on the hoof "to Camp in the most Expeditious Manner . . . to answer the present Exigency." He then wrote a blistering letter to Frank Lee and the other Virginia delegates in Congress,* complaining of the

---

* The Articles of Confederation and Perpetual Union, approved by the Continental Congress in 1777, established a league of states, each having one vote in a Congress granted power to make war but not allowed to raise money or troops except by requisitions upon the member states. Although Virginia ratified the Articles in December 1777, several small states, especially Maryland, withheld formal approval until conflicting state claims over western lands were settled. Meanwhile the Continental Congress, as organized by Henry and

threat the mismanagement posed to "the existence of american Liberty" and the burdens it had placed on Virginia.

Henry wanted it "earnestly . . . understood and remembered once for all" that the governor's office had nothing to do with the congressional commissary. The executive holds "itself guiltless of all the Mischiefs which in future may arise from Delinquency in that office," Henry declared, exonerating himself in advance from any charges that his bold action amounted to a meddlesome usurpation of power. "It will indeed be unworthy the Character of a Zealous American to entrench himself within the strict Line of official Duty, & there quietly behold the starving and dispersion of the American Army," Henry said, and added a concluding flourish, "The Genius of this Country is not of that Cast."

Henry worked hard to relieve "the pain which government feels" on the matter of supplies by supplanting the laggard agents in Virginia with men of his own choosing. "I exerted all my personal influence," Henry told R. H. Lee of his effort to get an old Hanover friend, John Hawkins, to take on the commissariat in Virginia; if Congress failed to approve the arrangement, it could not count on any more help from Henry. The congressional delegates, stung by Henry's uncharacteristic vehemence, secured a host of departmental reforms that brought some relief by spring. In April the governor and council indulged in a mild celebration by sending, through newly established channels, a shipment of fine rum to Washington and his staff. (Washington kindly thanked Henry for the "agreeable present" which, he said, "will find us in a humour to do it all manner of justice.")

Henry remained worried, however, by signs that Virginians had lost their patriotic fervor. In the trans-Allegheny counties frontier settlers had ignored Henry's steady appeals

---

others in 1774–75, continued to conduct business as if the Articles were in force. In 1781 Maryland finally endorsed this first constitution after Virginia agreed to surrender its claim to all territory north of the Ohio River. Congress organized this vast domain into the Northwest Territory by ordinances in 1784 and 1787.

and provoked quarrels with the Indians. With the Shawnee poised for a general attack, Henry reprimanded the county leaders in Botetourt for not bringing "the vile assassins" to trial. Those who brought on a frontier war just when "our whole Force was wanted in another quarter" had to be considered enemies to American independence. "Is this not the work of Tories," Henry raged, to "oblige our People to be hunting after Indians in the Woods instead of facing General Howe in the field." The governor insisted that the civil magistrates endeavor "at all hazards and to the last extremity" to bring the "traitorous" murderers of Indians to justice.

At the opposite end of the state, in the swampy regions south of Norfolk, a band of Loyalists led by a laborer named Josiah Phillips had engaged in months of pillaging and burning that now threatened to become a full-scale insurrection. Henry used his emergency powers to call out the militia against "the traitor Phillips" and his band. He also ordered the families supporting the insurgent removed to another part of the state. Some gentlemen regarded Phillips as a "common robber" who tried to cloak his depredations with the dubious protection of British citizenship, and to tighten the net, Jefferson (with Henry's backing) rushed a bill of attainder through the assembly that would pronounce Phillips guilty of treason if he did not surrender by a certain date. In convention Henry had raised the specter of a heinous criminal escaping the reach of ordinary law when he pressed the deletion of attainders from the Declaration of Rights. His sense of desperation and his renewed disposition to act unilaterally led him to endorse this extreme use of state power against Phillips, but it proved unnecessary. Phillips would be captured and tried in civil court on simple charges of robbery, not attainted treason, and the threat of rebellion eased.

The long and anxious winter had left Henry depleted and worn. "My strength will not suffice," he confided to Lee. "I am really so harassed by the great load of continental Business thrown on me lately, that I am ready to sink under my Burden." Henry's "thoughts of taking . . . rest," however, would remain idle ones, for on May 29 (Henry's forty-second birthday) the assembly elected him to a third term as governor. Henry reluctantly accepted "this fresh instance" of favor with a weary one-sentence promise that his "best endeavours shall be used to promote the public good."

As a sign of confident administration, however, Henry for the first time made a comprehensive report to the general assembly, advising it of executive actions taken and directing the legislature's attention to certain serious problems, preeminently those of recruiting, supplies, and public finance. Henry expressed alarm at the "shock to the public Credit" occasioned by depreciating paper money and the "truly alarming" rise in prices. Salt, for example, which had sold for twenty-six shillings a bushel in July 1776, now cost at least seven pounds. The governor's salary, fixed originally at one thousand pounds per year, would shortly be raised to three thousand pounds in an effort to keep pace with inflation. The assembly considered a variety of credit schemes but shied away from tightening the money supply through heavier taxation. R. H. Lee lobbied strenuously with Henry to endorse such a course, which the governor in turn "pressed warmly on some, but in vain." Most delegates drifted along on the hope, still nursed fondly by Henry, that loans from France and Spain would ease the problem less painfully. Expectations grew larger in midsession with the joyous news that, at long last, France would enter into a treaty of alliance and commerce with the newly independent states.

The "generous French," Henry thought, would pull America back from the "dreadful precipice," yet his outlook remained gloomy. The war had moved into its fourth arduous year with enlistments waning and profiteering on the rise. "The flesh pots of Egypt are still savoury to degenerate palates," Henry told Lee, and the British would do their best to corrupt Americans if they could not defeat them in battle. The moral reformation that Henry and Adams once expected to accompany political revolution had not yet occurred, and this melancholy realization left Henry despairing even as the military picture brightened.

The advancing French fleet threatened the British supply

lines along the northeastern seaboard, and General Clinton, who had replaced Howe as commander, decided to withdraw from Philadelphia and regroup his army in New York. Washington chased the retreating redcoats across New Jersey and encamped at White Plains. With the navies stalemated off Rhode Island and the armies checking each other at the Hudson River, it became clear that the British had not divided the continent and, indeed, had not gained an acre of territory in two years. The heroic effort of keeping the Continental Army in place had done its defensive work, and in the summer of 1778 Americans began to wonder, with France (and Spain) coming into the war, whether the British would sue for peace. It was not likely, the strategists realized, until the British had tried attacks from the south or west.

Henry understood that all the resources Virginia had sent north would now have to be redirected south, and that the Chesapeake itself might be the next target. For this reason he strenuously opposed Congress's plan of sending an expedition against Fort Detroit in midsummer 1778. Henry remonstrated that sufficient supplies could not be provided from Virginia and the staging area at Fort Pitt and that the season had advanced too far for a campaign to reach the Great Lakes before winter. His stubborn insistence led Congress to back off, and no one guessed that Governor Henry had tried to keep the Continental Army out because Virginia had its own secret expeditionary force in the region.

Henry waited all summer and long into the fall for news from Clark. Finally, in November, a wearied express rider named William Myers came from Illinois with Clark's news that he had taken Kaskaskia on the Fourth of July without loss of life. The populace had sworn allegiance to "the Republic of Virginia" and aided Clark in an equally successful capture of Vincennes. During the summer, Clark reported, he had made treaties with most of the tribes in the region, except for the implacably hostile Shawnee. He had enjoyed favorable commerce with the Spanish and given thought to establishing a trading post at St. Louis. With the Illinois country triumphantly obtained, Clark wanted attention directed to an attack on Detroit.

Henry reported this success to Congress solely in terms of frontier safety and Indian diplomacy. He thought Congress might want to know Clark's views on "the state of things in the Western country" and the commander's sense of Detroit's vulnerability. About the acquisition of territory and the Spanish trade, Henry said little, telling Congress somewhat disingenuously that "The french Inhabitants have manifested great Zeal & Attachment to our Cause & insist on Garrisons remaining with them under Col. Clarke." "I am induced to agree," Henry reported, "because the Safety of our own Frontiers, as well as that of these people demands a compliance with the Request."

The governor did not tell Congress that he would shortly ask the general assembly to extend Virginia county government to Illinois. Within the month Henry had appointed the civil officers for the new county, thoughtfully enclosing copies of the Declaration of Rights and the state constitution with their commissions. He also named Clark "commander" of an augmented Virginia force in Illinois and gave him extensive new orders to protect the country "and as occasions may serve, annoy the enemy." Henry granted Clark "general discretionary powers" but suggested that he might consider operations either against Detroit or against the Indians who remained hostile. "One great Advantage expected from your Situation is to prevent the Indians from warring on this side of Ohio," Henry said, while implying that Clark might initiate a war on the northern shore to either remove the "troublesome thorns" beyond the Great Lakes or "exterminate" them. "The same world will scarcely do for them and us," Henry said. A settler's mentality still lay beneath the diplomatic concern for Indian justice he had expressed, virtually as military necessity, earlier in the year.

Henry also asked Clark for a private favor. "I am very desirous to get two of the best Stallions that [may] possibly be found at the Illinois," Henry said; "I hear the Horses are fine." Clark should spare no expense in buying "the finest Horses of the true Spanish blood," from either the Indians or perhaps the Spanish commandant, and paying "handsome wages" to "good men" who would bring them safely and carefully to Hanover. The governor also wanted Clark to purchase eight mares for him "as large as you can get and not old" and have them sent to Colonel Christian's "by some good men coming in." "Don't loose a moment in agreeing for the Mares," Henry advised, "for vast Numbers of people are about to go out after them from here, & will soon pick them all up & raise the price very high." He would expect the mares immediately, since "they need not be picked with the Care to be used in finding out the finest Horses," Henry said, and then he added a two-page memo describing the qualities he desired in his stallions and concluding with the most rhapsodic words he would ever write. "There is something so striking & inexpressibly *Beautiful* in a *Fine* Horse, that must catch the Eye of every Beholder," Henry said, and while this is "impossible to describe," he would "premise" that "the parts wch Constitute Beauty, Constitute Strength, & the *Beautiful* Horse, is Always *Good*." Therefore, Henry would pay, in addition to expenses, a bonus of two hundred pounds for the diligent searcher who produced the longed-for stallions.

Dreams of prized horseflesh and the prestige of a postwar stud farm propelled Henry through the last six months of his term. The early spring brought yet another round of recruiting worries, for the expected British assault had begun in Georgia and South Carolina. He tried to expand the military horizon to embrace the Lower Mississippi and West Florida, but the Continental Army was too hard-pressed to consider it, and Henry had neither a second George Clark nor men in reserve for such a venture. Indeed, the thinness of the state's defenses became cruelly exposed in May 1779, when a British naval party stormed Portsmouth and Suffolk, capturing or destroying more than one hundred Virginia vessels and three thousand hogsheads of tobacco. The assembly called loudly for continental aid, and Henry took a number of measures to secure stores and mobilize the militia, but the British withdrew before they could be engaged.

The raid reminded Virginians of what Henry had insisted upon all spring. It was wrong, he said "to think that the contest is at an end, and to make money, and to get places, the only thing now remaining to do." If we corrupt ourselves, Henry told George Mason, the British will remain here "on tiptoe," waiting for our collapse. Nothing can save us but "a total reformation in our conduct" and an effort "to bring things back to first principles, correct abuses, and punish our internal foes."

Henry was calling for help. For three years he had borne the burdens of office despite recurring illness, and he had worn himself out in the cause. He craved rest, and he sought to shatter any illusion that he alone could save Virginia. When talk blossomed that the constitution ought to be amended to allow him a fourth term, or more, he squelched the idea immediately. The commonwealth had many gentlemen of abilities. "Let this voice," Henry cried to Mason and Jefferson, "call upon you, and others. Do not, from a mistaken opinion that we are about to sit down under our own vine, and own fig-tree, let our hitherto noble struggle end in ignominy. Believe me when I tell you there is danger of it."

Yet the vine and fig tree, the biblical image of contentment in Zion once swords are turned to plowshares,* dominated Henry's thoughts. At the end of May, as soon as the legislature chose Jefferson as his successor, Henry left Williamsburg to find surcease in the hinterland he had always regarded as liberty's ultimate refuge.

---

* Micah 4:3–4: "And they shall beat their swords into ploughshares, and their spears into pruning hooks; nation shall not lift up sword against nation, neither shall they learn war anymore; but they shall sit every man under his vine and under his fig tree, and none shall make them afraid."

CHAPTER 17

"To Do Good and Prevent Mischief"

Henry led the family's exodus from the capital. They went in a motley caravan of horses, two-wheeled chairs, and farm wagons, numbering about fifty people from the governor, his wife and baby, his married daughter and her child, his sisters, and his older children to the cluster of black slave families who served them all. The household goods accompanied them; the livestock, the plantation stores and tools, and the gangs of field hands had gone on earlier from Hanover.

They traveled nearly two hundred miles to the fresh land the patriarch had bought near the Carolina border in a new county named in his honor. The property—ten thousand acres of densely forested hillsides and moderately fertile bottom land—ran along Leatherwood Creek, a noisy, twisting, south-flowing branch of the Dan River. The land had a wild, un-tamed look, with towering hickories and oaks, great outcrops of rock, and striking western views toward the knobs and pinnacles of the Blue Ridge. The Henrys found some squatters already tucked away in Leatherwood's hollows, each in his own cabin, as Carolina folks said, eating his "Hogg and Hominee" and afraid of no one.

Fifteen years earlier Henry had pushed into a lightly settled county with a new family, and once again, despite his fatigue and his recurrent fever, he enjoyed the challenge of a fresh start. Getting cropland started and a decent farmhouse built drew his attention away from the affairs of state. He roamed and hunted the new land, taking its measure and making his plans. He might lop off the southern corner for Patsy's husband, John Fontaine, he thought, and he started thinking about the sections to be reserved for his ever-growing number of children. He also kept his eye out for some choice spots that he might yet want to purchase. Only one country project came to nothing: Clark had failed to find those handsome Spanish horses for his stable.

Henry had sold off large tracts in Botetourt and Kentucky in order to pay for Leatherwood on short credit; although the currency depreciation made it something of a bargain, he actually met one of his notes with tobacco certificates worth considerably more than Virginia's paper money. He had also sold Scotchtown for a good price, and thus he returned to self-sufficient farming with a small, depreciating stock of capital along with ample resources in slaves and livestock. (In 1782 Henry paid taxes on seventy-five slaves, a work force less than half the size of Jefferson's or Page's, each of whom owned more than two hundred Negroes, but large enough to make Henry a very substantial planter.) Yet Leatherwood's remote situation restricted Henry's access to market; he could ship tobacco on flatboats down the Dan into the poorly paying Carolina Piedmont, or he could have barrels rolled overland on an expensively long journey either east to the better Southside Virginia markets on the Appomattox or north into the Shenandoah Valley trade. None of his choices offered a high return, but they all gave enough to maintain the family in better than average circumstances.

Henry County had fewer than five thousand inhabitants, and its prominent men quickly nominated both Henry and his son-in-law for seats on the county court and the parish vestry. Henry declined all invitations to resume public service, including election by the general assembly to a term in Congress. The thought of exchanging Leatherwood's crisp autumn air and brilliantly colored hillsides for the crowded frustrations of Philadelphia held no appeal for Henry. "I am circumstanced so as to make my attendance on Congress impossible," Henry advised the Speaker of the House, Benjamin Harrison, in October 1779. Having undergone a "tedious illness," Henry explained, he now must pay close attention to business. Nor did he want to endure a long separation from his family.

In the spring, however, Henry quickly responded with gratitude to a polite note from Governor Jefferson, saying, "I have scarcely heard a word of public matters since I moved up in the retirement where I live." Henry unburdened himself of his "many anxieties for the commonwealth," chiefly the depreciating currency and the "mistaken avarice" that had given rise to profiteering. Men who had seemed "good whigs" now kept company with "disguised tories" who undermined the health of the state by stockpiling goods, inflating prices, smuggling British goods, and spreading rumors of disaffection. Such "wretches" ought to be "shunned and execrated" (in the absence of stern laws), but their acceptance in good company, Henry said, "while their guilt was clear as the sun, has sickened me, and made me sometimes wish to be in retirement for the rest of my life."

Henry would do his best to shake off such despondent thoughts. He promised, "if I am chosen," to return to the assembly. "My health," he told Jefferson, "will never again permit a close application to sedentary business, and I even doubt whether I can remain below long enough to serve in the assembly." Convinced, however, that the public required fresh encouragement to "virtue," Henry vowed that he would "make the trial." The county did elect its most distinguished citizen, but within a fortnight of taking his seat in the legislature Henry's health broke and forced his return to Leatherwood.

Henry tried hard to stay out of public affairs, but the war came almost to his front door. The British had made their expected assault upon the South, easily taking Savannah in 1779 and capturing Charleston after a two-month-long siege in May 1780. (Virtually the entire Virginia Continental Line, under Henry's former rival William Woodford, was taken as prisoners to New York, where Woodford died of pneumonia.) In August Lord Cornwallis, the British commander in the South, overwhelmed General Gates's command at Camden, South Carolina, and seemed poised to take North Carolina as well. The British had counted on Loyalist sentiment in the southern states to reassert political control in the wake of their military victories, but the expected Tory rising did not materialize. Instead vicious internecine warfare took place across the Carolina backcountry throughout the fall. Near Leatherwood, Henry wrote in August, "The Tories have been plotting," but he believed that the parties "out in pursuit" would soon have them "pretty well suppressed." At Kings Mountain, more than a thousand shirt men under the command of Henry's brother-in-law William Campbell (a wild-looking Scotsman with a shock of flaming red hair) decimated a large Loyalist band bent on terrorizing the countryside, but the fierce fighting did not stop Cornwallis's march. Continental troops under Nathaniel Greene played tag with the British on the Carolina-Virginia border in January and February 1781, and when Greene was obliged to ferry his troops across the Dan not many miles from Leatherwood, Henry's plantation supplied 167 bushels of corn for the army and forage for twenty-eight horses. Henry's messenger returned from Greene with an urgent appeal to send fifteen hundred volunteers immediately. "The present moment requires . . . the most spirited exertions," Greene told Henry; "You, I know, are equal to them."

Henry, faced once again with the desperate problem of recruiting, helped rouse a contingent of three hundred volunteers, including John Fontaine, who joined Greene in time for a decisive confrontation with Cornwallis forty miles south of Leatherwood at Guilford Court House, North Carolina, on March 15. The British held the ground, but, as at Bunker Hill early in the war, sustained such heavy losses that Cornwallis, rattled and unsure of himself, withdrew to the seaboard to regroup. Then he impulsively brought his army to the Chesapeake, where a vanguard under the traitorous Benedict Arnold had already frightened the Virginia Tidewater.

In January 1781, Arnold's regiment had moved swiftly to attack Richmond, which ironically had become the capital in 1780 because it appeared safer than Williamsburg. The notorious turncoat had destroyed public records, captured large quantities of ammunition and tobacco (still Virginia's best coin for purchasing war matériel abroad), and set fire to a large section of town. By the time Henry heard the news, Arnold had secured himself in winter quarters near Portsmouth, and Governor Jefferson's posting a large reward for Arnold's capture did little to revive sagging spirits. After nearly six years of supporting the battle elsewhere, Virginia had scant resources for the fight that now threatened its heartland.

Intrigued by the possibility of capturing Arnold, Washington dispatched several thousand Continental troops to Virginia under the young French officer Lafayette. Still badly outnumbered by the British, Lafayette tried to check their advances with feints and skirmishes but refrained from pitched battle. The British hit Williamsburg and the Chickahominy shipyards one week, burned supplies at Petersburg or Richmond the next. The armies crisscrossed Hanover County, and Lafayette camped for a time at Henry's father-in-law's plantation, not far from Mount Brilliant and Scotchtown.

By mid-May, when Henry set off for the assembly session scheduled now for the hamlet of Charlottesville, sixty miles west of vulnerable Richmond, the situation looked hopeless. Supplies and men were scarce, and disaffection had spread throughout the state. Crowds armed with poles and clubs had chased the military recruiter and quartermaster from several mountain counties, and on the eastern shore a thousand men had stormed the county court meeting to break up a draft lottery in process. Looting and plundering had increased, and in many places sheriffs could no longer collect taxes. On May 28, the day the legislature convened, Jefferson appealed to General Washington for direct help. Virginians, their governor said, believed they "retained some right" to their "beloved Countryman," to whom they "have ever looked up as their dernier resort in distress." Were Washington now to appear among them, "full confidence of salvation" would be restored and "would render them equal to whatever is not impossible. . . . The difficulty would then be how to keep men out of the field." Jefferson said he hinted at such a drastic step "at the sollicitations of many members of weight in our legislature which is not yet assembled to speak their own desires."

The next day the assembly, with Henry in a leading role, urged Jefferson to order as many militiamen as necessary into immediate service and set in motion repair of many existing defects in the militia and impressment laws. The assembly moved with unaccustomed dispatch, but before work had fairly begun on executing the barrage of well-intentioned measures, Colonel Banastre Tarleton's cavalry chased the legislature out of town.

Cornwallis, tired of fruitless maneuvering with Lafayette, had sent his cavalry on a double mission to destroy an important arms depot on the upper James and capture the governor and legislature at nearby Charlottesville. However, a Louisa County captain, Jack Jouett, spotted Tarleton's horsemen on their night march and raced forty miles to sound the alarm. Jefferson, the story goes, jumped up from the breakfast table to race away while Tarleton was ascending the lower slopes of Monticello.

"Such terror & confusion you have no idea of . . . Governor, Council, everybody scampering," the state treasurer's daughter, Betsy Ambler, wrote. While rushing to leave, the treasurer found himself accosted by Edmund Pendleton, who demanded that Ambler accept a huge bag containing twenty thousand pounds in nearly worthless paper money that Pendleton had just received from the long-delayed sale of land in the Robinson estate. Pendleton insisted upon discharging Robinson's remaining public debt with the windfall quickly, knowing that the legislature would soon void the paper as legal tender. Pendleton followed Ambler until the treasurer took the money.

Tarleton bagged seven slow-moving assemblymen. Then the British troops moved on to destroy the arms depot and wreak havoc on one of Jefferson's outlying plantations, where they burned the crops and departed with thirty slaves.

When the assembly reconvened, by prior arrangement, three days later over the mountains in Staunton, everyone laughed nervously as they swapped stories about the hullabaloo. Many claimed some connection with the heroic Jack Jouett. Without detracting from the soldier's glory, the Walker family wanted some credit, too. Tarleton's advance had gotten a delayed start, the Walkers insisted, because Dinah, the family cook, had served the intruding officers so delicious a meal of fried chicken that the commander had asked for more, which she obligingly—but slowly—prepared.

Henry's friend John Tyler, however, told the most engaging story. His quartet of fugitives included Speaker Benjamin Harrison, William Christian, and Patrick Henry. When they stopped late in the afternoon at a remote cabin and asked for food, the woman at the door questioned them narrowly. Henry explained that they were members of the legislature who had to leave Charlottesville because of the enemy's raid.

"Ride on, you cowardly knaves," the woman raged. Her husband and sons had gone to Charlottesville to fight, and she would feed no deserters.

"But here is Speaker Harrison," Henry explained. "You don't think he would have fled had it not been necessary, do you? It would not do to have the assembly broken up by the enemy."

"I always thought a great deal of Mr. Harrison until now," she replied, "but he'd no business to run from the enemy. Ride on."

Tyler interrupted to ask, "What would you say if I were to tell you that Patrick Henry fled with the rest of us?"

"Patrick Henry! I should tell you there weren't a word of truth in it. Patrick Henry would never do such a cowardly thing."

"But this is Patrick Henry," said Tyler.

The woman stared as Henry looked at her sheepishly. Then she opened the door.

"Well, then, if that's Patrick Henry, it must be all right," she said, and offered them whatever she had.

The story became a talisman that eased anxieties and used Henry's great prestige to transform the legislature's flight into a prudent act of statesmanship. Such yearning for reassurance underlay all the agitated talk about summoning General Washington or General Greene to serve as a temporary "dictator" who might see Virginia through its present trouble. The Romans had done it, declared young George Nicholas, the late treasurer's son, who was serving his first term as a delegate, when he proposed the idea in committee. In rising to second Nicholas's motion, Henry subtly made it more realistic. He thought it "immaterial" whether "the officer proposed was called a Dictator or a Governor with enlarged powers or by any other name." "Yet," Henry argued, "surely an Officer armed with such powers was necessary to restrain the un-bridled fury of a licentious enemy," especially at a time when virtue had collapsed. "P. Virtue gone," Henry had jotted on the back of the pending militia bill; "we must do what will put a lasting stop to the conquest of the enemy."

Henry recognized the value of strong leadership in a time of crisis, but he knew that talk of bringing the general home was folly. Over the next week Henry helped draft a bill that granted the governor broad powers to impress supplies, draft soldiers and appoint their officers, and discipline the civilian population. The law allowed the governor to arrest those suspected of "disaffection to the independence of the United States" and hold them without recourse to bail or a writ of habeas corpus. Moreover, he could forcibly remove those who refused Virginia's oath of allegiance to positions behind the enemy's lines and order the death penalty for those who refused to go. The law granted the governor power to extend recruiting and draft laws beyond their expiration dates and declared that persons forcibly disrupting recruitments or drafts would be decreed "civilly dead" and their property passed to their heirs.

If the delegates looked toward Henry as the most fit person to execute these harsh powers, he quickly discouraged them. The assembly chose instead Thomas Nelson, Jr., the Yorktown merchant who, despite his asthma, had become a sturdy militia commander. Much hostility existed toward Jefferson, who had earlier indicated that he did not want another term and did not join the legislature in Staunton. Jefferson later insisted that since his term had expired on June 2, the day before Tarleton's raid, he had no official reason to do so, but some felt that the gentleman had scarpered. Henry's cousin Edmund Winston had prepared an address of thanks to Jefferson for consideration by the Senate, but he withdrew it when the House, at the request of the impulsive George Nicholas, ordered "an inquiry into the conduct of the Executive for the past twelve months" in order to weigh responsibility for the state's "numberless miscarriages and losses."

The rash attempt to make Jefferson a scapegoat wounded him grievously, and on the strength of no discoverable evidence he attributed the insult to Patrick Henry. Henry's hand, Jefferson believed to his dying day, had manipulated Nicholas's "natural ill-temper." The stout Nicholas was "like the minners which go in and out of the fundament of the whale," Jefferson told an ally a few months later, "but the whale himself was discoverable enough by the turbulence of the water under which he moved." Furiously jealous that Henry had sufficiently recovered from the governorship to dominate the assembly while he had to bear the brunt of the wartime disintegration that had begun in Henry's term, Jefferson could not control himself. He did everything he could to perpetuate the impression that Henry had wanted to become dictator himself, and he resentfully nursed the grudge for years. The inquiry would be dropped six months later in the aftermath of victory, but no resolutions of praise could ease Jefferson's sore pride or his malevolence toward Henry. He persisted in privately castigating Henry as "being all tongue without either head or heart." When Henry held his tongue, remaining perfectly amiable toward Jefferson in public, his rival grumbled that the people's darling lacked enough "personal courage to shew hostility toward any man."

Before the legislature adjourned Henry drafted its appeal to Congress for "men, money, arms, and military stores." Rehearsing Virginia's proud record of contributions to the continental struggle and its dispatch of arms and soldiers to the more southerly states in the past two years, Henry declared that the enemy has "found us unprepared and exhausted." "Active zeal for the American cause has rendered us so," he said, imploring Congress to relieve "the sufferings of a Virtuous people." If Congress cannot comply, Henry concluded frostily, "we think it high time to call upon our European Allies and Friends for their most strenuous exertions."

Although it took the remainder of the summer, help did come. While Governor Nelson vigorously used his powers to repress dissent and maintain the militia in support of Lafayette, General Washington marched a combined American and French army toward Virginia. The French fleet arrived in Chesapeake Bay even before the army and blocked any hope that Cornwallis could either resupply or retreat. After a siege of several weeks the British army, trapped at Yorktown, surrendered to Washington, and everyone realized that the royal government would now be compelled to recognize American independence and negotiate a settlement.

Henry lived quietly at Leatherwood during the last months of fighting and the long winter before news of a preliminary treaty of peace arrived in spring 1782. With it there came new calls to action. General Horatio Gates, who had presided over the first great victory at Saratoga, praised Henry, along with Jefferson, Nelson, and R. H. Lee, for their heroic efforts: "Now, sir, may you exult with Cicero, 'Cedant Armae Togae' " and share in the "Glorious Opportunity" to establish "the happiness of the Present Generation . . . upon the Broad Basis of Civil Liberty."

George Mason, affectionately recalling the pleasures of collaboration and friendship with Henry, also asked him to resume public service. "It is in your Power, my dear Sir, to do more Good & prevent more Mischief than any Man in this State," Mason said. He shared Henry's conviction that "a Depravity of Manners & Morals" and a declining respect for "fundamental Principles of Justice" jeopardized the victory. "We are now to rank among the Nations of the World,"

Mason wrote, "but whether our Independence shall prove a Blessing or a Curse, must depend on our own Wisdom or Folly, Virtue or Wickedness."

In appealing for Henry to exercise "the great Talents with which God has blessed you, in promoting the public Happiness & Prosperity," Mason assumed a concord of opinion that did not exist. In politics "good" and "mischief" are relative, and measures well calculated for gentlemen planters seated on the flowing expanse of the Potomac might not suit Piedmont farmers on the upper reaches of the Roanoke. In the postwar years, from his retreat deep in the backcountry, Henry developed a social and political outlook that put him at odds with the other leading men of the commonwealth.

For Henry, as for the vast majority of his countrymen, land held the key to happiness and prosperity. Nine out of every ten Americans lived—and made their livings—on farms, and very few doubted the moral superiority of the agrarian way of life. To own land enough to feed and clothe the family and raise enough of a marketable crop to trade or sell for what the land could not yield seemed close enough to paradise for anyone. The crowds and corruption of city life, and the dubious manipulations of merchant princes, struck most yeomen as unsavory and threatening. After a few weeks on business in little Williamsburg or Richmond, Henry yearned for the peace and security of his plantation; aside from the brief trip to New York in 1770 and the two seven-week sojourns in Philadelphia at the Continental Congress in 1774 and 1775, Henry never traveled beyond the placid rural counties of Virginia.

Although he always sympathized with the modest farmer, Henry nonetheless had an ambitious commercial streak that lifted him from self-sufficiency into more complex transactions. He spent little on luxuries, however, preferring always to increase his land holdings; yet he moved about so often that he never assumed a place in the settled country squirearchy. He wanted to assure "seats" for his numerous sons, but, in the absence of cash, he used his numerous warrants and surveys in the distant West as a trading coin and a medium of exchange.

Henry measured personal wealth in land, not the accumulation of capital, and he judged continental prosperity by a similar rule.

Tracing the rivers of the beckoning Mississippi Valley on the map convinced Henry that "the finger of heaven" had marked out the course of settlement and "pointed the way to wealth." A surge of free white settlers, Henry indulgently thought, would obviate the need for slaves; although his vision of the West comprehended a succession of quiet, rural localities, in his mind's eye the landscape may have resembled New England more than his familiar Virginia.

In his eagerness to promote population growth, Henry would even welcome the return of Tory refugees to Virginia, for he regarded them as an "enterprising, moneyed people [who] will be serviceable in taking off the surplus produce of our lands." To those who feared their subversive presence, Henry replied grandly, "Shall we, who have laid the proud British lion at our feet, now be afraid of his whelps?"

The settlement of the West would expand the volume of trade, which, in Henry's view, should be "unfettered" and "as free as the air." He envisioned extensive commerce with the French and Spanish through New Orleans and wanted to avoid falling back into the old habits of dependence upon Great Britain. A diversified international trade and a thriving backcountry would create a commercial equilibrium and preserve republican prosperity indefinitely. Whether the states to be formed beyond the mountains would join the confederacy already established or form an amiable union of their own did not much trouble Henry.

Henry envisioned a tranquil society that would expand without changing. Such enlargement, however, could be endangered by rapid or unlimited development. While true liberty secured property and honest labor, abundant success might create a debilitating luxury and political decadence. If concentrations of capital led to the building of great cities, where factories employed hordes of landless poor, the countryside might find itself in thrall to a luxurious aristocracy of merchants and stock jobbers. Republican simplicity might decay into European corruption, Philadelphia might become as great a sinkhole as London, and an oppressive monarchy might take hold once again.

Henry's preoccupation with the decline of public "virtue" bespoke his anxiety for the fate of republican society in the face of its own prosperity. His friend Samuel Adams had talked of the American states as "a Christian Sparta," and Henry shared the understanding that a great deal of self-discipline and self-denial would be necessary to protect the society they wanted. This would come, Henry believed, through the encouragement of religion, especially the stern morality of the evangelicals, as both a spur to civic virtue and a curb upon decadent consumption. Republican society might also be protected by preserving the small-scale, local character of the economy and remaining indifferent to grandiose schemes of commercial development that required complex financial arrangements, large accumulations of capital, or great public expense.

Averse to formal, systematic thought, Henry articulated these assumptions only in the context of specific legislative proposals. He did not have a formal program, but rather a protective attitude toward the locally oriented, modest free-holders he represented, and he was eclectic and casual enough to swap one measure for another that seemed more important at the time. Elected to every assembly from 1780 on, Henry attended sporadically. Illness kept him away entirely in 1782; in the sessions of 1783 and 1784 he sometimes arrived late and left early, "sighing for home" in the languid way he had of expressing weariness.

In the House, however, his influence was "immense," but not, as his opponents sneered, simply because he could rouse delegates with a speech. As in the years of protest against Parliament, Henry's forensic talent did not so much sway the malleable or uncommitted as give shape and force to what the "generality" thought. Henry's voice could be decisive because he spoke principally to men who shared his outlook.

The legislature had ceased to be an exclusive gentlemen's club and had taken on the cruder, more open flavor of the tavern and the courthouse green. While the Tidewater counties had more representatives than they should have had, given the westward shift of population, there were enough western counties now to give the frontier element more weight than ever before. The legislature met in a ramshackle, barnlike structure on a muddy street in Richmond instead of the handsome brick Capitol in Williamsburg. Fine broadcloth and powdered wigs had disappeared, too; many delegates wore buckskin jackets and riding boots and looked as if they had just come in from the tobacco fields or a deer hunt. Although men of substance, they owned smaller farms and fewer slaves than their predecessors in the colonial House of Burgesses, and European visitors regarded them as simply "farmers . . . with little education or knowledge of the world." The assemblymen of the eighties, moreover, had much less experience than the burgesses; they came directly into the House from county participation in the Revolution and had not served long apprenticeships as magistrates or vestrymen. Jefferson complained of the "very low state" to which the legislature had sunk, with well-intentioned members who possessed "but little knowledge of the science to which they are called."

A German visitor found the assembly appallingly devoid of dignity. It must be a "trifling business to make laws," he concluded, when men lounge about during debate, read pamphlets, write letters, or stroll in and out of the chamber, talking of irrelevant matters. The doorkeeper loudly and "incessantly" called after the members to come in from the tumultuous anteroom, where they liked to "amuse themselves zealously with talk of horse-races, runaway negroes, yesterday's play, politics, or it may be, with trafficking."

The German observed that "a certain Mr. Henry" seemed to have "the greatest influence over the House." Henry, who used to be a "country schoolmaster," the German heard, had "a high-flown and bold delivery" but dealt "more in words than reasons." Other observers praised Henry's amiability, even when engaged in strong argument. A young Richmond lawyer named John Marshall thought Henry's "peculiar excellence" lay in his ability "to appear to be drawn unwillingly into the contest & to throw in the eyes of others the whole blame on his adversary." To this finely honed courtroom skill Henry added entertaining touches of wit and humor that verged on the burlesque. In protesting a tax bill more stringent than the straitened circumstances of the Piedmont farmers could bear, Henry contrasted their "severe toil" with the easy way of life in Tidewater, where people could harvest the rivers. Then Henry "presented such a ludicrous image of the [Tidewater] members who had advocated the bill . . . peeping and peering along the shores of the creeks, to pick up their mess of crabs . . . as filled the house with a roar of merriment."

The sectional division in the House did not run on a straight east-west line but along an axis that separated the northern Potomac and Rappahannock river valleys from the interior southwestern counties. The "Northern Neck"—with its great plantations, numerous tenant farms, and fine access to water transport—had a more developed, commercial outlook, while the "Southside"—a newer region with smaller, less developed holdings, and poor transportation—remained pre-occupied with maintaining self-sufficiency in the aftermath of the war. Henry lived in the heart of Southside and drew his strength in the legislature from its counties and those adjacent in the central Piedmont. This bloc consistently favored measures that eased the circumstances of small farmers: laws that postponed the collection of taxes and allowed them to be paid in commodities like tobacco, hemp, and deerskins, laws that "stayed" the execution of judgments for debt and allowed more time before sheriffs could seize property for nonpayment of taxes, laws that required seized property to be valued by sympathetic members of the community rather than outside creditors. Since large planters also found themselves in debt, Henry and his Southside friends could find allies for these measures in wealthier areas of the state, including the Northern Neck. Generally speaking, however, the delegates from that section favored a more aggressive use of government power. They gave more vigorous support to the various proposals that would strengthen the power of

Congress to regulate commerce and raise revenue by taxing imports, and they entertained ambitious schemes for linking the Potomac and Ohio rivers with a series of canals. They wanted taxes collected promptly so that interest on the huge public debt could be paid and the principal retired, and they disliked "tender laws" that allowed notes or commodities to be substituted for gold or silver in payment of obligations. They also wanted to institute a more comprehensive system of district courts to expedite lawsuits against debtors, but the proposals made little headway. John Marshall complained in 1784, "There are many members who really appear to be determined against every Measure which may expedite & facilitate the business of recovering debts & compelling a strict compliance with contracts."

Henry preferred an easy-money policy, and he believed that too rapid an extinguishment of the public debt through heavy taxes would depress trade and put an intolerable squeeze on most farmers. These views set him apart from old friends like Mason and Lee, who shared the creditor outlook of the Northern Neck, although they did not subscribe to some of the more extreme fears of the commercial-minded men that a popular majority might someday repudiate all debts and decree a redistribution of property.

These fears increased as economic conditions worsened in 1784 and 1785. They also grew as Henry remained fervently opposed to the repayment of the prewar debts Virginians owed to British merchants. During the war the assembly had closed the courts to suits by British creditors and had allowed Virginians to pay their British bills into an escrow account using the rapidly depreciating paper currency. In the aftermath of war, the creditors (who now included Virginia merchants who had taken over some of the British bills) wanted court judgments in their favor. They wanted the escrow account recalculated at par value in specie, and they demanded interest for the war years as well. The treaty of peace promised that the bona fide claims of British creditors would be honored in the United States, and Virginia's leading men, including Washington, Lee, and Mason, insisted that the nation's credit reputation would be severely jeopardized by a refusal to pay. However, Henry, backed by a majority of the legislature, refused to countenance any enabling legislation. He insisted that the claims could not be paid until Britain honored its promises to evacuate its frontier posts on the Great Lakes and return confiscated property, including slaves.

These legislative counterpunches did not obscure the deeper messages Henry intended. He deplored the postwar rush to purchase British luxury goods and by his intransigence on the debt question hoped to put a crimp in that trade and prevent the old habits of opulence from reasserting themselves. Henry did not want already scarce specie rushing back to Britain, and he feared the devastating impact the repayment of two million pounds would have on the state's struggling economy.

Henry owed no British debts himself, nor did most of his constituents, and his opposition puzzled some and worried others as an indication that Henry might challenge the sanctity of contracts in other circumstances closer to home. For Henry the opposition to British debts did provide a relatively safe way of challenging the commercial mentality, for behind all the high-sounding talk of national honor and prestige he heard the creditor's voice deploring any sign of fiscal laxness.

Henry had his way on the issues that most mattered to him, although as a practical politician he made his share of compromises. When he heard that James Madison would be returning to the legislature in May 1784 after three years in Congress, Henry moved at once to conciliate the young man, whose commitment to fiscal orthodoxy and formidable reputation as a parliamentary tactician made him the natural leader of the Northern Neck creditor bloc. Henry wrote very few letters from Leatherwood, but on the eve of the assembly session he dispatched an "affectionate" note to Madison that welcomed the prospect of his service. Although Madison's work had entitled him to a "respite," Henry urged that several matters "of the greatest Moment" forbade it. "Is not the federal Government on a bad footing?" Henry asked. "If I am not mistaken you must have seen & felt that it is." Other matters also needed "Correction and Improvement," Henry added, and he concluded by lamenting the mortification of seeing "a rich Harvest of Happiness" lacking only "Labourers . . . to gather it in."

Henry knew, of course, that Madison had worked strenuously for granting Congress increased powers, and Henry had supported a previous year's effort to allow a tax to be levied on imports. He reasoned that it would fall most directly on wealthy consumers and, by reducing the size of state requisitions for Congress, would further ease the tax burden on ordinary farmers. Yet not even Henry's support could overcome the legislature's suspicion that this would be an entering wedge by which Congress would tax citizens directly and intrude upon state sovereignty.

These fears, which Henry shared, were not chimerical. They stemmed from the extraordinary measures proposed over the past three years by Robert Morris, a Philadelphia merchant who had become the Confederation's secretary of finance in 1781. Morris had employed a variety of stratagems in his quest for a congressional taxing power, and in support of his plan he assembled a formidable coalition of army officers (who wanted all their promised pay) and holders of congressional loan certificates (who wanted regular interest and principal payments in hard money, not depreciated paper). "Every engine is at work here to obtain permanent taxes and the appointment of Collectors by Congress, in the States," reported Arthur Lee, one of Virginia's delegates in Congress. "The terror of a mutinying Army is played off with considerable efficacy," Lee said, and eventually General Washington put a stop to using the army as "mere Puppits."

In taking the army out of politics, however, the general put himself in by sending a circular letter to the states in which he deplored the "want of energy in the continental government" and warned that unless Congress had "supreme power" over "the general concerns of the confederated republic" the Union would be undone by "anarchy and confusion." Washington's support for the impost and other unspecified measures intensified hard feelings in Richmond, where legislators murmured "against what is called the unsolicited intrusion of his advice."

While Madison had tried to temper some features of Morris's financial plan, he generally shared its perspective, which unflinchingly sought national powers by elevating the interest of creditors in all the states above the mixture of interests represented in any state. In making overtures to Madison, Henry sought to brake the accelerating momentum of that ambitious plan by rallying support for some modest expedients. When the two men arrived in Richmond, they met amiably at a coffeehouse. Henry declared that the "only inducement" he had for attending the assembly lay in doing something to strengthen the powers of the federal government. If Madison and their mutual friend Joseph Jones would "sketch out some Plan," Henry said, he would "support it on the Floor." A "bold Example set by Virginia," Henry said, might influence the other states, each of which had balked at one aspect or another of previous plans. At minimum (and perhaps, at maximum) Henry thought Congress ought to have some way of compelling delinquent states to meet their requisitions.

The wary Madison doubted the depth, if not the sincerity, of Henry's commitment. Yet as long as Henry seemed willing to lead, Madison had to follow. The two men went on to cooperate on a number of issues. Henry supported a proposed revision in the Articles of Confederation that would apportion state quotas on the basis of population instead of land and another law desired by the friends of Congress that provided for the extradition of Virginians who made provocative attacks upon the Spanish or Indians in the Mississippi Valley. Henry also supported Madison's proposal to retaliate against the British merchants by confining their trade to a handful of Virginia ports. Both men worked unsuccessfully to obtain an acceptable version of the congressional plan to levy import duties, and they also tried (but failed) to get the assembly to grant a tract of land to Thomas Paine, the author of *Common Sense*, who had fallen upon hard times.

Their collaboration quickly reached its limits, however. Henry remained impervious to the various carefully worded compromises Madison put forward to settle the British debt problem, nor would he countenance the revisions in the state constitution Madison promoted on Jefferson's behalf. (When Jefferson, away in France as the American ambassador, heard of Henry's opposition, he grimly told Madison, "What we have to do I think is devoutly to pray for his death.")

Madison did not believe in prayer as an instrument of state. He reached his limit of cooperation with Henry when the latter proposed to assign a portion of state tax revenues to the support of religious groups.

The idea of imposing a general assessment to be distributed to the church designated by the taxpayer had fractured the legislature in 1776, when it had agreed that dissenters did not have to pay state levies to support the Church of England. At the same time the legislature had "suspended" the state-supplied salaries of the Anglican clergy, leaving their own vestries to provide. But the assembly exerted some control in ecclesiastical affairs by mandating that references to the king be removed from the Anglican prayer book used in Virginia churches.

Religious groups held divergent views on the wisdom of a general assessment. The Anglicans, now known as the Protestant Episcopal church, favored tax support for religion as a way of shoring up their tottering institution, but they put greater hope in the idea of having their church incorporated by the state, a move that would provide legal independence while confirming title to the extensive tracts of land assigned to church use throughout the colonial period. Dissenters (except for the Methodists, who remained as an evangelical sect within the Episcopal church) found the incorporation idea abhorrent and insisted that the Episcopalians should not gain exclusive control of property bought, in effect, by the entire community. From this position, however, two opposite conclusions followed. The Baptists insisted that the state should have nothing to do with religion, since any involvement, whether fiscal or theological, jeopardized the rights of conscience. Many Presbyterians, however, entertained the idea of a plural establishment; a general distribution of revenues by denomination, they believed, could assist religion without intruding the state into matters of creed and conscience.

Henry found this Presbyterian position a congenial one, especially as his friendship deepened with John Blair Smith, a Presbyterian clergyman who presided over Hampden-Sydney College in Southside's Prince Edward County. Smith, like James Madison, had studied at the College of New Jersey under John Witherspoon, who vigorously insisted that since a people could remain virtuous only with the aid of religion, "magistrates" had a clear duty to foster it while respecting freedom of conscience. Henry became a trustee of Hampden-Sydney (which the Presbyterians hoped would become the Princeton of the South) and sometimes worshiped in Smith's church. In 1784 Smith drew up a memorial for the legislature, endorsed by the influential Hanover Presbytery, that followed Witherspoon's teaching in calling for both "the inalienable rights of conscience" *and* "an equal share of the protection and favor of government to all denominations of Christians." In the tacit division of labor between Smith and Henry, the clergyman would rally church support for a general assessment, while Henry would persuade the Episcopal majority in the legislature.

Both men encountered a more obdurate opposition than they had anticipated. After private soundings in May 1784, Henry prudently decided to withhold the measure until the fall session, and it became clear to him that the Episcopalians expected him to support their incorporation bill in exchange. Henry did so and thereby greatly antagonized his ally, the Reverend Smith. The clergyman, meanwhile, had problems of his own. A substantial number of Presbyterian clergy from the Shenandoah Valley objected to the general assessment because the tax power, as all good Whigs should remember, could be grievously abused and the legislature might well impose certain theological constraints before disbursing the money.

Henry did not know the extent of Presbyterian division on the issue when he first asked the legislature in November 1784 to declare that "the people of this Commonwealth . . . ought to pay a moderate tax or contribution, annually, for the support of the christian religion, or of some christian church, denomination or communion of christians, or of some form of christian worship." Henry argued that religion promoted virtuous conduct and the state ought to support it as a means of self-defense. But Madison objected that, amid a welter of denominational differences, the state could not determine which societies were Christian without infringing upon matters of conscience. The true question, Madison emphasized, was not whether religion was valuable but whether a religious establishment was necessary for religion to flourish. Henry replied that the general assessment had nothing to do with theology or creed. It was not for religion's sake but for the state's that he proposed the plan, and he agreed with John B. Smith's qualification that the legislative role ought to be confined to "supporting institutions for inculcating the great fundamental principles of all religion, without which society could not easily exist."

Henry's motion passed by a vote of forty-seven to thirty-two, but he knew that Madison had made great headway with the contingent of Presbyterians in the House by raising the specter of state meddling with religious doctrine. Appointed head of the committee to draft a specific bill, Henry tried to blunt Madison's tactic by formulating a measure that would provide tax money only for "teachers of the Christian Religion." Since the "general diffusion of Christian knowledge" had a tendency to "correct the morals of men, restrain their vices, and preserve the peace of society," the bill's preamble declared, the state could provide for religious education "without counteracting the liberal principle heretofore adopted" of free exercise of religion. The bill would allow citizens who did not want to designate a religious denomination as recipient of funds to assign the money for the support of secular institutions of learning within their counties.

Henry had done what he could to draft a careful bill that answered his purposes while meeting the objections Madison had raised. Yet his coalition seemed to be dwindling away. A new round of Presbyterian petitions showed that support for Henry's bill had cooled among delegates from the valley. Madison used Henry's support of the Episcopal incorporation bill to tag him as a friend to church establishment but then turned around and supported the Episcopal bill himself in a shrewd bid to break up the alliance Henry had forged. The incorporation bill passed easily, and then eight Episcopalians joined Madison in voting to postpone a final vote on the religious teachers' measure until public opinion could be more fully sounded.

The maneuver might not have worked had Henry been on hand to expose it. However, he had accepted election to the governorship on November 17, and before the month ended he had gone up to Leatherwood to ready the family for the move to Richmond. Henry's departure greatly "disheartened" supporters of the assessment idea and left Madison smugly relieved that Henry was "out of the way" at last.

The choice, however, was Henry's. He had come into the session knowing that, with Harrison's third term at an end, the governorship could be his. "It is in the option of Mr. H.," Madison told R. H. Lee, "and I fancy he will not decline the service." Six months earlier Henry had sought to purchase a "seat" for his family closer to Richmond, for which he was reluctantly willing to give up some choice acreage near Norfolk. He had grown tired of the week-long journey between Leatherwood and Richmond, and Dolly found the situation there much too isolated and removed from her kinfolk. (In November 1783, Henry had told Annie Christian, "My wife wants to come downwards next spring.") Henry also wanted good matches for his two eligible daughters and had already sent the elder, Anne, to circulate at her Aunt Lucy's in Hanover). The desire for a richer social life after years in seclusion, when combined with some pending business propositions, made the prospect of town life appealing again, and in peacetime the duties of governor would hardly be as onerous as before. Although he believed strongly in the general assessment idea, he had always retreated from positions that public opinion would not accept. Since it seemed clear that his Presbyterian friends would back away from the scheme, Henry saw no reason to sacrifice his private interests by continuing a losing battle in the House. Election to the governorship offered him as convenient a means to withdraw as it afforded his opponents an easy way of removing him.

Over the next twelve months an avalanche of hostile petitions completely buried the general assessment idea. Thousands of Baptists and Presbyterians circulated and signed statements that condemned state interference with church affairs as contrary to both "the Spirit of the Gospel, and the Bill of Rights." Madison covertly drafted a remonstrance that restated the philosophical arguments for separating state from church. It attracted many fewer signatures than the evangelicals' petition, but it prepared the ground in the legislature for the successful passage in 1786 of the comprehensive statute on religious freedom drafted nearly a decade earlier by Thomas Jefferson.

It was an unlikely coalition of secular and pietistic forces. Madison and Jefferson sought to prevent the state from legislating over the human mind, whereas the evangelical sects sought the freedom to propagate the gospel without hindrance from the state. Henry shared Madison's argument that it would breed disrespect for the law to impose a general religious assessment upon an unwilling populace. Yet he retained a certain partiality for the evangelical attempt to influence social conduct, even through public laws. Henry sought, most of all, to ensure moral respectability, a self-discipline that would provide a bulwark against the corruption of a relatively homogeneous rural society.

Sectarian combat ended, but religion triumphed nonetheless. The fight over the general assessment proved to be part of the larger struggle between a traditional, provincial society and the cosmopolitan standards of the world outside. The settlement proved ambiguous. The state would not discriminate among beliefs yet would affirm the importance of a community unified by belief. Henry, like most Virginians, believed that the legislature in certain ways might act upon the religious beliefs of the great majority without rousing opposition. Shortly after passing the religious freedom bill the House assented to a law requiring the observance of Sunday as a day of rest, a measure that Henry regarded as similar in spirit to his 1783 effort to have the House open its sessions with a prayer "adapted to all persuasions." Nor did he see any prohibition upon advancing religious ideas while in public office. A few months after becoming governor, Henry read a pamphlet by Soames Jenyns, an English latitudinarian who defended Christianity by demonstrating the compatibility between reason and revelation. Henry liked it so well that he had several hundred copies printed and distributed at his own expense, thus acting upon his continuing belief that religion had a substantial role to play in preserving the fabric of society.

Governor Henry found life in Richmond congenial. The state supplied a house on the side of Shockoe Hill, adjacent to the massive marble Capitol (modeled after a Roman temple) then under construction. A larger kitchen had to be built on the back of the governor's lot, and Dolly tried to brighten the cramped quarters with new carpeting and china for the dining room, hair cloth for the passageways, and other amenities. Yet the Henry family preferred to pass great stretches of time at Salisbury, a plantation Henry rented in the open country just across the James.

Richmond had a white population of nearly fifteen hundred souls, including a variety of craftsmen and a sizable number of lawyers attached to the state courts. Gentry from the neighboring counties came in to town occasionally to attend dances (the ball on General Washington's birthnight being the annual favorite) or to see plays staged by a traveling company from Baltimore that had added the little capital to its itinerary.

Henry enjoyed mingling in this genteel provincial society. The family acquired a handsome coach, but the governor put on few airs himself. He often made his own fire, and sometimes he could be seen riding out to his farm on horseback with one of his toddlers propped on the saddle in front of him and another hanging on behind. Henry dressed in his habitual black suit, brightened only by a cloak lined with scarlet, and he wore a dressed wig in a prewar style that the town's young dandies found a trifle passé.

His term as governor, though generally happy, began in shadow. His mother died after months of an "inveterate cough" in November 1784; his brother William died early in January 1785, and his last surviving aunt died a few days later. Then, in what seemed a never-ending season of tribulation, Dolly's brother and mother died. "Thus is the last generation clearing the way for us, as we must shortly do for the next," Henry lamented. As a sickly man nearing his fiftieth birthday, Henry made up a will, telling his executors that any claims from British creditors would be spurious, for he had seldom contracted British debts and would immediately pay the one trifling sum outstanding. Henry gloomily worried about his children. He had always hoped that his sister Annie Christian and her husband could be entrusted with their care if he and Dolly died, but the Christians had moved to distant Kentucky, and he felt their absence keenly.

Public business did not weigh upon him as heavily as it had during the years of war, yet some of his work echoed his former preoccupations. The legislature had appropriated a decent sum for replenishing militia arms, and Henry labored in "this season of tranquility" to purchase a supply in France with the aid of the well-disposed Lafayette. A reorganization of the militia absorbed his time as well, since the law required him to replace long-entrenched officers by giving preference to men with Continental Army service. This pitched Henry into the politics of distant counties with only scanty knowledge of the situations, and he found it so exasperating—and the counties so recalcitrant—that he had to ask the assembly to repeal the law.

He also devoted much time to settling long-standing claims for payment from French merchants, local suppliers, and veterans, whose demands were made complicated by the destruction of state records in Arnold's 1781 raid. As governor, too, he heard petitions from those in desperate need of the state's clemency. He pardoned some criminals whose death sentences seemed "disproportioned" to the crime, and he ordered the attorney general, Edmund Randolph, to aid a distraught free black woman named Judy, whose child had been taken from her and unlawfully enslaved. The executive "owes them protection," Henry said, and he assured Randolph that he would receive a fifty-shilling fee from the "contingent fund" for assisting "this poor woman."

Henry also exerted diplomatic efforts to avoid renewed Indian warfare on the frontier. Settlers in western North Carolina, aggrieved at that state's insensitivity to their demands for tax relief and greater representation in the legislature, had broken away from that jurisdiction and set up an independent state of Franklin. Leaders in the adjacent Holston River area of Virginia also flirted with the Franklin secessionists, and Henry feared that the rebellious action would spill over into expansionist moves against the Indians. He urged Virginians in the area to observe a "strict neutrality" in the dispute between North Carolina and Franklin and to avoid anything that might "provoke" the Indians into war with the settlers or an alliance with the Spaniards. When Henry learned that the Washington County militia leaders had advocated secession, he replaced them at once with a new group headed by his newest brother-in-law, General William Russell, in order "to prevent the weight of office being cast in the scale against the state." Yet in reporting to the legislature in October 1785, he urged "lenient measures in order to reclaim our erring fellow citizens," since their "intemperance" stemmed from their continuing economic distress and had temporarily blinded them to the "mischievous consequences" of separation.

Although tobacco prices had started to fall, Henry had a generally buoyant outlook on the state's prospects. He endorsed plans for opening navigation on the upper Potomac and the James, with an eye to a canal connection into the Ohio Valley, and another, even more visionary scheme, for a canal across the Dismal Swamp that might draw the trade of eastern North Carolina into the rejuvenated port at Norfolk. Henry had land in that section and tried fruitlessly to enlist George Washington in a new venture to acquire even more along the route of the proposed canal.

"Virginia seems to me to concentre within its limits natural benefits not only enough to render her own people happy, but can also contribute largely to make her neighbors so, by inviting them to a participation," Henry told R. H. Lee. Yet when Madison helped to organize a conference with Maryland concerning joint development and use of the Potomac, Henry unaccountably mislaid the papers advising Virginia's commissioners of their appointment. George Mason learned of the meeting when the Maryland delegates stopped by his plantation on the way to Alexandria, and only he and his neighbor, General Washington, represented Virginia. Madison felt chagrined at missing the meeting, which he regarded as another opportunity to push for enlarging the commercial powers of Congress, and Edmund Randolph (the other gentleman who failed to attend) told him that their "inadvertant delinquency must be ascribed to the forgetfulness of our friend Henry." Madison did not miss the implication that Henry's enthusiasm for stronger "federal" measures had cooled.

In the fall assembly of 1785, which reelected Henry for another year as governor, Madison once more pressed the issue of transferring some of the state's power over commerce to Congress. When various expedients failed, however, he reluctantly endorsed a suggestion made by John Tyler that the states appoint commissioners to consult about the advantages of a "uniform system of commercial regulations" and make recommendations for the unanimous approval of Congress. Henry remained noncommittal on the idea, but this time he dispatched the circular letter to the states as requested and, in due course, carefully notified Madison, Randolph, and the other commissioners that the meeting would take place in Annapolis in early September, 1786.

Henry's mind was much distracted in the summer of 1786, however, by the news that William Christian had died in a skirmish with Wabash Indians in northwestern Kentucky.

"My heart has felt in a manner new & strange to me," he told his grieving sister Annie; "while I am endeavoring to comfort you I want a comforter myself." He wrote consolingly of the pious lessons "given us by our honored parents" and guiltily apologized that his "actions" had not "kept pace" with the affections expressed in his letters. "You never knew how much I love you and your husband," Henry said, with the startled realization that he might never see his sister again either. "Oh," he cried, "may we meet in that heaven to which the merits of Jesus will carry those who love and serve him."

To ease his aching heart Henry wrote a stinging letter to Congress the next day complaining about "the seeming neglect of Indian affairs" and the unpleasant necessity for seeking congressional approval for a retaliatory attack upon the Wabash towns. Congress had never sent agents to treat with the Wabash on the model pursued more successfully on Virginia's southern borders, and Henry had received no intelligence of their hostile disposition until yesterday's terrible news of "murders and depredations committed on our citizens." Such flailing greatly oversimplified the problem, as Henry recognized in subsequent, calmer letters, but it heightened all over again his sense of Virginia's sovereignty and his desire to protect its interests by unilateral action.

Henry's sour attitude toward Congress became balefully hostile in late August when he received some devastating political intelligence. Congress, he learned from James Monroe, stood on the verge of bartering away the American right to navigate the Mississippi in exchange for a favorable trade agreement with Spain. John Jay, the American plenipotentiary, believed a temporary surrender of the Mississippi for twenty-five years to be the only wedge that would pry a treaty out of the Spanish court, and according to Monroe, Jay had intrigued mightily among the northern states to procure instructions to himself along those lines. Monroe believed that commercial men on the eastern seaboard favored the closure so as to restrict the growth of the southern states and keep "the weight of government" with themselves. Congress stood at loggerheads on the subject, engaged in such procedural and substantive wrangles that the outcome could not be predicted. Monroe also reported that "committees" of New England and New York men had plotted the formation of a separate confederacy of their own and would use the Mississippi business to precipitate "the event."

Henry had cherished the dream of Mississippi Valley expansion for more than a decade, and as the vanguard of the Henry family's interest in Kentucky, William Christian had died for that dream. Governor Henry moved at once to stimulate protests from the assembly and elsewhere. Writing to Annie Christian about the painful subjects of mourning rings and her husband's tombstone, Henry let politics intrude for the first time in a letter to a woman. "I've exerted myself to prevent" Congress from giving up the Mississippi, he told her, and he supplied her with a list of "judicious men" he wanted advised to send petitions both to Congress and the Virginia assembly. "I have not time to explain this affair fully," he wrote, "but a firm protest . . . is I think necessary from y'r people."

In the midst of the Mississippi furor Henry paid scant attention to the trade conference at Annapolis. Only five states had attended. The twelve delegates present reported their opinion that "the power of regulating trade is of such comprehensive extent, and will enter so far into the general System of the federal government, that to give it efficacy, and to obviate questions and doubts concerning its precise nature and limits may require a correspondent adjustment of other parts of the Federal System." Behind the circumlocutionary phrases could be discerned an intent to consider general amendments to the Articles of Confederation. The Annapolis report recommended that the states appoint delegates to another meeting, set for Philadelphia in May 1787, "to devise such further provisions as shall appear to them necessary to render the constitution of the Federal Government adequate to the exigencies of the Union." The suggestions would be then submitted to Congress and "afterwards confirmed by the Legislatures of every State."

The Virginia assembly, under Madison's leadership,

accepted the idea and promptly named its delegation, with Washington, Henry, and Madison heading the list. Henry, who had declined a third term as governor, had left Richmond for yet another retirement, and no one knew for sure where he had gone. "My wife and self [are] heartily tired of the bustle we live in here," Henry told Annie Christian in October. "I shall go to Hanover to land I am like to get of Gen. Nelson, or if that fails, towards Leatherwood again."

Edmund Randolph, the new governor, wrote to Henry at Leatherwood, urging him to accept appointment to the convention. Matters had grown so perilous, Randolph argued, that "those who first kindled the Revolution" must now come forward again to devise the means of saving it. "The neglect of the present moment may terminate in the destruction of Confederate America," Randolph said.

Nearly three months passed without a reply from Henry. Finally, in mid-February 1787, writing from yet another new "seat"—this one in Prince Edward—Henry politely declined the invitation. He offered no reasons, and only later was he heard to say that he did not go to Philadelphia because "he smelt a rat."

CHAPTER 18

"Great Divisions Are Likes to Happen"

Henry fled the capital in his characteristic state of frantic collapse. Intractable public issues, such as the looming threat to the Mississippi and the onrushing sense of crisis fostered by those who favored constitutional reform, vexed him. The death of so many kinfolk had depleted him, his older boys had developed a reputation for wildness, and his finances had taken a precarious turn toward indebtedness. The expenses of stylish life in Richmond had run well ahead of the governor's annual allowance, and his extensive land holdings (paper castles of little immediate value) required a considerable outlay in taxes. The Leatherwood plantation had suffered from mismanagement and produced only a dozen hogsheads of tobacco for sale. At the shockingly low prices of the past two years the crop provided only scanty return. Even worse, every assay test and trial of soil he could think of had failed to produce evidence of the gold he had anxiously hoped might exist on his Botetourt County land, but Henry stubbornly held on to the idea and insisted on more costly exploration.

In the midst of all had come the harassment of providing dowries for his daughters. Seventeen-year-old Betsy had caught the fancy of Philip Aylett, a well-to-do young man from King William County whose late father had served Governor Henry as state quartermaster during the war. Philip was only nineteen, and the young man's guardian undertook the negotiation. He would not take Henry's word that he would make all his daughters equal in point of fortune and insisted on a written stipulation that Henry, in the unsettled state of his affairs, absolutely refused to make. Henry said that he thought the property willed to Betsy would be worth at least one thousand pounds, and while he promised to give what he could afford upon the marriage, he would not be bound to a fixed sum. The guardian countered by stating that Aylett would "relinquish all pretensions of forming the connexion," an outcome that Henry may have intended all along.

While these negotiations were going on, a Richmond politician and lawyer named Spencer Roane paid his addresses to Henry's older daughter, Anne. Roane wrote a formal letter to Henry stating his circumstances and (Roane said later) "leading him, delicately, if he so chose, to a disclosure of the portion he intended for his daughter." Again, Henry would put nothing in writing, but in an interview (without witnesses, Roane noted suspiciously) Henry promised to endow Anne with one thousand pounds upon her marriage and, upon his death, to divide his estate equally among the children of both his marriages.

Roane accepted the offer, and the match was struck. Anne had little to say in the affair, and to judge from the exceedingly overbearing letter Henry wrote to her shortly after the wedding, she went to the altar unwillingly. "You are allied to a man of honor, of talents, and of an open, generous disposition," Henry reminded her, and if she sedulously avoided "whim or caprice," and steadfastly resolved never to "control [her] husband by opposition, by displeasure, or any other mark of anger," happiness might yet be hers.

Betsy, meanwhile, was distraught at the loss of her engagement, and she persuaded her stepmother Dolly to intervene with Henry on her behalf. Henry then promised Aylett's guardian a dowry identical to what he had offered Roane. That sealed the bargain. Betsy happily married her beau six weeks after her sister's rather more somber wedding, and Henry did not write her a lengthy patriarchal valedictory.

With the daughters married off, and Henry obliged to pay out more than he intended, he still faced the problem of finding a place for his younger family to live. Both he and Dolly regarded Leatherwood as too remote, and a return to Hanover seemed impractical. Eventually Henry chose his friend John Blair Smith's neighborhood in Prince Edward County, a Presbyterian stronghold on the Southside, where Henry's sons could be reined in at Hampden-Sydney Academy. He picked out a hilly quarter rising back from the Appomattox River, totaling about sixteen hundred acres with farm tracts already cleared, and he patched together a purchase price consisting of tobacco, land warrants, Negroes, two horses, and a small amount of cash.

The new plantation could meet the family's considerable needs, but its earnings (like most Prince Edward holdings) would be very modest. "Your tongue will pay your debts," advised the man who had sold Henry the place and promised to give him a retainer for legal services. Henry started taking law cases for the first time in fifteen years, while an overseer supervised the daily farm routine. Family life remained haphazard, for in December 1787, Henry wrote daughter Betsy that he'd had to leave the assembly session for a while "to try to get some house to winter in." "At present your mamma & all our family live at one fire" without any kitchen house or other outbuilding to assist, Henry said, with the twinge of self-pitying optimism that used to mark his own father's letters. "We expect . . . something better soon, & hope to live a little more comfortably."

Henry's straitened circumstances underlay his "peremptory" refusal to attend the Philadelphia convention, as Governor Randolph reported to Madison, yet both men suspected that there was something more. "The refusal of Mr. Henry to join in the task of revising the Confederation is ominous," Madison said, and he speculated that Henry wanted to remain "unfettered." Henry would keep himself "free to combat or espouse the result of [the convention] according to the outcome of the Mississippi business," Madison predicted. After all, everyone in Richmond knew that Henry had said "he would rather part with the confederation" than relinquish navigation of the river, although John Marshall wittily ventured that Henry would invert the old maxim by being strong in manner but gentle in deed.

Henry did feel strongly about the looming threat to southwestern interests, and he was happy to know that "in Kentucky, Liberty or Death are in every one's mouth." Yet he also felt antagonized by the ugly shift in the political climate surrounding the meeting. The Annapolis address had circulated along with news of widespread political protest in New England. Backcountry farmers had petitioned unavailingly for legislative relief from burdensome and inequitable taxes, and, in the wake of several years of depressed prices, they demanded the full panoply of debtor relief measures, including emissions of paper money and postponements of suits for debt. In September 1786 crowds of farmers had paraded menacingly around the legislature's meeting place in New Hampshire, and in western Massachusetts a "regulator" movement tried to force suspensions of the court sessions that had mandated foreclosures and imprisonment for debt. When the legislature remained adamantly against reform and instead undertook repressive measures against the dissidents, thousands of farmers defiantly organized themselves into a militia and surrounded the state arsenal at Springfield. The rebels (called "Shaysites" by the newspapers after one of their numerous leaders, a Revolutionary War veteran named Daniel Shays) were overwhelmed by a state expeditionary force, financed by contributions from eastern merchants and creditors after efforts to secure congressional troops had failed.

Distorted and hysterical accounts of "Shays' Rebellion" spread alarm among the well-to-do that tax protests were but the pretext for a campaign to repudiate all debts and redistribute property. Proponents of constitutional reform insisted that weak government had brought the country to the brink of anarchy and that new ways must be found to restrain insurgent majorities and protect property. "There are combustibles in every State, which a spark might set fire to," George Washington warned, and writer after writer insisted that "the prevailing rage of excessive democracy" would have to be checked by a more energetic government. Old Dr. Franklin, in his typical fashion, reduced the issue to aphorism: "Having dreaded giving too much power to our governors, now we are faced with the danger of too little obedience in the subjects." Some professed to see Tory machinations behind the protest, and Madison recruited support for the convention by warning that, if it failed, monarchists might capitalize upon the discontent. "All the real friends of the Revolution," he said, must now exert themselves "to perpetuate the Union and redeem the honor of the Republican name."

Henry remained aloof from the panic. Having lived for years among hard-pressed farmers, he understood their grievances more than most public men and, for years, had championed the moderate relief laws that had eased the debtors' condition in Virginia and avoided (so far) the tumults that had erupted in New England. As the depression grew worse in 1786, he had developed some sympathy for a new emission of paper money, and as governor he had imperturbably counseled leniency and patience in dealing with the insurgent movement that sought independence from Virginia and North Carolina. As a private citizen, however, he engaged in no speculations or predictions about the convention's work, and he kept to himself any apprehensions raised by the harsh antidemocratic talk.

The Philadelphia convention observed a rule of secrecy during its summer of deliberation, and the newspapers did not much catch the drift of things. Most reports declared that the conference enjoyed a glowing unanimity, but as the weeks went by, word of disagreement surfaced, and occasionally a newspaper hinted that the delegates would be recommending an entirely new scheme of continental government instead of the anticipated amendments to the existing constitution.

On Saturday, September 15, 1787, the convention in Philadelphia approved the draft of a new Constitution and ordered it engrossed and printed. On Monday, September 17, when the delegates stepped forward to sign the formal copy, two Virginians—Governor Edmund Randolph and George

Mason—stood back and withheld their endorsements, as did Elbridge Gerry, a Massachusetts delegate. By the next morning, a Philadelphia printing office had five hundred copies of a six-page broadside text ready for distribution, and the delegates at once began mailing them to friends and colleagues in the states. James Madison sent one copy to his father (along with "a few plumb Stones from an excellent tree") and another to his mentor Edmund Pendleton. "If the plan proposed be worthy of adoption, the degree of unanimity attained in the Convention is a circumstance as fortunate as the very respectable dissent on the part of Virginia is a subject for regret," Madison told Pendleton gravely, while insisting that, as a draftsman, he could not properly comment on the plan's merits or faults.

George Washington announced the same rule of silence in transmitting the document to Virginia's former governors, including Henry. "Your own Judgment will at once descover the good, and the exceptional parts of it," he wrote on September 24, adding, "your experience of the difficulties which have ever arisen when attempts have been made to reconcile such variety of interests, and local prejudices as pervade the several States will render explanation unnecessary." Yet Washington went on to endorse the plan as "the best that could be obtained at this time" and he urged its adoption by the states. "The political concerns of this Country are, in a manner, suspended by a thread," Washington insisted, and he emphasized that "the reflecting part of the community" knew that if the convention had not agreed to something, "anarchy would soon have ensued—the seeds being richly sown in every soil."

Henry did not like such alarmist talk, but he replied with elaborate courtesy. "I have to lament that I cannot bring my mind to accord with the proposed Constitution," he told Washington. "The concern I feel on this account is really greater than I am able to express. Perhaps mature Reflections may furnish me Reasons to change my present Sentiments into a Conformity with the opinions of those personages for whom I have the highest Reverence," he wrote. "Be that as it may," he concluded, he wanted to assure Washington of his "unalterable Regard and attachment" and "as a Citizen" extend his gratitude "on account of the great Fatigue necessarily attending the arduous Business of the late Convention."

Beneath Henry's polite talk, however, ran deep feelings of betrayal, for he believed that the convention had vastly exceeded its authority. The Articles of Confederation had established a league of sovereign states equally represented in a Congress that dealt with a limited range of common concerns, especially the conduct of war and diplomacy and the management of the public domain. The system depended a great deal upon the voluntary cooperation of the states, and for some years Henry had believed that Congress ought to have some compulsory power over delinquent or uncooperative member states. He also believed that Congress ought to have jurisdiction over interstate commerce and be allowed some form of independent revenue through a tariff on imports. The Articles could be amended only with the unanimous consent of the states, and like most of his countrymen Henry expected that the Philadelphia convention would synthesize and improve the various proposals of the past few years and, in effect, mobilize enough support to expedite (or perhaps improve) the cumbersome amendment procedure.

Instead of strengthening the Confederation, however, the convention recommended that it be abolished and replaced by a national government that would have coercive power over individuals in every state. The proposed Constitution granted a national legislature a long list of enumerated powers over taxes, money, trade, diplomacy, and defense and then further extended its jurisdiction to "all laws which may be necessary and proper" for the tasks enumerated. The laws made pursuant to the new Constitution, moreover, would take precedence over state laws, and a national judiciary would be established to assure the "supremacy" of the new Constitution. Individual states would be prohibited from legislating on a number of specific issues, including the emission of paper money or any law (such as debtor relief measures) that impaired the obligation of contracts.

Henry objected to the principle of consolidated government and insisted that it violated the spirit of the Revolution. Each state, he believed, had formed its own independent government, allied with the others for common defense, and agreed to remain in "perpetual union" to achieve a limited number of objectives in peacetime. To shatter this alliance and replace it with a government whose national legislature and executive bore a worrisome resemblance to Great Britain's seemed an invitation to renewed oppression, Henry thought. When he learned that George Mason had refused to endorse the convention's work owing to its deliberate omission of a bill of rights that would secure personal liberty against the vastly enlarged powers of a more distant government, Henry grew even more convinced that the fundamental principles of the Revolution stood in jeopardy. He shared Mason's conviction that the plan, which already seemed "a moderate aristocracy," would ultimately "produce a Monarchy, or a corrupt oppressive Aristocracy."

Henry had theoretical objections to the principle of consolidated government. He also had a furiously antagonistic reaction to both the manner in which the plan had come forward and the method its advocates had chosen for its adoption. The Philadelphia convention insisted that the new Constitution should go into effect when three-fourths of the states had approved it in special ratifying conventions, elected by the people under direction of the state legislatures. This mechanism not only circumvented the Confederation's rule of unanimity but effectively bypassed the existing Congress. The convention merely recommended that the new Constitution "be laid before" Congress and "afterwards submitted" to the state conventions. When nine states had approved, Congress should fix a date for the requisite new elections and establish the time and place for "commencing Proceedings" under the new plan. In effect, the Philadelphia proposal established a rival government by rival means but, with the procedural scrupulousness of a debater's revolution, requested Congress to schedule its own demise.

Everything Henry heard from Philadelphia and New York confirmed his suspicions that a high-handed "junto" sought to curb popular sovereignty in what amounted to a coup. A delegation of convention men, led by a no-longer-constrained Madison, had rushed from the Philadelphia "conclave" to New York, where they resumed their seats in Congress and blocked R. H. Lee's determined effort to amend the plan with a bill of rights. Not long after that, the friends of the new plan, who cunningly styled themselves "Federalists" (a name that Henry properly thought belonged to those who supported the Confederation), caused a ruckus in Philadelphia by insisting that the state legislature, on the eve of adjournment, call for an immediate ratifying convention. Opponents of the new plan (who were smeared with the epithet "Anti-Federalists") thought that new elections might better reflect public opinion and deliberately stayed away from the session in order to prevent a vote. A Federalist mob, however, searched the city for the absentees and forcibly hauled two recalcitrant assemblymen into the House long enough to establish a quorum and thus validate the call for ratification. George Mason had warned that the convention men would try to stampede the affair, and R. H. Lee, furious at the "this, or nothing" attitude in Congress, denounced the "extreme intemperance" with which the advocates "push the business on with great dispatch . . . that it may be adopted before it has stood the test of Reflection & due examination."

Lee warned the friends of "civil liberty" that they faced "a coalition of Monarchy men, Military Men, Aristocrats, and Drones whose noise, impudence & zeal exceeds all belief— Whilst the [anticipated] commercial plunder of the South stimulates the rapacious Trader." To old associates like Mason and Henry in Virginia and Samuel Adams in Massachusetts (those with whom, Lee said, he had "long toiled . . . in the vineyard of liberty"), Lee urged a common insistence upon amendments—especially a bill of rights—prior to ratification. Otherwise the powerful new government would be, from the outset, an "elective despotism."

Henry never said that he would agree to an amended plan, but he repeatedly said that he could "never agree to the proposed plan without amendments." The idea of concerted amendments and a second convention to review them appealed to him, however, as the maneuver most likely to brake the driving force of "the great continental waggon." Henry went to the October 1787 assembly session determined not to debate the plan until the terms of consideration were altered.

"Every corner of the city resounds with politicks," a Richmond law student wrote. The new Constitution "affords matter for conversation to every rank of beings from the Governor to the door keeper," an assemblyman declared, adding, "the opinions appear to be as various as the persons possessing them." Henry had not seen the delegates so wrought up in years. "Such is the Warmth of all the Members of Assembly concerning the new Constitution, that no Kind of Business can be done 'til that is considered, so far at least as to recommend a Convention of the People," Henry told his brother-in-law in Botetourt County. "Great Divisions are likes to happen, & I am afraid for the consequences."

In his typically casual manner Henry asked, "Pray, how are politics your way?" and then indicated the answer he sought. "The Friends of Liberty will expect support from the back people," Henry told his kinfolk, and he expended considerable effort to rally westerners against the plan. The valley's Presbyterian leader, William Graham, had opposed Henry and Smith on the general assessment but now agreed with Henry that "a vigorous opposition will be necessary if we mean to claim the Privilege or even Name of freeman any longer." Graham, at the behest of "friends" whom he declined to name, planned to "open the Eyes of the People" with a pamphlet attacking the new Constitution as "arbitrary," "very expensive," and "inadequate to the End proposed."

Backcountry sentiment did run heavily against the plan. A favorite story circulating in Richmond on the eve of the assembly session told of the old Pennsylvania wagoneer who complained that the Federalists were trying to trick the people into accepting a plan that would oppress them. "It is for all the world like me and my waggon horses," the driver says. When they are grazing freely and need to get in harness, "I whistle to 'em, coax 'em, and stroke 'em, and makes as if I only mean to feed and curry 'em, and so let them go again." Just so, the Federalist gentleman "coaxes and wheedles and palavers us silly doodles, that this here newfangled government may catch us; telling us that we may go loose again when we please. But my mind misgives me. . . . When once we are caught, we shall be fast bridled and harnessed, like my horses." The story ends with the sound of the cracking whip and the cry, "Gee— you sons of bitches."

At least one western leader, however, the hot-tempered Shenandoah lawyer Archibald Stuart, thought the Constitution "our only hope" and deplored the partisan "Wars and Rumors of Wars" that had Richmond in turmoil. The Constitution's "friends and foes are like the Electors in Poland whose resentments carry them to the extreme of madness," Stuart complained. "Henry digresses from every subject to assaulting [the plan's] friends, [who] with equal ardor follow him for its protection."

The first official skirmish took place on October 25. Francis Corbin, the son of the Tory receiver general whom Henry had harassed about reparations for the gunpowder, proposed that the assembly call a state convention empowered to ratify the Constitution as the draft directed. In "an elegant and judicious speech" Corbin expressed his approval of the plan and emphasized that the Union had to be reestablished "on a firm and unalterable Basis."

Henry immediately objected. He did not "Question the Propriety or Necessity of calling a [ratifying] Convention," he explained, for "no Man was more truly federal than himself." However, he strongly believed it improper to confine the convention to the stark alternative of adoption or rejection. "It was possible that there might be some Errors in the new Government," Henry said. "Nay, he would not hesitate to declare that there were Errors and Defects in it," he emphasized, and the Virginia convention ought to be granted the power to alter it.

George Nicholas and Corbin both objected that Henry's proviso "would convey an idea to the people of this state, and to the whole continent" that Virginia's legislature believed that amendments ought to be made. Yet, as a newspaper account shrewdly noted, neither man "denied the Right of the Convention to propose Amendments." Henry wanted to give public opinion a signal, and the Federalists could not stop him without further confirming the antidemocratic charges already leveled against them.

Then George Mason, who had arrived in Richmond only that morning, made a dramatic statement in support of Henry's proposition. Although he was fully convinced that "some general Government" ought to be established, Mason considered the Philadelphia constitution "repugnant to our Highest interests." He would not commit the treasonable act of subscribing to the plan without amendments. Mason held his arm aloft and shouted, "I would have lost this Hand, before it should have marked my Name to the new Government."

The remark shocked the House and showed the Federalists that they would have to give some credit to the idea of an open convention. A compromise ensued. The assembly would submit the Constitution to a "Convention of the people for their full and free investigation, discussion, and decision." Elections would be held in March, and the convention would meet on the first Monday in June.

"This is a happy and politick resolution," Governor Randolph told Madison, who had remained in New York the better to rally Federalist efforts in the East. The all-or-nothing approach "propounded" from Philadelphia would, in Randolph's view, have doomed the Constitution in Virginia.

With the immediate question settled, the assembly moved on to other controversial business. The persistent economic depression had worsened in 1786 and, although prices had begun to pick up in 1787, the rural population had accumulated a chronic burden of indebtedness. Wholesalers and merchants, equally caught in the squeeze, accelerated the process of foreclosure and bill collection, only to face rising anger in the countryside. The first signs of a farmers' uprising had already appeared. In Greenbrier County 150 people agreed to "stand together" against seizures for debts or taxes, and their leader, Adjoniah "Black" Matthews, was arrested when he tried to disrupt the county court. In Henry County, and elsewhere, sheriffs reported that they feared mob violence if they collected taxes. A mysterious fire destroyed court records in King William, and another blaze entirely destroyed the courthouse in New Kent County. The arsonist, a disgruntled farm manager named John Price Posey, who had once worked for General Washington, received a death sentence from a Richmond judge just as the assembly session began.

Protest and banditry deeply alarmed the men of commerce. "I take for granted we are on the Eve of a Revolution," a Fredericksburg merchant wrote despairingly, for not even the new constitution will "entirely avert our fate." From Petersburg, a broker told his Philadelphia partner that over four thousand lawsuits lay unheard on the General Court's docket. "Where this will end the Lord only knows. . . . If the new Constitution should not be adopted . . . such is the Influence of Debtors in our State that everything will be at Risk."

Henry renewed his support of relief measures in the assembly. An antagonist complained that "Henry is loud on the distresses of the People and makes us tremble with the Apprehensions of a Rebellion if they are driven to despair." On every issue Henry "fired his shot" at the new Constitution, complaining especially that the proposal would prohibit Virginia from enacting a number of the relief laws that had given ease to the people. A clamor had arisen in the back-country for a new emission of paper money (more than half the states had undertaken this inflationary expedient), and Henry was recognized as its chief advocate in the legislature.

Despite Henry's strenuous efforts, however, he could not get the opponents of the Constitution to unite upon measures for economic relief. Indeed, George Mason proved the most implacable foe of all. He so vigorously led the condemnation of the paper money scheme as "corrupting" to morals and "injurious" to public confidence in laws and government that Henry had no choice but to abandon it. Mason also gutted a plan to allow debts to be paid in three installments by insisting that creditors must consent to it, although Henry did manage to protect small freeholders by securing a bill that would prevent property from being sold for debts at less than three-quarters of its value. Henry continued his campaign against extravagant purchases of European goods by sponsoring a bill to prohibit the importation of all spiritous liquors. "Mason and Henry have got Virginia politically d——k," a Federalist scoffed, "and are determined they shall never be physically so with anything but peach and apple brandy."

Mason had also disappointed Henry by reiterating that, although he greatly desired amendments, he would support adoption without them in preference to no government at all. This position gave too much away, Henry thought, for he believed that only unequivocal popular opposition might create pressure enough for amendments. They must occur before ratification, Henry believed, for he doubted that the partisans of such an energetic government would voluntarily undertake them once installed. Only a crazy man, Henry liked to say, would buy a defective machine in the hope of repairing it afterward. Henry insisted that the choice lay between Confederation and Constitution and did not want to accept the dichotomy industriously propagated by the Federalists that anarchy and disunion stood as the only alternative to the Philadelphia plan.

Having grown less certain about Mason, Henry turned his attention to Governor Randolph, who had also refused to sign the Constitution. Randolph had not yet issued his long-promised explanation, and many observers believed that the governor, whom Jefferson had long before dismissed as a "perfect chameleon," had hung back because he was "afraid of the democracy & Patrick Henry." Speculation as to Randolph's ultimate course ran high; some guessed that, like Mason, he would ultimately support the plan as a lesser evil, while others sensed that Randolph's willingness to talk about his "objections" increased as public opposition mounted and that he might remain in the opposition camp.

Henry held several "animated" discussions with Randolph. The governor lacked his uncle Peyton's resilience and charm, and he still felt the stigma of his father's loyal removal to England in 1775. Randolph was a stolid, thickset man who spoke and wrote in a dense style that perfectly modeled the thickness of his intellect. Predictably, he and Henry could not find common ground; "he recedes so far from me," Randolph said, "that we must diverge after a progress of a half a degree further."

Randolph's circling, however, gave Henry an idea. He sensed that the governor's wavering had led him to grasp at the idea of a second convention at which the various amendments proposed by the states could be weighed and incorporated into the plan. If Henry could get Randolph to hold the door open for amendments, and indeed to invite other states to walk through it as well, a concerted opposition might stand a chance.

Henry took advantage of a crucial oversight in the assembly's convention call. The resolution had not provided for the delegates' compensation and travel expenses and would have to be amended. In drafting the corrective legislation Henry slipped in allowances for the expenses of "deputys to a second federal convention in case such a Convention be judged necessary" and for the expenses of any commissioners dispatched to "confer with the Convention or Conventions of any other state . . . on the proposed plan of federal Government."

Henry's "art is equal to his talents for declamation," Light-Horse Harry Lee said ruefully, when this deftly contrived signal came before the House. In debate Henry suggested that the Speakers of the two houses "should form a committee of correspondence" with the other states, and he emphasized that "our southern neighbors might be driven to despair seeing no door open to safety should they disapprove the new Constitution." Although supporters of the Constitution strenuously contended for more neutral language, Henry's resolution—significantly supported by Mason—passed by sixteen votes. On a subsequent reading, however, the Federalists steadily diluted the resolution until it would merely subsidize "communications" with sister state conventions or other means of "collecting the sentiments of the Union respecting the proposed Federal Constitution."

Despite the harshest winter in half a dozen years, the politicking never let up. Neither side could yet see its way to a clear majority, which meant that every seat in the ratifying convention would be bitterly contested and the campaign would end with "elections made in phrenzy."

Federalists in Virginia took heart from the swift adoptions secured in the small states of Delaware, New Jersey, Connecticut, and Georgia. (Of the last General Washington had remarked, "if a weak state, with a powerful tribe of Indians in its rear & the Spaniards on its flank, do not incline to embrace a strong *general* government, there must . . . be either wickedness or insanity in their conduct.") Perhaps, one of Madison's lieutenants speculated, the late date of Virginia's convention might yet work to their advantage, for if the requisite number (or close to it) had approved, the pressure on Virginia to conform would be very great.

If anyone could resist such influence, it would be Patrick Henry. He repeatedly declared that even if twelve states should approve, he would keep Virginia independent until the plan's grave faults were corrected. "His language is, that the other States cannot do without us," Madison was told, "and therefore we can dictate to them what terms we please."

Another story went around that Henry's friend William Grayson had passionately addressed a courthouse crowd in Dumfries while holding a tiny snuffbox. "Perhaps said he you may think it of consequence that some other States have accepted of the new Constitution. What are they? When compared to Virginia they are no more than this snuff Box is to the Size of a Man." (When a friend asked afterward why Grayson had "risqued such an assertion," he laughed and said, "There was not any short-hand man present.")

North Carolina had decided to hold its convention after Virginia's (surely Henry's doing, the Federalists thought), and some kind of collaboration seemed afoot with the opposition in New York (also to meet in June). That might make three holdouts, and debtor-dominated Rhode Island would surely make a fourth. Pennsylvania had ratified in a close vote, but the Anti-Federalists had so loudly challenged the proceeding that a second convention might have to take place. Their denunciations of bullying tactics and specious arguments, moreover, might well influence the February vote in Massachusetts, where opinions on the Constitution mirrored Shaysite divisions between east and west, creditor and debtor.

Virginia's campaign thus took place in the midst of a continental political quarrel of unprecedented ferocity. The French chargé d'affaires in Philadelphia fairly summarized the controversy in a report to Paris: "On one hand, energy and national reputation, on the other, civil and political liberty, give the new Constitution either a favorable or alarming aspect."

Partisans used more agitated language. The Constitution, said the *Virginia Independent Chronicle*, is "the tree of Life, whose Fruit will enthrone this western Empire high among the Nations." Writing from Philadelphia, "Centinel" attacked the proposal as a "spurious brat . . . come forth under the veil of mystery" with "its true features being carefully concealed" to misrepresent this "daring attempt to create a despotic aristocracy" as "the genuine off-spring of heaven-born liberty."

Federalist writers lambasted the weaknesses of Congress and painted awful pictures of idle ships and unemployed hands languishing in poverty because of the government's ineptitude. They portrayed the new Constitution as the only means left to restore national honor and permit Americans to be "fellow citizens of one great respectable and flourishing empire." The new government would promote manufacturing and commerce and protect men of property from "domestic violence and the depredations which the democratic spirit is apt to make." The "evils" of state laws that undermined "private rights," Madison privately told Jefferson, "contributed more to that uneasiness which produced the Convention . . . than those which accrued . . . from the inadequacy of the Confederation." Writing under the nom de plume of "Publius," Madison made the point more luridly: "The pestilent effects of paper money on the necessary confidence between man and man . . . and on the character of republican government . . . constitutes . . . an accumulation of guilt which can be expiated no otherwise than by a voluntary sacrifice on the altar of justice of the power which has been the instrument of it."

The defenders could sound very harsh. More than one writer looked forward to "an impartial and sometimes a severe administration of justice" that would rebuke the "political empirics [who,] ever courting popularity, give to a distempered multitude whatever their depraved appetites may crave."

The Constitution, Federalists insisted, would be "a revolution effected by good sense and deliberation," and Americans had a duty to cultivate "a spirit of submission to the counsels of th[e] great patriot band" that had produced it. "Publius," in a more soothing voice, insisted that the Constitution continued the grand work of revolution begun in 1776; if those daring leaders, he said, "had erred most in the structure of the union," it might be excused as "the work most difficult to be executed."

Where the Federalists saw energy to do good, the Anti-Federalists smelled power to oppress liberty. Almost every writer took the absence of a bill of rights as a sign that people would be unsafe under a new government, and efforts in New York and Boston to suppress pamphlets critical of the proposed Constitution only confirmed the fears. We did not "throw off the yoke of Britain and call ourselves independent," said "Cato," in order to "let the rich and insolent alone be our rulers." The haughty methods used to promote ratification and the endless exhortation to defer to the convention's wisdom antagonized the democratic spirit. "Teach the members of the convention," "Cato" said, "that you are capable of a supervision of their conduct; . . . in politics, as well as in religious faith, every man ought to think for himself."

Many Anti-Federalist writers tried to strike a middle course between Shaysites and levelers, on the one hand, and aristocrats and "Morris-ites" on the other. They appealed, as "the Federal Farmer" put it, to "the weight of the community, the men of middling property . . . not in debt . . .

[but] content with republican governments, and not aiming at immense fortunes, offices, and power." This agrarian backbone of the nation resisted "a politer kind of government" as unnecessary and potentially dangerous as an instrument of economic or political domination. "The dazzling ideas of glory, wealth, and power uncontrolled, unfettered by popular opinions, are powerful to captivate the ambitious and the avaricious," warned R. H. Lee.

"Energy" in government, to the Anti-Federalists' way of thinking, always worked to the advantage of the few. "The aristocracy who move by system and design, and always under the colourable pretext of securing property, act . . . like the screw in mechanics," a Maryland "Farmer" wrote, "always gaining, holding fast what it gains, and never loosing, and in the event has ever proved an overmatch for the multitude, who never act but from their feelings, and are never permitted to feel *until it is too late.*"

Patrick Henry established himself as the democratic-minded sentinel against such concentrations of power. Yet as a paper-money man who spent much energy on the search for a gold mine, he did not lack in contradiction. Like most Anti-Federalist leaders, he possessed more property and had more commercial aspirations than most of his constituents. His political commitments, however, led him to prefer a slower kind of growth, less diverse, less cosmopolitan than the aspirations of the Federalists. This could be made compatible with liberty and majority rule in a way that he believed the Federalist plan could not. However alluring the vision of national, indeed imperial, prosperity might be, it seemed realizable only by a sacrifice of the local political independence that he had spent a lifetime in achieving.

Virginia's mercantile community recognized Henry as its enemy. "His influence has occasioned many of the Assemblymen to declare against it; they have carried his objections & prejudices with them to their counties where they have spread them so generally that I fear the consequences," a James River tobacco dealer complained; "we have so many rascals that I am very fearful it will be rejected." A Richmond merchant explained that the rascally opposition came in "two classes": "those who have power, & are unwilling to part with an atom of it" and "the people who . . . are very unwilling to pay [their debts and are] afraid this Constitution will make them *Honest Men.*" From Fredericksburg, a Scotch broker told his Liverpool employer that he "did not like the complexion of many of those elected. . . . The involved & worthless anti-federalists"—led by "that Scoundrel Henry and his Minions" —"have taken so much pains to poison and prejudice the lower order of People, that I am greatly apprehensive a majority of those will be returned." A broker in New York advised his Virginia connections to expect a rapid drop in the price of securities if the state failed to adopt. Be prepared to sell quickly, he said, rather than "trust to the Issue of what Convulsions may happen if Virga. holds out, which may be an Appeal to Arms & the Cause of a Civil War; and what probably will follow, not only disability to pay but real intention to Annihilate the former Domestick debt." (Of course, in the broker's way, he added that he "would not be surprised" to see the price double "for a little" if Virginia adopted the plan, in which case "it would be prudent to strike & be done with them.")

Never before had Virginians tried to organize a statewide canvass by positioning candidates in the various counties and keeping close track on their progress. When Fairfax County succumbed to the numerous hostile attacks upon George Mason and would not elect him to the convention, his friends, determined that "such a Man shou'd not be risqued at so important a crisis," found a way for him to run in a neighboring county where he also held property. When Madison hung back from standing for election in bitterly divided Orange County, his friends insisted that they could easily find him a place from one of the distant Kentucky counties.

Henry had no difficulty gaining election from Prince Edward, but his former ally John Blair Smith made trouble for him nonetheless. The Presbyterian college president, who now made common cause with his Princeton classmate Madison, rigged up a speaking exhibition at Hampden-Sydney. One student repeated, from shorthand notes, the speech Henry had recently made against the Constitution at the local courthouse, while another student delivered a vigorous rebuttal prepared by Smith himself, although neither author was credited. Henry, in the crowded audience as both college trustee and parent of two students, took offense at this "ill treatment" and loudly complained that Smith had embarrassed him. Smith asked if the speech had been reported fairly, and Henry said that he thought the student had done an excellent job of imitation and that his complaint had not to do with accuracy but with the attempt to debate through surrogates without prior notice or opportunity for rebuttal. Smith made no apology, but insisted that Henry's speech had become public property. Henry stalked from the room and refused to hear Smith's preaching ever again.

Henry's influence on the Southside remained supreme, however. Edward Carrington, the young man who had wanted to be buried at the scene of Henry's "liberty or death" speech, now condemned "the torrent of folly" that his former hero spoke. Traveling as Madison's scout in Henry's Southside and Piedmont neighborhood, Carrington found Henry's politics "so industriously propagated that the people are much disposed to be his blind followers." "The demagogues in the opposition suppose that their popularity is increased in proportion to the loudness of their clamors," Carrington complained, "whilst the Friends to the constitution think it prudent to suppress their opinions, or at least advance them with Caution." Even in the creditor strongholds of the Northern Neck, Carrington had found the opponents "pretty numerous and vociferous." Some supporters of the plan, moreover, had "weak characters," he warned Madison; there would be great "danger" if too many got into the convention, for no matter what they professed in advance, "there is no accounting for the effects with which Mr. Henries address and Rhetoric may have upon them" in Richmond.

The gloomy reports and fearful talk about Henry's influence eventually provoked his most able rival, Madison, into the contest. The ink had hardly dried on the Constitution before Madison began receiving letters urging him to run for the Virginia convention; George Washington had written first, but other political allies and his own family had followed. As the news grew more pessimistic, the clamor became insistent. For a time Madison hid behind the fastidious pose that the final decision on the plan should "proceed from men who had no hand in preparing and proposing it," a rule that had not prevented him either from blocking R. H. Lee's effort in Congress to add a bill of rights to the new plan or from spending the winter furiously writing (with Alexander Hamilton of New York) a series of anonymous newspaper articles in support of his handiwork.

Although Madison was a brilliant political operative, he remained a most reluctant public politician. He found even the discreet campaigning approved by Virginians "personally distasteful," "irksome," and something of an embarrassment. Bookish and theoretical, he shone best in legislative committees or in serious debate in plenary session, where his passion for planning, outlining, and systematizing could find adequate expression and his diligent attention to detail and capacity for indefatigable work made him indispensable. In small groups no one could exceed his persuasiveness; on a wider stage, however, he generally went overlooked, held back by a combination of shyness and intellectual hauteur. A Virginia belle, visiting in Philadelphia, found him "a gloomy, stiff creature." "They say he is clever in Congress," she wrote back home, "but out of it, he has nothing engaging or even bearable in his manners—the most unsociable creature in existence."

Madison did not want to go home, and he put off the commitment as long as he dared. Even when he finally decided to "submit" to the nearly frantic requests of his father and connections and return to Virginia for the March election, he procrastinated. He did not arrive at Montpelier, his father's Orange County estate, until the day before the election, having first stopped at Mount Vernon for a quick strategy conference with George Washington.

Although his father had spent the intervening weeks in careful politicking, feeling ran so deep against the Constitution, especially among "the Baptists & the ignorant part," that Madison felt obliged, for the first time in his life, to make a speech from the courthouse steps on election day. The morning was very cold and windy, with a flurry of snow, and Madison's voice did not carry very far.

Nor did he cut an imposing figure. Sickly and nervous as a child, he still looked like a youth fresh from college: short and wiry, with a delicate face, soft-featured and nearly beardless. "No bigger than half a piece of soap," someone had said of him when he first arrived in Philadelphia in 1779 as a delegate to the Continental Congress, and now only his receding hairline and his sober mien hinted at his thirty-seven years and his decade of public service. To many of the assembled crowd he must have still seemed Squire Madison's boy, young Jamie, but that was just the point. His father, after all, commanded attention as the foremost planter in a prosperous county filled with large estates and dominated completely by the wealthy. The Madisons held more than five thousand acres and one hundred slaves, and the old squire had served many years as a county magistrate and had presided over the local revolutionary committee during the independence movement. Now the son appeared to be making his mark on a grander stage, and the local folks did not want to be taken for granted.

The importance of the talk lay less in its substance than in the act of making it. Virginians did not like to elect absentees, and while happy to defer to the wisdom of their leaders, they wanted upon occasion to hear from them directly. It was a subtle test, but Madison had evidently passed. When the sheriff called everybody in for the poll, Madison received 202 votes to his opponent's 56. His father and his friends beamed with satisfaction. Perhaps they had overestimated the opposition, after all. But Madison graciously conceded that they had not erred in calling him home. "A very different result would have taken place," he said, "if the efforts of my friends had not been seconded by my presence."

Madison's election gave Virginia's Federalists the general

they had previously lacked. (Washington, who husbanded his political capital as carefully as he tended his vast acreage, would not become a delegate himself. He quietly interested himself—with a nod here and a tactful letter there—in the election of Federalist candidates and did not object to having his name mentioned as the likely first president in order to reassure those who feared the powers of the proposed executive.) With Washington out, Pendleton feeble, and Randolph uncertain, the Federalists depended upon Madison, the diminutive theoretician who had pressed the Philadelphia convention to a result that still fell short of his nationalist hopes. A dogged partisan but a reluctant leader, Madison knew that a dramatic, public confrontation with Patrick Henry was now as inevitable as the summer heat.

Yet no one knew how to read the election returns. Arthur Lee made a tally of elected delegates that showed sixty-seven for the Constitution and sixty-three opposed, but the total left thirty-eight votes uncounted, especially from the Kentucky and other trans-Allegheny counties. "Patrick Henry and old Grayson will strive hard to gain the back counties," one correspondent wrote. Kentucky had seemed favorable at first, but Madison complained, "As elsewhere, the torch of discord has been thrown in and has found the materials but too inflammable."

Henry made no predictions. Another Virginia Anti-Federalist, writing in a Philadelphia newspaper, claimed that Virginia "will, by a very decided majority, reject a measure that . . . will endanger those liberties for which America gloriously contended during an eight years war."

Madison, listening carefully now on home ground, termed himself "a very incompetent prophet." "The real sense of the people of this State cannot be easily ascertained," he told Jefferson. While people generally felt great attachment to the Union, only "the most intelligent and independent" citizens seemed to favor the plan under consideration, Madison realized. His neighbor, George Nicholas, however, thought the Federalists had a majority in the convention, but feared "it will be but a small one."

In New York the secretary of war, Henry Knox, who had founded the association of former army officers known as the Cincinnati, learned that Madison was pessimistic about Virginia and exclaimed, "I hope in God it will go in that State even if it rubs hard." And in Philadelphia, R. H. Lee's kinfolk heard that "in Virginia it will be one of the most nicely divided questions that ever came on."

CHAPTER 19

"I Speak the Language of Thousands"

The stagecoach company had put on extra carriages and advanced its schedule by a day so that it could get "the gentlemen going to the convention" into Richmond by Sunday evening. The tavern keepers and the livery stablemen had booked every available place weeks earlier, and an enterprising wholesaler had stored quantities of flour in his cellar to await the bakers' inevitable shortage. Brokers held on to their commercial paper, anticipating a quick rise in prices "the moment Virginia adopts."

Talk covered the town as thickly as the clouds of dust hanging over its drought-cracked streets. "Nothing but debate & altercation in all companies," a merchant wrote, for Richmond seemed more agitated now than it had during Benedict Arnold's raid in 1781. No one could remember when the great majority of delegates had arrived so early for a public assembly.

On only two points did the politicians agree: the fate of the Constitution, with seven states having ratified, rested with Virginia, and Virginia's convention appeared as neatly divided as it could be. Beyond that, every word had a partisan tinge. The latest issue of the Federalist newspaper reprinted George Washington's circular letter of 1783 calling for an energetic central government; Anti-Federalists murmured that the general had been "misled" into "a gilded trap" by the artful financier Robert Morris, with whom he lodged during the Philadelphia convention. An Anti-Federalist likened the convention to a ship with "one half the Crew hoisting sail for the land of Energy—and the other looking with a longing aspect on the Shore of Liberty." A Federalist merchant believed "all the objections may be reduced to two—debt and dignity—the dread of paying old debts and the fear of many losing their influence and consequence."

Supporters of the Constitution hailed their champion in verse: "Maddison, above the rest,/Pouring from his narrow chest/More than Greek or Roman sense,/Boundless tides of eloquence." And they mocked his "great adversary" in triple measure: "Public virtue—a gown/Ev'ry fiend must put on/To conceal his unlawful intention;/And his horns tho' so big/He may hide with a wig/And array'd thus appear in convention."

Henry rode down to Richmond in a topless stick gig, his attention torn between the impending contest and affairs of home. "I left my ever dear wife very unwell," he explained to daughter Annie; Dolly had felt sickly for months and now lay within days of delivering another child. "Nothing but a Sense of the Duty I owe my country at this important Crisis could have dragged me from her in such a situation," Henry said. Once before, in 1774, he had left an ailing wife to attend an urgent Congress and returned from Philadelphia to find that, while he had advanced the public cause, she had lost her reason.

Henry plunged directly into politics upon his arrival. He met his old friend Mason at the Swan, the town's finest lodging, up on Broad Street behind the handsome new Capitol. Pendleton, it turned out, also had taken rooms at the Swan, and he chirped greetings to all comers, professing good health while he admitted the lack of an antidote for the ailment of advancing age. The old judge had long since endorsed the Constitution, and Henry and Mason had to find a private corner to discuss their strategy.

The Federalists had tried hard to divide the two, portraying Henry as the implacable demagogue while courting Mason, along with Governor Edmund Randolph, as a reasonably moderate critic who would subordinate his objections to the demands of unity. In October, Mason had indeed sounded malleable, but the long campaign had hardened his opposition, and he reacted stiffly to the recurring charges that his objections stemmed from personal distemper rather than political principle. Mason and Henry grimly contemplated the rising sentiment for the ploy of "ratifying first and amending afterwards." "The idea," Mason scoffed, "appears . . . so utterly absurd, that I can not think any Man of Sense candid, in Proposing it."

On Monday morning, June 2, 1788, Henry and Mason, wearing suits of deepest black, strode out of the Swan together and walked, arm in arm, down the hill to the clapboard meeting house that still served as the commonwealth's temporary Capitol. The gleaming marble temple on the hilltop looked magnificent, but despite earnest effort and extra money from the assembly, the interior lacked finish enough to permit meeting there. Inside the old assembly chamber the hordes of eager spectators and the stifling heat quickened enticing rumors of a surprise vote and early adjournment.

By prior arrangement George Wythe nominated Pendleton to preside, a favor to the commonwealth's senior judge that no one could deny. Pendleton hobbled to the rostrum and, begging the convention's indulgence, sat down to read a brief address of thanks that concluded with a homily upon the necessity of "order and decorum in the deliberation of all Public bodies." "As Trustees for a Great people, the citizens of Virginia," Pendleton said, "let us calmly reason with each other, as friends having all the same end in view, the real happiness of our constituents, avoiding all heats, Intemperance, and Personal Altercation [and] finally decid[ing] as our Judgment shall direct."

After the convention agreed to open the daily sessions with prayers, Pendleton appointed a large committee on privileges and elections to examine the credentials of the delegates and review some disputed elections. The two dozen names, even as announced in Pendleton's pinched quaver, flowed as the litany of leadership, old and new, in Virginia: Harrison, Mason, Randolph, Tyler, Nicholas, Marshall, Carrington, Bland, Grayson, Monroe, Wythe, Corbin, Taylor, Blair, Lee. Only two names did not sound: Madison, who had not arrived, and Henry, who sat in the front row and looked unperturbed at yet another snub from Pendleton.

Then George Nicholas asked if any member would object if "the short-hand gentlemen should be suffered to take down the business of the house." George Mason would. They are "strangers," Mason said, and the task is too important to be left to men of uncertain reputation, for not only might the public be misinformed, but "a fatal stab might be given to a gentleman of the house from a perversion of his language." To show his good faith, however, and to prove that he did not want to take part in "another *conclave*" (the slap at secrecy in Philadelphia was unmistakable), Mason moved adjournment to the large and commodious theater on Shockoe Hill, where the public could witness the debates and a delegate could speak "the language of his soul." The delegates concurred and, relieved, walked from the close and fetid chamber into the tobacco-scented heat of a Richmond afternoon.

Madison arrived that night, astonished that the session had begun with a full house at its appointed hour, and he joined the body on Tuesday morning at the theater. The "New Academy," as Richmonders called it, had opened the year before; it was the brainchild of a French dancing master who conceived it as a grand ballroom, concert hall, and center for instruction in the all the finer arts. A "spacious & airy" building, it afforded space for the 170 delegates on the main floor, with hundreds of spectators arrayed above them in the boxes and galleries. "We have every day a gay circle of ladies to hear the debates," one delegate wrote, "and have the pleasure of believing them all Federalists."

Two unequivocally Federalist visitors also attracted attention. Financier Robert Morris and his business partner, Gouverneur Morris (no kin), had passed the spring ostensibly tending to their tobacco contracts in Virginia. Their presence in Richmond, however, demonstrated to the Anti-Federalists the heavy commercial lobbying behind the plan.

Tuesday's audience did not get much of a show as the delegates maneuvered briefly for position, then adjourned. Yet the astute observer could see the drama taking shape. First, Henry ("Light-Horse Harry") Lee, the heroic young cavalry leader who favored the Constitution as deeply as his absent uncle Ritt opposed it, challenged the seating of one of the Louisa County delegates, William White. A planter of modest holdings, White had voted consistently with Patrick Henry during his years in the legislature and always said that "the sense of his constituents" would be his only "rule of conduct." White had edged out Louisa's wealthiest planter, Richard Morris, by a handful of votes, and now Lee charged foul and asked the convention to reverse the results. The motion would go to the committee appointed on the previous day for a hearing. Every vote would count, and neither side neglected an opportunity to take a vote from the opposing column.

Next, Benjamin Harrison, the former governor and Speaker, moved that all the papers "relative to the Constitution" be read, a maneuver that heralded Henry's likely attack that the Philadelphia convention had violated its charge. But Mason preempted Harrison and urged the necessity of clause-by-clause discussion before any other question be put. Madison unexpectedly agreed. Mason wanted to avoid a quick vote, but Madison, who would not force a vote until he was more certain of the tally, sensed an opportunity to rein in Mason and Henry. He thought they might find it difficult to raise their objections to the fundamental conception of the plan if confined to debating each clause singly.

Henry had not yet said a word on the floor of the convention. On Wednesday morning, however, he served notice that he would do as he liked, regardless of strategy or rules. Henry labored under the tactical disadvantage of having agreed to the ratifying convention, which to a large extent mooted his complaint that the constitutional proposal was illegitimate. When Henry sought to read the charge to the Philadelphia convention, Pendleton cut off the intended polemic against the usurpation of authority. The old jurist argued pointedly, "We are not to consider whether the federal convention exceeded their powers." Congress had sent the report to the legislature, and the legislature had asked the people to send us here to determine "whether this government be a proper one or not." The act of assembly appointing the convention should be paramount and controlling, Pendleton argued, and as someone said, "Plant Pendleton on an act of assembly and no one can knock him down."

Henry withdrew his motion and sat glumly as the clerk read the preamble and the first two sections of Article I. They dealt with the composition of the House of Representatives, and for two hours George Nicholas defended it. Nicholas was a short, squat man who, people said, looked like a plum pudding with legs, but he spoke forcefully and held the convention's attention. He insisted that the House would not be too small, nor would it engross power, as the Anti-Federalists had charged, by abusing the control granted over the time, place, and manner of elections. A certain uniformity would be necessary, Nicholas insisted, but this would not be incompatible with liberty, and "as long as the people remained virtuous and uncorrupted," there could be no abuses by Congress, for the people would not tolerate them.

Henry heard his opportunity and seized it. A new kind of government, fraught with dangers, was being proposed without the consent of the people, he charged; if it could be foisted on a virtuous people now, what would prevent tyranny later when virtue declined and revolutionary ardor further weakened? Henry sailed into the speech he had intended to make earlier in the morning. He cast himself as "a sentinel" over the people's rights and happiness and explained that he had sought appointment to the convention because he "conceived the republic to be in extreme danger." The people, he said, were "exceedingly uneasy" at being brought from a state of "perfect repose" to "the present delusive appearance of things." This "fatal system"—a proposal to "sever the confederacy"—had placed the country in "fearful jeopardy," Henry insisted. It "goes to the utter annihilation of the most solemn engagements of the states and the treaties we have formed with foreign nations"—"and for what?" he asked in a tone of outraged innocence.

Henry paused. He looked around the hushed room and fixed his eye on Randolph, on Madison, on Mason. Then he asked grandly whether "these worthy characters" who had attended at Philadelphia could explain why they had formed "a great consolidated government instead of a confederation." "What right had they to say, 'We, the People?'" His "political curiosity," Henry said, led him to ask why they spoke in the name of the people when the states had sent them and the states formed "the characteristics and the soul of a confederation." "The people," said Henry, "gave them no power to use their name. That they exceeded their power is perfectly clear," Henry charged, and "I would demand the cause of their conduct, even from that illustrious man who saved us by his valour, I would have a reason."

Henry wanted to dispel the aura of enlightened, disinterested statesmanship the Federalists had assiduously created about the Philadelphia meeting. By putting the delegates on the spot, he hoped to elicit some damaging revelations about what had transpired in the convention, but he ran the great risk of receiving only a great barrage of Federalist attacks on the weaknesses of the Confederation.

The most vulnerable of the Philadelphia trio jumped at Henry's bait. Edmund Randolph's equivocal course had made him touchier than ever, and he jibed sharply at Henry's "enthusiasm" and popularity. Then he rehearsed again his reasons for not signing the proposal, emphasizing now his desire for amendments. With evident distaste, he admitted that Henry's queries deserved an answer and insisted that the old Congress had no means to enforce the powers that it possessed and had worked only when the dangers of war had forced cooperation from the states. But, Randolph said, in a direct slap at Henry, now Congress cannot even enforce the treaty that brought victory because some will not suffer to have debts paid to people on the other side of the Atlantic.

As to Henry's challenge to the phrase "We the People," Randolph rejoined, "Why not? The government is for the people; and the misfortune was, that the people had no sway in the government before . . . what harm is there in consulting the people on the construction of a government to which they are to be bound . . . ?" asked Randolph, inadvertently getting to the heart of Henry's objection that the new government held a coercive power over people that the Confederation had specifically forsworn.

Before Henry could exploit this advantage, however, Randolph sprang a surprise of his own. As much as he desired amendments, Randolph said, too many states had ratified to allow those changes to take place before the new government came into being. (Madison had urged this argument upon Randolph all spring and had cleverly asked him to distribute fifty bound copies of *The Federalist* essays to other men who shared his doubts.) To preserve the Union, Virginia would have to accept the Constitution, however faulty, and work for changes as the new plan prescribed. Those who persisted in opposition, Randolph charged, placed the Union itself in jeopardy. Randolph had now ended any doubt that he might vote with the Federalists, and the realization that a significant vote had just been announced raised a great stir in the galleries.

George Mason, the other Virginian who had not signed at Philadelphia, tried to bring attention back to Randolph's acknowledgment that the new government had consolidated power. Mason pointed to the mention of direct taxes in Article I, Section 2. No one would consent to double taxation, Mason charged, and the more powerful general government would "annihilate the states." The states, Mason emphasized, must not surrender this power; only they, and not a distant, inadequately representative, tiny general Congress, could know what the people could bear. Why not simply let Congress tax only those states that did not meet their requisitions? Although Governor Randolph had surrendered the hope of prior amendments, Mason said, he would not overcome his doubts until "the great essential rights of the people are secured." A restraint such as he proposed on the power of direct taxation would be "a *sine qua non* for adoption." Mason, in other words, still insisted upon amendments before Virginia ratified.

To divert attention from Mason's proposed amendment on taxation, Madison urged that discussion on it be postponed until the convention reached the section that enumerated the powers of Congress. He moved adjournment for the day.

The opponents of ratification met that evening to weigh the day's events. Henry had attacked from the heights and Mason from within, but Randolph's announcement had trumped them. Worse yet, the afternoon stage had brought news that South Carolina (the eighth state) had ratified and, following the stratagem first developed in Massachusetts, had placated the opposition by recommending a series of amendments to the attention of the new Congress.

These "two unlucky circumstances," wrote William Grayson, have made us "alarmed, though we do not despond." It would be harder to get Virginia to stay out of the new plan, but if they pressed for prior amendments, it was still not too late to influence ratification in the remaining states. With eight states in and three or four agreed on amendments, perhaps a compromise could yet be struck. Meanwhile the Anti-Federalists still believed that they might prevail with outright rejection in Virginia. "The district of Kentuckie is with us," Grayson wrote, "and if we can get over the four counties, which lye on the Ohio between the Pennsylvania line and Big Sandy Creek, the day is our own."

That night Madison wrote the first in his series of reports to General Washington. "The federalists are a good deal elated," he said, "for the governor has declared the day of previous amendments past, and throws himself fully into the federal scale." Madison drew comfort from the strategic differences he discerned between Mason's close attention to the text and Henry's wholesale attack on the conception. "They appeared to take different and awkward ground," he wrote, and he concluded that they had "made a lame figure." Yet he felt the outcome far from settled. "Kentuckie has been extremely tainted," Madison said, "and every piece of address is going on privately to work on the local interests and prejudices of that and other quarters."

In Thursday's session Henry intensified the attack with a speech of such length and vehemence that the Federalists consumed the next day and a half in rebuttal. Meeting in a theater suited Henry's histrionic talent. While other men declaimed, Henry dramatized; this day he presented the great spectacle of ordinary people defending their revolutionary principles against "refined" ideas and the "ropes and chains of consolidation." And he presented himself as both architect and guardian of the revolutionary legacy. "When I profess myself an advocate for the liberty of the people," he complained, I am called "a designing man" or "a demagogue," and "suspicions of my integrity" are raised. Twenty years ago, Henry said, such "suspicion" roused the country to the dangers posed by the Stamp Act. Some people then called me "the bane of sedition because I supported the rights of my country," he recalled, without hinting that Pendleton had been one of them and Edmund Randolph's father another. "Perhaps in these refined, enlightened days," he charged, "an invincible attachment to the dearest rights of man . . . may be deemed old-fashioned; if so, I am content . . . to become an old-fashioned fellow."

Others spoke of union, Henry said, but he would speak of liberty—"the greatest of all earthly blessings." "You are not to enquire how your trade may be increased, nor how you are to become a great and powerful people," Henry emphasized (to the gallery as much as to the delegates), "but how your liberties can be secured; for liberty ought to be the direct end of your government." "Those nations who have gone in search of grandeur, power, and splendor, have also fallen a sacrifice and been the victims of their folly," Henry warned, and he tried to call his audience back to the days when republican simplicity seemed the highest goal.

Henry reiterated his attack upon a consolidated government. He regarded it as a misguided lust toward greatness and power that would lead to large armies and navies, an expensive government of place men, colonels, courtiers, and tax gatherers that would design legislation to serve the interests of the "ambitious few." He ridiculed this "acquisition of strength" as a quest for "splendor," and he insisted that such a government would inevitably become tyrannical. Intended to prevent the "faction and turbulence" dreaded by creditors, it would aggrandize power and "oppress and ruin the people." "I dread the operation of it on the middling and lower classes of people," he said; "it is for them I fear the adoption of this system."

"In this scheme of energetic government," Henry warned, "the people will find two sets of tax-gatherers—the state and the federal sheriffs." Everyone knew the dreadful oppressions of the state sheriffs—"those unfeeling bloodsuckers"—who seized property and sold it for a fraction of its value, and how the "constant vigilance" of the legislature was necessary "to keep them from totally ruining the people." If these outrages were "dared" under "the watchful eye" of the state representatives, "what would they not have done if their masters had been at Philadelphia or New York?" Henry asked. "When these harpies are aided by excise men who may search at any time, your houses, and most secret recesses, will the people bear it? . . . Where I thought there was a possibility of such mischiefs, I would grant power with a niggardly hand."

Again and again, Henry drummed home his point that only a government small in scale, close to home, and broadly representative could operate without infringing upon liberty. Not that it would be more benign, Henry stressed, but it would be more accountable. "There is no true responsibility" in the new government, Henry emphasized, and "this, sir, is my great objection to the Constitution." Henry had a deeply skeptical attitude toward hierarchical authority, which derived from both the Whig and the evangelical traditions. Whigs insisted that power be subjected to limitation and review, always more feasible in smaller, local settings, and the evangelicals believed in the power of a homogeneous, beloved community to regulate itself. Both views pointed toward more democracy than the Constitution would permit.

When power is granted to the new government to suppress "sedition and licentiousness," Henry insisted, the proposal uses language that is "clear, express, and unequivocal." When the subject turns to rights and privileges, he warned, "there is an ambiguity, sir, a fatal ambiguity—an ambiguity which is very astonishing." Why, for example, does it say, in speaking about representation, that "the number shall not exceed one for every thirty thousand"? Henry wanted to know. Why not say "clearly and unequivocally" that the people shall be entitled to one representative for every thirty thousand, unless there was some artful intent, one day, to reduce the number as close to nullity as possible. "I confess this construction is not natural; but the ambiguity of the expression lays a good ground for a quarrel," Henry said. (Generally speaking, the Anti-Federalists considered the 1:30,000 ratio much too small a basis for decent representation, but that was not Henry's point here.)

Henry reminded Virginians that their bill of rights guaranteed that they would be taxed only with the consent of their representatives, but the new, consolidated government could tax them even if all ten of Virginia's congressmen said no. "Those feeble ten," he warned, cannot prevent passage of the most oppressive tax law so that, "in direct opposition to the spirit and express language of your declaration of rights, you are taxed not by your own consent, but by people who have no connection with you."

Henry saw only "specious imaginary balances" and "ridiculous ideal checks and contrivances" in the new system. The president, eligible for reelection as long as he lived, could easily become a despot, especially since he was given command of the army; the Senate, indirectly elected for long terms, could be dominated by a handful of members and become a sinkhole of corruption and the president's accomplice in diplomatic treachery; the national courts would not be bound, in all cases, to extend the protection of trial by jury.

Ordinary citizens needed protection against a consolidated government of such size, complexity, and power, and they had a right, nay a duty, to be suspicious of it. How could we punish abuses of power in such a government, without a bill of rights and sufficient powers retained by the states? "Will your mace-bearer be a match for a disciplined regiment?" Henry asked. Is it not likely that there will be a national riot act that will prohibit "a few neighbors" from assembling without "the risk of being shot by a hired soldiery"?

In a speech of such length and passion, Henry sometimes lost his way or explored arguments that failed to make his point. His efforts to show the malign influence of British ideas in the plan came across so clumsily that the Federalists threw charges of monarchism back at him. He expatiated at length on the difficulty of making amendments under the new plan, for example, which left him open to a long rebuttal from Madison on the paralysis of the Confederation owing to its even more rigid rules on amendments. Henry also went off, in an uncharacteristic fashion, to draw upon examples of effective confederacies in ancient and modern history, a fruitless exercise, given Madison's superior knowledge of the subject, and an entirely speculative one to boot.

Henry concluded by reiterating his opposition to adoption without prior amendment and insisted that Virginia could remain out of the new arrangement, for a time, without danger. He insisted also that "a great majority of the people, even in the [eight] adopting states, are averse to this government." Pennsylvania "has, *perhaps*, been tricked into it," he charged, and the other states "hurried on" despite substantial opposition. No government could proceed without "the affection" of the people," Henry emphasized, and he knew that the majority of Virginians had grave doubts about the new plan. "We are come hither to preserve the poor commonwealth of Virginia," Henry said. "Something must be done to preserve your liberty and mine." "I speak as one poor individual," he concluded, "but when I speak, I speak the language of thousands."

Over the next two days half a dozen Federalist speakers hammered away at Henry's speech. Pendleton disputed Henry's skeptical premise that to protect liberty the people had to retain power against government. "There is no quarrel between government and liberty," Pendleton insisted. "The war is between government and licentiousness, faction, turbulence, and other violations of the rules of society," he said, warning that "we ought to be extremely cautious not to be drawn into dispute with regular government." Madison went further and warned that the "abuse of power by the majority trampling on the rights of the minority" had frequently produced "the commotions which, in republics, have more frequently than any other cause, produced despotism." (Agrarian insurgency, Madison had warned for more than a year, would lead to monarchic repressiveness, unless a republican form of strong government could be developed. In the new Constitution Madison professed to find the means of controlling the majority while preserving republican forms. He thought the balance successful; Henry did not.)

Edmund Randolph, however, revealed the antidemocratic tendency in Federalist thought by disputing Henry's criticism that the House would be too small to be sufficiently representative. Virginia would have ten of sixty-five delegates, Randolph said. "I appeal to those who hear me, if they could not rely on the intelligence of ten men they could fix upon, sooner than upon any crowd they could have." Randolph insisted that he would cast no aspersions, but he argued: "There is a certain listlessness and inattention to the interest of the community, such indecision or faction in numerous bodies, that I would rather depend upon the virtue and knowledge of some few men than on ever so many."

Calling himself "a child of the revolution," Randolph tried to counter Henry's emphasis upon the legacy of liberty by stressing "the security of public justice" as the key to "the public happiness." With creditors wearied by endless delays, with commerce at a standstill in the seaports, with state laws endlessly changing and popular licentiousness on the rise, the country required a "national" government to protect itself, Randolph insisted. He then shifted the question from the virtues of consolidation to the necessity of "union." He berated Henry for jeopardizing Virginia's safety by contemplating a withdrawal from any confederation and painted a dreadful picture of the separate states warring against each other with such force and expense that republicanism would be destroyed.

Madison, looking pale and speaking in a voice so low

that the gallery missed much of what he said, tried to cut through all the speculative talk—"distorting the natural construction of language," he called it—to concentrate upon a single question: Will the new Constitution "promote the public happiness"? "Its aptitude to produce this desirable object ought to be the exclusive subject of our present researches," he said calmly. He insisted that the proposal did not grant power "to any particular set of men" but to "representatives responsible to the people." Madison insisted that the proposed government had a uniquely "mixed nature," partly federal and partly consolidated. The states would be directly represented in the Senate, in the process of choosing the president, and in the introduction of amendments. Were the government wholly national, Madison said, it would go into effect when a simple majority of the people approved; the ratification by states was a federal protection, he insisted, and he speciously claimed that the ratification by eight states signified that a majority of the population had already approved.

There had to be sufficient energy in government to perform its designated tasks, Madison emphasized, and if the tasks were necessary, then the power had to follow. We must either "submit to the inconvenience" of shifting power or "lose the Union." (Another speaker, George Nicholas, said that Henry's objections rested upon the insupportable premise that "the powers given to any government ought to be small," whereas the Federalists believed that they had to be proportionate to the ends.)

"Thirteen independent sovereignties," Madison warned, could be only "a solecism in theory and a mere nullity in practice." By analogy he pointed to the government of Virginia and wondered what would happen if each county were free to supply its quota of state revenue by requisition instead of taxation. Would not the commonwealth then be as feeble and disabled as the Confederation is now? he asked.

Madison defended the power to levy taxes, however, by insisting that it would not be much used. "It can be of little advantage to those in power to raise money in a manner oppressive to the people," he said, which brought the argument full circle to Henry's contention that the people were being asked to grant large powers on the mere chance that they would not be abused.

In closing the week's debates with a powerful rejoinder on Saturday afternoon, Henry talked about "certain political maxims which no free people ought ever to abandon." Henry identified these "poor little humble republican maxims" with "our bills of rights." These liberties now are "in our own hands," Henry said. "Let us not relinquish them," and especially, "Let us not adopt this system until we see them secure." Unlike Massachusetts, which endorsed the new government on the "mere possibility" of reform afterward, Virginia must cling fast to her creed and insist that the defects be remedied first. Henry would not accept the Federalist reassurance that civil liberties were protected by implication. Henry saw nothing but "danger" in the use of "constructive power." "If they can use implication for us, they can also use implication against us," he said. "We are giving power; they are getting power; judge, then, on which side the implication will be used!"

In Henry's view protection for popular liberty had remained uncertain in England until the Bill of Rights of 1689 spelled out procedures that had only been implied—and hence, debatable—before. The dispute with Great Britain, moreover, had taken place over Parliament's "implied" power to bind the colonies in all cases whatsoever. We successfully opposed this "constructive power," Henry said, and "the most important thing that could be thought of was to exclude the possibility of construction and implication" by making "a bill of rights."

No one in 1776, Henry emphasized, was satisfied to leave their rights to the vagaries of interpretation and argument. Now, after a week of fervent attack and denunciation, Henry at last named his price. A bill of rights was "indispensably necessary" before he could approve the Constitution. "A general positive provision should be inserted in the new system," he proposed, "securing to the states and the people every right which was not conceded to the general government" and doing away with "every implication." By concentrating attention upon a bill of rights, however, Henry implied that, with safeguards, a consolidated government might be made acceptable. He did not mean that, but it offered a powerful wedge to a politician as adroit as Madison.

Henry, Mason, and their most trusted supporters spent the weekend working on a list of possible amendments, spurred on by a sudden opportunity to coordinate their opposition with New York. Colonel Eleazer Oswald, a bluff soldier who had served with distinction at Ticonderoga and Monmouth and now stirred controversy with his Anti-Federalist newspapers in Philadelphia and New York, arrived in Richmond on the Saturday afternoon stagecoach with confidential letters for Henry and Mason. They came from General John Lamb, a New Yorker and Oswald's former commanding officer, who invited the Virginians to enter "a free correspondence" with the "federal republicans" of New York so that they "should understand one another on the subject of amendments and unite" in the ones proposed. Lamb believed that the New Hampshire convention, just resuming its deliberations after a four-month recess, would join a united front, and he hoped the Virginians had already explored North Carolina's desire to participate.

Henry's caucus of Anti-Federalists worked in high spirits. Mason, roused to new anger by Oswald's reports that Governor Randolph might have deliberately retarded previous correspondence with New York, provided determination. The old warrior Grayson, one of the few senior military officers in the country to oppose the Constitution, relieved the task with a steady stream of sarcastic jokes, delivered with a solemn face while his manservant, Punch, massaged his master's gouty feet. "Beau" Dawson, a spirited young bachelor from Fredericksburg, danced attendance on his senior colleagues and raced off in search of necessary books and documents. Henry, his mind eased by news that Dolly had safely given birth to another son, bragged a little about his young daughters' accomplishments and amiably agreed to pose, as time allowed, for an Italian sculptor who had come to

Richmond for the convention business. The likeness, in clay, emphasized Henry's calm determination, with chin thrust forward, thin lips set in the merest trace of a scowl, bushy eyebrows putting a slight canopy over his steady gaze. Yet in the wrinkled forehead, the long facial creases and the deep pouches under the eyes the sculptor felt the weariness and fatigue behind the visage of a champion.

With Mason wielding the pen, the Anti-Federal caucus reworked the Virginia Declaration of Rights of 1776 into a preface for the new Constitution. They expanded some of the more carelessly drafted protections in criminal proceedings and provided additional guarantees for the rights of speech and assembly. They also improved the article on religion to reflect the new consensus: in addition to protecting "free exercise," the declaration now specified: "No particular religious Sect or Society of Christians ought to be favored or established by Law, in Preference to others." (They would subsequently broaden this clause by deleting the phrase "of Christians.")

Moving beyond civil liberties to the powers of the new government, the caucus proposed a baker's dozen of restrictions. They gave pride of place to a sentence taken directly from the Articles of Confederation: "Each State in the Union shall retain its Sovereignty, Freedom, and Independence, and every Power Jurisdiction and Right, which is not by this Constitution expressly delegated to the Congress." There followed Henry's proposal that direct taxes not be levied unless duties on imports proved inadequate and not until the states had had an opportunity to comply with requisitions. Another proviso of Henry's explicitly guaranteed one representative for every thirty thousand persons until the whole number of representatives reached two hundred. Other amendments required two-thirds votes in Congress for all commercial regulations or treaties, the raising of armies in peacetime, or the personal assumption of military command by the president or vice-president.

As a mirror of Anti-Federalist discontents, the amendments revealed the concern to protect individual rights, to restrict the central government to expressly delegated tasks and otherwise preserve the autonomy of state governments, and to reduce opportunities for oppression by requiring a larger proportion of Congress to approve certain classes of action.

On June 9 Henry sent the newly drafted proposal off to New York via Colonel Oswald and in an accompanying letter to General Lamb pronounced the idea of cooperation "the only remaining chance for securing a Remnant of those invaluable Rights . . . yielded by the new Plan." Henry told Lamb what "a great consolation" it was to know that "the sentiments of a vast majority of Virginians are in unison with those of our northern friends." Although he was sure that four-fifths of the people (nine-tenths on Southside) opposed the Constitution, Henry said, the "numbers in convention appear equal on both sides." The "Friends and Schemers of Power, with their usual subtlety, wriggled themselves into the choice of the people by assuming shapes as various as the Faces of the Men they address[ed]," Henry complained, and so he could not predict whether the idea of prior amendments would carry. If the New Yorkers could send a delegation immediately to work out a joint statement, the "doubtful" members might be swayed by this tangible evidence of outside support.

If previous amendments failed, Henry indicated, the caucus was prepared to carry on as a committee of correspondence. The friends of liberty would have to "assimilate . . . views" and establish a coordinated system of opposition and mutual protection. Henry assured Lamb that the people in North Carolina, even more than in Virginia, seemed "ripe to hazarding all before they submit," and he thought that in addition to the state "republican societies" in contemplation, "perhaps lesser Associations dispersed throughout the State" might help to remedy the "inconvenience arising from our dispersed situation."

The Anti-Federalists made no immediate move to introduce the amendments in convention. Instead they lobbied privately, but without bothering to conceal their "advances" from the opposition. Arguing, in the words of Henry's friend

Theodorick Bland, that it would not be prudent "to mount a fiery high-blooded steed without a bridle," they hoped to attract the few "wavering" delegates with these "simple propositions." We only object to the powers that are "hurtfull," the line went in those earnest tavern and hallway conversations that kept Richmond buzzing day after day; "the government shall want no aid for its own support or execution provided that [there are] restraints . . . to support and ensure the state privileges and the liberty of the Individual against oppression."

Here and there the Anti-Federalists made headway. James Monroe, a stolid Fredericksburg lawyer who had served as a delegate to Congress and followed an equivocal course like Randolph's, came over to an insistence on previous amendments. ("Monroe may be slow," Henry remarked, "but give him time and he is sure.") But the Federalist phalanx remained implacable on the question of any amendments at all, and Madison, weakened by a "bilious attack" that kept him confined to bed on Sunday and Monday, worried that the protracted argument would end in a stalemated convention. That Oswald spent the weekend "closeted" with Henry and Mason seemed to Madison an ominous sign that the Virginians might contrive either to stall the debates or to seek a temporary adjournment until further word could come from New York.

Inside the convention chamber, the atmosphere grew even more heated. On Monday morning Henry immediately wove the thread of the weekend's efforts into a continuation of Saturday's speech. "It is a fact that the people do not want to change their government," he said. Echoing his private remarks to Lamb, Henry told the convention: "Four-fifths of the people of Virginia must have amendments to the new plan, to reconcile them" to the change. "Does it not insult your judgment to tell you, Adopt first, and then amend!" Henry asked. "Is your rage for novelty so great, that you are first to sign and seal, and then retract? . . . agree to bind yourselves hand and foot—for the sake of what? of being unbound? . . . go into a dungeon—for what? To get out. Is there no danger, when you go in, that the bolts of federal authority shall shut you in?"

Henry also pulled a surprise. The caucus had somehow procured the substance of a letter from "an illustrious citizen of Virginia, who is now in Paris," who (Henry claimed) "advises you to reject this government till it be amended." Ensconced amid "the splendor and dissipation" of the French court, Henry said, this citizen "thinks yet of bills of rights—thinks of those little, despised things called *maxims*." Randolph retorted that there was no letter, only "a report circulated through the town, that Mr. Jefferson wanted nine states to adopt, and the others to reject it, in order to get amendments." To Randolph's mind this meant that Jefferson wanted to "prevent a schism in the Union" and that Virginia, as the pending ninth state, must ratify. Henry responded that Virginia, as the most influential state, must lead the opposition, for no one would later pay attention to North Carolina, New Hampshire, or Rhode Island.

(The letter sounded like one Madison had received, although it turned out that the Anti-Federalists had obtained their intelligence from a copy Jefferson had sent to a friend in Maryland. Eventually Madison felt obliged to concede that Jefferson had expressed a mixture of views, but he did not read to the convention Jefferson's assertion: "A bill of rights is what the people are entitled to against every government on earth.")

In framing the rest of his remarks Henry swiped heavily at Randolph. Although Henry now professed an aversion to paper money (except in "extreme necessity"), he said that he could not subscribe to the idea that the state assemblies should not be trusted "with the private contracts of the citizens." The Philadelphia convention "had no business" with paper money, and Governor Randolph's idea that "the chosen ten" would know Virginia's interests better than "one hundred and eighty representatives [assembled as] the choice of Virginia" aroused nothing but "indignation." "If, sir, the diminution of numbers be an augmentation of merit," Henry said, "perfection must center in one."

Henry mocked Randolph's turnabout, and he made sport with Madison's "treatise on political anatomy." "In the brain it is national . . . some limbs are federal," he joked, then lashed out. "It is federal in conferring general powers, but national in retaining them. It is not to be supported by the states; the pockets of individuals are to be searched for its maintenance." Who cared about the "curious anatomical description," Henry charged, when common sense showed it to be "a great consolidation" that took all serious tasks away from the state governments.

"I look upon that paper as the most fatal plan that could possibly be conceived to enslave a free people," Henry said with a final flourish. "If such be your rage for novelty, take it and welcome; but you shall never have my consent."

As in the previous week the Federalists took several days to respond to Henry's exertions. Light-Horse Harry Lee sneered at Henry's "throwing those bolts which he has so peculiar a dexterity at discharging" and challenged Henry's criticisms of a standing army as rooted in a lack of battlefield experience. Lee begged for justice for "the military creditor," the soldiers compelled to receive worthless paper certificates instead of gold for their back pay, and grandly declared: "If Pandora's box were on one side of me, and a tender-law on the other, I would rather submit to the box than to the tender-law." Lee would accept any risk, he said, because he "dreaded more from the licentiousness of the people than from the bad government of rulers."

Governor Randolph intensified the attack on Henry. He tried to undermine the sincerity of Henry's concern for civil liberty by bringing up the old case of Josiah Phillips, the Tory insurgent against whom the legislature—at Jefferson's behest—had passed a bill of attainder. How could Henry claim liberty was safe in Virginia when such a dreadful proceeding had taken place during his own administration? (This was not the first time Randolph had tried to use the Phillips case. A few days earlier he had charged Henry with having Phillips hanged by attainder, to which Henry had carelessly—and unworthily—replied that the man was "not a Socrates." He could have replied—and eventually Benjamin Harrison did straighten the record—that Randolph himself had successfully prosecuted Phillips on ordinary charges of robbery for which a death sentence was imposed and that Henry had scant connection to the move to attaint.)

But now Randolph complained that Henry had attacked him "in the most illiberal manner." "I disdain his aspersions and his insinuations," Randolph said. They are incompatible with parliamentary decency and friendship, he charged, and added dramatically, "and if our friendship must fall, *let it fall, like Lucifer, never to rise again!*"

A shock ran through the theater. Randolph wanted to read aloud his old public letter to the legislature to prove the consistency of his course, but Henry interrupted him with a calm apology for having inadvertently wounded the gentleman's feelings in the course of doing his duty.

Randolph replied "that he was relieved by what the honorable gentleman had said; that, were it not for the concession of the gentleman, he would have made some men's hair stand on end, by the disclosure of certain facts."

Henry rose again to ask that if Randolph had anything to say against him he say it publicly and be done.

Randolph abruptly turned the question back to his own conduct. He waved his letter aloft. This, he said, would provide the information to vindicate his position, and with a flourish he threw it on the clerk's table, where, he said, it might lie "for the inspection of the curious and malicious."

Talk at Formicola's and Galt's and every other hostelry that evening centered on Randolph's outburst. Two Hanover men had already wounded each other in a duel (a postwar custom of rising popularity) a day or so earlier, and ripples of dread ran through the town with the rumor that Henry's friends had "waited" on Randolph. The night passed without incident, however, and, as if by arrangement, new voices assumed the next day's burden of debate.

They came from the rising generation. James Monroe, a carpenter's son who had come into politics on the strength of his military service, read a long, well-reasoned speech on the dangers of granting too much power to the general government. Then John Marshall, a carelessly dressed Richmond lawyer with the dashing look and daring reputation of a ladies' man, roused the audience with more spirited charges of disunion and yet another attack on Henry as a hypocrite for endorsing maxims of liberty while permitting Josiah Phillips to be "deprived of his life without benefit of law." Marshall countered with his own "favorite maxims of democracy"—"a strict observance of justice and public faith, and steady adherence to virtue."

On Wednesday morning, June 11, Madison presented a major defense of the tax power. He appeared recovered from his illness, his walk bouncy, and his manner as diffident as ever. He spoke from a single page of notes on which he had concisely outlined four main points—direct taxation was "necessary, practicable, safe, and economical"—which he intended to support with a total of twenty-nine subpoints.

Madison emphasized that punctuality and confidence must characterize the public credit. Requisitions, in his opinion, would not suffice because people paid slowly, if at all, when they suspected that others would not pay. To tax only as punishment for noncompliance, as Henry and Mason suggested, would unwisely excite "great clamors" and "hatred" against the government. Partial compliance, moreover, would complicate enforcement. Only direct taxation could secure adequate revenue in time of war, Madison argued, since trade would be disrupted and alternative revenue from an impost therefore diminished.

Moving on to his second point, Madison argued that, in practice, an assembly committee of not more than ten or fifteen men prepared the tax legislation for Virginia, so he did not see why that number could not adequately represent the state's interest in Congress. He thought Congress might adapt tax laws to fit the different circumstances of the states, much as Parliament had varying systems of land taxes for England and Scotland.

In addressing the compatibility of the general tax power with public liberty, Madison argued that elections from large districts would be more secure against corruption than small districts, which in the parliamentary system so easily turned into rotten boroughs, and that the states had a sufficient role in the creation of the national government to prevent their annihilation. If anything, Madison thought, the states remained too powerful and would advance local considerations at the expense of the general interest. (He had contended at Philadelphia for a national congressional veto upon state legislation. While this point never came out publicly during the convention, Henry almost certainly knew of it from Mason, and it greatly fed Anti-Federalist suspicions.)

Madison argued that direct taxation would be cheaper, for the general government would not have to chase down smugglers who evaded the impost, and the states, with a total of nearly three thousand assemblymen on public pay, would be spared the tediously expensive weeks spent deliberating upon requisitions.

George Mason disputed Madison's argument. Mason attacked Congress as insufficiently representative to be trusted with the tax power. Parliament, he pointed out, had 550 members; for a country ten times the size, the American Congress would have but 65. So small a body, in Mason's opinion, would sit at "aristocratic" remove from the people and have no "fellow-feeling" for them. So small a body, moreover, could be more easily bribed or corrupted than a large assembly and would be more likely to tax the poor in the interests of the rich. Mason produced an old letter in which financier Robert Morris urged Congress to levy a poll tax, a land tax, and a whiskey tax, all of which Mason insisted would fall lightly upon the rich and heavily upon the poor. A Philadelphia nabob would pay his six-shilling tax on one hundred acres worth one hundred pounds an acre, while a Virginia backwoodsman would pay the same six shillings for his hundred acres, worth no more than twenty shillings each.

Mason also attacked the underlying premise that revenue was needed to promote the government's power and respectability abroad. France was "the most powerful and respectable nation on earth," Mason said, but no Virginia farmer would swap his boots for the wooden clogs of the French peasant. The opposition tells us that "if we be powerful and respectable abroad, we shall have liberty and happiness at home." Secure liberty and happiness first, and respectability would follow, said Mason, and he likened the pretensions of those who lusted for splendor to the cat who was transformed into a fine lady, only to betray her origins by springing out of the chair when she saw a rat.

The talk turned to the state of the economy, and the florid William Grayson, in a speech filled with jocular asides, pointed to the sales of western lands as a decent source of revenue and said that while he served in Congress he knew that sixteen vessels had "sea letters" in the East India trade and two hundred vessels had cleared the French West Indies in a single year. He insisted that the debt could be redistributed and managed without so drastic a change in government if the Confederation were granted the much-discussed impost.

Henry chimed in with the observation that "no nation ever paid its debts by a change of government." "The want of money," Henry said, "[is] the source of all our misfortunes," and only hard work and frugality could remedy the problem. "You will never pay your debts but by a radical change of domestic economy. At present you buy too much, and make too little, to pay. . . . The evils that attend us lie in extravagance and want of industry, and can only be removed by assiduity and economy." "It sounds mighty prettily to gentlemen, to curse paper money and pay debts," Henry said, but "you will find in America there are thousands and thousands of contracts, whereof equity forbids an exact literal performance." "Pass that government, and you will be bound hand and foot" to pay depreciated paper at its face value, and you will be "carried to the federal court" if you don't.

The days wore on, and both delegates and spectators felt their attention droop. "Nine days spent ere they begin," scrawled Gouverneur Morris on a dinner invitation from John Marshall. The New Yorker's doggerel mocked "the Members come together/Melting with Zeal and sultry Weather/ . . . the next three Days they kindly dip yee/Deep in the River Mississippi."

Stumbling into a full-scale debate on the Mississippi gave

the Federalists a bad scare. Henry foxed them into it on Friday, June 13, when George Nicholas opened the session with an exasperated plea that the convention either follow the method of clause-by-clause discussion or rescind the rule. Henry suavely agreed. He had always favored an at-large examination, but if the gentleman wanted a topical discussion, why not consider "the business of the Mississippi" once and for all? Let the gentlemen who had served in Congress give the convention "the most authentic and faithful account of facts," Henry said. Nicholas could not oppose the suggestion without alienating the Kentucky delegates, for whose benefit Henry aimed the discussion.

Madison angrily jumped up to counter any insinuation that *he* had given an incorrect account. He had always believed the "relinquishment" of the river to be "unwise" and had opposed the "exceptionable mode" by which that policy had come on. Harry Lee, on the other hand, fiercely insisted that Jay's present policy offered the best chance of ultimately securing the river.

This claim set the stage for a long recital by James Monroe, which described in patient detail what he reported to Governor Henry nearly two years earlier: that Jay had asked Congress to refer the Spanish negotiations to a secret committee and that the committee be asked to allow him to consent to a treaty that would secure trading rights with Spain in exchange for an American promise to renounce the right to use the river for twenty-five or thirty years. In Congress a majority of seven states voted to support Jay's request to repeal the instruction barring him from negotiating a closure of the river, but Virginia and other affected southern states argued that if a two-thirds vote (nine states) were required to approve an instruction, how could a repeal by a simple majority be considered binding? On this "constitutional" point, Monroe said, the matter foundered, and the public uproar seemed to have put the project "to sleep."

Some Federalists argued that since Spain requested that the U.S. "forbear" the Mississippi for a short interval, this implied, by the law of nations, that she recognized the ultimate validity of the claim. "Will Grotius and Puffendorf relieve Kentucky?" Grayson asked scornfully, and he went on to argue that the Mississippi, already jeopardized in the Confederation, would be at greater risk under the new plan since the president could make a treaty without prior instructions, subject only to approval by a two-thirds vote in the Senate. With a quorum of fourteen, two-thirds would be ten, Grayson reckoned, and if seven states now were willing to "surrender that great and valuable right," the vast watershed would be surely lost when only five states could carry the vote.

Madison tried to blunt the force of this argument by insisting that he had secret information which showed conclusively that the project would not be revived. It stemmed from "a weak system," he said wanly; under the new government the nation would be strong enough to defend its rights without such negotiation. To counter Grayson's reasoning Madison argued that the House would "have a material influence upon the government," and since it would in all likelihood represent the "landed" as opposed to the "commercial" interest, its opinion would have some bearing on the president's course.

Henry, who with evident enjoyment had watched the Federalists squirm, now pounced. Did Madison mean to say, he wondered "that the House . . . will break through their balances and checks, and break into the business of treaties?" Were these vaunted checks "an impenetrable wall for some purposes and a mere cobweb" for others? There was no real security, Henry charged, for under the new system the senators could not be instructed and could not be recalled. "If you should see the Spanish ambassador bribing one of your senators with gold," Henry asked, "can you punish him?" Yes, he could be impeached before the Senate, Henry answered, and he let the implication linger.

"It is said that we are scuffling for Kentucky votes, and attending to local circumstances," Henry said, but he emphasized that the "interests of Virginia and Kentucky are most intimately and vitally connected." The Mississippi Valley held the key to America's destiny, in Henry's view, and he painted a glowing vision of widespread agrarian prosperity linked to a flourishing river trade.

The debate ran on all day and ended only when a thunderstorm blew open the windows and drowned out Randolph and Corbin's appeal to the western delegates to transcend all "partial," "narrow," and "local" considerations in order to secure the general interests of the Union. As the crowds left the Academy, one could hear mutterings that the tone would surely be different if the issue were the relinquishment of Chesapeake Bay.

CHAPTER 20

"Overpowered in a Good Cause"

"Matters are not going so well in this State as the Friends of America could wish," Gouverneur Morris informed the New York Federalist leader, Alexander Hamilton, from Richmond after Friday's debate. That night Madison, still seething at being "dragged into communication" on the Mississippi problem, told Washington: "The business is in the most ticklish state that can be imagined." He feared that the Kentucky votes, now considered to be largely negative, would be decisive. "The issue . . . is more doubtful than was apprehended when I last wrote," Madison informed a Massachusetts ally. The "chief mischief is effected . . . out of doors," he complained, but he also knew that delegates had wearied of the debates.

Although Henry and Mason had repeatedly emphasized their overriding concern that the Constitution granted power without sufficient safeguards against abuse, Madison would not acknowledge the existence of this argument. Summarizing the debates for a friend, he listed "the ostensible points of opposition" as "direct taxation, the imperfect representation in the H. of Reps.; the equality in the Senate, regulation of Trade by majority—& the Judiciary department. The first & last are dwelt on most."

Madison yearned for a vote on some tangential issue that might gauge the Federalists' strength. Yet when Pendleton fell sick before the Saturday morning session, Madison did not contest the nomination of Henry's friend John Tyler as temporary chairman. If the Federalists had the votes to defeat Tyler, there was no telling what retaliation might ensue, and if the vote showed that they did not, perhaps the Anti-Federalists would strike suddenly on the question of previous amendments. The Federalists applauded Tyler and hoped, successfully, for Pendleton's quick recovery.

Madison feared that the Anti-Federalists would deliberately prolong the debates until either their budding alliance with New York bore fruit or they fatigued the delegates into voting to recess or even adjourn without coming to a vote. Over the next few days, therefore, the Federalists tried to accelerate the tempo of debate by shortening their remarks (this involved curbing Governor Randolph's tendency to exculpate himself on every point) and insisting that the body move with dispatch from clause to clause.

Yet no one could control Henry. He continued "most warm and powerful in Declamation," Gouverneur Morris wrote, "being perfectly Master of Action Utterance and the Power of Speech to stir Men's Blood." Henry sensed that at last he had the Federalists on the defensive, and he would not moderate the intensity of his attacks.

After two weeks spent ostensibly on the first two paragraphs, the convention did pick up its pace, but Henry exploited every opportunity to preach against unguarded powers. "Too much suspicion may be corrected," he said. "If you give too little power today, you may give more tomorrow. But the reverse . . . will not hold. If you give too much power today . . . tomorrow will never come." Henry condemned the proposal as "a sort of mathematical government" that looked tidy on paper but would be impossible to control in practice. "The delegation of power to an adequate number of representatives, and an unimpeded reversion of it back to the people, at short periods, form the principal traits of a republican government," Henry said. However, the new government could be called republican only by a process of reasoning too deep for the ordinary citizen, he charged, since the governors would be masters, not servants, and the "infinitude" of both ends and means excluded every idea of "subordination." "When you give power," he warned again, "you know not what you give."

Bitter arguments continued to break out over the interpretation of nearly every clause. On Monday, June 16, the controversy centered on the dangers of a standing army and whether the power of Congress to "call forth the militia to execute the Laws of the Union" would unite "the purse and the sword" in a single branch of government, thus annihilating state control and creating another engine of oppression. Each speaker attempted a slightly different reading of one clause as construed and compared in light of another.

"Constructive reasoning," as Henry called the concept of implied powers, itself became the issue. Henry insisted upon clarity and wanted the Constitution to be "like a beacon, held up to the public eye, so as to be understood by every man." How can a constitution protect liberty, if it "cannot be understood, in many parts, even by its supporters"? "Poor people do not understand technical terms," Henry said. "Their rights ought to be secured in language of which they know the meaning."

The clouds of construction and inference obscured the entire matter of a bill of rights. When the debate turned to the "general welfare" and "necessary and proper" clauses, George Mason pointed out that nothing in the Constitution forbade the government from restricting the press. He offered a hypothetical example. "Suppose oppressions should arise under this government, and a writer should dare to stand forth, and expose to the community at large the abuses of those powers; could not Congress, under the idea of providing for the general welfare, and under their own construction, say that this was destroying the general peace, encouraging sedition, and poisoning the minds of the people . . . could they not, in order to provide against this, lay a dangerous restriction on the press?"

The Federalists, following an argument laid down the previous October by the Philadelphia lawyer James Wilson, insisted that Congress could not do as Mason feared because it had no power over the press. Wilson had postulated in a widely reprinted speech that, whereas the states had reserved certain powers to the people and granted everything else to their governments, in the new Constitution everything not enumerated was presumed to be reserved to the people. Anti-Federalist writers had condemned Wilson's argument as "flimsy sophistry" and "an insult on the understanding of the people." Many states had insisted on bills of rights because, under the British constitution, rights not expressly and un-equivocally reserved were assumed to be relinquished to the rulers. Nowhère in the Constitution was Wilson's dictum stated, the Anti-Federalists complained, and, besides, the enu-merated powers themselves seemed to them "sweeping" enough to cover everything that mattered.

Harry Lee explained the Federalist position as a theory of agency. If a man delegates an agent to do certain things, Lee said, it would insult common sense to think the agent could legally transact any business for his principal not spe-cified in the commission. George Nicholas added, "If I have one thousand acres of land, and I grant five hundred acres of it, must I declare that I retain the other five hundred?" He went on to rebut Mason. "It is agreed upon by all parties that the people have all power. If they part with any of it, is it necessary to declare that they retain the rest?"

"Why not?, asked Henry. "Is it because it will consume too much paper?" The people regard the principles of the bill of rights as too sacred and important to be left to "implica-tion," and if it suits their "genius" to have them stated, why not exclude "the possibility of dispute" by doing so?

The Federalists tried to argue, in response, that the Con-stitution itself was a bill of rights, for it declared and specified "the political privileges of the citizens in the structure and administration of government." Moreover, they said, to affix a bill of rights would be "dangerous" because it would con-tain "various exceptions to powers not granted . . . and would afford a colorable pretext" to claim the very powers upon which restraint was sought. "Why declare that things shall not be done for which there is no power to do?" asked "Publius" in a paper hastily added to the pamphlet edition of his *Federalist* newspaper articles.

If that were the case, retorted the Anti-Federalists, why did the Constitution mention the writ of habeas corpus and specify the right of jury trials in criminal cases? Did the draftsmen mean to exclude juries in civil cases, or think a free press—"the palladium of liberty"—unworthy of mention? Henry called the truncated bill of rights that appears in Article I, Section 9. too "feeble and few." "Every word of mine . . . is lost," Henry said, if gentlemen believe that this slender section will sufficiently secure their liberties. "I trust that gentlemen, on this occasion, will see the great objects of religion, liberty of the press, trial by jury, interdiction of cruel and unusual punishments, and every other sacred right, secured, before they agree to that paper," Henry said.

The Federalists belittled the significance of a bill of rights for the tactical reason that any concession of its importance would open the Pandora's box of amendments and jeopardize ratification. At a deeper level, however, the Federalists held firm against a bill of rights because they feared that scrupulous attention to individual liberties would impair the efficiency of the powerful government they wanted. Partisans of a bill of rights worked from a theory of limited government that, despite their professions, the Federalists did not share.

In the prohibition against the passage of ex post facto laws, however, Henry and Mason discerned not a sign of tenderness for civil liberty, but the hint of economic bias. "If no ex post facto laws be made, what is to become of the old Continental paper dollars?" Henry asked. If neither Congress nor the states can adopt a scale of depreciation, then the notes will have to be paid in gold and silver at their face value.

Henry had insisted throughout the convention that changing the government would not pay off the debt. Now he and Mason argued that speculators would profit from the change. Was it not true, he asked, that some northern states had "vast quantities of Continental paper packed up in barrels" and that stock jobbers had bought up for a pittance notes held by ordinary soldiers and farmers?

"Mr. Madison," noted the shorthand man, "admitted there might be some speculations on the subject." But, he said, he took the clause providing that the debts and obligations of the Confederation would be valid against the new government to mean that they would stand on the same footing as before: "as valid as they were, but no more so."

Mason considered that speculation of a theoretical kind. The prohibition on ex post facto laws would prevent the legislature from scaling down the debt. "We may be taxed for centuries to give advantage to . . . a number of rapacious speculators," he warned. Madison replied that in his opinion the "new rulers" could not enhance the value of the money without violating the Constitution. (Randolph, however, made a different argument. Ex post facto laws referred to criminal prosecutions only, he thought, and if the old Congress had power to scale the money down, then so would the new.) Both men agreed, however, that the note holders would be treated fairly, since they could not imagine that (as Madison put it) "a majority of the people of America . . . would wish to defraud the public creditors."

"A contest for money" exists, Henry said bitterly, along with "a contest for empire." The commercial states want to block off the Mississippi, and they want to enrich themselves by speculation. The debt will be transferred without the means of discharging it fairly, and if we accept the Constitution, we will be "bound hand and foot," judgments will be brought against us in federal court, and our property will be seized in taxes, "to satisfy this most infamous speculation."

Congress can be counted upon to "make such a regulation as will be just," Madison predicted.

Then we are getting "a government of men, not laws," Henry replied.

In this "nefarious business," as in all the other instances of discretionary or unguarded power, everything rests upon the character of the rulers, Henry emphasized. No good Whig can trust such a government; it smacks of noblesse oblige, and it violates the fundamental idea that any grant of power carries the seed of oppression that will grow and flower unless carefully watched and frequently pruned. All the good qualities of this government are founded on the supposition that the governors shall be honest, Henry said, but its defective construction opens the way to "the worst of mischiefs" if they are bad. Henry insisted that liberty could not rest upon the contingency of rulers being good or bad.

Day after day the partisans of energy and confidence collided with the adherents of liberty and skepticism. The nationalists sensed greatness in a large, diverse republic in which a wealthy elite would have a powerful voice. The Anti-Federalists set local autonomy ahead of national prestige; they sought to preserve the broadly based state assemblies as guarantors of the democratic hopes inspired by the Revolution.

Madison always spoke from the perspective of one who expected to run the government and tried to show how the rules could be made to work fairly; Henry always spoke from the standpoint of the citizen who would be affected by the rules. He regarded Madison as too theoretical, too preoccupied with forms to realize their practical effect, and he suspected that, like Washington's, Madison's republican integrity was being used by more artful commercial men to conceal their private, more aristocratic designs.

The debate and the speculation went on and on. By the middle of the third week, however, with the article on the judiciary still to be discussed, the delegates' energies had shifted to politicking outside. On Wednesday, June 18, Grayson realized that the opposition had not gained the votes it needed. "We have got ten out of 13 of the Kentucki members, but we wanted the whole," he said, "and I don't know that we have got one yet of the four upper counties." Both sides contended for these crucial votes "by every means in their power," Grayson knew. He could see "80 votes on our side which are inflexible," with "eight persons still fluctuating & undecided." They would need five of the eight to prevail.

The Federalists thought they needed to find only three more votes. Archibald Stuart's count showed "82 members immoveably fixed for it," with 74 opposed and "immoveable." Of the twelve remaining, Stuart saw five or six, including the three remaining Kentucky delegates, as likely to vote for adoption, but he warned his colleagues: "The fate of Virginia is suspended upon a single Hair."

The "scuffle" for the last few votes turned, in large measure, upon personalities. "Federalist" and "Anti-Federalist" were labels of a season that grouped men of varying dispositions and circumstances. They referred not to well-organized, disciplined parties but to loose constellations of men who shared a view on a single issue. Many came instructed by their counties or at least had been elected because their constituents knew where they stood. Others had secured election on the basis of habit or character without a clear statement of their views, and in the final search for votes these delegates stood out as prime targets.

Andrew Moore, a stout, tough horseman from Rockbridge County in the southern Piedmont, had fought at Saratoga and with Morgan's rifle company in Carolina, and ultimately he followed the convention's other soldier-delegates in supporting the Constitution, although his constituents did not favor it. His colleague, William McKee, went along, too, and claimed later that his county had only declared its opposition after he had been elected.

The Kentucky vote became complicated by the swirl of that district's internal politics, which shifted according to personalities and conflicting perceptions of how Kentucky's hopes for statehood would be served by the outcome of the federal contest. Humphrey Marshall, an irascible and flamboyant land speculator from Fayette County, decided to defy his county's instructions and vote for the Constitution. A cousin of John Marshall who had migrated west in 1781, Humphrey Marshall had long served Virginia's interests in Kentucky and had commercial connections with the group (including Washington and Harry Lee) seeking to develop the Potomac-Ohio connection in preference to the Mississippi. (He had even named his first son after John Jay.) A bullying personality, Humphrey Marshall exerted strong influence over the two Kentucky delegates from the commercial district around Louisville and brought both of them into the Federalist camp.

As for the upper Ohio River counties, the men there seemed most concerned about the hostile Indian tribes on their northwest flank and the continued British occupation of the Great Lakes forts. Henry's arguments about the threat to the Mississippi trade seemed less compelling than the Federalist claims that the new government would provide greater military protection in the area. (This argument worked on the Louisville men, too, along with the Federalists' hint that the long-delayed Kentucky statehood would be expedited under the new Congress.) Henry's hostility toward British debts told heavily against him, too, for the British were refusing to leave the northwestern frontier until the U.S. complied with the treaty provisions on debt repayment. If Henry didn't like the new government, the old soldier who represented Berkeley County grumbled, "let him go live among the Indians."

If all sectional appeals were exhausted, other subtle arguments could be made. Virginia had better come into the new government, the Federalists whispered, otherwise General Washington would be ineligible for the presidency. Virginia had better ratify by more than a single vote or two, lest the minority gain too great a foothold to continue its mischief. Henry and Mason, the rumor ran, would most surely continue their opposition, possibly into a secessionist league with North Carolina.

The Anti-Federalist appeal grew wilder, too. George Mason complained, on the one hand, that slave property had not received adequate protection in the Constitution and, on the other, that it was iniquitous to have allowed the slave trade a twenty-year grace period in which Congress could not legislate against it. Madison, who detested slavery as deeply as Mason and Henry, had the galling task of explaining how much more explicitly slavery was recognized and protected in the new government than the old. Henry declared his heartfelt desire for eventual emancipation but warned that under the "necessary and proper" clause, and with the aid of "constructive reasoning," the Congress could find ways of compelling manumission through heavy taxation. Slavery was a "local matter," he insisted, and ought not to be subject to congressional fiat. "They'll take your niggers from you," he is supposed to have shouted to great laughter in the hall. The argument, while pouring into the well of southern politics some of the poison that would afflict it for the next two centuries, carried little immediate weight, for everyone knew that the slaveholding states had gotten almost everything they had wanted at Philadelphia.

With Henry and Mason holding fast, the Federalists finally had to change their tactics. To attract or hold the wavering delegates, they would concede in a general way the necessity of amendments, but they insisted that they be made "subsequent" to ratification. A short list of suggestions started to circulate in competition with the lengthy array of "previous" amendments Henry and the others had shown around for several weeks. The question had come down to "previous or subsequent amendments," everyone agreed, and one Federalist wrote, "the grand object [now] is to convince the Antis that those amendments can as readily be procured after adoption as before." Henry insisted, however, that Virginia's power derived more from staying out than from coming in and that the state would forfeit all leverage for amendments once the Constitution had carried and the powerful new government went into effect.

Over the weekend of June 21–22 the final strategies took shape. Henry would propose a bill of rights and other amendments as a condition of ratification; if that failed, the Anti-Federalists would press for an adjournment until autumn. The supporters of the Constitution would counter with "a peculiar form of ratification." Governor Randolph would draft the resolution: it would be prefaced with what Madison called "a declaration of a few obvious truths which cannot affect the validity of the act" and be followed with recommendations for "a few amendments to be pursued in the constitutional mode." This "expedient," Madison calculated, would "conciliate some individuals who are in general well affected, but have certain scruples drawn from their own reflexions, or from the temper of their Constituents." (The formula, as Madison knew, had already worked in Massachusetts.) As Madison lay in his room, "much indisposed" and frustrated at his inability to "cooperate in the business," he received optimistic reports. His predictions of a "bare majority" on Friday, increased to "3 or 4" on Saturday, and by Sunday he thought, "perhaps 5 or 6."

In convention, however, the Anti-Federalists demonstrated enough strength to reject a committee report that would have unseated their delegate from Louisa County, and Madison went back to thinking his majority would be either "bare" or overset by a freak accident. Rumors circulated that subsequent amendments were a sham; the supporters of the Constitution planned to quit town on various pretexts before the amendments could be named.

Henry and Mason also despaired. Mason warned the convention of "popular resistance" to operations of the new government. Before the packed galleries Henry said it would be "my duty, if this government is adopted before it is amended, to go home." When Randolph accused him of encouraging "secession," Henry denied the implication. He said that he "would have no hand in subsequent amendments; that he would remain and vote, and afterwards he would have no business here." A few days earlier, however, Henry had declared, "Old as I am, it is probable that I may yet have the appellation of rebel," and, as always, the aura of uncertainty augmented his power.

On Tuesday, June 24, George Wythe, who had served in the Virginia House since 1758 and numbered at least a dozen convention delegates among his former law students, moved that the convention ratify the Constitution and recommend whatever amendments it desired to the wisdom of the new Congress. Wythe admitted the "propriety" of amendments but urged that "the extreme danger of dissolving the Union" made it necessary to defer change until the new system went into effect. The preamble to Wythe's resolution declared the powers granted under the proposed Constitution to be "the gift of the people" and asserted that powers not granted remained with them. No branch of the new government, the preamble declared, could cancel, abridge, restrain, or modify the rights of the people "except in those instances in which power is given by the Constitution for those purposes," and the resolution named "among other essential rights, liberty of conscience, and of the press."

The conciliatory language did not impress Henry. He looked at Wythe, the man who had signed his law license nearly thirty years before, and shrugged. The resolution was "premature" and its premises "unenforceable," Henry said, and he attacked it on all the grounds he had laid out over the past three weeks. He then moved a substitution that would refer a declaration of rights and certain other amendments to the other states in the Confederation "previous" to ratification by Virginia.

Madison objected that previous amendments were "but another name for rejection." He described a dizzying pyramid of parliamentry and legal complications that might ensue if Virginia insisted on so unorthodox a move. He appealed to the spirit of compromise that had animated the gentlemen at Philadelphia, and he said that insofar as Henry's amendments "are not objectionable, or unsafe . . . they may be subsequently recommended. Not because they are necessary but because they can produce no possible danger, and may gratify some gentlemen's wishes."

Randolph strode up and down, reading each clause of Henry's proposal and insisting that either the Constitution already secured the right or Congress had no power to abridge it. Henry's forty amendments were utterly unnecessary, Randolph charged.

"The bill of rights [in twenty clauses] is but one amendment," Henry retorted, as he launched into a final appeal. People say that he could reconcile the disaffected to the new plan, Henry recounted, but "were I to ask them to apostatize from their native religion, they would despise me." A majority is opposed, Henry insisted, warning the proponents that they did not enjoy "solid reality—the hearts and hands of the men who are to be governed." The other gentlemen foresee "important blessings" from the adoption of this system, he said, as the auditorium grew dark with shadows. "I see the awful immensity of the dangers with which it is pregnant. I see it. I feel it. I see beings of a higher order anxious concern-

ing our decision." When Heaven weighed "the political decisions and revolutions which, in the progress of time, will
happen in America," Henry solemnly declared, the account
would depend "on what we now decide." As Henry spoke,
lightning and a thunderclap startled the crowd, and the storm
clouds that had darkened the hall suddenly poured forth a
storm of such torrential violence that even Henry's voice
could not prevail. He had never, not even in 1775 at the
church on Richmond Hill, issued so resounding a call to
judgment. On Wednesday they would vote.

"Thunders Roll and lightenings flash . . . both in the
Natural and Political Atmosphere," an Anti-Federalist wrote,
and Spencer Roane told Philip Aylett that their father-in-
law had "given exemplary proofs of his greatness, and in the
opinion of many, his virtue. I have myself heard some Touches
of Eloquence from him which would almost disgrace Cicero
or Demosthenes." Others marveled at how Henry had held
the galleries in rapt attention day after day, although the
spectators talked and milled about when anyone else was
speaking.

"I do not know that either party despairs absolutely,"
Madison told his brother on the eve of the vote. Yet just
before the roll call, Henry told the House: "If I shall be in
the minority, I shall have those painful sensations which arise
from a conviction of *being overpowered in a good cause.*"
He would be "a peaceable citizen," Henry promised, and
would "wait with hopes that the spirit which predominated
in the revolution is not yet gone, nor the cause of those who
are attached to the revolution yet lost."

Henry formally moved acceptance of his motion: "*Resolved,* That, previous to ratification of the new Constitution
of government recommended by the late federal Convention,
a declaration of rights, asserting, and securing from encroachment, the great principles of civil and religious liberty, and
the unalienable rights of the people, together with amendments to the most exceptionable parts of the . . . Constitution . . . ought to be referred by this Convention to the other
states in the American confederacy for their consideration."

The delegates rose from their seats and pressed toward the lobby for the vote. They moved in two equally unruly clumps, and it took an agonizingly long moment for them to form in single files so that they might be counted by the doorkeepers. Each side looked anxiously to see where the doubtfuls now stood, but nothing certain could be known until the tally sheets were passed back to the chair and the delegates resumed their places.

It was half past two o'clock before Pendleton solemnly announced that by a vote of eighty ayes and eighty-eight nays, Mr. Henry's motion had failed.

In the hubbub that broke an awful silence Henry asked for the floor. He wanted the roll to be called, and he listened intently as the drone of voices confirmed what he already knew: three votes shy in Kentucky, no votes at all from the four upper counties; and the loss of all but one of the six last doubtfuls, a Richmond lawyer named William Ronald who represented a Southside county but who had come under heavy pressure from Marshall and his other colleagues at the bar.

The second vote, this time on Wythe's resolution for ratification with subsequent amendments to be recommended, seemed perfunctory. One Southsider, David Patteson, changed his vote to accord with the majority, so that the final vote for ratification became eighty-nine ayes and seventy-nine nays.

The town remained quiet that night. The inhabitants were "either wise enough, or polite enough, to make no procession or parade," a newspaper observed. "There is no rejoicing on account of the vote of ratification," Roane told Philip Aylett. "It would not be prudent to do so, and the federalists . . . do not exult in their success." Madison told Washington that the vote was "without flaw or pretext for it, and there is no doubt that acquiescence if not cordiality will be manifested by the unsuccessful party." "*Two* of the leaders," Madison could not resist adding, "betray the effect of the disappointment, so far as it is marked in their countenances."

There remained the question of recommended amendments. Pendleton put both Henry and Mason on the committee in charge of preparing them, but there is no record of their service. The document the Anti-Federalists had sent off to New York, however, did become the basis of the committee's report. On Friday, June 27, with the theater so crowded that the delegates could hardly get to their seats, the convention adopted the proposed bill of rights without dissent.

The remaining amendments proved "highly objectionable" to Madison. The statement of reserved powers, the provision for two-thirds votes on commercial laws and treaties, limitations on the president's term, a different method for impeaching senators, and other concrete limitations of power privately galled him, but he did not think they would get far enough to cause trouble. But the insistence that direct taxes be prohibited unless the states failed to comply with requisitions Madison regarded as too grave an "error" to go unchallenged.

He angrily moved that the article be stricken from the list, but he could get only sixty-five votes for the deletion. Randolph, Marshall, and Nicholas supported him, but Pendleton voted with Henry to retain the amendment. Enough Federalists followed along, either from a wish to conciliate or to express their own opposition to the tax power, to rebuke Madison's effort.

"Notwithstanding the fair professions made by some, I am so uncharitable as to suspect that the ill will to the Constitution will produce . . . every peaceable effort to disgrace and destroy it," Madison told Hamilton. He fully expected that Henry would lead an effort to engage the state legislatures "in the task of regularly undermining the government."

That "great adversary," pensive in defeat, stood quietly as Pendleton made a brief appeal for patience and urged the delegates "to breathe peace and hope to the people." After declaring the convention adjourned sine die, Pendleton hobbled from the chair and took a seat on a front bench, where he tearfully bade goodbye to the delegates crowded around him.

Henry clasped Pendleton's hand, then called for his horse and went home.

CHAPTER 21

"Playing the After Game"

Richmond saved its celebration for the Fourth of July. Townspeople gathered at the Eagle Tavern to hear a thirteen-gun salute and to drink toast after toast to "unanimity." "May discordant opinions cease," went one refrain, "and the friends and opponents of the new government meet on the firm basis of American union and public liberty." Another toast hailed "the year 1788—may its civil revolution form the great epoch of American honor, happiness, and glory." At the end of the day, ten guns were fired in tribute to the states that had adopted the Constitution. (New Hamsphire, ratifying on June 21, had beaten Virginia for the honor of being the decisive ninth state, though no one in Richmond knew that when the convention voted its approval on June 25.)

The maritime community of Portsmouth put together a joyful pageant of prosperity, in which the town's artisans—sailmakers, joiners, caulkers, and carpenters—joined the pilots, merchants, and captains in a procession behind the replica of a ship, *Federalist*, drawn through the streets by ten beribboned horses. As in other coastal towns, the waggish printers inserted in the shipping news a political item: "Arrived safe in port, the ship *Federal Constitution*, Perpetual Union, commander, from Elysium," passengers including "Flourishing Commerce . . . gen. Prosperity and National Energy." "Same day sailed the snow, *Old Confederation*, capt. Imbecility, for the old world . . . no passengers, as she is known to be a weak vessel. . . . The sloop *Anarchy*, we are told, is ashore on the Rock of

Union, and cannot be got off, the crew has perished and the owners have broke." At the upper end of Chesapeake Bay the Baltimore newspaper expressed confidence that "the Revolution of 1788 will be attended with much more important consequences to the interests of mankind in general, than that of 1688 was to Great Britain in particular."

The interior counties had more subdued reactions. Some back counties held mock funerals for liberty and, in the words of one Henry ally, continued to "weep over the corpse of dying republicanism." In far-off Maine a dour farmer scrawled an echo of the local complaint on a blank page in his almanac: "I see by the Publick Print such show & ostentation taking Place in Virginia & nine states more such rejoicing as I think is imprudent if not sinful as we are placing too much confidence in means as Must be Displeasing to God."

In the Southside counties "the discontents are said to be loud," Governor Randolph reported to Madison, who had returned to New York to ensure that the lame-duck Congress would make a decent transfer to the new government; "but it does not appear that any of the opponents, who were of the convention, are active by word or deed in fomenting them." Madison remained skeptical, however, warning friends in the seaboard towns he passed: "There is a regular correspondence between the Anti-Federalists of the different States." He feared that they "are yet acting in Concert" and "that there is in Contemplation a settled System of Opposition to the Government."

At home in Prince Edward, Henry passed a quiet summer enlivened principally by a terrible wind and rainstorm at the end of July that whipped down cornfields and drowned the tobacco crop. August, however, brought favorable political news. The North Carolina convention had refused to ratify until the amendments proposed by Virginia were made part of the Constitution. (Henry's opponents quickly assumed that he had engineered this verdict, but they could never prove it.) While New York had ratified by a margin of only three votes, that convention had hedged its decision with various conditional resolutions, a list of amendments that closely followed the draft brought by Colonel Oswald from Virginia, and—most gratifying to Henry—a call for a second convention.

In a circular letter to the states, signed by New York's convention president (and governor) George Clinton, the New Yorkers declared that some parts of the Constitution "appear so exceptionable to a majority of us, that nothing but the fullest confidence of obtaining a revision of them by a general convention, and an invincible reluctance to separating from our sister states, could have prevailed upon a sufficient number to ratify it, without stipulating for previous amendments." Clinton emphasized that since no government "can operate well" without the "confidence and goodwill of the body of the people," he hoped that "sound policy" would lead even those states "content with every Article" to join the call for a new convention "to gratify the reasonable desires of that numerous class of American citizens" who anxiously felt the necessity of amendments.

Such strong language from New York thrilled Henry. "He grows in violence against the constitution," Edmund Randolph's cousin reported after a visit to Prince Edward in September, "and is much pleased at the idea of a new convention." The circular letter "will be eagerly caught by Mr. P. Henry who in our next assembly will be greatly an over match for any federalist that I know," an Orange County ally predicted to Madison. Henry's "having the whole game to play in the Assembly" painfully alarmed George Washington, who lamented to Madison: "To be shipwrecked in sight of the Port would be the severest of all possible aggravations to our misery."

Madison agreed. The proposal for a second convention "has a most pestilent tendency," he told Edmund Randolph, who seemed well disposed toward the idea as a means of conciliating the opposition and securing the changes he had always desired. Madison tried to disabuse him. A convention would be "extremely dangerous." As "the offspring of party and passion," it would become "the parent of error and public injury." Radical changes would be "extorted by menaces" or "obtained by management." No changes should be contemplated in a fevered atmosphere, Madison emphasized; "the delay of a few years" will point out the faults that really need amendment, he thought, and "assuage the jealousies" artificially created by "designing" politicians like Henry. Madison regarded public opinion as too unsettled to risk a convention. A majority favors the Constitution "as it stands," he claimed to Randolph, but he then modified the assertion: "or at least are not dissatisfied with it in that form; or if this be not the case it is at least clear that a greater proportion unite in that system than are likely to unite in any other."

Madison's reasoning had some effect on Randolph's "doublings and turnings," but public opinion in Virginia strongly rallied to the idea of a second convention. As the October assembly session drew near, the Federalists, lacking a "competent commander," feared not only a convention endorsement but an attempt to subvert the pending elections for the new Congress.

Henry did not disappoint those who dreaded his influence. He has come to Richmond "but keeps himself close," a friend advised Madison on the assembly's opening day. "I have not seen him," Randolph reported, "but I am told, that he appears to be involved in gloomy mystery. Something is surely meditated against the new constitution, more animated, forceful and violent, than a simple application for calling a convention."

The great adversary waited nearly a week to make his first direct move, but by mounting a successful challenge to the seating of Madison's lieutenant, Edward Carrington, on opening day Henry served notice that he would give no quarter. Then came the annual deluge of private petitions and the excitement of moving the House from its temporary shed along the waterfront to a spacious "apartment" in the new Capitol on Shockoe Hill. Praise for the new building combined with wonderment at the simultaneous opening of John Mayo's pontoon bridge across the James (the man was collecting at least seven pounds a day in tolls from a steady parade of wagons) preempted politics for a few days.

Then Henry declared himself. He "would oppose every measure tending to the organization of the Government, unless accompanied with measures for the amendment of the Constitution." He moved that another general convention of the states be held "as soon as practicable" to formulate amendments "for quieting the minds of the good citizens of this commonwealth, and securing their dearest rights and liberties, and preventing those disorders which must arise under a government not founded on the confidence of the people."

"The Cloven hoof begins to appear," a Federalist exclaimed at the "dreaded" resolution. The "Non-Emendo-Tories," as one of Henry's allies derided the Federalists, had no hope of defeating Henry's call, especially since Governor Randolph gave every sign of "joining the mutineers either to trim the Ballast of the new government or put the ship about." They could only try to "divest [Henry's text] of its inflammatory dress" or plead for a postponement of a convention until the government had had "a fair trial." But since Henry was "old in parliamentary science and supported by the prejudice" of many members, the "young and inexperienced" Federalists considered themselves "a feeble band."

Of the fifty ratifying convention delegates who were returned to the fall assembly, eighteen were Federalist and twenty-six Anti-Federalist, but while the Antis numbered Henry, Grayson, Monroe, and Harrison among their leaders, none of the Federalist speakers, save young Francis Corbin, had come into the assembly. Without Madison, Nicholas, Pendleton, and Marshall, the Federalists were indeed outclassed. They also stood badly outnumbered. Of the seventy-five assemblymen who had not served in the June convention, approximately fifty favored amending the Constitution.

This clear sign of the public's opinion emboldened Henry, and he insisted that whatever individual delegates might believe, they ought to conform to the wishes of the people. He said that he regarded his own opinion as nothing when compared to his constituents and felt willing "at all times . . . to bow, with the utmost deference, to the majesty of the people."

This proved too much for Francis Corbin. He challenged Henry's claim that the majority of people wanted amendments and charged that Henry had run counter to public opinion on the Constitution from the very beginning. The people wanted it ratified, and the votes of their delegates in the convention proved it. How can the gentleman tell us, Corbin asked, that he bows "to the majesty of the people"? Corbin, who had spent his youth studying in England and had not returned to Virginia until after the war, accompanied his repetition of Henry's phrase with a deep bow in the most elegant, courtly style anyone could imagine. For many minutes he rang changes on Henry's phrase, mocking it at every repetition with another charming bow. "It was of little importance," Corbin said, "whether a country was ruled by a despot with a tiara on his head, or by a demagogue in a red-cloak & caulbare wig . . . although he should profess on all occasions to bow to the majesty of the people." Corbin bowed again with another flourish.

Henry's friends were appalled, while Corbin's allies did their best to smother their laughter. A silence fell over the House. Henry had looked indifferent during the performance, but now he rose, with an "affected awkwardness," to reply.

"I am a plain man, and have been educated altogether in Virginia," Henry said quietly. "My whole life has been spent among [farmers], and other plain men of similar education, who have never had the advantage of that polish which a court alone can give, and which the gentleman over the way has so happily acquired." Indeed, Henry said, while we at home engaged in "the toils of revolution," that gentleman took happy advantage of his "splendid fortune" to acquire a "foreign education, basking in the beams of royal favor at St. James." Henry stooped very low in a most obsequious and sycophantic bow, then stood upright and paused. "I will not therefore presume to vie with the gentleman in these courtly accomplishments, of which he has just given the house so agreeable a specimen; yet such a bow as I can make, shall ever be at the service of the people."

Henry then made a rustic's bow, so ludicrously clownish that it pitched the entire house into gales of laughter. "The gentleman, I hope, will commiserate the disadvantages of education under which I have labored, and will be pleased to remember that I have never been a favorite with that monarch, whose gracious smile he has had the happiness to enjoy."

Corbin "sank at least a foot in his seat," Spencer Roane recalled.

It was many minutes before the "Non-Emendo-Tories" could regroup and introduce Corbin's substitute motion urging Congress to recommend pursuant to Article V of the Constitution that the states ratify "a bill of rights, and . . . certain articles of amendment [proposed by Virginia]" and that, until such ratification, "Congress do conform their ordinances to the true spirit of the said bill of rights." To parry the convention idea, the Federalists felt compelled to endorse some degree of amendment, although their absent leader Madison remained adamantly opposed to any immediate action.

Corbin's motion failed by a vote of thirty-nine ayes to eighty-five nays. Then the House passed Henry's call for a second convention by voice vote and placed him at the head of the committee that would draft the necessary documents.

Attention turned over the next week to the question of elections. Henry, much to the Federalists' relief, turned down all importuning to accept a seat in the new U.S. Senate. He was "unwilling to submit to the oath," capital gossips whispered, although Henry for years had declined any post that would take him away from home for more than a few weeks.

Henry endorsed William Grayson and R. H. Lee for the two Senate seats. The Federalists countered by nominating Madison, who had confided to Randolph that he would prefer a seat in the new House of Representatives since he lacked the financial resources to live on the grand scale that might be expected of senators. Henry wanted Madison kept out of the Senate for other reasons, declaring frankly in debate that he believed Madison too "unfriendly to amendments" to justify Virginia's trust. The Federalists, Henry told Lee, "urged Madison's election most warmly, claiming as a sort of right the admission of one Federal member," but Henry successfully resisted the idea. "For to no purpose must the efforts of Virginia have been expected to procure amendments, if one of her members had been found adverse to that scheme," Henry explained. "The universal cry is for amendments & the Federalists are obliged to join in it; but whether to amuse, or conceal other views seems dubious," Henry said. "You have been too long used to political measures not to see the grounds of this doubt." We cannot depend on such "occasional conformity," Henry warned, nor trust "the contest" "to those whose late proceedings, if they do not manifest enmity to public liberty, yet show too little solicitude or zeal for its preservation."

Madison received seventy-seven votes, trailing Lee by twenty-one and Grayson by nine votes. Harry Lee later claimed that Henry prophesied bloodshed if Madison were elected and the campaign to secure amendments failed as a result. Although Mrs. Lee considered her friend Madison's defeat "a dreadful blow," her husband, after consulting with "the Sachem" at Mount Vernon, declared it for the best, since now Madison could go into the general's cabinet.

But Madison wanted a seat in the new Congress, and he did not want to campaign for it. To Randolph he expressed hope that "the arrangements for the popular elections may secure me against any competition which would require on my part any step that would speak a solicitude which I do not feel, or have the appearance of a spirit of electioneering which I despise."

Henry, however, intended to make Madison face up to public opinion. The congressional elections would take place from ten districts apportioned on the basis of the white population without allowances for the large numbers of slaves in certain sections; the candidates, moreover, would have to be residents of the district. (Those provisions had come from Corbin, who believed that the Federalists had to support "a liberal election law" to appear as "true democrats," lest Henry and his "myrmidonum" be "open-mouthed against aristocracy.") Henry did not serve on the committee that drafted the election law, but he certainly endorsed the partisan effort that "counterpoized" Madison's Orange County with avow-edly Anti-Federalist neighbors. The committee reached across the James for several Southside strongholds. Madison would have to run in a lopsided eight-county district that stretched at least eighty miles along the Piedmont foothills and was heavily "tainted" with Anti-Federalism. His friends had found "the *Antes* too strong" when they tried at the last minute to add one more friendly county, and they exclaimed bitterly at the "uncommon" manner in which "the majority bent its utmost efforts against an individual." They execrated Henry as a "tyrant" and claimed that he had more power than an Ottoman ruler or the king of France. "He has only to say let this be Law—and it is Law," Washington lamented. This assembly was "the worst set, ever were collected, before or since the Revolution," a Fredericksburg merchant wrote; "Henry did just as he pleased with them."

In an age that regarded partisanship as factious and un-principled, Henry's methods seemed not only unorthodox but wicked. After his attack on Madison, a Shenandoah Valley assemblyman complained: "Hereafter, when a gentleman is nominated to a public office, it is not his virtue, his abilities, or his patriotism we are to regard, but whether he is a federalist or an antifederalist."

The writer regarded dissent as inherently suspicious. "In a free state there can be no government if the voice of the majority is not submitted to; it is as essential to the existence of liberty that ninety-nine should obey one hundred, as that one should submit to ninety-nine—the only difference is, that where the majority is small, a door of hope is left open to ambitious men, that by fomenting the discontents of the people, they may gain the ascendancy—subvert the govern-ment, or aggrandize themselves."

Throughout his career Henry had forged a new kind of politics. He had sparked the Revolution by an unorthodox mobilization of public opinion, and now he protested new restrictions on that democratic upsurge with unabashed parti-sanship. Supporters of the Constitution, of course, had done the same thing but had more consistently cloaked their new tactics with the familiar claims of disinterested patriotism. They would suppress partisanship by creating what they regarded as a temporary party of national unification. Henry, too, rose above "party" to justify his opposition by the time-honored "Whig" appeal to fundamental principles. In this way he honored conventional assumptions, yet his instinct that men might openly compete for power by organizing themselves into parties that sought majority support for specific ideas and programs would become commonplace in another generation.

The Federalists, however, quite explicitly sought to restrain power exercised by a majority. Indeed, in his first contribution to *The Federalist* series, Madison had bluntly stated that the great advantage of "the extended republic" envisioned by the Constitution would be the "greater obstacles opposed to the concert and accomplishment of the secret wishes of an unjust and interested majority. . . . A rage for paper money, for an abolition of debts, for an equal division of property, or any other improper or wicked project, will be less apt to pervade the whole body of the Union than a particular member of it. . . . The influence of factious leaders may kindle a flame within their particular States but will be unable to spread a general conflagration through the other States."

Undaunted by the aspersions cast either upon partisanship or upon majority rule, Henry crowned his month-long effort to keep Virginia on the mark toward amendments by drafting the response to Clinton's circular letter and a parallel appeal to Congress for a second convention. Virginia's objections to the constitution, he declared, "were not founded in speculative theory, but deduced from principles which have been established by the melancholy example of other nations—so they never will be removed, until the cause itself shall cease to exist." The campaign for amendments "we consider as a common cause [that] will ill admit of delay," Henry wrote. "Since concessions have been made from political motives, which *we* conceive may endanger the republic," Henry emphasized, "we trust that a commendable zeal will be shown for obtaining those provisions, which experience has taught us, are necessary to secure from danger the unalienable rights of human nature." The House approved the draft and ordered it sent to Congress and printed as a broadside for circulation in the counties.

Henry left for home the next day. "I have not a moment to spare," he told his daughter Betsy, in explaining why he could not ride over to King William to see her ailing young family. "Your Aunt Christian is come in from Kentucky with all her children, & waits to see me, I expect, with great impatience." A contest had arisen over her husband's will, and Henry's best legal efforts were required to protect his sister's interest and the funds intended for her children's education. "I must see her directly," Henry said. He hoped Betsy and her children would come up to Prince Edward as soon as their health permitted. His "dear little Family were all well" when he last heard from Dolly, Henry said; her sister Fontaine has a new son, and added, "I have a son also, four months old."

The Federalists mocked Henry's early departure from the session. Washington's private secretary, Tobias Lear, set the tone: "After he had settled everything relative to the government wholly . . . to his satisfaction, he mounted his horse and rode home, leaving the little business of the State to be done by anybody who chose to give themselves the trouble of attending to it."

Henry had no interest in politics beyond the question of amendments. Just before leaving Richmond, he wrote a long letter to R. H. Lee, in which he disavowed any interest in "deliberations held out of this state, unless in Carolina, from which I am not very distant and to whose politics I wish to be attentive." If Congress does not "give us substantial amendments," Henry said, he would consider moving to North Carolina. "I am indeed happy where I now live . . . for in near 20 adjoining countys I think at least 19/20ths are antifederal, and this great extent of country in Virginia lays adjoining to No. Carolina, and with her forms a great mass of opposition not easy to surmount." It is "the wish of my soul," Henry went on, that the opposition remain "wise, firm, & temperate," but he did not think it could remain so if Congress withheld amendments. The "American union depends on the success of amendments," he said; "God grant I may never see the day when it shall be the duty of whiggish Americans to look for shelter under any other government than that of the United States."

Henry had done what he could, and he hoped Lee and Grayson would now carry on the struggle. Much depended, of course, on whether they would have to contend with Madison in Congress. For the second time in ten months Madison found himself overwhelmed by increasingly agitated appeals to return to Virginia for a political campaign. The prospect of "electioneering [is] not a little grating to me," Madison replied, and he winced at the thought of jouncing hundreds of miles along muddy roads while "much indisposed with the piles."

"For the interest of our Country *you must* take some trouble however disagreeable it may be to you," an ally told Madison. He had a formidable opponent in James Monroe, the Baptists remained extremely concerned about religious freedom under the new government, and the "Antis" had everywhere spread the idea that Madison remained opposed to any amendment whatsoever.

Madison bowed. He returned to Virginia shortly after Christmas prepared to canvass actively in his district. Public opinion proved so hostile that he felt obliged to make a campaign pledge. While freely acknowledging that he had "never seen in the Constitution . . . those serious dangers which have alarmed many respectable Citizens," Madison conceded that he now believed something might be done to assuage those fears. "Circumstances are now changed . . . ," he admitted publicly, "and amendments, if pursued with a proper moderation and in a proper mode, will be not only safe, but may serve the double purpose of satisfying the minds of well meaning opponents, and of providing additional guards in favour of liberty." Accordingly, he told an influential Baptist minister in a letter intended for public circulation: "It is my sincere opinion that the Constitution ought to be revised, and that the first Congress . . . ought to prepare and recommend to the States . . . the most satisfactory provisions for all essential rights, particularly the rights of Conscience in the fullest latitude, the freedom of the press, trials by jury, security against general warrants &c . . . the periodic increase of the number of Representatives . . . [and] sundry other alterations which are either eligible in themselves, or being at least safe, are recommended by the respect due to such as wish for them."

Madison studiously avoided any mention of the amendments adopted by the Virginia convention, but he insisted that Congress would be a more "expeditious" forum than a second convention, which might be dominated "by insidious characters" and likely to "spread a general alarm . . . and turn every thing into confusion." (Some amendments from Congress, Madison privately told Jefferson, would separate "the well meaning from the designing opponents, fix on the latter their true character, and give to the Government its due popularity and stability.")

The statement proved highly effective. Madison and Monroe, in a great departure from traditional Virginia practice, campaigned actively despite the January cold and once found themselves attending a Lutheran church service together in bitterly contested Culpepper County, after which they each "addressed" the people outside and got a touch of frostbite. Monroe carried the "extra" counties added to the district along with his own home county, but he received only 9 votes to Madison's 216 in Orange. Madison's astute letter had carried the Baptists in Culpepper, and his hundred-vote margin there proved decisive in giving him the victory.

Henry watched Madison's skillful volte-face with bemusement. "Federal and anti seem now scarcely to exist," he wrote in March to William Grayson, already in New York for the opening of the new Congress. "Our highest toned Feds say we must have the amendments, but the Enumeration stops at Direct Taxation Treatys Trade &c. &c. so that I perceive it will be a question of prudence." From his "secluded situation," Henry said that he could not guess whether "the Temper of the Times" would be apprehensive enough to "extort concession to any salutary purpose." "You perhaps can tell me how far appearances tend that way," Henry added.

From Prince Edward, Henry played only a minor role in launching the new government. His district chose him to serve as its presidential elector, and he went down to Richmond to cast his vote, as did every elector in the country, for General Washington. Then he defiantly voted for New York's Governor Clinton as vice-president, while the majority (by pre-arrangement) chose John Adams. The political gossips had whispered that the Antis would support a Henry-Clinton ticket as a means of subversion, but Henry would neither seek national office nor challenge the invincible Washington.

The gossips, however, would not let Henry alone. Throughout the winter and spring a series of newspaper articles by "Decius" attacked Henry as "a despot under the disguise of republican rags" who has employed "all the horrors of a gloomy imagination to affright us . . . and all the powers of mimicry . . . to laugh us out of our sober senses." An American tyrant, "Decius" predicted, would be "a man . . . calculated to soothe, and not to threaten the populace; possessing a humiliating, and not an arrogant turn; affecting an entire ignorance and poorness of capacity, and not assuming the superiorities of the illumined . . . a man whose plainness of manners and meannesses of address, first should move our compassions; steal upon our hearts; betray our judgments; and finally run away with the whole."

"Decius" attacked Henry on every conceivable ground; he scurrilously charged him with desertion during the war, corruption during his governorship, wanton indebtedness, and devious partisanship in the legislature that would have "deprived us of the services of the only man, almost, who could render the new system different in its operations from what [Henry] foretold it would be." The writer attacked the jut of Henry's chin and the dark shadow of his beard, and described him as "hideous in outward appearance, but moderate in courage and slow of motion"; he could be "justly drawn with a fox's head on a bear's shoulders, and a mouse's heart in a wolf's stomach."

Henry's friends wrote vigorous rebuttals. For two things only, said "Junius-Brutus," "His triumphing over the British aristocracy before the war, and his defence of the people's liberties since . . . I freely forgive him all his faults . . . let him be artful, or designing, or even the OLD-BOY himself." Every responsible Virginian deplored "Decius," and Edmund Randolph especially objected to the articles as an untimely insult to the "general calm" that had settled upon Virginia politics after the elections. Henry turned aside the attacks with the modest statement that had "Decius" known him better, he would have had many truthful deficiencies to mention. Privately, however, he told Grayson that while "the dirty scribbler" would be "disowned" by his party, Henry had no doubt that "Decius" had received covert encouragement as one of those "political understrappers who follow the footsteps of power and whine and fawn or snarl a bark as they are bid."

The attacks on Henry went on too long to be dismissed as the vituperative work of a crank. They formed part of the design to discredit Henry as a fanatic while appealing to the "better element" among the Anti-Federalists with the promise of amendments. The Federalists had won seven of the ten congressional seats, an encouraging sign that Madison's strategy would work. When Theodorick Bland, an ally of Henry's, presented Virginia's call for a second convention to the new Congress, the overwhelmingly Federalist House refused to refer it to a committee and, after an ill-tempered debate, agreed only to record it as "filed."

Madison had publicly promised to seek amendments from Congress, but the House did not seem inclined to help. The Virginian had to cajole his colleagues into granting a hearing; in his first presentation on June 8 he asked only that the House listen long enough that "our constituents may see we pay proper attention to a subject they have much at heart." When finally given the floor, Madison spoke from an outline urging adoption on four grounds:

"1. to prove fedts. friends to liberty
2. remove remaining inquietudes
3. bring in N.C. & R.I.
4. to improve the Constitution"

He insisted that he did not want "to see a door opened for a re-consideration of the whole structure of government" but only wanted "to incorporate those provisions for the security of rights, against which I believe no serious objection has been made." Madison backed away from the Federalists' standard arguments against a bill of rights by admitting that the government had "certain discretionary powers with respect to the means, which may admit of abuse to a certain extent." He did, however, reiterate his view that the greatest threat to liberty lay not in government but "in the body of the people, operating by the majority against the minority." Nonetheless, Madison argued that even "paper barriers . . . have a tendency to impress some degree of respect for them, to establish the public opinion in their favor, and rouse the attention of the whole community." Madison thus indirectly endorsed Henry's insistence that the Constitution promote fundamental "maxims" of government." "No harm," Madison now emphasized, could come from obtaining "the confidence of our fellow citizens" by fortifying "the rights of the people against the encroachments of the government."

In preparing his amendments Madison had, with characteristic thoroughness, reviewed the nearly two hundred recommendations made by seven ratifying conventions. Many were similar; North Carolina's and New York's closely followed the Virginia master text. Madison limited himself to points he regarded as "important in the eyes of many and . . . objectionable in those of none." He wanted "nothing of a controvertible nature" because he sought measures whose passage would be absolutely assured. He ignored all the recommendations that addressed the powers of government: nothing on taxation as a last resort (a provision that appeared on every list), nothing on two-thirds votes for treaties, trade laws, or standing armies in peacetime, nothing toward the prohibition of monopolies (urged by every state except Virginia). There was nothing that looked like the grand charter of rights Mason and Henry had envisioned as a preface to the Constitution; Madison proposed that additional clauses be inserted at appropriate places in the text itself.

Madison's amendments covered nineteen points. He began with a preface on the fundamental rights of the people, drawn from the opening paragraph of the Virginia Declaration of Rights. He then answered with an explicit ratio Henry's objection to the ambiguous phrasing of the clause on representation. He enumerated the rights of conscience, speech, press, and trial by jury in both civil and criminal cases, and he proposed protections against arbitrary searches, excessive bail, double jeopardy, and other elements of due process of law. Additional amendments stated that rights and powers not enumerated would belong to the people or states. Madison, who had originally wanted a national veto on state legislation, saw a new opportunity to promote uniformity, and he proposed that the states also be prohibited from infringing the fundamental rights of conscience, press, and trial by jury. ("The most valuable amendment on the whole list," Madison called it.)

"Last Monday a string of amendments were presented to the lower House," Grayson reported to Henry on June 12, 1789. "Their object is . . . unquestionably to break the spirit of the party by divisions." The measures only treated "personal liberty . . . leaving the great points . . . to stand." Even these proposals were opposed by Georgia, New Hampshire, and Connecticut, small states that "are afraid of touching a subject which may bring into investigation or controversy their fortunate situation." Grayson told Henry that Madison was "so embarrassed in the course of the business" that he almost withdrew the motion and succeeded in getting it referred to committee more from "personal respect than a love of the subject introduced." Grayson wanted to counter Madison by bringing Virginia's proposed amendments directly to the floor of the Senate, but R. H. Lee had persuaded him to wait for the House's action. Lee, however, told Henry that he would do everything possible "to effect . . . the wishes of our legislature." The convention call having failed, Lee said his wish to "more effectually secure civil liberty" formed his "sole reason" for accepting a seat in the Senate. "I agree perfectly with you," he told Henry, "that your time of life and mine, after the turbulence we have passed through, renders repose necessary to our declining years."

Henry squinted narrowly at Madison's amendments and pronounced them intended only "to lull suspicion" and provide "guileful bait" to North Carolina and Rhode Island. Pointing to Congress's recent decision that the president had the discretionary power to remove appointive officers, Henry grumbled, "See how rapidly power grows; how slowly the means of curbing it." He told Lee, "While impediments are cast in the way of those who wish to retrench the exorbitancy of power granted away by the constitution from the people, a fresh grant . . . is made in the first moments of opportunity."

Madison's amendments languished in committee for most of the summer. The House finally debated them in mid-August and decided to reorganize them into seventeen articles to be appended to the text of the Constitution as a supplement. The phrasing of some articles, especially the clauses on religious freedom, was strengthened and the preface deleted, but the lengthiest debate took place over a last-minute attempt by Thomas Tudor Tucker, a South Carolina congressman, to add the recommended limitation on the tax power. The House defeated this, thirty-nine to nine, and sent the seventeen proposals to the Senate, which removed some remaining ambiguities in the texts and deleted Madison's proposal that the states be uniformly prohibited from abridging the rights of conscience, free press, and trial by jury. A preamble was affixed declaring the amendments a response "to the conventions of a number of the states having . . . expressed a desire, in order to prevent misconception or abuse of [the Constitution's] powers, that further declaratory and restrictive clauses should be added."

The Senate condensed the remaining measures into twelve articles, which, after a few more changes in conference with the House, were jointly approved on September 25, 1789, and submitted to the states for ratification.

Debate in the Senate proved desultory. Some argued that the whole matter should be postponed for at least one year, while others denigrated the importance of the subject. Lee raised objections to the preamble, which he said allowed "a careless reader . . . to suppose that the amendments desired by the states had been graciously granted. . . . But when the thing done is compared with that desired, nothing can be more unlike." When Lee and Grayson proposed that the text affirm the people's right to instruct their representatives, theirs were the only votes in favor, and their submission of Virginia's full list of recommendations as an alternative met defeat without a roll call.

"We might as well have attempted to move Mount Atlas upon our shoulders," Lee told Henry on September 14. "In fact, the idea of subsequent amendments was delusion altogether, and so intended by the greater part of those who arrogated to themselves the name of Federalists. I am grieved to see too many look at the rights of the people as a miser examines a security, to find a flaw in it." Lee conceded, "some valuable rights are indeed declared," but feared that Congress still had so much discretionary power that violations would easily occur. Our only remedy now, Lee thought, is "to fill our state offices with men of known attachment to radical amendments . . . whose firmness and abilities may serve as a counterpoise."

"The extraordinary doctrine of playing the after game" has turned out as badly "as I apprehended," Grayson told Henry two weeks later. Grayson believed the Senate had "so mutilated and gutted" the "safeguards" proposed by the lower house that "in fact they are good for nothing, and I believe, as many others do, that they will do more harm than benefit." The Congress is dominated by "a set of gentlemen" who intended "to make up by construction what the constitution wants in energy," Grayson wrote, and left Henry to draw his own gloomy conclusions.

Lee and Grayson promptly transmitted the twelve proposed amendments to the Virginia assembly with a stiff note manifesting their displeasure at the omission of "those radical amendments proposed by the convention." "It is impossible for us not to see the necessary tendency to consolidate empire in the national operations of the Constitution if not further amended," they warned, and they predicted, "Unless a dangerous apathy should invade the public mind it will not be many years before a constitutional number of Legislatures will be found to *demand* a convention for the purpose."

The House found the senators' language intemperate and declined Henry's motion to commend them for their efforts to secure the Virginia package. With Randolph, Harry Lee, and John Marshall in their places, the Federalists had strong leadership again, and Henry found himself stymied. He proposed that the amendments be deferred for one year until the people "might give their sentiments whether they were satisfactory, alledging that in his opinion they were not." Enough Anti-Federalists, however, thought the amendments worth taking while offered, and Henry's proposal was tabled. Edward Carrington told Madison what followed: "Mr. H—— was disposed to do some antifederal business, but having felt the pulse of the House on several points and finding that it did not beat with certainty in unison with his own, he at length took his departure about the middle of the session without pushing any thing to its issue."

After Henry left, a large majority of the House agreed to the first ten amendments,* but Randolph raised some impenetrably foggy objections to the proposals that described "rights retained" by the people and powers "reserved" to the states. Then George Mason's nephew persuaded the usually subordinate state Senate to reject the amendments dealing with freedom of religion, the press and trial by jury as being too weak. (George Mason himself, preoccupied with business affairs, appreciated Madison's achievement but said it would take "two or three" further "material amendments" before

---

* Congress had sent out twelve proposals. The first would have fixed the ratio for expanding the size of the U.S. House of Representatives, and the second would have deferred congressional salary increases until after an election had intervened. These two amendments failed to receive the requisite three-fourths vote in the states. Article III on the list, dealing with the freedom of religion, speech, assembly, and press, thus became the "first" amendment of the ten known collectively but unofficially as "the Bill of Rights."

he could "chearfully put my Hand and Heart to the new Government."

A Madison lieutenant conjectured that Anti-Federalists in the Senate wanted to hold the most popular civil liberties ransom in hopes of still obtaining the strong reforms they desired. In the end, with the two houses in disagreement, ratification had to be postponed. Virginia was the first state to consider the amendments but the last to accept them, ratification not being accomplished until 1791.

Back home in Prince Edward, Henry threw the pamphlet containing the twelve amendments on his office table and told his law clerks that "Virginia had been outwitted." Yet he still held out. North Carolina's ratification of both Constitution and amendments in November 1789 demonstrated that Madison's ploy had broken the momentum of protest. But Henry never liked to admit the necessity for compromise, although Lee had decided, "If we cannot gain the whole loaf, we shall at least have some bread." Lee was sorry Virginia had not ratified the amendments because, weak as they were, they served "one great object" of such declarations by inculcating "upon the minds of the people, just ideas of their rights," so that "it will always be hazardous for rulers, however possessed of means, to undertake a violation of what is generally known to be right." "By getting as much as we can at different times," Lee said gently, "we may at last come to obtain the greatest part of our wishes."

Henry found it hard to agree. Madison had successfully divided the opposition, and it was Henry's fate to have been both "well-meaning" and "designing." He wanted so much more that he could not even grudgingly accept what only his strenuous efforts had goaded Madison to produce.

When William Grayson died in March 1790, Henry declined to stand for appointment to the vacant place in the Senate. "My mind recoils," he told Beau Dawson. "I cannot find those resolutions [?] within my breast which I deem necessary" for service in the government, he said. "Some of its leading principles are subversive of those to which I am forever *attached*, while its practices seem equally at variance with republican sentiments. Could I believe that my poor efforts would work a change I would sacrifice everything to go there—but the utmost which I see possible to effect is . . . to improve some of the lesser movements of the system, while the [illegible] errors remain."

Henry doubted that an opportunity for what he regarded as genuine reform would come in his lifetime, and he remained convinced that fundamental change would occasion "so much horror" that people will "hesitate" and "perhaps finally desist" from attempting it. He had hopes, however, that the yet-to-be-settled Southwest would remain a bastion of liberty.

Henry's antagonists still charged him with nurturing hopes of founding his own southwestern confederacy, but he dreamed only of backwoods repose under his vine and fig tree. "A comfortable prospect of the issue of the new system would fix me here for life," he told R. H. Lee. "A contrary one sends me southwestward [to newly purchased land on the edge of Georgia]. For if our present system grows into tyranny is not a frontier possession most eligible?" Henry felt anxious for his family, he said, "besides the concern common to every citizen." Then he softened. "I am refining perhaps too much," he mused, "and looking to a period too distant in my estimate of things."

Then, early in 1791, having served for the last time in a public body, Henry suddenly let go. He wrote an avuncular letter to Virginia's new senator, James Monroe, in which he confessed that while "The Form of Government into which my Countrymen determined to place themselves, had my Enmity, yet as we are one & all embarked, it is natural to care for the crazy Machine, at least so long as we are out of Sight of a Port to refit. I have therefore my Anxieties to hear & know what is doing, & to what point the State pilots are steering, & to keep up the Metaphor, whether there is no Appearance of Storms in our Horizon."

Henry asked Monroe to write regularly and hoped that there would be enough news from his own remote corner "to spin it out into the Size of a Letter" in response. He would hold himself in check, Henry declared, and not "criminate" everything. "The little Stock of good Humour which I have towards . . . the present proceedings ... . is increased by reflecting that some Allowances ought to be made, & some Hopes indulged of future amendment," Henry wrote. "All I can promise you is, that I will be sparing of Complaints against the Government, & find Fault as little as my fixed Habits of thinking will permit."

EPILOGUE

"My Secluded Corner"

Once again he became a country lawyer. With a plantation cabin for his office and several nephews as his clerks, Henry worked at home, reviewing complaints and preparing "writings" for his clients' use. He no longer rode from county to county with a saddlebag full of fifteen-shilling pleas. A district court system had supplanted the old county magistrates, and now the judges, including his son-in-law Spencer Roane, rode the circuit, bringing a greater knowledge of the law and more uniform standards to the counties. Henry confined his trial practice to nearby district courts in Prince Edward and Bedford, although if the fee were large enough and his health permitted, he would ride down to Richmond or over the mountains to Greenbrier for a compelling case.

Stories mounted quickly of Henry's forensic triumphs. Juries, judges, and spectators all thrilled to his performances in both "the tragic and the comic line." No listener could ever forget how Henry drew shivers by reminding jurors that "blood is concerned" in their decision. Nor could people forget how Henry spiked the testimony of a woman who had witnessed something through a keyhole.

"Which eye did you peep with?" he asked. When the laughter had subsided, he turned from the flustered witness to the court, flung out his arms and said, "Great God, deliver us from eavesdroppers!"

When a Scotch merchant named John Hook sued one of Henry's neighbors for the value of two steers impressed during the war, Henry spoke feelingly of the wartime sacrifices patriots had made and described the joyous celebration that followed the British surrender at Yorktown. What notes of discord disturbed the general joy? Henry asked, and he convulsed the courtroom with the answer, "They are the notes of John Hook, hoarsely bawling through the American camp, 'beef! beef! beef!' " For years afterward someone in the courthouse crowd would be sure to greet Henry with a happily mooing cry of "beef! beef!" and relish every opportunity to tell the story over and over again.

When opposing counsel spoke, Henry made a show of taking ample notes. He would then rise to make his objections. If they were to be brief, he would read from the notes, but "if he was ever seen to give his spectacles a cant to the top of his wig," people said, "it was a declaration of war and his adversaries must stand clear."

Henry turned down a good many cases, including a plea from one of the Randolph families to defend a young scion who had got caught up in a scandalous case of bastardy and infanticide. They had offered a fee of 250 guineas, but Henry replied that he felt too sickly to ride the sixty miles to Cumberland Court. Then a messenger returned with word that John Marshall would prepare the case if Henry would agree to examine the witnesses. The family offered to double the fee. After consultation with Dolly, Henry accepted the offer and got from the Randolphs 500 guineas, the same sum that Peyton Randolph had long ago wanted to pay for a single vote against the obstreperous lawyer.

Only occasionally did Henry's law practice lead him to the brink of politics. In 1791 he joined John Marshall and several other luminaries of the Richmond bar in defense of Dr. Thomas Walker, an Albemarle physician and planter being sued for recovery of prewar debts owed to a British merchant house. Walker insisted that he had paid the debt into the Virginia loan office as permitted by the commonwealth's wartime legislation. Henry had opposed the payment of old British debts for more than a decade, and he prepared the case with extraordinary care. He had his grandson ride sixty miles to borrow a copy of Vattel's *Law of Nations*, and the family remembered how Henry rehearsed his arguments while walking up and down in the locust grove beyond his office.

The trial, with enormously complex pleadings and conflicts over applicable law, went on for weeks, but for the three days that Henry spoke no other business took place in Richmond. The shops emptied, and the legislature could not make a quorum. With Marshall, Henry developed ingenious arguments in support of Virginia's sovereign power to discharge the debt itself, and he rehearsed again the British treaty violations that must end before repayment could be considered. Between his speeches Henry, wrapped in a greatcoat against the courtroom chill, rested his large bald head against the bar in a display of weariness that, as with all great actors, grew from a blend of artifice and truth. Then, in one last grand effort, he recollected yet again the grievances of the Revolution and the successful issue of the war that in his mind made the debt collection both unlawful and odious. "He is Shakespeare and Garrick combined," young John Randolph marveled, but oratory did not carry the day. The case went through endless permutations and reargument and ultimately was decided in the merchants' favor by the U.S. Supreme Court in 1796, two years after Henry had ceased to practice.

"I am obliged to be very industrious . . . to my great fatigue to clear myself of debt," Henry told his daughter Betsy while in Richmond for the British case in the winter of 1791. "I hope to be able to accomplish this in a year or two if it please God to continue me in health." It took him three years. Poor crops, a "sharp attack of a fall fever," and long patches of hip trouble spun out his affairs. Finally, in September 1794, he told Betsy that he would "give out the law & plague myself no more with business, sitting down with what I have. For it will be sufficient employment to see after my Flock, & the management of my plantation."

Henry had several families and plantations under his care. His sister Annie Christian had died of consumption in 1790, leaving to Henry the "great anxiety" of supporting and educating her three young children along with his own. The burden became more difficult when a portion of their income passed to the control of a second, somewhat improvident executor in distant Kentucky. Henry's eldest daughter Patsy, a matronly forty now, and her younger children had also come back into the circle after the death of her husband John Fontaine, and Henry integrated the management of her farms with his own. "What a weight of worldly concerns rest upon this old man's shoulders," a neighbor wrote in 1792 after a day's visit. (Henry was fifty-six, but everyone, himself included, had an impression of aged decline.)

Henry had traded his Prince Edward seat in 1792 for a new estate called Long Island, thirty-five miles southwest in the foothills of Campbell County. Then he acquired a second plantation, Red Hill, eighteen miles below Long Island in the Staunton River Valley, where the family increasingly spent its time. Henry liked Long Island's "very retired" situation, but even he admitted it was "so much so as to disgust Dolly & Sally," the eldest daughters of his second marriage, who suddenly stood at the brink of womanhood. "As we go to Red Hill in August for five weeks," he told Betsy Aylett, "they will be relieved from this Solitude, as that is a more public place."

Henry meant only that the neighborhood was more thickly settled. Red Hill occupied a serene portion of the ridge dividing the Staunton and Appomattox valleys and lay not too far from an east-west road; Lynchburg, a good twenty miles away, had only two dozen houses and a main street still filled with stumps and grubs, but it could get nearly a hundred people to come in for balls at Christmas, Washington's birthnight, and other festivals.

At Red Hill the family lived in a small one-and-one-half-story farmhouse, as simple as the frame cabin Henry and his first young family had occupied on Roundabout Creek thirty years before. The older daughters found a more sociable life at Red Hill, and soon twelve-year-old Kitty (the third of the children with Dorothea) joined in their flirtatious games. Henry would be summoned to hear her verses: "The Lillys now their fragrance sheds/And all their sweets disclose/The pink perfumes, the violet beds/Are not compared with Rose." The girls would run off in gales of laughter, leaving Henry to puzzle out for himself that the verse referred to one of their beaus, "the handsome, sensible, witty, & accomplished Peter Rose."

Henry's six young sons (counting babies Winston, born in 1794, and John, born in 1796) had the run of the place, and visitors used to catch Henry with a group of "little ones climbing over him in every direction, or dancing around him with obstreperous mirth, to the tune of his violin, while the only contest seemed to be who should make the most noise."

Anxiety for his sons' prosperity led him into an endless variety of land schemes. He wanted to leave each boy a country seat, and he could not entirely abandon his hopes of finding wealth in distant western lands. He held on to some Kentucky property and bought an interest in a huge Georgia tract, only to lose it through fraudulent manipulations by that state's legislature. He had Carolina property, too, though the taxes on it proved a continuing harassment. And he always had an ear for the grandiose ideas of Harry Lee, who acquired heavy stakes in western land with hopes of quick resales to European investors. Neither Lee nor Henry, however, had the skill or temperament for financial manipulation. Henry had a speculator's desire but a householder's mentality. His social vision remained the utopian hope of the Revolution that yeomen would find contentment under their vines and fig trees; that is how he chose to end his days, and that is what he wanted for his sons.

Henry also grew more religious, beginning every day with a period of Bible reading and declaring to visitors his "misfortune" that he had not "found time to read it with the proper attention and feeling till lately. I trust in the mercy of Heaven that it is not yet too late." He purchased copies of sermons by the great English divines of the early part of the century, and on Sunday evenings he would read portions aloud to the family, after which they sang hymns to the obbligato of his violin. He still had copies of the tract by

Soames Jenyns that he had printed up while governor, and in his last months at the bar he distributed them on district court days, laughingly warning the judges not to take him for "a travelling monk." "I find much cause to reproach myself that I have lived so long and have given no decided proofs of my being a Christian," he told his daughter in 1796, giving intimations of an evangelical "new birth" that never occurred.

His growing piety afforded consolation amid the onrushing infirmities of age, the deaths of his melancholy sons John and Ned (who had possibly inherited his mother Sallie's illness), and the grim signal heard when George Mason died in 1792 and R. H. Lee followed two years later.

Religious feeling complicated his response to politics. He had stayed aloof from the early battles in the Washington administration. Yet he took a sour satisfaction at seeing his worst predictions confirmed. Under the bold leadership of Treasury Secretary Alexander Hamilton, the national government advanced creditor interests, assumed and refunded at par the state and federal certificates, found justification by implied powers for the creation of a national bank, took on a high-toned social style in which Washington presided at kingly levees, and tilted toward Great Britain in both trade and the complex European diplomacy that followed the French Revolution. These measures ultimately drove Madison and Jefferson into opposition, and their new "Democratic-Republican" party drew in most of the Virginians who had considered themselves Anti-Federalist in 1788.

Henry would not follow. In the fierce party conflicts of the 1790s the Federalists' British predilections had generated a Francophilia among the Republicans that Henry did not share. He made fun of Jefferson's French chef but then more grimly pointed to the French Reign of Terror as the inevitable consequence of deism and impiety.

The force of personal enmity made accommodation impossible. Jefferson had hated Henry for years and would not draw him into the party. Henry harbored a great hostility toward Madison, who had bested him not once but twice, and he remained astonished at Madison's naiveté in cooperating with a commercial elite whose program endangered the agrarian society Virginians cherished. (Madison, in fact, shared the agrarian outlook, but his brilliance made him too intellectually cosmopolitan to accept the limitations of the homogeneous and rustic community that Henry and his own father cherished.) Madison made no effort to bring Henry into his newly organized cause; indeed, in 1791 he had rebuffed Henry's offer to correspond. When an intermediary tried to arrange a meeting between Jefferson and Henry, neither man showed up.

Henry's estrangement from the Republican leaders, if not from the major tenets of the party's positions, made him an attractive catch for the Federalists. ("He grows rich every hour," Edmund Randolph said of Henry, "and thus his motives to tranquility must be multiplying every day.") They began to talk about him as a candidate to succeed Washington in 1796 instead of the unpopular John Adams, and the president, after a good deal of diplomatic coaxing by Harry Lee, began to entice Henry into his administration. In 1794 he offered to send Henry as ambassador to Spain to conclude, at long last, a favorable treaty on the Mississippi navigation. Henry politely declined. The next year Washington offered him a cabinet position as secretary of state, which he turned down, and then the post of chief justice, which he also rejected.

Henry's replies breathed cordiality and respect but spoke feelingly of the distress that removal to Philadelphia would cause. With eight children and "Mrs. Henry's situation [pregnancy] now forbidding her approach to the smallpox," he would add "other considerations arising from loss of Crops and consequent derangement of my finances" and the "decisive weight" of his own failing strength. He did assure Washington that he had "bid adieu to the distinction of federal and anti-federal ever since the commencement of the present government, and in the circle of my friends have often expressed my fears of disunion amongst the States from collision of interests, but especially from the baneful effects of faction."

He jibed at the Republicans more than he embraced the Federalists. Yet he shrank from the partisanship that he had once done much to foster. "Although a democrat myself, I like not the late Democratic Societies," Henry told Washington, but he added, "As little do I like their suppression by law." Although Henry shared the prevailing southern opposition to Jay's commercial treaty with Britain, he disliked the Republicans' maneuver in the House to withhold funds for the treaty's execution. It violated the separation of powers, and Henry chided those who now challenged the Senate's power. "What must I think of those men, whom I myself warned of the danger of giving the power of making laws by means of treaty, to the president and senate, when I see these same men denying the existence of that power, which they insisted, in our convention, ought properly to be exercised by the president and senate, and by none other?" he said to Betsy Aylett in an effort to vindicate himself from charges of apostasy. "It seems that every word was watched which I casually dropped [on a visit to Richmond], and wrested to answer party views," he complained, but he said he cared nothing: "I no longer consider myself an actor on the stage of public life."

But the public wouldn't let him go. The Federalists wanted him, and the Republicans berated him for the court their opponents paid, although in 1796 they, too, offered him the Virginia governorship to keep out a popular Federalist.

The actor worried about his reputation. He asked a neighbor to assist him in getting rid of a man who had pestered him for months about a stray calf Henry's overseer had taken up. Now the man threatened to sue, and this "vexed" Henry more than anything. "I was never sued in my life on my own account," Henry said, "and now to be sued & cast by this man would concern me more than fifty times the value of the steer." Since Henry was "afraid to ride out on account of my health," would the neighbor be so kind as to settle the affair, by offering him "full satisfaction either in cash or cow kind."

Sorting through his papers at about the time he made out his will, Henry found a rough draft of the Stamp Act resolutions of 1765. He wrote out a brief message on the reverse side, then put the sheet in an envelope, which he sealed with wax and placed with his will.

In 1799, George Washington, now retired, sought his services again. Partisan controversy had reached new ferocity during the Adams presidency, as the country became embroiled in a quasi war with France that was accompanied by large expenditures on the army and navy and harsh prosecution (under a new Sedition Act) of newspaper editors who criticized the administration. The Virginia Republicans passed resolutions that denounced the Sedition Act as unconstitutional and threatened to interpose the state's authority to prevent its enforcement. These actions filled Washington with grave fears that political opposition once again threatened the Union.

Washington did two things. He asked John Marshall, just returned from France where he was part of the American delegation from whom Talleyrand's agents had tried to extort a bribe, to run for Congress. Then he asked Patrick Henry to run for the assembly to stem the tendency toward disunion. "Ought characters who are best able to rescue their country from the pending evil to remain at home?" Washington asked Henry.

Before Henry had answered Washington's call, Marshall's friends asked Henry for an endorsement. He replied ambiguously, "Tell Marshall I love him, because he felt and acted as a republican, as an American," and filled the rest of his four-page letter with remarks against French infidelity and with homilies on "virtue, morality, and religion" as "the great pillars of all governments." He deplored any attempts to dissolve "the confederacy" and stated his fears that the "measures lately pursued" would lead to that end.

Although he felt himself "too old and infirm ever again to undertake public concerns," he did ride to Charlotte Court House in March 1799 to stand unopposed as a candidate for the assembly. He went in homage to Washington and to the remembered ideals of the Revolution, and he spoke less as a partisan than as an embodiment of political virtue. He lent himself at last to the Federalist opposition, but no one really knows to what degree he embraced the cause. Many moderate Republicans had doubts about the heated resolutions passed in 1798 that had Washington so alarmed, and Madison himself had sensed some need for reconsideration. Henry was a maverick all his life. No one knows where he would have stood in the House or whether he would have felt any sense of affinity or vindication in reading Madison's broadside, just making its way into the counties, that indicted the Federalist politics of the decade. Madison in 1799 sounded like his great adversary of ten years earlier in condemning the creation of an aristocratic fiscal system, a swarm of civil and military officers, a legislative attack upon freedom of speech and press, and "such a mode of construing the Constitution as will rapidly remove every restraint upon federal power."

No one knows, either, what the voters wanted him to do. They saw a pale, frail man who had answered his old commander's call, and they cheered him not as Federalist, not as Republican, but as their remembered "Pahtrick," the old governor, a firebrand in his youth and in his age, the son of thunder who spoke the language of thousands and won the people's hearts.

Henry never took his elected place in Richmond. He died at Red Hill of stomach cancer on June 6, 1799, twelve weeks after his last appearance on a courthouse green.

Later generations tried to give his final hours a Roman cast: the physician hands him a vial that will either ease his pain or kill him instantly and without hesitation the old senator downs the draft and expires. But his beloved Dolly told it in a different way to her stepdaughter Betsy. "Oh my dear Betsy what a scene have I been witness to—I wish all the Heroes of the Deistical Party could have seen my Ever-Honored Husband pay his last debt to Nature," Henry's widow said. "My loss, my dear Betsy, can never be repaired in this life. But oh that I may be enabled to imitate the virtues of your Dr. & honored Father; & that my end may be like his—He met death with firmness and in full confidence that through the merits of a bleeding Saviour his sins would be pardoned."

Henry's will left detailed instructions for the division of numerous tracts of land so that his sons would each have a decent provision, and he gave Dolly the task of supervising the boundaries and making the assignments. He left money and dowry slaves to his daughters, including the "something" he had promised Roane and Aylett years before. Dolly got the rest, along with permission, "if she chooses," to "set free one or two of my slaves." The estate was appraised at nearly six thousand pounds, with the thirty-eight adult slaves and numerous children valued at four thousand pounds and the horses, cattle, hogs, and sheep accounting for another one thousand pounds of the total. A few pieces of silver plate, some walnut chairs, a set of damask curtains, and a fortepiano proved the most substantial of the household goods, along with the four-horse "chariot" valued at one hundred pounds. "This is all the inheritance I can give to my dear family," Henry had written. "The religion of Christ can give them one which will make them rich indeed."

Dolly's earthly legacy, the patriarch ordered from the grave, would be void if she remarried, but she got round that by marrying the executor, Henry's cousin Edmund Winston, whose son had married their eldest daughter Dorothea. So Henry's widow became, in the inlaid way of Virginia families, her daughter's mother-in-law. When she died in 1831, however, she was buried alongside Patrick Henry at Red Hill.

Next to Henry's will the executors found the small envelope sealed with wax. On the back of his draft of the Stamp Act resolves Henry had written a brief account of their passage. It emphasized how he had acted in opposition to "the men of weight" and claimed that he had written them "alone, unadvised, and unassisted, on a blank leaf of an old law book." He recalled the abuse he received, and how the resolutions had initiated the successful revolution that had established American independence. "Whether this will prove a blessing or a curse, will depend upon the use our people make of the blessings which a gracious God hath bestowed on us." "Righeousness alone can exalt them as a nation," he concluded: "Reader!, whoever thou art, remember this; and in thy sphere practice virtue thyself and encourage it in others." That was his testament.

The newspapers put black borders around his death notice. "Mourn, Virginia, mourn! your Henry is gone!" lamented the *Gazette*, "Ye friends to liberty . . . drop a tear." The *Argus*, a Republican newspaper, praised Henry's revolutionary patriotism and "prophetic mind." "[He] pointed out those evils in our Constitution . . . against which we now complain. . . . If any are deposed to censure Mr. Henry for his late political transition, if anything has been written upon that subject, let the Genius of American Independence drop a tear, and blot it out forever!"

When the assembly met, however, Henry's name occasioned controversy one more time. The Federalists proposed a memorial resolution for Henry, whose "unrivalled eloquence and superior talents, were in times of peculiar peril and distress, so uniformly devoted to the cause of freedom and of his country." On a strictly partisan vote the measure failed, fifty-eight to eighty-eight.

Henry had forged a popular and partisan political style whose democratic implications took another generation to realize fully and accept. His career pointed the transition from the political squirearchy of the eighteenth century to the mass politics of Andrew Jackson's day, by which time the agrarian ideal of vine and fig tree had to compromise with steamboat and factory.

His son John, a three-year-old when his father died, lived on at Red Hill, where he rebuilt the simple Virginia cabin into a suitably Victorian manse. John Henry also hedged the family cemetery with boxwood trees and placed a stone on his father's previously unmarked grave. In this way he countered the well-wishers who sought to rebury Patrick Henry in a massive tomb they planned for the Richmond churchyard where Henry once had triumphed.

To find Patrick Henry today one leaves the interstate highway and drives for many miles on two-lane state roads through the farmlands and piney woods of Southside to the tranquil meadow at Red Hill. An ancient Osage orange tree spreads its boughs in front of the farmhouse, now restored, and the flags of state and nation flank the graveyard gate.

Henry lies beneath a stone slab whose faded letters proclaim, in words chosen by the son who barely knew him, "His Fame His Best Epitaph." Red Hill remains a secluded corner, far from the surge of modern life, and visitors come only by the handful and the hundred in search of the man who once spoke the language of thousands.

NOTES

References are supplied for most direct quotations and for exceptionally obscure or debatable statements. (They are referred to by page numbers and key words.) I have not thought it necessary to annotate topics generally covered in the standard histories and biographies of the period, but I have supplied a note when my view of the evidence differs substantially from previous writers.

The world does not need another bibliography on colonial Virginia or the American Revolution, but for the benefit of readers interested in pursuing topics in more detail, I have incorporated in the notes the titles found most useful in my own research.

Previous biographies of Henry require special mention. Early in the nineteenth century William Wirt collected memoranda from Henry's contemporaries which provided a relatively factual underpinning for Wirt's highly colored biography (1817) depicting Henry as a "forest-born Demosthenes." Much of Wirt's material found its way into the more comprehensive, three-volume "life and times" (1891) prepared by Henry's grandson, William Wirt Henry. A short, judicious volume by Moses Coit Tyler (New York, 1887) used W.W. Henry's work to sort out some of Wirt's excesses. R.D. Meade uncovered much new material for his two volumes (1957–69), which lack an interpretive focus. Richard Beeman's short study (New York, 1974) integrates Henry's life more successfully into the political history of the period, but insufficiently appreciates the significance of Henry's political style.

Passing details of Henry's life not otherwise cited may be assumed to come from Meade. Since W.W. Henry printed extracts of documents without indicating his editorial emendations, I have checked his versions against the surviving manuscript sources whenever possible.

Abbreviations for
Works Frequently Cited

AHR *American Historical Review.*
  BT Bancroft Transcripts [Virginia Official Correspondence], Library of Congress.
DHR John P. Kaminski and Gaspare J. Saladino, eds., *Documentary History of the Ratification of the Constitution* (Madison, Wisc., 1976–).
EDV Jonathan Elliott, ed., *Debates of the State Conventions on the Adoption of the Federal Constitution* . . . Philadelphia, 1866), Vol. 3 [Virginia].
EHD Merrill Jensen, ed., *English Historical Documents*, (*American Colonial Documents to 1776*) Vol. 9 (London and New York, 1955).
Force Peter Force, ed., *American Archives* . . . Fourth Series (6 vols., Washington, D.C., 1837–46).
GWFi John C. Fitzpatrick, ed., *Writings of George Washington* . . . (39 vols., Washington, D.C., 1931–44.)
GWFr Douglas Southall Freeman, *George Washington* (6 vols., New York, 1948–54).
  JCC Worthington C. Ford, ed., *Journals of the Continental Congress 1774–1789* (34 vols., Washington, D.C., 1904–37).
  JHB John Pendleton Kennedy and H.R. McIlwaine, eds., *Journals of the House of Burgesses* (13 vols; Richmond, 1905–15.) Not numbered consecutively by volume, but with chronological titles, e.g., *JHB 1766–69*. Since dates are clearly known from the text, this portion of the title is not given in the note.
  JHD *Journals of the House of Delegates of Virginia* . . . (Williamsburg, 1776–81; Richmond, 1781–).
  JNC *Journal of Nicholas Cresswell, 1774–1777* (New York, 1924).
  LC Library of Congress.
LCDi Jack P. Greene, ed., *The Diary of Colonel Landon Carter of Sabine Hall, 1752–1778* (2 vols., Charlottesville, 1965).
LDC Paul H. Smith, et al., eds., *Letters of Delegates to Congress, 1774–1789* (Washington, D.C., 1976–).
LFP Lee Family Papers, University of Virginia.
LPEP David J. Mays, ed., *Letters and Papers of Edmund Pendleton* (2 vols., Charlottesville, 1967).
  MG *Maryland Gazette.*
Mays David J. Mays, *Edmund Pendleton 1721–1803* (2 vols., Cambridge, Mass., 1952).
Meade Robert Douthat Meade, *Patrick Henry* (2 vols., Philadelphia and New York, 1957–69).

Morgan George Morgan, *The True Patrick Henry* (New York, 1907).

NYPL Rare Books and Manuscripts Division, New York Public Library, Astor, Lenox, and Tilden Foundations.

OL H.R. McIlwaine, ed. *Official Letters of the Governors of the State of Virginia. Vol. l: Patrick Henry* (Rich., 1926).

PGM Robert A. Rutland, ed., *The Papers of George Mason, 1725–1792* (3 vols., Chapel Hill, 1970).

PMHB Pennsylvania Magazine of History and Biography.

PJM William T. Hutchinson, et al., *The Papers of James Madison* (Chicago and Charlottesville, 1962–).

PTJ Julian P. Boyd, ed., *The Papers of Thomas Jefferson* (Princeton, 1950–).

Ran.Va. Arthur H. Shaffer, ed., Edmund Randolph, *History of Virginia* (Charlottesville, 1970).

Rev.Va. William J. Van Schreeven, comp., Robert L. Scribner and Brent Tarter, comps. and eds., *Revolutionary Virginia: The Road to Independence, A Documentary Record* (7 vols., Charlottesville, 1973–83).

RHLB James C. Ballagh, ed., *The Letters of Richard Henry Lee* (2 vols., New York, 1911–14).

Tr.Va. Rhys Isaac, *The Transformation of Virginia*, 1740–1790, (Chapel Hill, 1982).

UVa Manuscript Department, University of Virginia Library.

VG *Virginia Gazette*; (P) Purdie (PD) Purdie & Dixon (Pi) Pinckney (R) Rind, used to designate editions of similar date.

VHS Virginia Historical Society.

VIC *Virginia Independent Chronicle.*

VMHB *Virginia Magazine of History and Biography* (Rich., 1894–).

VSL Archives Branch, Virginia State Library, Richmond.

WWH William Wirt Henry, *Patrick Henry: Life, Correspondence, and Speeches* (3 vols., New York, 1891).

WMQ *William & Mary Quarterly*, series 1, 2, and 3.

Prologue

9. "INDIFFERENT" SOIL: 6–8 Jun. 1791; *GW Diaries* (Fitzpatrick, ed.) 4:197–98. Herbert C. Bradshaw, *History of Prince Edward County, Virginia* (Richmond, 1955); Norman K. Risjord, *Chesapeake Politics, 1781–1800* (New York, 1978). 45–61.

10. "DEMOCRATIC CHIEF"; Ran. Va., 168, 178.

12. PH DESCRIPTION: Archibald Alexander (1794), WWH 2:495; St. George Tucker (1773), WWH 1:126–27; Ran.Va., 180–81. PH

SPEECH: No copy of the speech survives. Henry's views are reconstructed from his speeches generally and commentary in correspondence. For flavor, direct quotations are borrowed from the ratifying convention debates, EDV 21, 44, 48, 52–57.

15. "TRUMPET OF DISCORD": GW to JM, 5 Feb. 1788, PJM 10:469; paragraph quotations: ER to JM, 27 Dec. 1787, PJM 10:346; JM to TJ, 19 Feb. 1788, PJM 10:520; J.B. Smith to JM, 12 Jun. 1788, PJM 11:120; Edw. Carrington to JM, 10 Feb. 1788, PJM 10:493–94; JM to ER, 10 Apr. 1788, PJM 11:19. "I CAN NOT FIND": Carrington to JM, 10 Feb. 1788, PJM 10:493–94; DHR 14:156–58 on separatist charges. "STRIKE AT ESSENCE" & "GREAT ADVERSARY": JM to TJ, 9 Dec. 1787, PJM 10:312.

16. ELECTION: sheriff's writ, 17 March 1788, VSL; Charles Sydnor, *Gentlemen Freeholders* (Chapel Hill, 1952). "OLD FELLOW": Hugh B. Grigsby, *The Virginia Convention of 1776* (Richmond, 1885), 152.

Chapter 1

19. "AIR OF OPULENCE": Edward Kimber (July 1746), WMQ (ser. 1) 15:223. GOVERNOR'S PALACE: Thomas Waterman, *The Mansions of Virginia, 1706–1776*, 31–44; Hugh Jones, *The Present State of Virginia* (1724), ed. Richard L. Morton (Chapel Hill, 1956), 189–90. Other mansions: Waterman, *passim*. The gentry's "state of emulation with one another in buildings": *American Husbandry* (1775) ed. Harry J. Carman (New York, 1939), 170.

22. "ALL THE WEALTH": Lewis Evans (1756), John Noble Wilford, *The Mapmakers* (New York, 1981), 191. Virginia's westward expansion: Richard L. Morton, *Colonial Virginia* (Chapel Hill, 1960), II, Chs. 13–14.

25. BYRD AT STUDLEY: 7–8 Oct. 1732, "A Progress to the Mines," Louis B. Wright, ed., *The Prose Works of William Byrd of Westover* (Cambridge, 1966), 375–76.

27. "BETWIXT DECKS": Edward M. Riley, ed., *The Journal of John Harrower* (Williamsburg, 1963), 24–25.

28. "AS BLACK": id. 76.

29. ST. ANDREW'S DAY: VG 7 Oct. 1737. Malcolm H. Harris, "The Port Towns of the Pamunkey," WMQ (ser. 2) 23:503–10, R.B. Lancaster, *A Sketch of the Early History of Hanover County, Virginia* (Hanover, 1976).

Chapter 2

32. "RED HOT COMET" and "RUEFUL CONFLAGRATION": Isaac Stiles (1743), Alan Heimart, *Religion and the American Mind* (Cambridge, 1966), 106.

33. "KIND OF LETHREGIE": Mary Dulaney to George Fitzhugh, 3 May 1787, Daniel Blake Smith, *Inside the Great House* (Ithaca, 1980), 78. "GENERAL STRAIN": Samuel Davies, *The State of Religion Among the Protestant Dissenters in Virginia* (1751), 8. Hanover revival: Donald G. Matthews, *Religion in the Old South* (Chicago, 1977), 14–22; William H. Foote, *Sketches of Virginia* (1850), 121–25, 134–37, 160–61; Wesley M. Gewehr, *The Great Awakening in Virginia*, (Durham, 1930), 40–67. "OUR PEOPLE": Heimart, 208.

34. "A STRANGER": Rev. Patrick Henry to Bishop of London, 13 Feb. 1744/45, WMQ (ser. 2) 1:263. "GOOD CHRISTIANS": Jones, *Present State*, 13. "NEW PREACHERS": WMQ (ser. 2) 1:261, 265. "A SET OF INCENDIARIES": Gewehr, 82. Rhys Isaac, "Religion and Authority: Problems of the Anglican Establishment in Virginia in the Era of the Great Awakening and the Parsons' Cause," WMQ (ser. 3) 30:3–36.

35. WHITEFIELD'S VISIT: Rev. Henry to Bishop of London, 14 Oct. 1745, WMQ 1:266–67. "THE CHURCH ITSELF": Lawrence A. Cremin, *American Education: The Colonial Experience* (New York, 1970), 271. "SCREW UP THE PEOPLE": Rev. Henry to Bishop of London, 8 June 1747, WMQ 1:273.

36. "INTEREST WITH COURT": Rev. Henry to Bishop of London, 22 Aug. 1751, WMQ 1:275. "AMBASSADOR": Foote, 221. "SWARMS": Matthews, 20. Davies: Gewehr, 68–99; George W. Pilcher, *Samuel Davies, Apostle of Dissent* (Knoxville, 1971). "WHERE I GO": (5 Sept. 1755), Pilcher, 86. PH and DAVIES: WWH 1:15; Meade 1:70–74.

37. "WILL BE FIXED": Davies, "The Universal Judgment," *Sermons on Important Subjects* (New York, 1854), 1:368. "UNEXPECTED SEPARATIONS": Davies, 1:371. "COLD OR HOT": Davies, "The Danger of Lukewarmness in Religion," 1:281. Evangelical oratory and Davies: Heimart, 223–233. "SKILLFUL PLEADER": Foote, 302. ORATOR: Morgan, 57–58.

38. ST. PAUL'S GALLERY: C.G. Chamberlayne, ed., *Vestry Book of St. Paul's Parish*, 187 (21 Jun. 1745). Anglican church-going, Tr.Va., chs. 4 and 6.

39. "ENCHANTING SOUND": Heimart, 228.

40. PH CHARACTER SKETCH: Spencer Roane and Samuel Meredith memos, printed in Morgan, 431–54, esp. 431, 437. Recollections of Nathaniel Pope and Charles Dabney are in Morgan, 30–31.

41. "ARE MORE INCLINABLE": Jones, 44; PH LEARNING: Roane, in Morgan, 448; Meade 1:55.

42. "KNEW HIS HORACE": VMHB 33:44–45. Nathaniel Pope to William Wirt, 27 Sept. 1805 (Wirt Papers, LC).

43. "RELUCTANCE TO CONFINEMENT": Harold Soltow, "Scottish

Traders in Virginia, 1750–75," *Economic History Review* (ser. 2) 12:83–98. *See also* Jacob Price, "The Rise of Glasgow in the Chesapeake Tobacco Trade," WMQ (ser. 3) 11:194–99.

44. SARAH SHELTON: Sketch in PH Museum, Red Hill, Va., artist and date unknown; R.D. Meade interview with William Shelton reports many generations of brown-eyed, brown-haired Sheltons, Meade Papers, n.d., Red Hill. Virginia courting: Smith, *Great House*, 130 ff. "EVERY GENTLEMAN HERE": "Letters from Lawrence Butler," VMHB 40:267.

45. LAND PROMISE: Louisa County Deed Books A & B, 22 Apr. 1758, VSL.

46. TOBACCO FARM: Blair Niles, *The James* (New York, 1935), 79–83.

47. "POOR PEOPLE": Francis Jerdone to Hugh Crawford, 10 Feb. 1756; "LAYING WASTE": Jerdone to Alex Spiers, 15 May 1756. Jerdone Letterbook, Swem Library, College of William and Mary. DAVIES SERMON: "Religion and Patriotism" in *Sermons* 3:43–44, 51–52.

48. "GENERALLY CLAD": William Winston, Meade 1:91. STOREKEEPING: reconstructed from PH Ledger Book, VSL.

50. TJ RECALLED: TJ to Wm. Wirt, 5 Aug. 1815, in PMHB 35:408.

Chapter 3

51. LAW TRAINING: Anton H. Chroust, *Rise of the Legal Profession in America* (Norman, Okla., 1965), 30–37, 262–93.

52. "I DO WISH": TJ to John Page, (25 Dec. 1762) PTJ 1:5.

53. "A LAWYER MUST": Catherine D. Bowen, *John Adams and the American Revolution* (Boston, 1950), 142–43.

54. "VIRTUOUS YOUNG MAN": Winston's memoir, VMHB 69:37.

55. WYTHE'S MILDNESS: Alonzo T. Dill, *George Wythe, Teacher of Liberty* (Williamsburg, 1979), 12.

56. WYTHE'S SIGNATURE: attested in Goochland County Order Book, 15 Apr. 1760, reprinted in *Tyler's Quarterly* 9:97. PH's license is not extant, but that of his contemporary, Paul Carrington, (also signed by Wythe in 1755) is at VHS, TJ's insistence in 1815 that Wythe had "absolutely refused" to sign the license (WWH 1:22) misled Wirt, Morgan, and many other biographers. Either TJ's memory failed him or he refused to entertain the idea that his own beloved teacher had once helped the man TJ had come to hate. RANDOLPH EXAM: Judge Tyler to Wirt, n.d., WWH 1:22–23.

57. SWEARING-IN: *Tyler's Quarterly* 9:97; Meade 1:98–99. On Court day and oaths: Tr.Va., 88–94. WINSTON WILL: Meade 1:103–4. FLYLEAF: WWH 1:10.

58. ACCOUNTS: Meade 1:112; Clement Eaton, "A Mirror of the Southern Colonial Lawyer," WMQ (3rd ser.) 8:520–34.   "EXCEPT

WHEN PATRICK": WWH 1:48.

59. PARSONS' CAUSE: WWH 1:32–46; Arthur P. Scott, "Constitutional Aspects of the Parsons' Cause," *Pol. Sci. Q.* 31:558–77; Glenn C. Smith, "The Parsons' Cause, *Tyler's Q.* 21:140–71, 291–306.

60. "AN ENTIRE STRANGER": Fauquier to Board of Trade (5 Jan. 1759), Morton 2:785.

61. "EACH INDIVIDUAL": Maury to John Fontaine, 15 June 1756, Ann Maury, *Memoirs of a Huguenot Family* (New York, 1853), 402. THOMAS JOHNSON: Rev. Maury had previously quarreled with his church warden Johnson, who caused a stir in church by ordering black slaves who had brought their children forward for baptism to step back until the ceremony for whites had ended. Maury to Rev. J—— D——, 10 Oct. 1759, Maury Papers, LC. PRESIDING JUDGE: Col. John Henry was not an attorney, but a justice of the peace in the tradition of the country squirearchy. *See* A.G. Roeber, "Authority, Law, and Custom: The Rituals of Court Day in Tidewater Virginia, 1720 to 1750," WMQ (3rd ser.) 37: 29–52.

62. JURY SELECTION: Rev. Maury to Rev. John Camm, 12 Dec. 1763, *Memoirs*, 419–20.

64. "AN INSTANCE OF MISRULE": Edmund Winston's paraphrase, VMHB 69:37. "THEIR OWN SAFETY": id. Henry's argument is also summarized in Maury to Camm, 12 Dec. 1763, *Memoirs*, 421–22.

65. "RAPACIOUS HARPIES": WWH 1:41.

66. "RECEIVED NO CHECK": Rev. William Robinson to Bishop of London, 17 Aug. 1764, in Perry, ed., *Historical Collections* 1:497. "PATRICK SPOKE": Winston recollection, VMHB 69:37. "UN-LOCKED THE HEART": Ran.Va., 179; Rhys Isaac, "Preachers and Patriots: Popular Culture and the Revolution in Virginia," in Alfred Young, ed., *The American Revolution* (Dekalb, Ill., 1976), 151–54.

Chapter 4

67. "WE IN AMERICA": quoted in *JHB 1761–65*, liii–liv. "I LOOK UPON": Morton 2:475–6.

68. HOUSE OF BURGESSES: S.M. Pargellis, "The Procedure of the Virginia House of Burgesses," WMQ (2nd ser.) 7:73–86, 143–157; Jack P. Greene, *The Quest for Power* (Chapel Hill, 1963); Greene, "Society, Ideology, and Politics: An Analysis of the Political Culture of Mid-Eighteenth Century Virginia," in Richard Jellison, ed., *Society Freedom, and Conscience* (New York, 1976), 14–64.

71. "ADMITTED TO HOUSE": JHB, 344–45. DOMINANT FAMILIES: Greene, "Foundations of Political Power in the Virginia House

of Burgesses," WMQ (3rd ser.) 10:485–506. Robinson: WWH 1:76; Ran. Va., 173–74; LCDi 1:83–86.

73. "Holds the Lamb": JHB *1756–61*, 90; "Whistle": Grigsby, *Convention of 1776*, 14.

74. "Remarkable exhibition": TJ account, WWH 1:76–77. "Men of rank": Ran.Va., 167.

75. "In conclave": Paul Carrington to Wm. Wirt., 3 Oct. 1815, Wirt Papers, LC.

76. "Nothing is further": House committee to the colony's agent in London, 12 Jul. 1764, VMHB 12:10. Petitions of November 1764: Rev. Va. 1:10–14. Edmund and Helen Morgan, *The Stamp Act Crisis* (Chapel Hill, 1953) remains standard; E. Morgan, ed., *Prologue to Revolution* (Chapel Hill, 1959) collects the documents.

78. Resolutions: The text presented here is a synthesis. The first five propositions come from the draft, in the handwriting of John Fleming, found among Henry's papers by his executors and bearing PH's endorsement on the reverse side. This draft is reprinted in Rev. Va. 1:17–18 and Morgan, *Prologue*, 48. The last two propositions appear in MG 4 July 1765, where they are clearly intended as clauses equally dependent upon the "Resolved therefore" that begins the final resolve in the draft endorsed by PH. His five propositions take up the full sheet; whether he lost a second sheet containing the remaining text is a matter of conjecture. I am convinced, from the Maryland text and surviving commentary discussed below, that the draftsmen conceived of the three clauses as a unit and submitted all (in one motion) to the House. Two centuries of argument among scholars as to whether five, six, or seven resolutions were introduced can be simplified, if not settled, by realizing that the "fifth" had three parts which may have fared differently once debate began. The tangled historiographic questions are surveyed in GWFr 3:592–95 and Morgan, *Crisis*, 124–32.

Chapter 5

81. "Immediately to consider": JHB *1761–65*, 358. Debate: Carrington to Wirt, 3 Oct. 1815, Wirt Papers, LC; TJ, WWH 1:82–83.

83. Excised preamble: My conjecture. The preamble appears neither in the House Journal nor PH's copy, but is printed in *Newport* (R.I.) *Mercury*, 24 Jun. 1765, reprinted Morgan, *Prologue*, 49. "In custody": JHB, 359.

84. Amended Fourth Resolve: Compare PH draft copy, Rev. Va.,

1:18 with JHB, 360. "Cool and deliberate" & "Paper'd resolutions": EP to JM, 21 Apr. 1790, *Md. His. Mag.* 66:76. Richard Bland, *An Inquiry into the Rights of the British Colonies* (1766), gives the moderates' argument, Rev. Va., 1:28–44, esp. 41–42.

85. "Torrents" & "Homer": TJ, WWH 1:82–83. "Plucked the veil" & "Style": Ran. Va., 168, 180.

86. "He had read": "Journal of a French Traveller in the Colonies, 1765," AHR 26:745. As reconstructed by Wirt, PH is supposed to have said "and George III may profit by their example!" Jefferson endorsed Wirt's version, but the Frenchman's account, written down that night rather than recalled forty years later, must take precedence. Carrington's recollection of "Mr. Henry's presence of mind in reply" to the Speaker's interruption is consistent with either version. Nowhere else does the record reveal an instance of wit comparable to what is attributed to PH in this speech. Further, it is not likely in 1765 that a colonist would have referred to the reigning monarch by name. PH's traditional retort, "If this be treason, make the most of it!", is equally spurious.

87. "If he had": AHR 26:745. "By God": TJ to Wirt, 4 Aug. 1805, in PMHB 34:389. Different results: Rev. Wm. Robinson to Bishop of London, 12 August 1765, Perry, *Historical Collections* 1:514–15, reported that the "concluding" resolve (which he quoted accurately) was rejected. The Frenchman heard this resolution discussed on the floor, but thought a majority approved it. AHR 26:746. TJ's reconstruction, to Wirt, 14 Aug. 1814, PMHB 34:398–99. The only major piece of evidence that contradicts the conclusion that all the known clauses went before the House is Governor Fauquier's report that the sponsors had two more stringent resolutions "in their pockets" which the close vote [on the "fifth"] deterred them from introducing. Fauquier to Board of Trade, 5 Jun. 1765, in JHB, lxvii–lxviii. No definitive solution is possible, but I suggest that Robinson might have deceived the governor on this point as part of the ensuing cover-up.

88. "Thumbing over": PMHB 34:399.

89. Missing page: Carrington to Wirt, 3 Oct. 1815, LC. "Uneasy, peevish": Fauquier, 14 Jun. 1765, C.O. 5/1345, BT. "Disappointed": AHR 26:746. "Young, hot & giddy": JHB, lxvii–lxviii.

90. "Sent to Tower": *London Gazette & Advertiser*, 13 August 1765, Meade 1:178. "Not Sparing Insinuations": *Historical Collections* 1:514–15. "Noble Patriot": AHR 26:747.

91. "Feasting": AHR 27:72; Boston toast: AHR 27:73.

92. "Alarm-bell": WWH 1:99; "Came Abroad": Mays 1:164. Colonial unity: AHR 27:75.

93. GAGE: reports to Secretary of State, 11 Oct., 4 Nov. 1765, *Corr. Gen. Gage* (Carter, ed.), 1:69–71.

94. "PREVENT ILL IMPRESS": House Committee, 14 Sept. 1765, reprinted in *Va. Hist. Mag.* 9:359. "GENIUS" & "PREVENT": MG 22 Nov. 1765; DUMFRIES PARADE: MG 12 Sept. 1765. WESTMORELAND: MG 17 Oct. 1765; Pauline Maier, *The Old Revolutionaries* (New York, 1980), 195–97.

95. "APPEARANCE OF COURTS": Pendleton to James Madison, Sr., 11 Dec. 1765, Mays 1:169. "A FERMENT": letter from *Bristol Journal* (10 Aug. 1765), VMHB 73:147. FAUQUIER: letters of 5 Jun., 14 Jun., 3 Nov. 1765, BT.

96. MERCER: Fauquier report, 3 Nov. 1765, JHB, lxviii–lxxi.

97. "NOT TREASON": MG 22 Aug. 1765; "VOLUNTARY PAYERS": Landon Carter, 30 Nov. 1765, VMHB 76:286. MAURY: to J. Fontaine, 31 Dec. 1765, *Memoirs*, 424. INTIMIDATE: John C. Matthews, "Two Men on a Tax," in Rutman, ed., *The Old Dominion* (Charlottesville, 1964), 96–108. "GREAT AND GLORIOUS": VG(P) 2 May 1766.

98. NORFOLK: VG(PD) 6 Jun. 1766. "LOYAL TOASTS": Mays 1:173.

Chapter 6

102. HUNTING: Morgan, 114: TJ to Wirt, 4 Aug. 1805, PMHB 34:394; LOUISA: Malcolm H. Harris, *A History of Louisa County* (Richmond, 1936). "PAHTRICK": Meade 1:342 cites this spelling on a Louisa County court document. *See* George Ancram to PH, 1775 in VHS, addressed to "Partrick Henry, Esq." The pronunciation still survives among Virginians. "NAITERAL PARTS": WWH 1:28. FEES: WMQ (3rd ser.) 8:532.

103. COURT CIRCUIT: *Virginia Almanac for 1766* (Williamsburg). "ORDINARY ENOUGH": JNC, 20.

104. "MAKE IMMEDIATE PAYMENT": VG(PD) 13 Jun. 1766; Scandal: Mays 1: Ch. 11, and Joseph Ernst, "The Robinson Scandal Redivivus," VMHB 77:146–73. "NO GREAT COMMAND": VG(PD) 15 Aug. 1766.

105. NEW NAMES: Mays 1:180–84.

106. NICHOLAS: to Col. Wm. Preston, 21 May 1766, Preston Papers, Draper Collection 2QQ97, is a sample of letter to burgesses; public pledge, VG (PD) 23 May 1766. FAUQUIER: to Board of Trade, 5 Jun. 1765, 11 May, 22 May 1766, BT.

107. "THE TREASURY OUGHT": Bland to RHL, 22 May 1766 (LFP, Reel 1). Bland said "the People" long suspected Robinson of making improper loans. "VIEWS OF CHAIR": Fauquier, 7 Apr. 1766, BT. *See* Greene, "The Attempt to Separate the Offices of Speaker and Treasurer in Virginia, 1758–1766," VMB 71:11–18. "CONFEDERACY": David Boyd to RHL, n.d., in Ernst, VMHB 77:166. "SALUTARY EFFECT": *NY Journal* 27 Nov. 1766.

108. "Is it not": VG(PD) 20 Jun. 1766. J. A. L. Lemay, "Robert Bolling and the Bailment of Col. Chiswell," *Early Am. Lit.* 99–142, and Carl Bridenbaugh, *Early Americans* (New York, 1981), Ch. 8.

109. "Must look": VG(PD) 19 Sept. 1766. "Most unhappy": VG (PD) 4 July 1766; diagram reprinted in Bridenbaugh, 190. "Partiality": VG(PD) 18 July 1766. Further quotations in paragraph from same source.

110. "Distrust": VG(PD) 12 Sept. 1766. "In parties": John Wayles to Farrell & Jones, 30 Aug. 1766, in VMHB 66:305.

111. "Nervous fits": VG(PD) 17 Oct. 1766. "Blood": Fauquier to Board of Trade, 8 Oct. 1766, BT.

112. "Last day": 20 Oct. 1766, in VG(PD) 11 Dec. 1766. Committees: JHB 1766–69, 14–15.

113. "Shall not": JHB, 24. RHL speech: Meade 1:210. Randolph's chagrin: VMHB 77:167.

114. "The advantages": JHB, 21, 55.

115. "He was pleased": 12 Dec. 1766, JHB, 74.

Chapter 7

116. "Wild colts": Morgan, 242.

117. "Never saw": TJ to Page, 20 Jan. 1763, PTJ 1:7. "The match": Henry to Christian, 12 Jan. 1768, WWH 1:222. "Greatly distressed": PH ledger memo, WWH 1:121.

119. "Neglects": to Crawford, 21 Sept. 1767, GWFi 2:467–71.

120. "Pardon me": PH to Fleming, 10 Jun. 1767, Henry Family Papers, VHS.

121. Shelton land: Lewis Summers, *History of Southwest Va.*, (Richmond, 1903), 45; copies of deeds in Chalkley, *Chronicles of Scotch–Irish Settlement in Va.* (Baltimore, 1905), 3:462, 478. "After many": PH ledger memo, WWH 1:121. Frontier trip: Route and quotations from "Journal of Dr. Thomas Walker, 1749–50," reprinted in Summers, 796–807.

123. "Precisely twenty": petition, 19 Dec. 1768, VSL.

124. "For fertility": James T. Flexner, *George Washington: The Forge of Experience* (Boston, 1965), 291. Curt reply: JHB, 287. "In obedience": VG(PD) 28 Dec. 1769.

126. "Sallie": Sarah Henry to Annie Christian, 13 Sept. 1771, W.W. Henry Papers, VHS.

127. "He could" & "better pleased": Roane, in Morgan, 439.

128. "A new path": Ran.Va., 178.

Chapter 8

129. "That side": GM to Committee of Merchants in London, 6 Jun. 1766, PGM 1:65–66. "Many acts": 6 Nov. 1766, JHB, 12.

130. "They have become": Fauquier to Shelburne, 27 Apr. 1767, C.O. 5/1345, BT. Declaratory act: EHD 9:695–96. "Experiment": PGM 1:70.
131. Grenville oath: Jensen, *The Founding of a Nation* (New York, 1968), 226.
132. Bland: Rev.Va. 1:41. "Snare" & "bird": *The Farmer and Monitor's Letters* (Williamsburg, 1769; Evans 11239), letters VII, XI. "Virtual obedience": Monitor, Letter III. "Flaming sword": 27 Mar. 1768, RHLB 1:26–27. "Flagitious attempt": EHD 9:716–17.
133. "A parcel": Jensen, *Founding*, 256. "Corruption": "Fabricus," VG(R) 19 Jun. 1768: Reprint: VG(PD) 4 Feb. 1768. "Five or six": 22 Jul. 1768, *Corr. Geo. III* (Fortescue ed.), 2:36. Instructions: 21 Aug. 1768, C.O. 5/1346, BT. Botetourt's appointment: John Brooke, *The Chatham Ministry* (New York, 1956), 366–69.
134. "All ranks": VG(PD) 27 Oct. 1768. Ode: VG(R) 3 Nov. 1768. Portrait of Botetourt, VMHB 63:378.
135. "I like": Bot., 1 Nov. 1768, C.O. 5/1346, BT. Cautionary notes: RHL to Dickinson, 26 Nov. 1768, RHLB 1:30–31; "Lip-loyalty": VG(R) 2 Feb. 1769. "Time-serving" & "silence": RHLB 1:30–31.
136. Atticus: VG(R) 4 May 1769.
136. "If the paper": 5 Nov. 1768, C.O. 5/1347, BT. "Never willingly": 17 Feb. 1769, C.O. 5/1347, BT.
138. "Lay claim": JHB, 188. Address: JHB, 188–89. Cf. Hillsborough's draft, 21 Aug. 1768, C.O. 5/1346, BT. "Wisdom": JHB, 199.
139. Four resolutions: 16 May 1769, JHB, 214.
140. Draft address: JHB, 215–16.
141. "I have heard": JHB, 218.
142. "Social privileges": RHL to Shelburne, 31 May 1769, RHLB 1:37. "Should scruple": GW to GM, 5 Apr. 1769, PGM 1:96.
143. Association: text and proceedings, Rev.Va. 1:73–77; evolution of plan, PGM 1:94–106. "Starving": "Atticus No. II," VG(PD) 11 May 1769.
144. Buys book: *Diaries of George Washington*, ed. Donald Jackson (Charlottesville, 1976–), 2:152–3.
145. PH recognized: mss. fragment, n.d., WWH 1:115–16.
146. "Don't you think": Meade 1:273. GW: GWFi 2:512–14. "If the acts": James Madison, Sr., to London merchants, 4 Aug. 1769, Madison Coll., Presbyt. Hist. Soc. Clavichord: TJ to Thos. Adams, 1 Jun. 1771, PTJ 1:71–72. Customs figures: Jensen, *Founding*, 355–57. Brave chain: "The Remembrancer, No. III," VG(R) 22 Feb. 1770.
147. "The Persons": Sainsbury, "The Pro-Americans of London,

1769 to 1782" 35 WMQ (3rd ser.) 433. PATRIOTIC NUMBER: Many radical groups attempted to drink forty-five toasts to "Wilkes and Liberty." Pauline Maier, *From Resistance to Revolution* (New York, 1972), 162–70.

148. "OPINIONS": 23 May 1769, C.O. 5/1347, BT. "THE KING WISHES": 17 July 1769, C.O. 5/1347, BT. "CONTRARY": 7 Nov. 1769, JHB, 227.

149. "A TRUE SENSE": VG(R) 5 Apr. 1770.

150. "SOME STATE TRICK": RHL to Arthur Lee, 5 Apr. 1770, RHLB 1:41.

150. "MEET PARLIAMENT HALF": LCD 1:418.

151. NY JOURNEY: based on journal of Dr. Robert Honyman (1775), published as *Colonial Panorama* (San Marino, 1939).

153. "WILKES OF AMERICA": Roger Champagne, *Alexander McDougall & the American Revolution in New York* (Schenectady, 1975), Ch. 3. PH MEETING: McDougall, "Diary of Political Activities in New York City, May–July 1770," McDougall Papers (reel 1), New York Historical Society.

154. FORTY-FIVE FRIENDS: Jensen, *Founding*, 343. COLDEN: to PH, 11 July 1770, C.O. 5/1349, BT. 12 July 1770, Minutes of Meeting, BT.

155. BOTETOURT FUNERAL: 18 Oct. 1770 VG(PD); Tr.Va., 326–28.

156. FATE HAD REMOVED: TJ recollections of 1825, *Writings* (Ford, ed.) 10:330.

Chapter 9

157. ANOTHER REVIVAL: Rhys Isaac, "Evangelical Revolt: The Nature of the Baptists' Challenge to the Traditional Order in Virginia, 1765–1775," WMQ 31:345–68; Tr.Va., 161–177; Gewehr, 106–37.

158. "WE ARE VERGING": VG(R) 5 Sept. 1771. "FORSAKE THEIR CHURCH": [John Randolph] "Address to the Anabaptists Imprisoned in Caroline," VG(PD) 20 Feb. 1772, L. P. Little, *Imprisoned Preachers and Religious Liberty in Virginia* (Lynchburg, 1938), 259.

159. JOHN IRELAND: Little, 163; JOHN WALLER: Little, 229–31. CHRONICLED MARTYRDOM: Little, 516–21.

160. PH DEFENSE: Foote, *Sketches*, 317. WEATHERFORD CASE: WWH 1:218.

161. "MAN OF MODERATION": Rachel Wilson diary notes, in M. Conway to W. W. Henry, 18 Sept. 1891, VHS. "HERBS OF HYPOCRISY": "Recipe to make an Anabaptist Preacher," VG(PD) 31 Oct. 1771.

162. RANDOLPH: "Address to Anabaptists," Little, 256–57. "INTOLERABLE": Gewehr, 128. "GENERAL TOLERATION": PH mss. fragment, n.d., WWH 1:112–116, is source for this paragraph; the crucial phrase "free exercise" is used by PH at WWH 1:116.

163. Henley: Isaac, Tr.Va., 219–20.

164. "It was represented": Nicholas, "To Hoadleianus," VG(R) 10 Jun. 1773. "Revolutions in opinion": "To A.W.," VG(R) 5 Mar. 1772. Nicholas reply: VG(R) 10 Jun. 1773.

165. Religious bill: text in VG(R) 26 Mar. 1772. Legislative history: VG(R) 10 Jun. 1773.

166. "Is there man": mss. fragment, n.d., WWH 1:116.

167. "Check so pernicious": JHB, 283–84. Overseer hostage: VG (R) 25 Jan. 1770.

168. PH on slavery: The most complete text is Meade 1:299–300, obviously copied from the mss., but no citation given. The version in WWH 1:152–53 is abbreviated without indication.

171. Wife's Illness: Meade 1:280. "Proper name": GM, 6 Dec. 1770, PGM 1:127–28. The story: Rev.Va. 2:3–5. Dunmore to Dartmouth, 31 Mar. 1773, in JHB, ix–xi.

173. "Damn Virginia": William Smith, *Historical Memoirs* (Sabine ed., New York 1969), 107. "Very goodnatured": Hugh Wallace to Wm. Johnson, 3 Jun. 1770, *Johnson Corr.* 7:711. Pranks: Richard Bland to Thomas Adams, 1 Aug. 1771, VMHB 6:127. "Great folks": John Watts to Wm. Johnson, 5 Jun. 1770, *Johnson Corr.* 7:713.

174. "As the proceedings": 10 Mar. 1773, JHB, 20. "Old members": TJ, "Autobiography," *Writings* (Library of America, ed., New York, 1984), 6. Resolutions: Rev.Va. 1:91.

175. "The duty": JHB, 22. Dunmore reply: JHB, 33.

176. "Use your endeavours": JHB, 36. Tucker: WWH 1:126–27.

177. Roane: Morgan, 442. "His imagination": Ran.Va., 179. "Boanerges, Son of Thunder": Roger Atkinson to Samuel Pleasants, 1 Oct. 1774, VMHB 15:356. "Boanerges" is Hebrew or Aramaic in origin; it had come to be used as a synonym for vociferous preaching or loud oratory. The Oxford English Dictionary records a 1778 usage with a distinctly political slant: "Boanergy on Mobs to make an Impression."

Chapter 10

181. "Hampden" & "Plan of Union": VG(PD) 11 Nov. 1773.

182. "Vociferators": *Journal and Letters of Philip Vickers Fithian, 1773–1774* (Farish ed., Williamsburg, 1965), 57. "The lords": VG(PD) 6 Jan. Boston news: VG(PD) 20 Jan. 1774.

184. "Ritt" Lee: Nickname used in William Shippen, Jr. to Thomas Lee Shippen, 29 Nov. 1787, Shippen Papers, LC. "Well-deserved fate": RHL to Sam Adams, 24 Apr. 1774, RHLB 1:106. "Tyrannic": RHL to Adams, 8 May 1774, RHLB 1:110.

185. "Bull-baiting" & rumors: VG(PD) 12 May 1774.
186. "Dangerous commotions": "Epitome of the Boston Bill," VG (PD) 19 May 1774. "Shock . . . astonishment": RHL to Adams, 26 Jun. 1774, RHLB 1:114. "Whenever they dare": VG(PD), 19 May 1774. Lord North: Arthur Lee to RHL, 18 Mar. 1774, in Force 1:228–29. "Gunpowder Tea" & "American Turkies": VG(PD) 26 May 1774.
187. Pendleton's view: EP to Jos. Chew, 20 June. 1774, LPEP 1:93–94. "Prepared with privacy": GM to Martin Cockburn, 26 May 1774, PGM 1:190.
188. Lee's sketch: RHL to S. Adams, 26 Jun. 1774, RHLB 1:115. "Rummaged": TJ, *Writings*, 8. Text: Rev.Va. 1:94–95.
189. "Not above" & "scheme calculated": R. C. Nicholas, *Considerations on the Present State of Virginia Examined*, Rev.Va. 1:283. "Your passions": PGM 1:190.
190. Dissolution: JHB, 132; TJ, *Writings*, 8. Dunmore to Earl of Dartmouth, 29 May 1774, Force 1:352. "Traitorously": Rev.Va. 1:96. Association: Rev.Va. 1:97–98.
191. "Feeble" & "dirty": RHL to S. Adams, 26 Jun. 1774, RHLB 1:114. "We flatter ourselves": 31 May 1774, Rev.Va. 1:102. "Piecemeals" & "god knows": GW to Geo. Fairfax, 10 Jun. 1774, GWFi 3:224.
192. Bundle of documents: texts, Rev.Va. 2:71–81; background, David Ammerman, *In the Common Cause* (New York, 1975), 24–34.
193. Division over tactics: James Parker to Charles Steuart, 7 Jun. 1774, Steuart Papers (microfilm) VSL; original collection in National Library of Scotland. Mason resolutions: PGM 1:191–92. Mobilization: VG(R) 16 Jun. 1774; *Pa. Journal* 7 Sept. 1774. Tr.Va., 243–55.
194. "Truth": VG(R) 14 Jun. 1774. County meetings: Rev.Va. 1: 109–69 gives reports from thirty-one counties; the proceedings of at least nine others are not extant. Caroline, Rev.Va. 1:114–16; Hanover, Rev.Va. 1:139–41.
196. "To feel how" & "greatest men encouraging": David Wardrobe to Archibald Provan, 30 Jun. 1774, Rev.Va. 2:135–36. Wardrobe's censure and apology, Rev.Va. 2:165. Randolph appeal: *Considerations on the Present State of Virginia*, Rev.Va. 1:206–18, esp. 207, 216–17.
197. Protesters' response: "W.H.O.," VG(R) 30 Jun. 1774; "The British American," VG(R) 16 Jun., 30 Jun., 28 July 1774, series reprinted, Rev. Va. 1:168–203. "Does it not": GW to Bryan Fairfax, 4 July 1774, GWFi 3:228–29. "A deeper tone": Ran.Va., 176–77, 181. Isaac, Tr.Va., 266–69. Harry S. Stout, "Religion,

Communications, and the Origins of the American Revolution," WMQ (3rd ser.) 34:519–41.

198. DUNMORE ORDERS: 10 Jun. 1774, Reuben Thwaites and Louise Phelps Kellogg, *Documentary History of Dunmore's War* (Madison, 1905), 33. JOINT SURVEY PARTY: Surveyor's journal, Thwaites and Kellogg, 110–33.

199. "EXPERT RIFLEMEN": Rev. Va. 1:199. THE SAME HORSES: GWFr 3:269–70. "HEAVEN ONLY KNOWS": Fithian, *Journal*, 122, 172–73.

200. "THE CONVENTION": J. Franklin Jameson, "On the Early Political Uses of the Word Convention," AHR 3:477–87. WHIG PRINCIPLES: Gordon S. Wood, *The Creation of the American Republic, 1776–1787* (Chapel Hill, 1969), 1–118. Lois G. Schwoerer, *The Declaration of Rights, 1689* (Baltimore, 1981). Trevor Colbourn, *The Lamp of Experience* (Chapel Hill, 1965).

201. AGREED TO CONGRESS: Rev.Va. 1:223–24. TWO RELATED PAPERS: Association (6 Aug. 1774), Rev.Va. 1:231–35; Instructions (6 Aug. 1774), Rev.Va. 1:236–39. A third document, purporting to be a draft of instructions but actually a bold pamphlet by TJ, was transmitted by messenger when TJ fell ill on his way to the convention. Excerpts were read to an approving audience one night at Peyton Randolph's house, but TJ was annoyed that PH (to whom he had sent a duplicate) did not formally ask the convention to endorse his paper. TJ, *Writings*, 9–10; Ran.Va., 205. Published immediately as *A Summary View of the Rights of British America*, the pamphlet had a great success and PH took copies with him to Philadelphia. Text in *Writings*, 105–22.

202. "PRESENT UNHAPPY SITUATION": Rev.Va. 1:231.

203. CONVENTION BALLOT: Rev. Va. 1:227–29.

204. AN INVITATION: GW to RHL, 7 Aug. 1774, GWFi 3:236.

Chapter 11

205. PH AT MT. VERNON: GW Diaries (ed. Jackson) 3:271–73; Flexner, *Forge*, 285–86. "LIKE A SPARTAN": Mays 1:278.

206. LYRICAL SEND-OFF: "Hail Sacred Liberty," VG(R) 1 Sept. 1774. HARD PACE: GW Diaries (ed. Jackson) 3:274–75.

207. "MASTERLY MAN": John Adams Diary [JADi], 3 Sept. 1774, LDC 1:7. "AS TRUE A TROUT": VMHB 15:356. STOUT VIRGINIA TALK: JADi, 2 Sept. 1774, LDC 1:7. CONGRESS DETRACTORS: [Jonathan Boucher] *Letter from a Virginian to Members of the Congress* (1774), 15 and passim.; T.B. Chandler, *The American Querist* (1774), 4.

208. PHILADELPHIA COMMITTEE: Rev.Va. 2:137–38, 145–55. Richard A. Ryerson, *The Revolution Is Now Begun* (Phila., 1978), 39–115.

209. PLAN UNFOLDED: JADi, 5 Sept. 1774, LDC 1:9–10; Robert Paine Diary, LDC 1:13. James Duane's Notes, LDC 1:25; Silas Deane to

Elizabeth Deane, LDC 1:20–23, which includes Randolph description. Lynch: Deane, 7 Sept. 1774, LDC 1:34.

210. DUANE INITIATIVE: LDC 1:10, 26. PH TOOK FLOOR: Thomson, WWH 1:219, delegate, LDC 1:62.

211. "ONE WOULD PROPOSE": Thomson, WWH 1:220. "THIS WAS THE FIRST": PH's speech and responses, JADi, LDC 1:10. "GRAND WITTENAGEMOOT": William Smith (1774), in Jack N. Rakove, *The Beginnings of National Politics* (New York, 1979), 38.

212. "MERE MILKTOASTS": Joseph Reed, Morgan, 157. "MORE SENSI-BLE": Caesar Rodney to Thomas Rodney, 9 Sept. 1774, LDC 1:58. "THE COMPLEATEST SPEAKER": Silas Deane to Eliz. Deane, 10 Sept. 1774, LDC 1:62. TUESDAY DEBATE: JADi, LDC 1:27–29; Duane's Notes, LDC 1:30–31.

214. "THE MINUTIAE OF RECTITUDE": Adams quotes PH as saying, "We must aim at the Minutiae of Rectitude" (LDC 1:29), but in context PH is ridiculing the claim that precise numbers were necessary. JOURNAL NOTED: JCC 1:25. BOSTON NEWS: LDC 1:27–49, *passim*.

215. PRAYER MOTION: JA to Abigail Abams, 16 Sept. 1774, LDC 1:74; JADi, 7 Sept. 1774, LDC 1:33; Deane, LDC 1:34.

217. COMMITTEE STALEMATE: Ammerman, 53–101, and Rakove, 42–62, interpret congressional politics. CONGRESS CONFINE ITSELF: 24 Sept. 1774, JCC 1:42.

218. PHILADELPHIA NEWSPAPERS: "Thieves, Pirates," *Pa. Packet* 3 Oct. 1774; "Very inoffensive," *Pa. Journal* 21 Sept. 1774; others reported, *Pa. Packet* 19 Sept. 1774; Wilkite crowd story, *Pa. Journal* 7 Sept. 1774. TO AWE COLONIES: *Pa. Journal* 7 Sept. 1774. "RUIN-OUS SYSTEM": JCC 1:76.

219. MILITANT PREPARATIONS: *Pa. Journal* 28 Sept. 1774; RHL to Wm. Lee, 20 Sept. 1774, LDC 1:87–88. "FIFTY . . . TEMPERS": JA to AA, 18 Sept. 1774, LDC 1:79. "WE SHALL SETT": Samuel Ward to Samuel Ward, Jr., 9 Sept. 1774, LDC 1:59. "GENTLEMEN . . . ENTERTAINING": Caesar Rodney to Thomas Rodney, 12 Sept. 1774, LDC 1:67. "MOST SINFULL FEAST": JADi, 8 Sept. 1774, LDC 1:45.

220. "MEMBERS OF CONGRESS": JA to AA, 8 Sept. 1774, LDC 1:49. STATE HOUSE PARTY: *Pa. Packet*, 19 Sept. 1774; Silas Deane to Eliz. Deane, 18 Sept. 1774, LDC 1:65.

221. WHARTON BREAKFAST: Thos. Wharton to Thos. Walpole, 23 Sept. 1774, PMHB 33:444–46. DINNER AT CHEW's: JADi, 22 Sept. 1774, LDC 1:90. "SLOW AS SNAILS": JA to AA, 25 Sept. 1774, LDC 1:99.

222. POSSIBLE ACTION: JA Notes, LDC 1:93–94. "WE DON'T MEAN": JA Notes, 26 Sept. 1774, LDC 1:104. PH & GALLOWAY: JA Notes, 28 Sept. 1774, LDC 1:111.

223. "LOYAL ADDRESS": 1 Oct. 1774, JCC 1:53. LEE'S MOTION: 3 Oct.

1774, LDC 1:141. DEBATE: Silas Deane Diary, 3 Oct. 1774, LDC 1:138–39. All PH quotations from this source, except "The present measures . . . ," which he first used in debate on 28 Sept., LDC 1:111.

225. "ART & ADDRESS": JA to AA, 29 Sept. 1774, LDC 1:128. "HORRID OPINION": JADi, 11 Oct. 1774, LDC 1:173.

226. CALLED THEIR BLUFF: JA to Edward Biddle, 12 Dec. 1774, LDC 1:265–66. Mass. delegates' view, JA to William Tudor, 7 Oct. 1774, LDC 1:156–57. "A GOOD UNDERSTANDING": 11 Oct. 1774, JCC 1:61. "BROUGHT OVER": Pa. Gazette 26 Oct. 1774. "AVOID WAR, IF POSSIBLE": JA to AA, 7 Oct. 1774, LDC 1:155.

227. "NIBBLING AND QUIBBLING": JADi, 24 Oct. 1774, LDC 1:236. "DRIVE US NOT TO DESPAIR": PH draft petition, LDC 1:222–25. Edwin Wolf 2nd, "The Authorship of the 1774 Address to the King Restudied," WMQ (3rd ser.) 22:189–224.

228. "ELEGANT ENTERTAINMENT": JADi, 20 Oct. 1774, LDC 1:221. "STRUGGLING THROUGH LIFE": JADi, 11 Oct. 1774, LDC 1:173. PH/JA FAREWELL TALK: JA to Wirt, 23 Jan. 1818, WWH 1: 239–40.

229. HAWLEY'S LETTER: "Broken Hints," C.F. Adams, Works of John Adams (Boston, 1856) 9:641–43. PH OUTBURST: WWH 1:239. "SENSIBLE OF PRECIPICE": JA to TJ, 12 Nov. 1813, Works 10:78. "ALTHO' OUR BELLIGERENT POW'RS": "Hail Sacred Liberty," VG (R) 1 Sept. 1774.

Chapter 12

230. "I ASSURE YOU": Sarah W. Henry to Anne Fleming, 15 Oct. 1774, WWH 1:249. "MY BROTHER PAT": Annie Christian to Anne Fleming, 15 Oct. 1774, Fleming Papers, Washington & Lee University. WIFE'S ILLNESS: Meade 1:280–83.

231. CHRISTIAN RECOUNTED BATTLE: based on William Christian to William Preston, 15 Oct. 1774, Thwaites and Kellogg, 261–66; Preston to PH, 31 Oct. 1774, Thwaites and Kellogg, 291–95.

232. "VERY ANIMATED SPEECH": Dabney to Wirt, 21 Dec. 1805, WWH 1:251–52. PH AT OVERTON'S: WWH 1:207–8.

233. "OUR PATRICK": Roger Atkinson to Samuel Pleasants, 1 Oct. 1774, 15 VMHB 356. LANDON CARTER HEARD: LCDi 2:860.

234. "SACRED TIES OF VIRTUE": James City County Committee, 25 Nov. 1774, Rev.Va., 2:177. "BUSY VOICE OF PREPARATION": William Eddis, Letters from America, ed. Aubrey C. Land (Cambridge, Mass., 1969), 100. "LIBERTY-MAD": JNC, 57. "THE SOLE RULE": Rev.Va., 2:177. "GOD DAM THE KING": VG(DH) 28 Jan. 1775. COMMITTEE SYSTEM: Rev.Va., 2:101–331 gives committee reports, Nov. 1774–Mar. 1775. Ammerman, 103–24. Isaac, "Dramatizing

the Ideology of Revolution: Popular Mobilization in Virginia, 1774–1776," WMQ (3rd ser.) 33:357–85.

235. "A LITTLE GOLD": 1 Dec. 1774, Rev. Va., 2:180–81. "UNGUARDED HEAT": 12 Nov. 1774, Rev.Va., 2:169–70. "CAN'T POOR DOGS": Mays, 1:227.

236. "UNSUPPORTABLE WEIGHT": 13 Oct. 1774, Rev.Va., 2:161. "THE GENTLEST MEASURES": Randolph to Henry Tazewell, 13 Feb. 1775, Rakove, 51. "AT A LOSS": Lord Dartmouth to Dunmore, 3 Mar. 1775, C.O. 5/1353, BT. CRITICS CHARGED: "trumpet," Chandler, 24; "inquisition," A. W. Farmer [Samuel Seabury], *The Congress Canvassed* (New York, 1774), 11, 17.

237. "AN ENTHUSIASM IN POLITICS": Jonathan Sewell to General Haldeman, 30 May 1775, Greene, ed., *Colonies to Nation: A Documentary History* (New York, 1967), 267. "TO PUBLIC SPEAKERS": Jonathan Boucher, *A View of the Causes and Consequences of the American Revolution* . . . (London, 1797), 320–21. "ACT THE HYPOCRITE": JNC, 46, 57. "RESUME IT & PLACE IT": John Adams, "Novangulus," 23 Jan. 1775, Robert J. Taylor, ed., *Papers of John Adams* (Cambridge, Mass., 1977) 2:230.

238. CITIZEN-SOLDIERS: George Mason, "Remarks to Fairfax Independent Company," ca. 17–26 Apr. 1775, PGM 1:229–31. Lawrence D. Cress, *Citizens in Arms* (Chapel Hill, 1982). "A WELL REGULATED MILITIA": VG(PD) 29 Dec. 1774; Rev.Va., 2:187. Fairfax County, 17 Jan. 1775, Rev. Va., 2:242–43.

239. DEANE LETTER: to PH, 2 Jan. 1775, *Collections of New York Historical Society*, 19:33–42. "ANOTHER TIER OF COLONIES": Deane's views on western settlement expressed earlier, to Samuel Adams, 13 Nov. 1774, LDC 1:261–62. FINCASTLE ADDRESS: 20 Jan. 1775, Rev. Va. 2:255–56. "PREPARED FOR EVERY": Rev. Va., 2:325. "MOST FORMIDABLE INFANTRY" etc: RHL to Arthur Lee, 24 Feb. 1775, LDC 1:313–14.

240. "OTHER PURPOSES OF PUBLIC SECURITY": id. LDC 1:314. "NOT A JUSTICE": Dunmore to Dartmouth, 24 Dec. 1774, Force, 1:1062. "DISTRAUGHT OLD MAN": Meade 2:16.

241. "THE POOR CALEDONIANS": Virginius Dabney, *Richmond: The Story of a City* (New York, 1976), 21. CONVENTION DELEGATES: Rev. Va., 2:334–36.

242. "A ROD IN PISS": Adam Stephen to RHL, 1 Feb. 1775, LFP. RUMORS FLEW: Dunmore to Dartmouth, 14 Mar. 1775, C.O. 5/1353, BT. James Parker to Charles Steuart, 6 Apr. 1775, Steuart Papers (microfilm), VSL.

243. "WE ARE TO BE TREATED": Peyton Randolph to Landon Carter, 6 Jan. 1775, Rakove, 69–70. PH PROPOSED: Convention Journal, 23 Mar. 1775, Rev.Va., 2:366.

244. FIERCE DEBATE: Rev.Va., 2:368; EP to William Preston, 30 Mar.

1775, LPEP 1:100; Parker to Steuart, 6 Apr. 1775. "THE ILLUSIONS OF HOPE": Quotations in this paragraph and the two following are from the version prepared by Wirt from St. George Tucker's recollections, WWH 1:261–64. "DOOM OF FATE": Tucker, WWH 1:265. "HIS PURE SELF": Ran.Va., 212.

245. "A TYRANT, A FOOL": This paragraph from Parker to Steuart, 6 Apr. 1775. "SHALL WE GATHER": This paragraph, and the four following, from WWH 1:265–66. Gestures described, WWH 1:268–70. "LIBERTY OR DEATH": David A. McCants, "The Authenticity of William Wirt's Version of Patrick Henry's 'Liberty Or Death' Speech," VMHB 87:387–404, defends the accuracy of Wirt's reconstruction, which I have followed, with the exception of one interpolated passage derived from Parker. For the authenticity of gestures, see Gilbert Austen, *Chironomia, or A Treatise on Rhetorical Delivery* (1806) eds. M.M. Robb and L. Thonssen (Dekalb, Ill., 1966). For this reference, as well as stimulating conversation on baroque gesture and style, I am indebted to Nicholas McGegan.

246. "DIGNITY OF CATO": Tucker, WWH 1:264. "AWFUL CADENCE": John Roane, WWH 1:270. "QUESTION" & "ACT": WWH 1:262. "LET ME": Edward Carrington's wish was granted at his death in 1810, WWH 1:270. DEBATE RESUMED: Ran. Va., 212. AMENDMENT: Rev.Va., 2:369, italics in original.

247. COMMITTEE PLAN: Rev.Va., 2:374–75. "FLATTENED THEIR ARDOR": Parker to Steuart, 6 Apr. 1775. CONVENTION BUSINESS: Three resolutions, Rev.Va., 2:376.

248. "YOU NEVER HEARD": Parker to Steuart, 6 Apr. 1775. "THIS IS NOT": Samuel Adams to RHL, 21 Mar. 1775, LDC 1:321–22.

Chapter 13

250. "FIRST PUBLIC INSULT": Hugh Mercer to GW, 25 Apr. 1775, Force, 2:387. DUNMORE'S ANGER: Deposition of William Pasteur, 14 Jun. 1775, JHB, 231. "THE GOVERNOR CONSIDERS": Peyton Randolph to Mann Page, Jr., et al., 27 Apr. 1775, Rev.Va., 3:63–64.

251. PROCLAIMED APPOINTMENT: 28 Mar. 1775, Rev.Va., 3:29. "EVERY MAN": Michael Wallace to Gustavus Wallace, 14 May 1775, Wallace Family Papers, UVa. "BAND OF ASSASSINS": James Parker to Charles Steuart, 12 Jun. 1775, Steuart Papers (microfilm), VSL.

252. "TO BE IN READINESS": 29 Apr. 1775, Rev. Va., 3:71. "THE THIRD DAY": Michael Wallace, 14 May 1775. "TELL THEM": WWH 1:279.

253. "1500 MEN": Richard Caswell to William Caswell, 11 May 1775, LDC 1:339. "INVESTED HUNTING SHIRT": Samuel Meredith's nar-

rative, n.d., Morgan, 205–7, also describes the ensuing march. Hanover Committee narrative, 9 May 1775, Rev.Va., 3:110–12.

254. "ALL WELL ACCOUTRED": VG(P) 5 May 1775. "RAPID RECURRENCE": 3 May 1775, Rev.Va., 3:80–81. THREATS: Dunmore to Dartmouth. 1 May 1774, JHB, xix.

255. "GOOD OLD SPEAKER": VG(P) 12 May 1775. BRAXTON: Rev.Va., 2:342–43.

256. HENRY REFUSED: Meredith narr., Morgan, 206–7. "MAN OF DESPERATE": Dunmore, Rev. Va., 3:9, 11.

257. HENRY'S RECEIPT: 4 May 1775, Rev. Va., 3:87–88. "AFFAIR . . . NOW SETTLED": PH to Nicholas, 4 May 1775, Rev. Va., 3:88. "FRIEND TO ORDER": "Civis," 29 Apr. 1774, Force, 2:442. Nicholas "is in a terrible panic, writing letters all over the Country, to prevent" protests. Parker to Steuart, 6 May 1775, Steuart Papers, VSL.

258. "JUDGED IT BEST": Hanover report, 9 May 1775, Rev. Va., 3:111. "ELOQUENT EXPRESSION": Philip Mazzei, *My Life and Wanderings*, ed. Margherita Marchione (Morristown, N.J., 1980), 217. DUNMORE OFFICIALLY: Proclamation, 6 May 1775, Rev.Va., 3: 100–101.

259. "PHRENZY OF REVENGE": TJ to William Small, 7 May 1775, PTJ 1:165–66. HENRY IMPLORED LEE: PH to Francis L. Lee, 8 May 1775, LFP.

260. "GREAT NUMBER": Charles Dabney to Wirt, 21 Dec. 1805, LC. "WE TAKE THIS": Orange Co. Committee to PH, 9 May 1775, PJM 1:147. PH REPLY: 11 May 1775, PJM 1:147 n.1. "GAINED HIM GREAT HONOR": JM to Bradford, 9 May 1775, PJM 1:144–45.

261. "MARTIAL SPIRIT": LDC 1:340, 344, 364. "THEY HAVE 28": Richard Caswell to William Caswell: 11 May 1775, LDC 1:340. "CARRIED AWAY" & "UNIFORMS": JA to James Warren, 21 May 1775, LDC 1:364. "DRUM & FIFE": Silas Deane to Eliz. Deane, 12 May 1775, LDC 1:347.

262. "WITHOUT DRAWING": Thomas Johnson, Jr., to Samuel Purviance, Jr., 18 May 1775, LDC 1:357. "AS I NEVER": GW to Fairfax Committee, 16 May 1775, LDC 1:354. "MEN WOMEN & CHILDREN": William Hooper to Samuel Johnston, 23 May 1775, LDC 1:399.

263. "THE ANSWER": John Dickinson to Arthur Lee, 29 Apr. 1775, LDC 1:331. "BILL OF RIGHTS": Silas Deane Diary, 23 May 1775, LDC 1:371. "LOST HIM CONFIDENCE": Meade 2:60. PENDLETON RECOMMENDED: EP to William Woodford, 30 May 1775, LPEP 1:103.

264. "I AM NOT": Thomas Johnson, Jr., to Horatio Gates, 3 May 1775, LDC 1:334. "NOT INCOMPATIBLE": JCC 2:65. SMALLPOX: LDC 1:407, 420. A Rhode Island delegate, Samuel Ward, took no treatment and died of smallpox while attending Congress in

March, 1776. "He never would harken to his Friends who have been constantly advising him to be inoculated ever since the first Congress began." JA to AA, 29 Mar. 1776, LDC 3:460.

265. INDIAN AFFAIRS: JCC 2:93, 174–77.

266. "GELD ALL MALES": Franklin, in Charles Royster, *A Revolutionary People At War* (Chapel Hill, 1979), 10. "A LARGE FLEET": JA to AA, 17 Jun. 1775, LDC 1:497. "IS ALL EXTRAVAGANT": JA to James Warren, 24 July 1775, LDC 1:658.

267. "MAKE YOURSELVES SHEEP": BF to Humphrey Marshall, 23 May 1775, LDC 1:395. "IN THE FLUCTUATION": PH to GW, 31 July 1775, WWH 1:305.

Chapter 14

268. "HARD DUTY": GM to Martin Cockburn, 24 July 1775, PGM 1:241. "PARTYS & FACTIONS": GM to GW, 14 Oct. 1775, PGM 1:255.

269. "WE ARE OF": Robert Carter to Landon Carter, 5 Aug. 1775, Sabine Hall Papers, UVa. "IT IS CONSIDERED": Id., 29 July 1775. "WAS VERY UNFIT": "Cato," Force, 4:1519.

270. "A GREAT PUSH": GM to Cockburn, 5 Aug. 1775, PGM 1:245. "WE HAVE CHOSEN": Carter, 5 Aug. 1775. "A VERY IMPROPER PERSON": Walker Maury to St. George Tucker, 24 Aug. 1775, Tucker–Coleman Papers, William & Mary College. "PURCHASED A TON": Carter, 10 Aug. 1775, Sabine Hall Papers, UVa.

271. "KNOWS US BETTER": 19 Jun. 1775, Rev.Va., 3:209. "A CERTAIN PATRICK": VG(Pi), 25 May 1775. "EVERY ORDINANCE": GM to GW, 14 Oct. 1775, PGM 1:255.

272. "FATHER AND MOTHER": GM to William Ramsey, PGM 1:239; on election, GM to Cockburn, 22 Aug. 1775, PGM 1:250. "ARTFUL TALK": Rev.Va., 3:422 n.3. "THE NECESSITY FOR": Carter, 10 Aug. 1775.

273. "THE RISEING WORLD": Royster, 8. SUPPORTER INNOCENTLY SAID: "Cato," Force 4:1519. "IN THE BEGINNING": JA to AA, 13 Feb. 1776, LDC 3:241.

274. "FAITHFUL AND TRUE": *Proceedings of the Convention of Delegates, July 1775* (Richmond, 1816), 39. PARCHMENT COMMISSION: Rev.Va., 4:125; text, Rev.Va., 3:498. "PAID HIM EVERY": WWH 1:320.

275. "AT LEAST FIVE FEET": recruiting form, 1775, LPEP 1:146. NOSE-SHAPED TARGET: John Harrower, 28 Aug. 1775, Journal, 111. "THE PEOPLE RIPE": JNC, 127. "A PARTICULAR OBSERVANCE": PH, 10 Oct. 1775, "The Orderly Book of the 2nd Virginia Regiment, 1775–76," ed. Brent Tarter, VMHB 85:165. Tarter, 156–183, for

orders cited in this paragraph, and the four following. Royster, 25–60.

278. "TO BE ATTENTIVE": Orders to Woodford, 24 Oct. 1775, Rev.Va., 4:271. "SAME REGARD": Tarter, VMHB 85:175. "MARK OF SUSPICION": Page to PH, 4 Nov. 1775, Rev. Va., 4:321.

279. "FATHER OF HIS COUNTRY": VG(Pi) 1 Jun. 1775. HENRY ORDERED: Tarter, VMHB 85:180. DUNMORE'S PROCLAMATION: 7 Nov. 1775, Rev.Va., 4:334. "LAWLESS BANDITTI": George Rae to John Rae, 7 Nov. 1775, Rev.Va. 4:337. On Randolph, Robert Shedden to John Shedden, 9 Nov. 1775, Rev. Va. 4:354. "BRACING UP": EP to TJ, 16 Nov. 1775, LPEP 1:130. "FATAL TO PUBLICK": PH broadside, 20 Nov. 1775, Rev.Va. 4:435–36.

280. "RESENT POINTING": Cary to RHL, 24 Dec. 1775, LFP. "NOT HEARING": PH to Woodford, 6 Dec. 1775, Rev.Va. 5:68.

281. "GREATEST PART": Woodford to EP, 4 Dec. 1775, Rev.Va. 5:50–51. "WHICH NO DOUBT": Woodford to PH, 7 Dec. 1775, Rev.Va. 5:77–78.

282. "TREAT THE BUSINESS": Jones to Woodford, 13 Dec. 1775, WWH 1:341. "INTERRUPTED BY": EP to Woodford, 7 Dec. 1775, Rev.Va. 5:76. "SECOND BUNKER'S HILL": Woodford to EP, 10 Dec. 1775, Rev.Va. 5:105 n.19. "THAT COLONEL WOODFORD": 22 Dec. 1775, Rev.Va. 5:221.

283. "INTERMEDDLE . . . LEST": EP to Woodford, 24 Dec. 1775, LPEP 1:141. "AN INDISPOSITION": PH to EP, 23 Dec. 1775, WWH 3:5.

284. "I THINK MY COUNTRYMEN": GW to Joseph Read, 7 Mar. 1776, WWH 1:345. PH FAREWELL: VG 1 Mar. 1776, Force 4:1516.

285. "NOISE IN COUNTRY": EP to Woodford, 16 Mar. 1776, LPEP 1:158. "YOUR ELOQUENCE FIRST": Force 4:1516–17. "THE FRINGE": LPEP 1:158. "OCCASIONED PRINCIPALLY": Leven Powell, Mays 2:91. "ENVY SOUGHT": "An Honest Farmer," VG(P) 8 Mar. 1776, Force 4:1518–19. "ABLE STATESMAN": Id.

Chapter 15

286. "THE TIME HATH FOUND US": Thomas Paine, *Common Sense* (ed. Isaac Kramnick, Penguin, 1976), 100. Subsequent quotations in this paragraph, and the three following, are from pp. 81, 91, 81, 78, 98, 91, 120.

287. "A GREAT NOISE": 19 Jan. 1776, JNC, 136.

288. "THE SOUND DOCTRINE": GW to Joseph Reed, 31 Jan. 1776, William B. Reed, *Life of Joseph Reed* (Philadelphia, 1847), 1:148. "SHALL WE NEVER": Col. Stephen Moylan to Joseph Reed, 30 Jan. 1776, Reed, 1:160. "BUT GENTLY TOUCHED": Nelson to Page, 13 Feb. 1776, LDC 3; 249. "OUR ARMY": Page to RHL, 12 Apr.

1776, LFP, for all quotations in paragraph, except "Stupid Security," to RHL, 19 Feb. 1776 (LFP).

289. "DESPERATELY INFECTED": Charles Lee to RHL, 5 Apr. 1776, LFP. "WHEN INDEPENDENCE WOULD": VG(P) 12 Apr. 1776. "A GOOD NIGHT": Cumberland County Comm., 22 Apr. 1776, Rev.Va., 6:433. "MUCH PUSHED" & "MANY NEW ONES": Robert Brent to RHL, 28 Apr. 1776, LFP.

290. "YOU WILL FIND": Thomas Lee to RHL, 13 Apr. 1776, LFP. "I AM WELL": RHL to PH, 20 Apr. 1776, LDC 3:563–65. All quotations in this paragraph and the next. "THOSE WHO WISH DELAY": RHL to Charles Lee, 11 May 1776, LDC 3:655.

291. "WE CONTINUE": JA to Joseph Palmer, 2 Apr. 1776, LDC 3:473. HENRY UNDERSTOOD: PH to JA, 20 May 1776, WWH 1:412–13. ADAMS REPLIED: JA to PH, 3 Jun. 1776, LDC 4:122–23. "THE HIGHEST OPINION": Charles Lee to PH, 7 May 1776, Collections of New York Historical Society, 5:1–3.

292. "PERMIT ME": EP to Convention, 6 May 1776, Rev. Va. 7:27. RESOLUTION HENRY DRAFTED: WWH 1:394–95.

293. "WITH THE CORDIALITY" & PH SPEECH: Ran.Va., 250. "SAYING A GREAT DEAL": J.A. Washington to RHL, 18 May 1776, LFP. "I think almost every Man except the Treasurer is willing to declare for independency." John Page to RHL, 12 Apr. 1776, LFP.

294. "HAD HELD HIS TONGUE": Washington, 18 May 1776, LFP. PENDLETON COMPOSITE: 15 May 1776, Rev.Va. 7:142–43. "TO CONTRADICT": GM to RHL, 18 May 1776, PGM 1:271. "Not QUITE SO POINTED": PH to JA, 20 May 1776, WWH 1:412. "TEDIOUS": GM to RHL, PGM 1:271. "IT MIGHT HAVE BEEN": Washington, 18 May 1776, LFP. "THAT PEREMPTORY": Thomas Lee to RHL, 18 May 1776, LFP. "PRINCIPLES NOW STALKED": Ran.Va., 251.

295. IMPROMPTU CELEBRATION: Thomas Lee, 18 May 1776; VG(P) 16 May 1776. FAST DAY: Id.; Rev.Va. 7:63–64 n.13. "GRAND WORK" & "TOO GREAT A BIAS": PH, 20 May 1776, WWH 1:411. "MY MOST ESTEEMED": PH, 20 May 1776, WWH 1:413. "A CERTAIN JUNTO": Thomas Lee to RHL, 1 Jun. 1776, LFP. BRAXTON MODEL: [Carter Braxton] An Address to the Convention of . . . Virginia . . . By A Native Of That Colony, (Philadelphia, 1776), Rev.Va., 6:518, 521.

296. "A DEMOCRACY CONSIDERED": EP to Carter Braxton, 12 May 1776, LPEP 1:177. "I SUSPECT HIS": PH to JA, 20 May 1776, WWH 1:413. "DELUSIVE BAIT": Braxton to Landon Carter, 14 April 1776, LDC 3:522. "TO FORM OUR PORTRAIT": PH, 20 May 1776, WWH 1:413.

297. "THE DONS": JA to PH, 3 Jun. 1776, LDC 4:123. "I OWN MYSELF": PH, 20 May 1776, WWH 1:411. "GREATEST LAWGIVERS": Adams, "Thoughts," Rev.Va., 6:413. "NO COLONY": JA to AA, 17 May 1776, LDC 4:18.

298. "IT IS CERTAIN": JA to James Sullivan, 26 May 1776, LDC 4:73. "REMEMBER THE LADIES": AA to JA, 31 Mar. 1776, *Adams Family Correspondence*, ed. Lyman C. Butterfield (Cambridge, 1963) 1:370. JA reply, 14 Apr. 1776, LDC 1:520. "OLD AND YOUNG": JA, 26 May 1776, LDC 4:73. "ALL THE MISCHIEFS": Braxton, Rev.Va. 6:522. "THE MOB": Gouverneur Morris to John Penn, 20 May 1774, EHD 9:861–62.

299. "AS THE BASIS": Declaration of Rights, draft, 27 May 1776, Rev.-Va. 7:271. "ALL MEN ARE BORN": Id. Remainder of paragraph, Rev.Va. 7:271–72.

300. "STUMBLING AT THE THRESHOLD": Thomas Lee, 1 Jun. 1776, LFP. NICHOLAS OBJECTIONS: Rev.Va. 7:454 n. 16; Ran.Va., 253. "NUMBER OF ABSURD": Thomas Lee, 1 Jun. 1776, LFP. Ran.Va., 253.

301. "TO VARY THE LANGUAGE" & PENDLETON FORMULA: Rev.Va. 7:454 n.16.

302. "GREAT LAW OF NECESSITY": PGM 1.278, 281. "HAVE AND ENJOY": VG(R) 26 Mar. 1772.

303. "DIABOLICAL HELL": JM to William Bradford, 24 Jan. 1774, PJM 1:106: MADISON'S AMENDMENT: PJM 1:174–75. The editors designate the interlinear text as "B." A separate paragraph Madison wrote at the bottom of the sheet is designated "A." It is a slight variant of the "free exercise" amendment, with a second clause prescribing that "no men or class of men ought, on account of religion, to be invested with peculiar emoluments or privileges, nor subject to any penalties or disabilities unless under &c." In the margin JM wrote, many years later, "Suggested by J.M. & follows the clause finally agreed to." By hypothesizing that "follows" may be read as "includes," the editors conclude that this amendment must have been written earlier. (PJM 1:179 n.5 and photograph of the manuscript sheet, PJM 1:164.) My view is that JM worked on the "emoluments" clause after the substitution of "free exercise" was accomplished, but this later suggestion never came to the floor. I think that designations "A" and "B" should be reversed. Madison's own recollection, while confused in some respects, emphasizes his primary concern for altering "toleration" to "free exercise." PJM 1:177. "HENRY SPONSORED": Ran.Va., 254. The much-repeated argument that PH backed away from supporting what PJM terms "A" (the "emoluments" clause) and that Madison then turned to Pendleton for help on the less comprehensive "B" proposal is purely conjectural. Rev.Va. 7:457 n.33 thoroughly discounts Pendleton's involvement; Randolph says plainly that the free exercise clause was sponsored by PH. "MADE BY THE REPRESENTATIVES": Rev.Va., 7:499. "SHOULD NOT . . . VIOLATE": Ran.Va., 255.

304. "HETEROGENIOUS, JARRING": GM, 18 May 1776, PGM 1:271. "READ WITH GREAT": PH, 20 May 1776, WWH 1:411.

305. "THERE IS NO GOOD": [John Adams], *Thoughts on Government* (Philadelphia, 1776), Rev.Va. 6:408–14, for this, and quotations in the following paragraph. "IT WILL BE SAFEST": JA, *Thoughts*, Rev.Va. 6:410. "ALL MEN": Declaration of Rights, Rev.Va. 7:449. "SHALL REMAIN": Plan of Government, 29 Jun. 1776, Rev.Va. 7:651.

306. "VERY MUCH OF": RHL to Charles Lee, 29 Jun. 1776, RHLB 1:203. For the synonymous use of "republican" and "democratic," *see* Willi Paul Adams, *The First State Constitutions* (Chapel Hill, 1980), 106–12. "WHERE ANNUAL ELECTIONS": Adams, *Thoughts*, Rev.Va. 6:411. HENRY CONTESTED: Ran.Va., 255–56.

307. "FOR THOSE WHO PUSHED" & REPLY: WWH 1:446. "I LAMENT MY": PH to Convention, 1 July 1776, Rev.Va. 7:666.

308. "IF HE SHOULD": Page to TJ, 6 July 1776, PTJ: 1:455. GOVERNOR'S OATH: *Proceedings of the Convention of Delegates . . . 1776* (Richmond, 1816), 7.

Chapter 16

311. "WE SHALL NOW": 3 Jul. 1776, LCDi 2:1052. "WE OUGHT TO LOOK": 13 Jul. LCDi 2:1057. CARTER'S JEALOUSY: 14 Jul. 1776, LCDi 2:1057.

312. "UNSPEAKABLE PLEASURE": 12 Aug. 1776, WWH 1:455. PH REPLY: 13 Aug. 1776, WWH 1:456. "ONCE HAPPY UNDER": WWH 1:453. WOODFORD'S NOTE: VG(P) 9 Aug. 1776; WWH 1:454. "THE REMEMBRANCE": WWH 1:454.

313. PUBLIC READINGS: VG(DH) 10 Aug. 1776.

314. "AS A LAWYER": PH to RHL, 20 May 1776, WWH 1:410.

315. "A DETACHED PEOPLE": "George Rogers Clark Papers, 1771–1781," *Collections of Illinois State Historical Library*, 8:213. "IF A CUNTRY": Id.

316. "THE SPICE": Roane memo, Morgan 448.

317. "FROM MORNING TILL": PH to RHL, 9 Jan. 1777, OL, 90.

318. "DIGNITY" & "HENRY-TOWN": Carter to GW, 31 Oct. 1776, Force (5th ser.) 2:1305–6. "SON ALTESSE ROYALE": Moses Coit Tyler, *Patrick Henry* (New York, 1887), 271. "TINSEL EPITHETS" & "IF I SHOULD": Charles Lee to PH, 29 Jul. 1776, WWH 3:9. "NOT QUITE SO": Roger Atkinson to Samuel Pleasants, 23 Nov. 1776, 15 VMHB: 357.

319. "LOW STATE": 30 Oct. 1776, OL, 59.

320. "ONE HUNDRED SAIL": 21 Nov. 1776, OL, 65. "THE GOVERNOUR": OL, 66. "THE GAME IS": GW to J.A. Washington, 18 Dec. 1776, GWFi 6:398. "OUR WORTHY COUNTRYMEN": PH to TJ, 19 Dec. 1776, PTJ 1:658. (Copies to every county).

321. "THE PRESENT DANGER": draft resolution, 21 Dec. 1776, PGM

1:326. "ADDITIONAL POWERS": PGM 1:327 n. "OUR PEOPLE": PH to RHL, 9 Jan. 1777, OL, 90. "EVERY POSSIBLE METHOD": PH to RHL, 20 Mar. 1777, OL, 126.

322. "CAN YOU TELL US": PH to RHL, 28 Mar. 1777, OL, 129. AD-DRESSED APOLOGIES: PH to GW, 29 Mar. 1777, OL, 130–31. "UN-EASY, IMPATIENT": GW to PH, 13 Apr. 1777, WWH 3:60–61. "BY COERCIVE METHODS": GW to PH, 17 May 1777, WWH 3:70. "GREAT EXERTIONS": PH to Adam Stephen, 31 Mar. 1777, OL, 133.

323. TUCKER WAITED UPON: WWH 2:37. "ON THE CHEAPEST": PH to county lieutenants, 29 Mar. 1777, OL, 131–32. "IF THE INDIANS": PH to Col. David Rogers, 27 Mar. 1777, OL, 128.

324. "BUT OUR FAMILY": Annie Christian to PH, 22 May 1777, WWH 3:72–73.

325. "ENJOY[ED] HER OWN": Dorothea Dandridge to Frances Thornton, 12 Jun. 1778, VHS. "I CAN'T THINK": Christian to PH, 12 Aug. 1777, WWH 3:88.

326. "THE CRADLE BEGAN": Hugh B. Grigsby, History of Virginia Federal Convention of 1788 (Richmond, 1891), 1:42 n. 48; Meade 1:280. "HEARTY CONGRATULATIONS": VG(DH) 31 Oct. 1777.

327. "CANNONS ROARING": Pvt. Elisha Stevens, Sept. 1777, Royster, 225. JOHN HENRY: Meade 2:167–68, 493. "I SUPPOSE I": PH to govs. of Cuba and New Orleans, 18 Oct. 1777, OL, 195–96.

328. "KEEP IT CLOSE": PH to RHL, 10 Nov. 1777, OL, 202. CLARK TOLD PH: Clark to PH, 1777, in Ill. Coll. 8:30–32; Clark, "Memoir, 1773–1779," Ill. Coll. 8:218–19.

329. CLARK KEPT SILENT: Clark to GM, 19 Nov. 1779, Ill. Coll., 8:116. "GREAT THINGS HAVE": Clark to PH, 3 Feb. 1779, Ill. Coll., 8:99. PH QUESTIONED: Ill. Coll. 8:219. "CRUEL TO DENY": PH to RHL, 18 Dec. 1777, OL, 219. RHL to PH, 7 Jan. 1778, WWH 3:140, indicates that illness prevented RHL from arriving soon enough to participate in the Clark decision.

330. PRIVATE LETTER: to Clark, 3 Jan. 1778, PGM 1:408–9. "SET ON FOOT": 2 Jan. 1778, OL, 222. SECRET ORDERS: PH to Clark, 2 Jan. 1778, OL, 223. "TAKING A BODY": Clark's Diary, 3 Jan. 1778, Ill. Coll. 8:27. "HE DID NOT" & "SET FORWARD": Clark Memoir, Ill. Coll. 8:219. "SHOULD NOT BE CONFIN'D": PH to Clark, 15 Jan. 1778, OL, 230.

331. "THE ECLAT": PH to RHL, 28 May 1778, OL, 175. "DESCRIBE TO THAT GENTLEMAN": PH to Col. Rogers, 14 Jan. 1778, OL, 227. "NATURALLY YOUR EXCELLENCY": PH to Gov. of Louisiana, 14 Jan. 1778, OL, 228. "A CERTAINTY": PH to Capt. Young, 26 Jan. 1778, OL, 227. "SO IMPORTANT A NATURE": PH broadside, 13 Dec. 1777, OL, 217.

332. "MUST INEVITABLY": GW to Pres. of Congress, 23 Dec. 1777,

GWFi 10:192–93. "I assure you" & "not easy": GW to PH, 27 Dec. 1777, WWH 3:137. "We have experienced": GW to PH, 19 Feb. 1778, WWH 3:148. "Several thousand beeves": PH to Va. Cong. Delegates, 20 Jan. 1778, OL, 231–32, for quotations in this paragraph and the next.

333. "The pain which": Id. "I exerted all": PH to RHL, 7 Apr. 1778, OL, 260. "Agreeable present": GW to PH, 16 May 1778, WWH 3:167. The General also remained deeply obliged to PH for passing along intelligence of an officers' cabal against him. WWH 3:545–51.

334. "Vile assassins": PH to William Fleming, 19 Feb. 1778, OL, 244–45, for all quotations in this paragraph. "The traitor Phillips": 1 May 1778, OL, 267: Bill to Attaint Josiah Phillips, ca. 28 May 1778, PTJ 2:189–93. "My strength will not": PH to RHL, 7 Apr. 1778, OL, 261.

335. "This fresh instance": PH, 30 May 1778, OL, 285. Shock to public": PH to Speaker of House, 13 May 1778, OL, 273. "Pressed warmly": PH to RHL, 18 Jun. 1778, OL, 292, for quotations in this paragraph and the next.

336. "Republic of Virginia": Hugh F. Rankin, George Rogers Clark (Richmond, 1976), 14.

337. "The state of things": PH to Va. Cong. Delegates, 14 Nov. 1778, OL, 324. "Commander": PH to Clark, 12 Dec. 1778, OL, 338–40. "Troublesome thorns": PH to Clark, 1 Jan. 1779, OL, 350, for remaining quotations in paragraph. "I am very desirous": PH to Clark, 12 Dec. 1778, OL, 340–42, for all quotations in paragraph.

338. "To think . . . contest": PH to GM, 27 Mar. 1779, WWH 3:45–47 for all quotations in this paragraph and the next.

Chapter 17

341. The Southern corner: Charles P. Blunt IV, *Patrick Henry: The Henry County Years* (Danville, 1976), 31–36, reviews Leatherwood land transactions. "I am circumstanced": PH to Speaker, 18 Oct. 1778, WWH 2:43.

342. "I have scarcely": PH to TJ, 15 Feb. 1780, WWH 2:48–49, for all quotations in this paragraph and the next.

343. "The Tories": PH to [?], 23 Apr. 1780, NYPL. "The present moment": Nathaniel Greene to PH, 10 Feb. 1781, Huntington Library.

344. "Retained some right": TJ to GW, 28 May 1781, 6:32–33. Military affairs, Hugh F. Rankin, *The War of the Revolution in Virginia* (Williamsburg, 1979). Social conditions, Hamilton J. Eckenrode, *The Revolution in Virginia* (Boston & New York, 1916), 246–59.

345. "SUCH TERROR": Betsy Ambler to Mildred Smith, [June] 1781, Dumas Malone, *Jefferson the Virginian* (Boston, 1948), 358–59. PENDLETON DEMANDED: Mays 1:222–23.

346. TYLER'S STORY: Tyler, *Patrick Henry*, 281–83.

347. PH SECONDS MOTION: Archibald Stuart recoll., PTJ 6:85. "P. VIRTUE GONE": PH notes, n.d., VHS. BILL THAT GRANTED: W.W. Hening, comp. *Statutes at Large* (13 vols., Richmond, 1809–23) 10:414.

348. "AN INQUIRY INTO THE CONDUCT": 12 June 1781, JHD, 15. Archibald Cary to TJ, 19 June 1781, PTJ 6:96–97. "NATURAL ILL-TEMPER": TJ to Isaac Zane, 24 Dec. [1781], PTJ 6:143. "BEING ALL TONGUE" & "PERSONAL COURAGE": TJ to George Rogers Clark, 26 Nov. 1782, PTJ 6:205. "MEN, MONEY, ARMS": [PH], Address to Congress, 22 Jun. 1781, WWH 2:154.

349. "Now, SIR, MAY YOU": Horatio Gates to PH, 10 May 1782, WWH 2:173. Cicero's maxim: "Let military power be subject to civil authority." "IT IS . . . POWER": GM to PH, 6 May 1783, PGM 2:769–73, for quotations in this paragraph and the next.

350. AGRARIAN WAY OF LIFE: Drew McCoy, *The Elusive Republic: Political Economy in Jeffersonian America* (Chapel Hill, 1980). Jackson T. Main, *The Sovereign States*, 1775–1783 (New York, 1973).

351. "FINGER OF HEAVEN" & "POINTED THE WAY": WWH 2:193. "ENTERPRISING" & "SHALL WE": WWH 2:196. "UNFETTERED": WWH 2:192.

352. "CHRISTIAN SPARTA": Wood, *Creation*, 114–18. "SIGHING FOR HOME": Edmund Randolph to JM, 21 Jun. 1783, PJM 7:186. "IMMENSE": John Marshall to James Monroe, 12 Dec. 1783, *Papers of John Marshall*, ed. Herbert A. Johnson (Chapel Hill, 1974) 1:111. LEGISLATURE HAD CEASED: Jackson T. Main, "Government By The People: The American Revolution and the Democratization of the Legislature," WMQ (3rd ser.) 23:391–407.

353. "FARMERS WITH LITTLE": Johann D. Schoepf, *Travels in the Confederation*, ed. Alfred J. Morrison (Philadelphia, 1911) 1:57. "VERY LOW STATE": TJ to Edmund Randolph, 15 Feb. 1783, PTJ, 7:247. "TRIFLING BUSINESS": Schoepf, 1:55. "PECULIAR EXCELLENCE": Marshall, 12 Dec. 1783.

354. "PRESENTED A LUDICROUS": Archibald Stuart recoll., WWH 2:213. SECTIONAL DIVISION: Jackson T. Main, *Political Parties Before the Constitution* (Chapel Hill, 1973), 244–67.

355. "THERE ARE MANY": John Marshall to Charles Simms, 16 Jun. 1784, *Papers*, 1:124.

356. "AFFECTIONATE" NOTE: PH to JM, 17 Apr. 1784, PJM 8:18.

357. MORRIS STRATAGEMS: E. James Ferguson, "State Assumption of Federal Debt During the Confederation," *Mississippi Valley*

Historical Review 38:403–24; Ferguson, "The Nationalists of 1781–83 & The Economic Interpretation of the Constitution," *Journal of American History*, 56:241–61. "EVERY ENGINE": Arthur Lee to Samuel Adams, 29 Jan. 1783, DHR 13:19. "MERE PUPPITS": GW to Alexander Hamilton, 4 Apr. 1783, DHR 13:20. CIRCULAR LETTER: GW, "To the Executives of the States," 15 March 1783, DHR 13:62–70.

358. "AGAINST WHAT IS CALLED": ER to JM, 28 Jun. 1783, PJM 7:200. "ONLY INDUCEMENT": William Short to TJ, 14 May 1784, PTJ 6:257; JM to TJ, 15 May 1784, PJM 8:34.

359. "WHAT WE HAVE TO DO": TJ to JM, 8 Dec. 1784, PTJ, 6:558.

360. SMITH & PH: Charles Sellers, "John Blair Smith," *Journal of the Presbyterian Historical Society* 34:211.

361. "PEOPLE OUGHT TO PAY": 11 Nov. 1784, JHD, 19. Thomas F. Buckley, *Church and State in Revolutionary Virginia, 1776–1787* (Charlottesville, 1977), 71–112 is a full account. "TRUE QUESTION": JM, Notes for Debates, 1784, PJM 8:198. "SUPPORTING INSTITUTIONS": Presbytery of Hanover, Memorial, October 1784, in Charles F. James, *Documentary History of the Struggle for Religious Liberty in Virginia* (Lynchburg, 1900) 234–35. "TEACHERS OF CHRISTIAN RELIGION": Text in Buckley, 188–89.

362. "DISHEARTENED": JM to James Monroe, 4 Dec. 1784, PJM 8:175. "OUT OF THE WAY": JM to TJ, 9 Jan. 1785, PJM 8:229. "IT IS THE OPTION": JM to Monroe, 14 Nov. 1784, PJM 8:137. "MY WIFE WANTS": PH to Annie Christian, 13 Nov. 1783, WWH 2:228. Land purchase near Richmond, PH to John Tabb, 22 May 1784, Box 10, McGregor Coll., UVa.

363. "SPIRIT OF GOSPEL": Buckley, 148.

364. "ADAPTED TO ALL": ER to JM, 15 May 1783, PJM 7:46.

365. "THUS IS THE LAST GENERATION": PH to Bart Dandridge, 21 Jan. 1785, WWH 2:252. "SEASON OF TRANQUILITY": 30 Mar. 1785, PH to Lafayette, WWH 3:289.

366. "OWES THEM PROTECTION": PH to ER, 21 Jun. 1785, WWH 3:303–4. "STRICT NEUTRALITY": PH to Joseph Martin, 16 Apr. 1785, WWH 3:294–95. "TO PREVENT" & "LENIENT MEASURES": PH to Speaker of the House, 17 Oct. 1785, WWH 3:327.

367. "VIRGINIA SEEMS": PH to RHL, 9 Jan. 1785, WWH 3:266. "INADVERTANT DELINQUENCY": ER to JM, 17 July 1785, PJM 8:324. "UNIFORM SYSTEM": PJM 9:116–18; PH to Executives of the States, 23 Feb. 1786; DHR 1:180–81.

368. "MY HEART HAS FELT": PH to Annie Christian, 15 May 1786, W. W. Henry Papers, VHS. "THE SEEMING NEGLECT": PH to Va. Cong. Delegates, 16 May 1786, WWH 3:350–52. HE LEARNED FROM MONROE: Monroe to PH, 12 Aug. 1786, WWH 2:291–98.

369. "I've exerted myself": PH to Annie Christian, 20 Oct. 1786, WWH 3:379–80. "The power of regulating trade": Report of the Commissioners at Annapolis, DHR 1:184.

370. "My wife and self": PH, 20 Oct. 1786. "Those who first kindled": ER to PH, 6 Dec. 1786, Moncure D. Conway, *Omitted Chapters of History* . . . (New York, 1888), 63. PH reply, 13 Feb. 1787, WWH 2:311. "He smelt a rat": Grigsby, *Virginia Convention of 1788*, 1:32 n.36.

Chapter 18

371. Every assay test: PH to Thomas Madison, 16 Jun. 1786, NYPL.

372. "Relinquish all Pretensions": Brief of Case: *Roane v. Henry*, c. 1809, Virginia Court of Appeals, printed excerpt, Huntington Library. "Leading him delicately": Id. "You are allied": PH to Anne Henry Roane, [1786], WWH 2:305–9.

373. "Your tongue will": Winston memoir, VMHB 69:40. "To try to get": PH to Betsy Aylett, 12 Dec. 1787, WWH 2:330. "Peremptory": ER to JM, 1 Mar. 1787, PJM 9:301. "The refusal": JM to ER, 25 Mar. 1787, PJM 9:331. "Unfettered": JM to GW, 18 Mar. 1787, PJM 9:316. "Free to combat": JM to TJ, 19 Mar. 1787, PJM 9:319. "He would rather part": John Marshall to Arthur Lee, 5 Mar. 1787, Papers, 1:206.

374. "In Kentucky liberty": Letter from Louisville, 6 Dec. 1786, *Maryland Journal*, 3 July 1787, DHR 13:154. "There are combustibles": GW to Henry Knox, 26 Dec. 1787, GWFi 29:122. "Prevailing rage": Albany Gazette, 21 Jun. 1787, DHR 13:141, and generally, 91–93. David P. Szatmary, *Shays' Rebellion: The Making of an Agrarian Insurrection* (Amherst, 1980).

375. "Having dreaded giving": Benjamin Franklin to M. LeVeillard, 17 Feb. 1788, Albert H. Smyth, ed., *Writings of Franklin*, 9:638. "All the real friends": JM to EP, 24 Feb. 1787, PJM 9:295.

376. "A few plumb stones"; JM to James Madison, Sr., 30 Sept. 1787, PJM 10:178. "If the plan proposed": JM to EP, 20 Sept. 1787, PJM 10:171. Pendleton read with characteristic thoroughness and discovered a typographical error in Article V; the printers (Dunlap and Claypool) had inadvertently made the text say that Congress could not prohibit the slave trade "prior to the year one thousand seven hundred and eight." Andrew J. Donelson Papers, LC. "Your own judgment": GW to PH, 24 Sept. 1787, WWH 2:319–20. "I have to lament": PH to GW, 19 Oct. 1787, WWH 2:320–21.

378. "A moderate aristocracy": GM, "Objections to the Constitution," Sept. 1787, PGM 3:993. "Be laid before": Convention Resolution, 17 Sept. 1787, DHR 13:210.

379. "THIS, OR NOTHING": RHL to GM, 1 Oct. 1787, RHLB 2:438–40, for quotations in this paragraph. "COALITION OF MONARCHY": Id. "LONG TOILED" & "ELECTIVE DESPOTISM": RHL to Samuel Adams, 5 Oct. 1787, RHLB, 2:444–47.

380. "GREAT CONTINENTAL": *Philadelphia Independent Gazetteer*, 25 Sept. 1787, DHR 13:229. "EVERY CORNER RESOUNDS": James Breckinridge to John Breckinridge, 31 Oct. 1787, Family Papers, LC. "AFFORDS MATTER": George Lee Turberville to Arthur Lee, 28 Oct. 1787, DHR 13:505. "SUCH IS THE WARMTH": PH to Thomas Madison, 21 Oct. 1787, William L. Clements Library, Schoff Washingtonia. "A VIGOROUS OPPOSITION": William Graham to Zachariah Johnston, 3 Nov. 1787, Fleming Papers. Washington & Lee Univ. "Graham has sounded the Bell of Sedition & raised an uncommon commotion." Stuart to Breckinridge, 1 Mar. 1788, LC. WAGON DRIVER'S STORY: VIC 7 Nov. 1787.

381. "OUR ONLY HOPE": Stuart to John Breckinridge, 21 Oct. 1787, L.C. OFFICIAL SKIRMISH: *Va. Journal* 8 Nov. 1787, for quotations in this paragraph and the three following.

382. "A CONVENTION OF THE PEOPLE": Resolution of 25 Oct. 1787, JHD. "THIS IS A HAPPY": ER to JM, 29 Oct. 1787, PJM 10:230. RISING ANGER: DHR 13:96.

383. "I TAKE FOR GRANTED": Matthew Maury to James Maury, 10 Dec. 1787, Risjord, 177–78. "WHERE THIS WILL END": Logan & Story to Stephen Collins, 2 Nov. 1787, Collins Papers, LC. "HENRY IS LOUD": Stuart to JM, 9 Nov. 1787, PJM 10:246. PH ADVOCATES PAPER: John Dawson to JM, 25 Sept. 1787, PJM 10:173. ". . . as the advocate of a paper emission, he cannot be friendly to a Constn. wch. is an effectual bar." GW to JM, 10 Oct. 1787, PJM 10:190. GM OPPOSES PAPER: PGM 3:1008–12.

384. "HAVE GOT VIRGINIA": Samuel Otis to Theodore Sedgwick, 25 Dec. 1787, DHR 15:91. "AFRAID OF PH": Robert Milligan to William Tilghman, 20 Sept. 1787, DHR 13:219.

385. "HE RECEDES SO FAR": ER to JM, 29 Oct. 1787, PJM 10:230. SLIPPED IN ALLOWANCES: PH draft, 4 Dec. 1787, Papers of House of Delegates, 1787, VSL. Stuart to JM, 2 Dec. 1787, PJM 10:291. "ART IS EQUAL": Henry Lee to JM, 7 Dec. 1787, PJM 10:295. FEDERALISTS DILUTED: *An Act Concerning the Convention. . .* , 12 Dec. 1787, Broadside, Evans 20842.

386. "ELECTIONS MADE IN PHRENZY": Edward Carrington to JM, 8 Apr. 1788, PJM 11:15. "IF A WEAK STATE": GW to Samuel Powell, 18 Jan. 1788, GWFi 29:386. "HIS LANGUAGE IS": Carrington to JM, 18 Jan. 1788, PJM 10:383. "PERHAPS SAID HE": Hugh Williamson to John G. Blount, 3 Jun. 1788, Blount Papers, Duke University.

387. "ON ONE HAND, ENERGY": Louis Guillaume Otto to Comte de

Montmorin, 20 Oct. 1787, DHR 13:422. "Tree of life": VIC 26 Sept. 1786, DHR 13:255. "Spurious brat": "Centinel" No. IV, 30 Nov. 1787, DHR 14:321. "Daring attempt": "Centinel" No. I, 5 Oct. 1787, DHR 13:332. "Fellow citizens": *The Federalist*, No. 14, 30 Nov. 1787, DHR 14:316. "Domestic violence": Alexander Hamilton, "Conjectures about the new Constitution," Sept. 1787, DHR 13:277. "Evils" of state laws: JM to TJ, 24 Oct. 1787, PJM 10:212. "The pestilent effects": *The Federalist*, No. 44, 25 Jan. 1788, DHR 15:470.

388. "An impartial": *Albany Gazette* 21 June 1787, DHR 13:144.

388. "A revolution effected": *New York Daily Advertiser* 24 Sept. 1787, DHR 13:225. "A spirit of submission": Id., DHR 13:224. "Had erred most": *The Federalist*, No. 14, 30 Nov. 1787, DHR 14:317. "Throw off the yoke": "Cato," 11 Oct. 1787, DHR 13:370. "Teach the members": "Cato," 27 Sept. 1787, DHR 13:256–57. "To the weight" & "Politer kind": *Letters from the Federal Farmer*, 8 Nov. 1787, DHR 14:50–51.

389. "The dazzling ideas": RHL to [?], 28 Apr. 1788, RHLB 2:464. "The aristocracy who move": "Essay By a Farmer," MG 29 Feb. 1788, Herbert J. Storing, ed., *The Complete Anti-Federalist* (Chicago, 1981) 5:20. Less Diverse, Less Cosmopolitan: Kenneth A. Lockridge, "Social Change and the Meaning of the American Revolution," *Journal of Social History* 6:403–39. Lee Benson, *Turner & Beard* (New York, 1960), 215–28. Jackson T. Main, *The Anti-Federalists* (Chapel Hill, 1961). Storing, *What The Anti-Federalists Were For* (Chicago, 1981). "His influence": Richard Morris to James Maury, 11 Feb. 1788, Morris Papers, UVa.

390. "Those who have power": Minton Collins to Stephen Collins, 16 Mar. 1788, LC. "Did not like the complexion": James Duncanson to James Maury, 11 Mar. 1788, Maury Papers, UVa. Broker in New York: Collin McGregor to Neil Jamieson, 2 Apr. 1788, McGregor Letterbook, NYPL. "Such a man": James Mercer to John Francis Mercer, 12 Dec. 1787, Mercer Papers, VHS.

391. A speaking exhibition: William Hill, "A Narrative of the Revival of Religion. . . . ," 25–26, mss., Union Theological Seminary. "Torrent of folly": Carrington to Henry Knox, 12 Jan. 1788, Knox Papers, Mass. Hist. Soc. "So industriously": Carrington to JM, 10 Feb. 1788, PJM 10:493–94, for all quotations in this paragraph.

392. "Proceed from men": JM to Ambrose Madison, 8 Nov. 1787, PJM 10:244. "A gloomy, stiff creature": M. Bland to Frances Bland Tucker, 30 Mar. 1781, Box 8, Tucker-Coleman Papers, William & Mary College.

393. "THE BAPTISTS & THE IGNORANT": Francis Taylor Diary, 26 Feb. 1788, VSL. "No BIGGER THAN": Merrill D. Peterson, ed., *James Madison* (New York, 1974), 121. "IF THE EFFORTS": JM to Eliza House Trist, 25 Mar. 1788, PJM 11:5.

394. LEE'S TALLY: Henry Knox to Jeremiah Wadsworth, 12 Apr. 1788, Wadsworth Papers, Connecticut Hist. Soc. PH & GRAYSON: Id. "AS ELSEWHERE": JM to GW, 10 Apr. 1788, PJM 11:20. "WILL . . . REJECT": extract of letter, 30 Mar. 1788, *Philadelphia Independent Gazetteer*, 16 Apr. 1788. "THE REAL SENSE": JM to TJ, 22 Apr. 1788, PJM 11:28–29. "IT WILL BE SMALL": George Nicholas to David Stuart, 9 Apr. 1788, French Coll., Mass. Hist. Soc.

395. "I HOPE": Henry Knox, 12 Apr. 1788. "IN VIRGINIA IT WILL BE": William Short to Thomas Lee Shippen, 31 May 1788, Shippen Papers, LC.

Chapter 19

396. "THE GENTLEMEN GOING": *Va. Gazette & Adv.* 22 May 1788. ENTERPRISING WHOLESALER: 31 May 1788, Hollingsworth Co., Letterbook, Hist. Soc. Pa. "THE MOMENT VIRGINIA ADOPTS": Coxe and Frazier to Walter Livingston, 12 June 1788, Coxe Papers, Hist. Soc. Pa. "NOTHING BUT DEBATE": James Duncanson to James Maury, 7–13 June 1788, Maury Papers, UVa. "MISLED . . . TRAP": William Shippen to Thomas Shippen, 29 Nov. 1787, Shippen Coll., LC.

397. "ONE HALF THE CREW": Theodorick Bland to Arthur Lee, 13 Jun. 1788, LFP. "ALL THE OBJECTIONS": James Duncanson, 7–13 Jun. 1788. "MADDISON, ABOVE": *Pa. Packet* 25 Jan. 1788. "PUBLIC VIRTUE A GOWN": *Pa. Packet* 22 Jan. 1788. "I LEFT MY DEAR": PH to Anne H. Roane, 15 Jun. 1788, NYPL.

398. "RATIFYING FIRST" & "THE IDEA": GM to TJ, 26 May 1788, PGM 3:1046. "ORDER AND DECORUM": EP Address, 2 Jun. 1788, Andrew J. Donelson Papers, LC.

399. "THE SHORTHAND GENTLEMAN": Fredericksburg, *Virginia Herald*, 5 Jan. 1788, all quotations in paragraph. "SPACIOUS" & "WE HAVE": Alexander White to Mrs. Wood, 10 Jun. 1788, LC.

400. "THE SENSE . . . RULE": William White to Garitt Minor, 13 May 1782, Watson Papers, UVa.

401. "WE ARE NOT": EP, 4 Jun. 1788, EDV 5. "PLANT PENDLETON": Grigsby, *Convention of 1788*, 1:77. "AS LONG AS THE PEOPLE": George Nicholas, 4 Jun. 1788, EDV 14. "A SENTINEL": PH, 4 Jun. 1788, EDV 21–23, quotations in this paragraph and the next.

402. "WHY NOT"?: ER, 4 Jun. 1788, EDV 28–29.

403. "ANNIHILATE THE STATES": GM, 4 Jun.. 1788, EDV 29. "GREAT ESSENTIAL" & "SINE QUA NONE": GM, EDV 33–34.

404. "Unlucky circumstances": William Grayson to Nathan Dane, 4 Jun. 1788, Dane Papers, LC. "The Federalists": JM to GW, 4 Jun. 1788, PJM 11:77.
405. Speech of such length: PH, 5 Jun. 1788, EDV 43–65. [For this and other extensive speeches, an inclusive reference is given and only highlights cited separately.] "Bane of sedition": PH, EDV 45.
406. "I dread the operation": PH, EDV 54. "Energetic government": PH, EDV 57–58. "No true responsibility": PH, EDV 61.
407. "Fatal ambiguity": PH, EDV 47. "Those feeble ten": PH, EDV 56.
408. "A great majority": PH, EDV 63. "We are come": PH, EDV 46. "I speak as one": PH, EDV 63. "There is no quarrel": EP, 5 Jun. 1788, EDV 37.
409. "The abuse of power": JM, 6 Jun. 1788, EDV 87. Balance successful: John M. Murrin, "The Great Inversion, or Court versus Country: A Comparison of the Revolution Settlements in England (1688–1721) and America (1776–1816)," in J.G.A. Pocock, *Three British Revolutions: 1641, 1688, 1776* (Princeton, 1980), 368–453. "Without contending for a nationalist conspiracy or coup d'etat in 1787, let us nevertheless concede what Beard rather clumsily argued, that the United States Constitution was very much an elitist solution to the problems left by the Revolution and the popular turbulence of the 1780s. . . . In a word, the Federal Constitution shifted the entire spectrum of national politics several degrees to the right." (403). "I appeal to those": ER, 7 Jun. 1788, EDV 125. "A child of revolution": ER, 6 Jun. 1788, EDV 65.
410. "Distorting the natural": JM, 6 Jun. 1788, EDV 87–90. "Submit to inconvenience": JM, 6 Jun. 1788, EDV 95. "The powers given": George Nicholas, 6 Jun. 1788, EDV 98. "Thirteen independent": JM, 7 Jun. 1788, EDV 129. "It can be little": JM, 6 Jun. 1788, EDV 95.
411. Powerful rejoinder: PH, 7 Jun. 1788, EDV 137–50. "Certain political maxims": PH, EDV 137. "If they can use": PH, EDV 149. "Bill of Rights . . . necessary": PH, EDV 150.
412. "Free Correspondence": [John Lamb] to PH, 18 May 1788, VHS.
413. The likeness, in clay: Bronze cast copy, Patrick Henry Foundation Collection, Red Hill, Virginia. Caucus reworked: Resolutions [ca. 8 Jun. 1788], PGM 3:1054–57; Proposed Amendments . . . by Anti-Federal Committee of Richmond, [ca. 11 Jun. 1788], PGM 3:1068–71. Source for this paragraph and the two following.

414. "THE ONLY REMAINING": PH to John Lamb, 9 Jun. 1788, Lamb Papers, NYHS, for quotations in this paragraph and the next. "ADVANCES": Theodorick Bland to Arthur Lee, 13 Jun. 1788, LFP, for all quotations in paragraph.

415. MONROE MAY BE SLOW": Grigsby, *Virginia Convention of 1788*, 1:68 n.149. "BILIOUS" & "CLOSETED": JM to Alexander Hamilton, 9 Jun. 1788, PJM 11:101. "IT IS A FACT": PH, 9 Jun. 1788, EDV 151. "DOES IT NOT INSULT": PH, 9 Jun. 1788, EDV 174.

416. "AN ILLUSTRIOUS CITIZEN": PH, EDV 152. "RANDOLPH REPLY: ER, 10 Jun. 1788, EDV 200. "A BILL OF RIGHTS": TJ to JM, 20 Dec. 1787, PJM 10:337; TJ to William Short, 2 Feb. 1788, DHR 14:500; TJ to JM, 6 Feb. 1788, PJM 10:474. "HAD NO BUSINESS": PH, 9 Jun. 1788, EDV 156. "DIMINUTION OF NUMBERS": PH, EDV 167.

417. "TREATISE ON ANATOMY": PH, EDV 171. "I LOOK UPON": PH, EDV 176. "THROWING THOSE BOLTS": Henry Lee, 9 Jun. 1788, EDV 177. "IF PANDORA'S BOX": Lee, EDV 179. "DREADED MORE": Lee, EDV 185. "NOT A SOCRATES": PH, 7 Jun. 1788, EDV 140.

418. RANDOLPH COMPLAINED: ER, 9 Jun. 1788, EDV 187–89, for all quotations in this and the four paragraphs following.

419. "DEPRIVED" & "MAXIMS": John Marshall, 10 Jun. 1788, EDV 222–23. "NECESSARY, PRACTICABLE": JM, Outline of Speech, 11 Jun. 1788, PJM 11:105. Speech in EDV 242–61.

420. MASON DISPUTED: GM, 11 Jun. 1788, EDV 262–73.

421. "SEA LETTERS": William Grayson, 11 Jun. 1788, EDV 276. PH CHIMED IN: Quotations in this paragraph fuse PH remarks of 9 Jun., EDV 157, 161, with 12 Jun. 1788 speech, EDV 318–19. "NINE DAYS SPENT": Morris, [11 Jun. 1788], *Papers of John Marshall*, 1:271.

422. "BUSINESS OF THE MISSISSIPPI": PH, 13 Jun. 1788, EDV 333. MADISON ANGRILY: Id.

423. "WILL GROTIUS": William Grayson, 13 Jun. 1788, EDV 350. MADISON TRIED: JM, 13 Jun. 1788, EDV 347–49. PH POUNCED: PH, 13 Jun. 1788, EDV 354–55. "SCUFFLING FOR": PH, EDV 351.

424. RANDOLPH & CORBIN: EDV 361–65.

Chapter 20

425. "MATTERS ARE NOT": Morris to Hamilton, 13 Jun. 1788, Harold C. Syrett, ed., *Papers of Alexander Hamilton* (New York, 1961–), 5:7. "THE BUSINESS IS": JM to GW, 13 Jun. 1788, PJM 11:134. "THE ISSUE" & "OSTENSIBLE POINTS": JM to Rufus King, 13 Jun. 1788, PJM 11:133.

426. "MOST WARM": Morris, 13 Jun. 1788. "TOO MUCH SUSPICION":

PH, 14 Jun. 1788, EDV 384. "MATHEMATICAL GOVERNMENT": EDV 396.

427. "LIKE A BEACON": PH, 23 Jun. 1788, EDV 579. "POOR PEOPLE": PH, 20 Jun. 1788, EDV 541. "SUPPOSE OPPRESSIONS": GM, 16 Jun. 1788, EDV 441–42.

428. "FLIMSY SOPHISTRY" & "INSULT": "Centinel" No. II, 24 Oct. 1787, DHR 13:459, 457. Wilson's speech, 6 Oct. 1787, DHR 13:337–44. "A Federal Republican" called Wilson's argument "a distinction of which the votaries of scholastic philosophy might be proud" but inappropriate for "the political world, where reason is not cultivated independently of action and experience . . ." 28 Nov. 1787, DHR 13:275. "IF I HAVE" & "IT IS AGREED": George Nicholas, 16 Jun. 1788, EDV 444. "WHY NOT?": PH, 16 Jun. 1788, EDV 448. "THE POLITICAL PRIVILEGES": "The Federalist" No. 84., *The Federalist Papers*, Clinton Rossiter ed., (NY, 1961), 513–15.

429. "FEEBLE" & "EVERY WORD": PH, 17 Jun. 1788, EDV 461–62. "VAST QUANTITIES": PH, 17 Jun. 1788, EDV 475. "MADISON ADMITTED": EDV 471–73.

430. "WE MAY BE TAXED": GM, 17 Jun. 1788, EDV 473. "A CONTEST FOR MONEY": PH, 17 Jun. 1788, EDV 475. "MAKE SUCH A REGULATION": JM, 17 Jun., EDV 480. "OF MEN, NOT LAWS": PH, 23 June 1788, EDV 577.

431. MADISON TOO THEORETICAL: Roane memo, Morgan, 450. Arthur Lee to Thomas Shippen, 25 Apr., 1790, LFP, gives the harsh Anti-Federalist view that Madison, "without being a knave . . . has always been the supporter of public knaves . . . [he] has had such vanity as to suppose himself superior to all other persons . . . in consequence he has been duped by the artful management of the rapacious Morris . . ." "WE HAVE GOT": William Grayson to Nathan Dane, 18 Jun. 1788, Dane Papers, LC. THREE MORE VOTES: Stuart to Breckinridge, 19 Jun. 1788, LC.

433. "LET HIM GO": Adam Stephen, 23 Jun. 1788, EDV 580. "THEY'LL TAKE": Grigsby, *Convention*, 1:157 n.142; slavery discussion, 17 Jun. 1788, EDV 455–59.

434. "THE GRAND OBJECT": James Breckinridge to John Breckinridge, 13 Jun. 1788, LC. "PECULIAR FORM": Thomas Willing to William Bingham, [Jun. 1788], LC. "A DECLARATION OF A FEW": JM to Rufus King, 22 Jun. 1788, PJM 11:167.

435. "BARE MAJORITY": JM to GW, 23 Jun. 1788, PJM 11:168. "MY DUTY IF": PH, 24 Jun. 1788, EDV 595. "WOULD HAVE NO HAND": PH, EDV 597. "OLD AS I AM": PH, 20 Jun. 1788, EDV 546. WYTHE'S MOTION: 24 Jun. 1788, EDV 586–87; preamble text, EDV 653.

436. "PREMATURE": PH, 24 Jun. 1788, EDV 587–95. "BUT ANOTHER NAME": JM, 24 Jun. 1788, EDV 619. "ARE NOT OBJECTIONABLE":

Id. EDV 622. "But one amendment": PH, EDV 625. "Were I to ask": PH, EDV 592. "I see the awful immensity": PH, EDV 625.

437. "Thunders roll": Bland to Lee, 13 Jun. 1788, LFP. "Has given exemplary": Roane to Aylett, 26 Jun. 1788, NYPL. "I do not know": JM to Ambrose Madison, 24 Jun. 1788, PJM 11:170. "If I shall be": PH, 25 Jun. 1788, EDV 652. PH motion: EDV 653. Roll call, EDV 653–54.

438. "Either wise enough": extract of Richmond letter, 25 Jun. 1788, in *New York Journal*, 8 July 1788. "No rejoicing": Roane, 26 Jun. 1788. "Without flaw": JM to GW, 25 Jun. 1788, PJM 11:178.

439. "Highly objectionable": JM to Hamilton, 27 Jun. 1788, PJM 11:181. "Not withstanding the fair": Id. Also, JM to GW, 27 Jun. 1788, PJM 11:181–82. "To breathe peace": Grigsby, *Convention*, 1:354.

Chapter 21

440. Richmond celebration: VIC 9 July 1788. Portsmouth Pageant: *Pa. Packet* 21 July 1788. "Arrived safe in port": Fredericksburg, *Virginia Herald*, 24 July 1788.

441. "The Revolution of 1788": *Md. Journal* 15 July 1788. "Weep over": William Nelson, Jr., to William Short, 12 July 1788, LC. "I see by the Publick": Jonathan Saybrook, 22 July 1788, Diaries, American Antiquarian Society Coll. "The discontents": ER to JM, 27 July 1788, PJM 11:208–9. "There is a regular": Robert Smith to Tench Coxe, 31 July 1788, Hist. Soc. Pa.

442. Circular letter: 28 July 1788, Elliot, *Debates*, 2:414. "He grows": ER to JM, 12 Sept. 1788, PJM 11:251. "Will be eagerly caught": James Gordon to JM, 31 Aug. 1788, PJM 11:245. "Having the whole game": GW to JM, 24 Sept. 1788, PJM 11:262. "Has a most pestilent": JM to GW, 11 Aug. 1788, PJM 11:230. "Extremely dangerous": JM to ER, 22 Aug. 1788, PJM 11:237–38, for remainder of paragraph.

443. "Doublings and turnings": Francis Corbin to JM, 21 Oct. 1788, PJM 11:311. "Keeps himself close": Carrington to JM, 22 Oct. 1788, PJM 11:312. "I have not seen him": ER to JM, 24 Oct. 1788, PJM 11:314. "Would oppose every": PH, 29 Oct. 1788, WWH 2:416.

444. Motion for convention: PH draft, House of Delegates Papers, VSL; JHD, 16. "The cloven hoof": George L. Turberville to JM, 27 Oct. 1788, PJM 11:319. "Non-Emendo-Tories": Theodorick Bland to RHL, 9 Nov. 1788, *Southern Literary Messenger* 28:43. "Old in parliamentary": Richard Bland Lee to JM,

29 Oct. 1788, PJM 11:323. "At all times to bow": PH, WWH 2:419.

445. Corbin/PH clash: WWH 2:420–22.

446. Corbin motion: JHD, 13; MG 13 Nov. 1788. "Unwilling to submit": ER to JM, 23 Oct. 1788, PJM 11:311. "Unfriendly to amendments": Turberville to JM, 16 Nov. 1788, PJM 11:346. "Urged madison's election": PH to RHL, 15 Nov. 1788, LC.

447. "A dreadful blow": Henry Lee to JM, 19 Nov. 1788, PJM 11:357. "The arrangements": JM to ER, 17 Oct. 1788, PJM 11:305. "A liberal election": Corbin to JM, 12 Nov. 1788, PJM 11:342. Partisan effort: ER to JM, 10 Nov. 1788, PJM 11:338–39; Turberville to JM, 13 Nov. 1788, PJM 11:343; Carrington to JM, 14 Nov. 1788, PJM 11:345.

448. "He has only": GW to JM, 18 Nov. 1788, PJM 11:351. "Hereafter, when a gent": Md. Journal 28 Nov. 1788.

449. "Greater obstacles": The Federalist, No. 10, 22 Nov. 1787, DHR 14:181. "Were not founded": WWH 2:424–25.

450. "I have not a moment": PH to Betsy Aylett, 11 Nov. 1788, WWH 2:434. "After he had settled": WWH 2:433. "Deliberations held out": PH to RHL, 15 Nov. 1788, LC.

451. "Electioneering": JM to Henry Lee, 30 Nov. 1788, PJM 11:372. "Much indisposed": JM to GW, 2 Dec. 1788, PJM 11:377. "For the interest": Burgess Ball to JM, 8 Dec. 1788, PJM 11:385. "Never seen": JM to George Eve, 2 Jan. 1789, PJM 11:404–5. Election overview, PJM 11:301–4.

452. "The well meaning": JM to TJ, 8 Dec. 1788, PJM 11:383. "Federal and Anti": PH to William Grayson, 31 Mar. 1789, VMHB 14:203.

453. "A despot under": Decius, Letters on the Opposition to the Constitution in Virginia (Richmond, 1789), 13–14. "Have deprived us": Decius, 61. "Hideous": Decius, 64. "For two things": Junius-Brutus, in Decius, 104.

454. "General calm": ER to JM, 27 Mar. 1789, PJM 12:31. "Dirty scribbler": PH, 31 Mar. 1789, VMHB 14:203. "Our constituents may see": JM, 8 Jun. 1789, PJM 12:193. Robert A. Rutland, The Birth of the Bill of Rights (Chapel Hill, 1955), 191–218. Outline: JM, 8 Jun. 1789, PJM 12:193. Speech, 196–209.

455. "Important in the eyes": JM to ER, 15 Jun. 1789, PJM 12:219.

456. "The most valuable": JM, Speech to House, 17 Aug. 1789, PJM 12:344. "Last Monday": WG to PH, 12 Jun. 1789, WWH 3:391–92. "To effect the wishes": RHL to PH, 28 May 1789, WWH 3:388.

457. "To lull suspicion": Edward Fontaine recoll., mss. Cornell University. "See how rapidly": PH to RHL, 28 Aug. 1789, WWH 3:398. "To the conventions": Senate Journal, 25 Sept.

1789, in Bernard Schwartz, *The Roots of the Bill of Rights* (New York, 1980) 5:1164.

458. "A careless reader": RHL to PH, 14 Sept. 1789, WWH 3:400. "We might as well": Id., WWH 3:399. "To fill our state": RHL to PH, 27 Sept. 1789, WWH 3:402. "The extraordinary doctrine": WG to PH, 29 Sept. 1789, WWH 3:406. "Those radical amendments": RHL and WG to Thomas Tinsley, 28 Sept. 1789, VHS.

459. "Disposed to do": Carrington to JM, 20 Dec. 1789, PJM 12:463–64. "Two or three": GM to TJ, 16 Mar. 1790, PGM 3:1189.

460. Hold the most popular: Hardin Burnley to JM, 5 Dec., 28 Dec. 1789, PJM 12:456, 460. "Virginia outwitted": Edward Fontaine recoll., Cornell University. "If we cannot gain": RHL to Charles Lee, 28 Aug. 1789, RHLB 2:499. "One great object": RHL to PH, 10 Jun. 1790, WWH 3:422. "My mind recoils": PH to John Dawson, 20 Mar. 1790, LC.

461. "A comfortable prospect": PH to RHL, 29 Jan. 1790, WWH 3:414. "The form of government": PH to James Monroe, 24 Jan. 1791. WWH 2:460–62.

Epilogue

463. "Tragic and comic": Roane recoll., Morgan, 445. Courtroom anecdotes: WWH 2:484–92.

465. "Shakespeare and Garrick": WWH 2:493. "I am obliged": PH to Betsy Aylett, 30 Oct. 1791, VHS. "Sharp attack": PH to Anne Roane, 19 Sept. 1792, NYPL. "Give out the law": PH to Betsy Aylett, 8 Sept. 1794, WWH 3:424. "Great anxiety": PH to William Fleming, 3 July 1790, VHS.

466. "What a weight": May 10, 1792, Richard Venable Diary, VHS. "Very retired": PH, 8 Sept. 1794, WWH 3:423.

467. "The lilys now": verses by Martha Catharine Henry, c. 1794, VSL. "Little ones climbing": Tyler, *Patrick Henry*, 384–85. Grandiose ideas: Charles Royster, *Light-Horse Harry Lee* (New York, 1981), 172–77; PH to Henry Lee, 1 Feb. 1794, UVa; Henry Lee to PH, 4 Feb. 1795, Huntington Library. "Found time to read": Dabney recoll., WWH 2:519.

468. "Travelling monk": Winston recoll., VMHB 69:41. "I find much cause": PH to Betsy Aylett, 20 Aug. 1796, WWH 2:570. Opposition politics: Richard R. Beeman, *The Old Dominion and the New Nation* (Lexington, Ky., 1972); Lance Banning, *The Jeffersonian Persuasion* (Ithaca, 1978).

469. Madison rebuffed: William Madison to JM, 3 Dec. 1791; JM to Wm. Madison, 13 Dec. 1791, PJM 14:137, 149. "He grows rich": ER to GW, 24 Jun. 1793, WWH 2:537. "Mrs. Henry's situation": PH to GW, 10 Oct. 1795, WWH 2:558–59.

470. "ALTHOUGH A DEMOCRAT": PH to GW, 27 Jun. 1795, WWH 2:551. "WHAT MUST I THINK": PH to Betsy Aylett, 20 Aug. 1796, WWH 2:569. "I WAS NEVER SUED": PH to Philip Payne, March 1798, WWH 3:425–26.

471. "OUGHT CHARACTERS WHO ARE": GW to PH, 15 Jan. 1799, WWH 2:603. "TELL MARSHALL I LOVE": PH to Archibald Blair, 8 Jan. 1799, WWH 2:592–93.

472. "SUCH A MODE OF CONSTRUING": Address to Congress from the [Va.] General Assembly, 22 Jan. 1799. A ROMAN CAST: Tyler, 421–22. "OH MY DEAR BETSY": Dorothea Henry to Betsy Aylett, n.d., VSL. PH WILL AND INVENTORY: Morgan, 455–59, 461–73.

473. "THIS IS ALL": PH will, Morgan, 457. MESSAGE ON STAMP ACT RESOLVES: Tyler, 84–85.

474. "MOURN VIRGINIA MOURN": *Virginia Gazette & General Advertiser*, Richmond, 14 Jun. 1799, VHS. "PROPHETIC MIND": *Virginia Argus*, 18 Jun. 1799, VHS. "UNRIVALED ELOQUENCE": 13 Dec. 1799, JHD.

ACKNOWLEDGMENTS

Since writing is a solitary vocation, it is a pleasure to express appreciation for those who extend help along the way.

Not everyone can be named, but I want to thank especially Glenn Cowley, my agent, and Peggy Tsukahira, my editor, for their faith in this book; Kenneth Kann, Emily Leider, and Lisa Rubens, for their steady encouragement from beginning to end; Dr. Janet Kimbrough, V. R. Shackleford, Jr., and Patrick Daily, for hospitality in Virginia; John Kaminski and Gaspare Saladino, editors of the Documentary History of Ratification project, for allowing me extraordinarily generous access to the Virginia files; and Christina Spaulding and Peter Waldman for research assistance.

I am grateful also for the many librarians and institutions who have shared material and granted permission for quotation.

I want to pay tribute to the child-care providers—Harriet Walker, Ann Larsen, Denise Colbert, Dora Halperin and the Rainbow School staff—whose faithful care of Eleanor and Tommy made working hours possible.

To my wife Betsy, who believes that support for the arts begins with supporting an artist at home, I am immeasurably grateful for the companionship and delight only hinted at in the dedication.

INDEX